Is the Welfare State Justified?

In this book, Daniel Shapiro argues that the dominant positions in contemporary political philosophy – egalitarianism, positive-rights theory, communitarianism, and many forms of liberalism – should converge in a rejection of central welfare-state institutions. He examines how major welfare institutions, such as government-financed and -administered retirement pensions, national health insurance, and programs for the needy, actually work. Comparing them to compulsory private insurance and private charities, Shapiro argues that the dominant perspectives in political philosophy mistakenly think that their principles support the welfare state. Instead, egalitarians, positive-rights theorists, communitarians, and liberals have misunderstood the implications of their own principles, which support more market-based or libertarian institutional conclusions than they may realize. Shapiro's book is unique in its combination of political philosophy with social science. Its focus is not limited to any particular country; rather it examines welfare states in affluent democracies and their market alternatives.

Daniel Shapiro is associate professor of philosophy at West Virginia University. A specialist in political philosophy and public policy, he has published in *Public Affairs Quarterly*, *Social Philosophy and Policy*, *Journal of Political Philosophy*, and *Law and Philosophy*. In the spring of 2003, he was a Distinguished Visiting Humphrey Lecturer at the University of Waterloo.

Dedicated to all academic supporters of the welfare state.
And, of course, to Kathy, Genevieve, Brandi, Peter, and Kirsten.

Is the Welfare State Justified?

DANIEL SHAPIRO

West Virginia University

CAMBRIDGE
UNIVERSITY PRESS

CAMBRIDGE UNIVERSITY PRESS

Cambridge, New York, Melbourne, Madrid, Cape Town, Singapore, São Paulo

Cambridge University Press

32 Avenue of the Americas, New York, NY 10013-2473, USA

www.cambridge.org

Information on this title: www.cambridge.org/9780521860659

First published 2007

Printed in the United States of America

A catalog record for this publication is available from the British Library.

Library of Congress Cataloging in Publication Data

Shapiro, Daniel, 1954–
Is the welfare state justified? / Daniel Shapiro.
p. cm.
Includes bibliographical references and index.
ISBN-13: 978-0-521-86065-9 (hardback : alk. paper)
ISBN-10: 0-521-86065-2 (hardback : alk. paper)
ISBN-13: 978-0-521-67793-6 (pbk. : alk. paper)
ISBN-10: 0-521-67793-9 (pbk. : alk paper)
1. Welfare state. 2. Free enterprise. I. Title.
JC479.S53 2007
330.12'6–dc22   2006029240

ISBN 978-0-521-86065-9 hardback
ISBN 978-0-521-67793-6 paperback

Contents

v

Preface

In the last dozen years or so, my philosophical writings have had two main themes: (1) political philosophers who have different philosophical principles actually are closer on institutional matters than they realize and (2) one cannot really make a sound or decisive argument for institutional change unless one has made a comparative institutional analysis of different, feasible alternative institutions. I think this view originated, in part, in my late teenage years, when I changed from what would be roughly described as a liberal view – in the modern American sense of the term, wherein one favors individual freedom and distrusts the government on "personal" or on civil liberties matters but favors a vigorous role for the government in restricting or regulating free markets and providing for the unfortunate – to a libertarian view that the government's sole role should be to protect the right to life, liberty, and property and keep its hands off the free market, which operates just fine if the government gets out of the way. When I looked back at this change, I thought that in one sense I had not changed at all. Once I realized how free markets really worked, and how government programs that were supposed to realize their seemingly compassionate or just goals didn't really do so, I realized that the attitude of distrust I had toward government power or the view I had about the value of individual freedom really applied to economic as well as personal matters. So at some level I came to think that my liberal friends who disagreed with me – and when I became an academic most of my fellow academics who opposed libertarianism – could come to agree with me, if they would just understand how free markets really work and how government programs, specifically welfare-state programs, really work (or don't work). Thus, in an embryonic form, I had the view that people with seemingly different philosophical principles actually could converge on institutional matters.

So I began to write articles such as "Why Rawlsian Liberals Should Support Free Market Capitalism" (*Journal of Political Philosophy* 3, March 1995), in which I argued that those who followed John Rawls's philosophical framework, which apparently opposed libertarianism, could actually, following their own principles, end up with more libertarian institutional conclusions than they realized. Perhaps this just represented a temperament of optimism – even if we disagreed about philosophical principles, we could come to agree on institutional matters if we could incorporate social theory or social science about how alternative institutions worked (or didn't) – but it also, I suspect, grew out of a frustration that during decades of philosophical disagreements about basic principles few minds were changed and the realization that many of my students' complaints about political philosophy – "they don't focus on the real world!" – had a point. You couldn't, I came to realize, after reading the writings of N. Scott Arnold (e.g., *Marx's Radical Critique of Capitalist Society*, Oxford University Press, 1990) and David Schmidtz (e.g., *Social Welfare and Individual Responsibility: For and Against*, Cambridge University Press, 1998), really make a sound argument for institutional change without doing social science, that is, without showing that there was some feasible alternative institution that could actually get rid of the injustice that was supposedly present in an existing institution. I owe Scott and David an enormous debt for the clarity and insight of their books and for their friendship and guidance over many years and their helpful criticism of earlier versions of this book. (I owe Scott a particular debt, as he read the entire manuscript and made detailed comments.) I also want to thank Christopher Morris and Eric Mack for their friendship and philosophical guidance over the years, and for comments on earlier parts of the manuscript. In addition, Jeffrey Friedman's journal, *Critical Review*, constantly stressed the need for political philosophers to look at how institutions really functioned, and I want to thank him for that journal as it also influenced my approach to political philosophy.

This book came about, in a way, almost by accident. In the spring of 1995 I was looking for some external support during an upcoming sabbatical year to write some articles that the welfare state is not, by the standards used in mainstream political philosophy, just or fair, and I contacted Jeffrey Paul of the Social Philosophy and Policy Center at Bowling Green State University and asked him who might support such a project. He invited me to spend a year at the Policy Center, and the idea of writing articles turned into this book, which, in a nutshell, argues that the dominant nonlibertarian philosophical principles prevalent in contemporary political philosophy provide good reasons for supporting a change from present welfare-state institutions to feasible market alternatives. I want to thank Jeffrey Paul, Ellen Paul, and Fred Miller, who all run the Policy Center, for providing such a congenial and supportive place to work and for supporting my book throughout the many years it has taken to complete it. They provided financial support during my sabbatical year (1995–6), but also during the last phase of the writing in the spring of 2006. In addition, they gave me the opportunity to present earlier versions of some of the chapters at three of their conferences. At a conference on "The Welfare State Reconsidered," I presented an early version of Chapter 5, later published as "Can Old Age Insurance Be Justified?" (*Social Philosophy and Policy* 14, Spring 1997). At a conference on "New Directions in Libertarian Thought," I presented an early version of Chapter 3, later published as "Why Even Egalitarians Should Support Market Health Insurance" (*Social Philosophy and Policy* 15, Spring 1998). At a conference on "Should Differences in Income and Wealth Matter?" I presented an early version of Chapter 6, later published as "Egalitarianism and Welfare State Redistribution" (*Social Philosophy and Policy* 19, Winter 2002). And last, but not least, Ellen Paul provided invaluable editing suggestions during the final phase of completion of this manuscript.

Other institutions and persons gave me financial support and the opportunity to present my work and arguments, and I want to thank them as well. The Earhart Foundation of Ann Arbor, Michigan, gave me support during the fall of 1998, which enabled me to do additional work on my chapters on health insurance and retirement pensions. In the fall of 1998, Peter Boettke of the economics department of George Mason University invited me to give a talk on health insurance, which enabled me to find out if my work was economically literate. Gerald Gaus invited me to present "Communitarianism and Social Security" to the International Economics and Philosophy Society in the summer of 1998, which was later incorporated into my chapter on retirement pensions. Michael Tanner of the Cato Institute invited me to a debate on Social Security in the fall of 1998, which led to a publication for the Cato Institute ("The Moral Case for Social Security Privatization," *The Cato Project on Social Security Privatization* 14) that gave me my fifteen minutes of fame until the news of President Clinton's impeachment focused the media's attention elsewhere. In the spring of 2003, during another sabbatical, Jan Narveson of the University of Waterloo invited me to a give a series of talks that enabled me to get most of the chapters of this book closer to their present form. (Most of the statistics or empirical information in the book stem from that period of spring 2003, although the last chapter has information on the financial ills of the U.S. Social Security system that applies through the year 2005.) Then, in the spring of 2005, in what I thought was icing on the cake, I was given the chance to present a synopsis of the main arguments in the book, in a paper entitled "Egalitarianism and Libertarianism: Closer than You Might Think" at the Association for Private Enterprise Education and at the World Congress of Philosophy of Law and Social Philosophy in Granada, Spain, where I presented my arguments to an international audience.

I thought at the time, "The book is just about finished. It has been accepted by Cambridge University Press, and I will finish it up in the fall of 2005 and be done." But life has a way of surprising you, and now, to use the commentator Paul Harvey's phrase, here is the rest of the story.

I fell seriously ill in July 2005. It has become a cliché in prefaces to thank one's spouse and family. In this case, the word *thanks* is so inadequate that words fail me. Without the support, love, and encouragement of my wife Kathy, I would not have made it. She helped me when I fell ill, got better, fell ill again, and then made what we hope is the start of a complete recovery. My daughter, Genevieve, who is now fifteen, handled her father's illness with aplomb and a maturity far beyond her years. My mother has been incredibly generous and supportive, and my brother, Mark, has been a source of support and comfort and superlative long-distance diagnoses. I also want to thank a long list of health-care providers who helped me during this period: Nicole Gauthier-Schatz, Raymond Hearn, Ryan Kurczak, Terra McColley, Terry Miller, Erika Pallie, Jim Slaymaker, the late Kimberly Stearns, Michael Todt, and Jacob Teitelbaum and his assistants Cheryl Alberto and Denise Haire. And during this period I was also fortunate enough to have an empathic and understanding chair of my department, Sharon Ryan.

Finally, during the last six weeks of writing this manuscript, two research assistants, Nikolai Wenzel and Diogo Costa, helped me with some of the economics and technical matters necessary to write the last chapter about a just transition from Social Security to a private-pension system. (Michael Tanner of the Cato Institute complemented their work by patiently answering a barrage of e-mails about these matters.) Their assistance greatly improved the final chapter. My brother- and sister-in-law, John Pepple and Sarah Blick, helped with the bibliography, and my wife Kathy again stepped in and provided final editing advice and assistance.

I am truly grateful to all the people and institutions mentioned in the preceding text.

1

Introduction

Suppose justice requires reducing or minimizing certain inequalities, those that arise through no choice or fault of one's own. Or suppose that justice requires providing everyone, particularly the most vulnerable, with guarantees that the most basic goods needed to lead a decent and secure life will be provided. Or suppose a good or just society will reinforce or sustain a sense of community or solidarity among all members of society. Then on all of these views of a just or good society, it seems to follow straightaway that we should support government-financed and -administered health insurance, retirement pensions, and various government programs for the poor and needy. This seems to be the consensus among contemporary political philosophers. The aim of this book is to argue that this consensus is mistaken. According to the principles and values that are central in contemporary political philosophy, welfare-state institutions fail to be justified when compared with viable, more market-based alternatives – specifically, private compulsory insurance and private charities. Private compulsory insurance means the state requires all citizens to purchase insurance, and supplies a safety net, but otherwise leaves insurance to the market. Private charities are voluntary organizations devoted to helping the poor or the unfortunate. I will argue that private compulsory insurance is clearly superior to government-financed and -funded insurance, when judged by the standards prominent in contemporary political philosophy, and that private charities are superior to some government programs for the poor and no worse than others. If the welfare state is composed of government-provided insurance and aid for the poor, then, taken as a whole, the welfare state is unjustified when compared with market alternatives. If the welfare state is broader than government-provided insurance and aid to the poor, then the argument of this book is that major welfare-state institutions are unjustified when compared with market alternatives.

My arguments in this book are different from most of the debates about the welfare state that have occurred in (close to) the last thirty years in contemporary political philosophy. Many of those debates concern disputes about relatively abstract political values or principles. So, for example, libertarians argue that basic political principles should focus on individual liberty, while egalitarians argue for a principle of equality or fairness. Liberals say that the basic unit of political concern is the individual; communitarians say that it is the community. By contrast, I bypass these debates. In this book, I do not challenge or criticize any basic political principle or value. Instead, I work within them, so to speak, and show that the dominant mainstream views should converge on supporting some market alternatives to the welfare state and not opposing other market alternatives to the welfare state. (Because libertarianism supports market alternatives to the welfare state, another way of putting this is that I show the dominant mainstream, nonlibertarian political principles have institutional implications that are more free market or libertarian than they realize.) This difference explains, in part, my disagreement with the consensus in mainstream contemporary political philosophy in favor of the welfare state. That consensus consists of people who disagree among themselves about which basic political values or principles are true or most plausible but agree that all or almost all of the institutional implications of these principles point to supporting the welfare state.[1] In this book I take no stand on disputes about basic political principles or values but argue that, whatever these principles, the institutional implications of mainstream principles point against the welfare state.

1.1 Justification in Political Philosophy

Another way to mark out the differences between my view that the welfare state is unjustified and the consensus in mainstream political philosophy that it is justified is to show that we have different

---

[1] Because libertarianism opposes the welfare state, from now on when I say "consensus" or "mainstream" view I exclude libertarianism.

understandings of justification. Justification in political philosophy is largely a matter of presenting the best arguments for certain normative claims when the focus is disagreement about the best or most plausible basic political values or principles. Empirical and social scientific questions about the way institutions work (or don't work) thus come to be seen as separate matters. Of course, because political principles or goals can only be instantiated or achieved by some kind of institutional arrangements, institutional questions are always relevant, but they do not take the foreground on this way of understanding justification in political philosophy. Another way to put this point is that for most political philosophers the object of justification – what gets justified – are principles or values, whereas on the model presented in this book, the object of justification is institutions.

In one sense, this model of justification is satisfactory. Political philosophy obviously is concerned with fundamental normative questions about the just or good society. A problem arises, however, when political philosophers use normative arguments as reasons for changing institutions, as it is not uncommon for them to do. After all, principles of justice or basic political goals are meant to establish the standards by which we should judge a political order, and if present institutions fail to meet these standards, then criticism of the existing order naturally follows straightaway.[2] From that criticism the claim that we should act to abolish or alter the institution also seems to follow straightaway. However, it does not. Identifying a very bad or unjust feature of an institution, even an essential feature of that institution, gives one no conclusive or sufficient reason to abolish or reform it, because the reformed or new institution may be no better. A joke illustrates the problem. A Roman Emperor asked to hear the best singers in his kingdom. The finalists were narrowed down to two. The emperor heard the first one, was unimpressed, and promptly announced that the award goes to the other finalist, because the next singer must be better than the first one. Of course, that's wrong: the second one could be no better or worse. The emperor needs to hear both singers to make a proper judgment.[3]

---

[2] Of course, principles can also be used to support institutions, but the points I wish to make here are more obvious when I focus on the principles' critical function.

[3] Peter J. Boettke, "James M. Buchanan and the Rebirth of Political Economy," in *Against the Grain: Economic Dissent in the 20th Century*, Steve Pressman and Ric Holts, eds. (Brookfield, VT: Edgar Elgar, 1997), 9–10.

This fallacy – call it the *nirvana fallacy*[4] – teaches us an important lesson. If political philosophy aims to give us good reasons to change or abolish an institution, it cannot limit itself to normative theory or arguments. Normative arguments by themselves only provide us with reasons to believe that a certain feature of an institution is unjust or seriously defective. Without some social-science arguments that there is some institution that will lack or lessen the injustice or social evil, we have no reason, or at least no particularly weighty reason, to abolish or alter the institution.[5] The injustice or evil could be a necessary evil. It could be a sad truth about human affairs that we are stuck with that evil or injustice.

Few philosophers explicitly commit the nirvana fallacy, although it does occur.[6] Most philosophers mention, at least implicitly, some kind of alternative institution that is supposed to lessen or get rid of the injustice or social evil. However, for these arguments to succeed the argument for an institutional alternative must specify what mechanisms or processes are likely to bring about the proposed change. Failure to specify how alternative institutional mechanisms or processes are likely to achieve justice or lessen present-day injustice is, unfortunately, a common problem in political philosophy, particularly in arguments that welfare-state institutions are needed to overcome injustices caused or embodied by markets. For example, John Rawls in *A Theory*

[4] The term comes from Harold Demsetz, "Information and Efficiency: Another Viewpoint," *Journal of Law and Economics* 12 (1969): 1–22.

[5] Someone might argue that X is not an injustice unless there is a feasible institutional alternative that would lack or lessen X. Perhaps that is correct. If it is correct, my point can be restated in one of two ways. Normative political philosophy is incomplete without a claim that some feasible institution will lack or lessen the injustice, or normative political philosophy describes serious institutional defects, describing them as injustices only if some feasible institutional alternative will lack or lessen these defects.

[6] Ronald Beiner, "What Liberalism Means," *Social Philosophy and Policy* 13 (Winter 1996): 203, says the following: "A liberal is someone who says that the present social order in contemporary, Western, democratic, individualistic and pluralistic societies is basically okay, apart from a need for improvements in equality of opportunity and more equitable social distribution. A critic of liberalism like myself will say this is nonsense. To this, the liberal will reply: 'Okay, this isn't good enough; what's your alternative?' It is both necessary and legitimate for me to claim that I don't need to answer this question. . . . That's not my job. My job as a theorist is to criticize the prevailing social order." Thus Beiner claims he can engage in legitimate criticism without specifying any institutional alternatives that will do a better job.

of Justice argues that a society is unjust if market institutions dominate and government's role is limited, because free markets without state correction allow too much of a person's lot in life to be a result of luck, that is, by one's inherited natural abilities and fortuitous social circumstances.[7] Rawls argues for the difference principle, which says, roughly, that social and economic inequalities are justified only if they work to the greatest advantage of the most unlucky or the least advantaged. But how is the difference principle to be institutionalized? Rawls answers by listing the *aims* of various branches of government.[8] However, institutions cannot be adequately characterized by their aims. In the real world, political decision makers do not simply have intentions to achieve a just society that they can simply implement. They have agendas and interests of their own. Furthermore, even if the decision makers were extremely committed Rawlsians, they would face informational constraints, such as their ignorance about most of the facts that are relevant for a decision, the difficulties in evaluating the relevant evidence, and our uncertainty about predicting the consequences of various policies.[9] It may be that trying to instantiate the

---

[7] John Rawls, *A Theory of Justice*, 2nd ed. (Cambridge, MA: Harvard University Press), 1999, 62–4.

[8] Ibid., 244–5. It's worth noting that Rawls, in *Justice as Fairness: A Restatement* (Cambridge, MA: Harvard University Press, 2001), 135–40, claims that the institutions or regime needed to support or sustain his two principles of justice would be a "property owning democracy" (or perhaps "liberal socialism"), not a welfare state. The difference between a property-owning democracy and a welfare state seems to be that the former relies more on a widespread redistribution of assets and wealth rather than income. Because Rawls's remarks seem to suggest that a property-owning democracy maintains social-insurance programs (ibid., 139–40), it seems to me that a property-owning democracy is a welfare state of a certain kind, but in any event, this semantic disagreement is irrelevant for my purposes. The point is that whether we call Rawls's proposed institutions for instantiating or sustaining the difference principle a welfare state or something else, Rawls never shows that his favored institutions will sustain or instantiate the difference principle better than alternative, less interventionist or more market-based institutions. Rawls does concede that although he outlines "a family of policies aimed at securing background justice over time. . . . I make no attempt to show that they will actually do so. This would require an investigation of social theory" (ibid., 135). However, without this social theory an argument that free markets are unjust and ought to be restricted or regulated by government programs has no force.

[9] For a thorough account of these sorts of epistemic problems, see Gerald Gaus, "Why All Welfare States (Including Laissez-Faire Ones) Are Unreasonable," *Social Philosophy and Policy* 15 (Summer 1998): 16–19. Ironically, Rawls recognized these kinds of epistemic problems in his discussion of "the burdens of judgment," which is his attempt to explain the sources of reasonable disagreement. See John Rawls, *Political Liberalism*

difference principle by government produces more inequalities than Rawls believes come about by the result of unfettered markets. Certainly our experience with welfare-state policies in the last half-century indicates that welfare-state programs do backfire and produce something quite different from their intended results.[10]

Similar problems infect Ronald Dworkin and Norman Daniels's criticisms of market health insurance (MHI). To simplify greatly (Dworkin and Daniels's views are discussed in Chapter 3), they argue that MHI is unjust because it prevents the poor and the unlucky from attaining adequate access to health care. National health insurance (NHI) is prescribed as the cure, but as Daniels and Dworkin recognize, that typically requires government rationing. They do not discuss how this rationing will improve the situation of those who are supposedly blocked from adequate health care in the market. It may turn out – I argue it does turn out – that the poor and unlucky's access to rationed services (surgery, high-tech equipment, etc.) in NHI is much worse than the affluent's access to such services, in which case that kind of insurance may be more unjust than MHI.

A sound argument for institutional change must avoid jumping between the real and the ideal. An argument that an institution is bad or unjust in some way is presumably about a real institution. Hence, an argument for changing or abolishing that institution must specify a real or realistic alternative.[11] It is a mistake to condemn a real institution

---

(New York: Columbia University Press, 1993), 56–7. However, he never seemed to realize that the burdens of judgments also apply to government agencies and that simply explaining that these agencies intend to carry out Rawlsian justice is a far cry from showing that these agencies will do a better job than if these agencies didn't exist or had a different task.

[10] I do not discuss Rawls's views in later chapters, because he doesn't provide detailed defenses of specific existing welfare-state programs. I mention him here because some defenders of the welfare state take their inspiration from Rawls, e.g., Norman Daniels.

[11] I say "real or realistic" because there may be no alternative in existence anywhere in the world. However, provided the alternative is realistic, i.e., could work as advertised without assuming substantial changes in human nature, and is similar to how real institutions work (or at least is not terribly dissimilar), using a nonexistent alternative to compare with an existing one is acceptable. In such cases, however, one is intellectually obligated to refute any arguments that such institutions could not exist and/or to explain why such alternatives are not now in existence. So, e.g., I argue in Chapter 3 that MHI is superior to government-provided versions of these insurances. This argument requires me to explain why existing private health insurance is not genuine MHI.

by some ideal without showing that there are institutional processes that have at least a decent chance of instantiating that ideal in the real world.[12] Of course, there is nothing wrong with evaluating an ideal in terms of another ideal, but that is irrelevant for the topic at hand here because welfare-state institutions are obviously real institutions.

This suggests the following argument for institutional change:

1. Institution X manifests or produces injustice or social evil E.
2. Institution Y has processes or mechanisms that make it likely that it will lack E or manifest or produce less of E than X does.
3. If an institution produces or manifests more injustice or evil than a feasible alternative, it ought to be altered or abolished.
4. Therefore, we should abolish or alter X and bring about Y.

This still isn't quite right, because even if Y produces or manifests less of E, the change from X to Y might produce or manifest such side effects or so much injustice that it would be wrong to change X and try to bring about Y.[13] In any event, the preceding argument gives a rough idea of how I will show that the welfare state is not justified. I will argue that core welfare-state institutions, when compared with

---

[12] In some cases, it is so obvious that the institutional alternative will eliminate the injustice or social evil that we don't bother to specify the former. Consider, e.g., such horrible injustices as slavery and genocide. If the evil or injustice simply consists of people being enslaved or murdered because of their ethnicity, race, class, etc., then the institutional alternative that eliminates these evils is simply the cessation of slavery and genocide. We don't have to specify anything further, because simply abolishing the institution eliminates the injustice or evil, and even if other injustices or evils come about as a side effect of that abolition, we tend to think that this is irrelevant because simply eliminating that injustice or social evil was our aim, and abolishing the institution eliminated the injustice or social evil. It may be that obvious cases like this mislead some thinkers into believing that identifying an institution as manifesting or containing an injustice or social evil is sufficient to support an argument for its alteration or abolition. However, in most cases the injustice or social evil of a certain institution doesn't just consist in the existence of the institution, but in some further feature the institution manifests or brings about, and so simply ceasing to have that institution doesn't show that an alternative institution will manifest or produce less injustice or social evil. Notice, also, that for those who think the evil of slavery consists not just in the existence of slavery but what it brings about (e.g., a gross diminution of welfare or well-being) then specifying an institutional alternative does become essential. That is why those who oppose slavery on the utilitarian grounds that it reduces human welfare have a more complicated argument for its abolition than those who think human enslavement is simply a gross injustice.

[13] I call this the *transition problem* in Chapter 8.

real market alternatives, produce or manifest more injustice or social harms, or, to put it positively, market institutions are more just or better than present welfare-state institutions. I will call this kind of argument *comparative institutional evaluation* or *comparative evaluation.*

1.2 Internal Versus External Arguments

My use of comparative evaluations will also avoid external arguments and use internal arguments. To illustrate that distinction, consider a debate between an egalitarian defender of the welfare state and a libertarian critic. The egalitarian might defend the welfare state on the grounds that it produces less of certain inequalities than market institutions, and the libertarian might object that those inequalities are not unjust or that there are more important values or principles than reducing certain inequalities, such as protecting individual rights or maximizing individual liberty. Notice that in this type of argument the libertarian does *not* contest the view that the welfare state will produce less of certain inequalities than market institutions – or to put it another way she seems to accept, at least for the sake of the argument, that market institutions produce more of certain inequalities than the welfare state – and instead rejects the egalitarian view of justice and argues that libertarian values are more important than egalitarian ones. In this example, the libertarian is making what I call an external argument, because she argues from a normative standpoint outside of the egalitarian's view. Similarly, if the libertarian defended free-market capitalism on the grounds that it maximized individual liberty and the egalitarian did not contest that claim but argued that there are more important values than individual liberty, then the egalitarian would be making an external argument. Most political philosophers today use external arguments. The use of external arguments explains why much of political philosophy places social-science considerations in the background. After all, if political philosophers disagree about whether or not markets are superior to welfare-state institutions (or to certain welfare-state institutions) because they disagree about which principles of justice or political values are the most plausible and important, then it is unsurprising that they will tend to ignore the question of whether the institutions work the way that their opponents assume that they do.

Although there is nothing wrong with external arguments, and they are appropriate for philosophical concerns with fundamental issues, they have an important disadvantage – they tend not to produce any resolution of the disagreement. Even though disagreement about principles can be and often is reasonable, it is hard to convince one's opponents that their fundamental principles in political philosophy are mistaken. My aim in this book is to convince defenders of the welfare state that they are mistaken; therefore I will eschew external arguments and use internal arguments. I will argue that the principles that defenders of the welfare state take to support welfare-state institutions do not do so because these institutions do not work the way egalitarians and other defenders of the welfare state think that they do, because egalitarians and other defenders of the welfare state have misunderstood the implications of their principles, or both.[14]

Internal arguments of this kind may seem insincere. If one does not accept the opponent's principles or values, isn't it wrong to argue on the basis of that principle or value for a certain conclusion?[15] However, if a principle or value one does not accept yields a conclusion that *also* follows from a principle or value one does hold, there is nothing wrong with an internal argument. One is simply arguing that you and your opponent converge on a certain conclusion, though you begin from different premises. Furthermore, if one can show that this conclusion

---

[14] One might wonder why I make the distinction between internal and external arguments, rather than relying on the familiar logical terms of validity and soundness. After all, it might be said, an external argument is simply another name for an argument that is valid (conclusion follows from premises) but unsound (at least one premise is false), and an internal argument is simply another name for an argument that is invalid (the conclusion doesn't follow from the premises). However, the familiar logical terms aren't illuminating for the purposes of the book for a couple of reasons. First, they don't reveal that the premises are political principles or values and the conclusions concern institutions. Second, they don't reveal a point I go on to make in the text, that if all or almost all reasonable principles or values in political philosophy converge on supporting certain institutions, then that institution has far more solid support then if it were merely supported by one principle.

[15] I say internal arguments *of this kind* raise the issue of insincerity because other internal arguments would not. Consider two people who share a common premise or perspective but think that different conclusions follow from that premise or perspective. In that case, while the argument is an internal one – one is arguing from within one's opponent's perspective and not taking issue with it – because one shares a common ground with one's opponent, no one could reasonably maintain that one is being insincere. The issue of insincerity arises when one argues from within a perspective that one does not genuinely accept.

follows from *any* (or virtually any) reasonable premises or principles, then one will have provided far more solid support for the conclusion than if the conclusion followed only from one premise or principle – for even if some of the principles supporting the conclusion turn out to be false or implausible, there will be some true or plausible principles from which one can derive the conclusion. When applying this point to the institutional question of the welfare state versus market alternatives, support for the latter becomes quite strong if it is compatible with or entailed by most plausible normative principles or perspectives in political philosophy. If market alternatives to welfare-state institutions are supported by most or all plausible normative principles in political philosophy, then the debate will, or should, no longer be the welfare state versus those alternatives but what form of market institutions are the best.

My aim here is to shift the debate in just that way. I will provide internal arguments that the welfare state must be rejected in favor of market alternatives. The principles and goals that I will use to compare welfare-state programs with market alternatives are mainstream in contemporary political philosophy, specifically those principles and goals that are used to argue that welfare states are just or are part of the good society. (As I shall explain in Chapter 2, these principles or perspectives are egalitarianism, positive rights theory, communitarianism, and a requirement of liberalism I call *epistemic accessibility*.) Thus, this book aims to marry two kinds of literature that are often treated separately: normative arguments of political philosophers, and social-science analysis of institutions.

1.3 Clarifying the Institutional Alternatives

My arguments require that we be very clear about the nature of, and the differences between, welfare-state institutions and market alternatives. This is a bit tricky because definitions of the welfare state tend to be contentious.

1.3.1 Social Insurance and Means-tested Benefits
Government-financed and -administered insurance programs are often labeled as social insurance. They are insurance in the sense

that these programs protect against common risks of loss of income when or if certain events come to pass – retirement, illness, disease and injury, and unemployment, for example. The modifier *social* is meant to indicate a contrast with market insurance in three respects. First, social-insurance programs are compulsory, not voluntary; second, rates are not determined by actuarial considerations: beneficiaries are not charged on the basis of expected risk (the *raison d'être* of market insurance); third, because competition is absent or significantly restricted, consumers have little or limited choice of types of policies or benefits.

Social-insurance programs are universal, or nearly so, in the sense that all or virtually all citizens receive the benefits when or if the relevant contingency comes to pass. Old-age social insurance (Social Security or SS) and NHI are the most nearly universal; unemployment insurance and programs for injured or disabled workers (workers' compensation) are less so because not everyone works or works for an employer. As insurance programs, eligibility for benefits is based on contribution (by beneficiary and/or employer), and because these are government programs, contribution means paying taxes for some period of time. However, virtually all social-insurance programs are supplemented by or contain within them benefits for those who have never contributed. Even the elderly who never worked get government retirement benefits, and "free" medical care is provided to those who don't pay taxes. These supplemental programs increase the number and extent of the beneficiaries and make the programs more universal. Provided these supplemental, noncontribution-based programs do not dominate the contribution-based benefits, these programs as a whole remain based on contribution.

Whereas social-insurance programs are based (for the most part) on contribution, other welfare-state programs are based on need. As this is usually financial need, these are often labeled as means-tested programs. The word *means* usually refers to income, but sometimes income and assets are considered. Sometimes no effort is made to "test" or ascertain a recipient's need, and this is inferred from her status – so, for example, those who are eligible for unemployment assistance after their unemployment insurance benefits expire are not required to reveal their income, but it is reasonable to infer that they are not affluent. Because most people in affluent democracies are not poor, means-tested programs are not universal but selective (although if the income cutoff is high enough or need defined broadly enough, these turn into virtually universal programs).

Means-tested programs are often equated with government welfare. This is a bit misleading. The word *welfare* has the connotation of providing cash benefits to able-bodied adults who need not (at present) be working; yet some means-tested programs require work as a condition for receiving benefits, and others provide in-kind aid rather than cash. Provided one keeps these qualifications in mind, however, there is no harm in equating means-tested benefits with government welfare. It is important, however, to distinguish between unconditional welfare, which provides aid without requiring work from the able-bodied or nondisabled, and conditional aid, which does require work, or at least requires a serious attempt to enter the work force and sharply reduces or eliminates benefits for the able-bodied who fail to do so.

One final point about social insurance and means-tested benefits: unless I say otherwise, my focus will not be on any particular country. There are enough similarities among different welfare states' social-insurance schemes and means-tested benefits that one can meaningfully abstract from the differences. This same point applies to my discussion of market alternatives to welfare-state institutions, although here I sometimes rely upon specific proposals or policies that have been or are used in specific countries.

1.3.2 *Narrow Versus Broad Definitions of the Welfare State*

I define the welfare state as consisting of social insurance and means-tested benefits. In so doing, I exclude two other sets of programs that sometimes are considered to be part of the welfare state. First, although state schooling is an obviously important function of modern states, its existence predates the expansion of the state's role in modern capitalism, and the arguments for state schooling are, to a significant extent, different from the arguments for social insurance and means-tested benefits. Second, I will, for the most part, exclude the whole panoply of programs and regulations that interfere with or heavily regulate voluntary contractual agreements between employers and employees, such as minimum wage laws, maximum hour regulation, health and safety regulations, and the like. It is defensible to include these regulations as part of the welfare state. They emerged at about the same time as social-insurance programs, and the rejection of employment at will – the doctrine that employment may be terminated by either the employer or employee without cause – was a central feature of arguments against free-market capitalism. However, social-insurance and means-tested programs are what most people think about when they debate the "welfare state." For those who insist that these regulations are an essential part of the welfare state, then this book's arguments need to be recast: rather than aiming to show that the welfare state is unjustified, they aim to show that major welfare-state programs are unjustified when compared with market alternatives.

1.3.3 Choosing the Relevant Market Alternatives

A natural assumption is that market insurance is the direct opposite of social insurance. Because social insurance is compulsory, nonactuarial insurance with little choice of plans or policies, then market insurance would have to be voluntary, actuarially sound, and provide a wide range of plan choices. However, market insurance need not be understood as the direct opposite of social insurance. We can distinguish between voluntary, completely free-market insurance, and compulsory private insurance. The latter does remove the choice about whether to take out an insurance policy, but the management and financing of insurance are, for the most part, left to market arrangements, which means they are generally actuarially sound.[16] It is this kind of insurance that, I will argue, is justified from virtually every central normative perspective in contemporary political philosophy. Although I believe that voluntary, purely free-market insurance is superior to compulsory private insurance, I will not argue for that view in this book, because I do not believe the former can be justified internally from the point of view of the political values that predominate in contemporary political philosophy. Though I do not argue for the direct opposite of social insurance, the adoption of compulsory private insurance would mean

---

[16] Compulsory private insurance also contains a safety net for the indigent and those with uninsurable risks that are not wealthy. These subsidies are structured in such a way as to not interfere with the actuarial soundness of private insurance, as I shall discuss in later chapters.

the abandonment of central welfare-state institutions. Social insurance dominates the budgets of all contemporary welfare states, and thus it is quite significant if most normative perspectives in political philosophy should favor its abandonment.

Is there an analogue of private compulsory insurance in the realm of welfare? Not really. Compulsory private welfare would mean that individuals would be forced to maintain some kind of savings for times of misfortune or to keep them out of extreme poverty or deprivation. However, the proposal is a nonstarter because not everyone works or has discretionary income. Hence private charity is really the only viable alternative to state welfare.[17]

Now because I will argue that some versions of state welfare (those that require able-bodied citizens to work in order to receive benefits) and private charity are equally justifiable from the perspective of mainstream contemporary political philosophy, this might seem to imply that my arguments, if successful, do not show that the welfare state is unjustified – even using a narrow definition of the welfare state that excludes health and safety regulations and wage and hour regulations, for example. At this point, the issue may be largely a semantic one. Some writers make a distinction between an institutional welfare state,[18] which is mainly composed of universal social-insurance programs, and a residual welfare state, which is mainly composed of means-tested benefits or programs for the poor. If we use this distinction, all present welfare states are institutional welfare states,[19] and my arguments in this book, if successful, show that from the standpoint of the dominant values or principles in contemporary political philosophy, this kind of welfare state is unjustified. However, my arguments

[17] A qualification is needed here. Historically, private charity is not the only alternative to state welfare. Mutual-aid or fraternal societies were equally important alternatives in the late-nineteenth-century and early-twentieth-century United Kingdom and the United States. I discuss this in an appendix to Chapter 6, where I express skepticism that mutual-aid societies are viable in contemporary affluent societies.

[18] See Norman Barry, *Welfare*, 2nd ed. (Buckingham: Open University Press, 1999), ch. 8.

[19] Means-tested benefits are, as a budgetary matter, the lesser part of today's welfare states. See Nicholas Barr, "Economic Theory and the Welfare State: A Survey and Interpretation," *Journal of Economic Literature* 30 (June 1992): 742–5, 755, and Neil Gilbert, "Renegotiating Social Allocations: Choices and Issues," in *Targeting Social Benefits*, Neil Gilbert, ed. (New Brunswick, NJ: 2001), 213.

show that residual welfare states are justified or at least are permissible from that standpoint.[20]

1.4 Coming Attractions

Before I compare specific welfare-state institutions with market alternatives, I set out, in Chapter 2, the dominant perspectives in contemporary political philosophy that frame my arguments: egalitarianism, positive-rights theory, communitarianism, and a requirement of liberalism I dub *epistemic accessibility*. Chapters 3 through 5 discuss insurance programs, specifically the ones that both dominate welfare-state budgets as well as contemporary discussion: health insurance and retirement pensions. Chapters 6 and 7 discuss welfare programs. In Chapter 8, I take stock of what has been accomplished and discuss a possible way defenders of central welfare-state institutions might respond to my justification of feasible alternative market institutions: that even if my arguments are sound, they are incomplete, because I also need to show that the transition from unjust welfare-state institutions to feasible just alternatives would not produce such injustice during the transition process that it would be better to remain with the status quo. In the final chapter, I begin to address this challenge by explaining how a just transition can be made from the current SS in the United States to a compulsory private-pension (CPP) system.

---

[20] The reason I say "justified or at least permissible" is that my arguments, if successful, show that private compulsory insurance is justified, whereas some forms of state welfare are permissible (i.e., neither required nor forbidden). It is unclear as to which of these programs would be more important were the changes I recommend to happen, and so it is unclear whether residual welfare states are justified or simply permissible.

2

Central Perspectives in Political Philosophy

The bases for my comparative institutional evaluation are those principles and values that predominate in contemporary political philosophy, in particular those that are used to justify welfare states. These are egalitarianism (and a cousin, prioritarianism), positive-rights theory, communitarianism, and epistemic accessibility, a requirement common to many forms of liberalism. Before I describe these, some preliminaries are needed.

First, I do not discuss *every* major principle or value in contemporary political philosophy. I ignore, for example, socialism. Socialist principles and values either support abolishing welfare-state institutions (perhaps because they are too tainted with or constituted by the evils of market capitalism) or support welfare-state institutions as an adjunct to socialist institutions. If the former is correct, then socialist concerns are not relevant for my project because the institutional choices under consideration in this book are welfare states versus more market alternatives. If the latter is correct (which is more likely because most socialists today do not favor abolishing all market institutions),[1] then the principles or values that they rely on are likely to be the ones I will discuss – in particular, egalitarianism and communitarianism. I also

---

[1] For a discussion of market socialism among socialists, see Bertell Ollman, ed., *Market Socialism: The Debate among Socialists* (New York: Routledge: 1998); Christopher Pierson, *Socialism after Communism: The New Market Socialism* (University Park: Pennsylvania State University Press, 1995); and John E. Roemer, *A Future for Socialism* (Cambridge, MA: Harvard University Press, 1994).

will not spend time discussing libertarianism because it is quite obvious that libertarians will prefer market-based alternatives to welfare states. (Of course, libertarians would prefer pure free-market institutions to the qualified form of market institutions that are the focus of this book, but that is a separate matter).

Second, my discussion of these principles and values that are dominant in contemporary political philosophy does not focus on whether they are correct. However, I will sometimes explain how proponents of these values attempt to justify them because that explanation is often necessary to show why one would think these are important and reasonable political principles and values. That explanation, however, will stop before I get to their ultimate foundations or justifications.

2.1 Justice, Equality, and Fairness

2.1.1 Egalitarianism, Strictly Speaking

Many justifications of the welfare state appeal to principles of justice or fairness. Egalitarian principles of justice dominate many of these arguments, so I begin with them. Strictly speaking, egalitarian principles of justice are those that value or defend (some kind of) substantive material equality as such (i.e., consider it a noninstrumental value).[2] By *substantive* material equality I mean to distinguish egalitarianism from views that value or defend equality only in a formal sense – for example, views that require that everyone have equal rights or that there be equality before the law. (Henceforth, when I refer to equality I will mean equality in this substantive sense.) The reason I say that egalitarians value or defend (some kind of) equality *as such* is to distinguish egalitarianism from views that value or defend equality only as a means to an end, for example, to helping the worst off members of society. To illustrate the difference between egalitarianism, strictly speaking, and views that focus on or favor giving priority to the worst off, consider a comparison between (1) a redistribution from the better off to the worse off (however these terms are defined) and

---

[2] On this conceptual or terminological matter, I have been influenced by Larry S. Temkin, *Inequality* (New York: Oxford University Press), 7–8. T. M. Scanlon, *The Diversity of Objections to Equality* (Lawrence: The University of Kansas Lindley Lecture, 1997), 1–7, has a helpful catalog of arguments that seem to be egalitarian but, strictly speaking, are not.

(2) identical gains for the worse off with equal (or even greater) gains for the better off and suppose that the kind of inequality between the groups is the kind that egalitarians consider objectionable. If so, then an egalitarian will consider the first option better because there is less inequality between the better and worst off. (This ranking is defeasible because egalitarians will almost certainly not consider equality to be the *sole* value).[3] However, someone whose focus is on improving the situation of the worst off will be indifferent between the first and second option because the absolute position of the worst off is identical in both cases. Although "egalitarian" is often predicated on principles of justice, such as John Rawls's difference principle, which states that social and economic inequalities are to be arranged so that they are to the greatest benefit of the least advantaged,[4] it will be clearer if such principles are not described as egalitarian, and the label of egalitarianism is affixed only to views that consider equality a noninstrumental value. Views that give priority or significant weight to improving (at the limit, maximizing) the plight of the worst off and are only concerned with equality as a means to or as a by-product of improving the lot of the worst off will be labeled as prioritarianism or the priority view.

The reason I said that egalitarians value *some kind* of equality as such is that there are many inequalities and many respects in which one's life may go better or worse than another, and so any egalitarian theory must specify which kind or kinds of inequalities or disadvantages are its concern. Contemporary egalitarianism, in the last twenty years or so, has generally focused on unchosen or involuntary inequalities.[5] The root idea – endorsed by Richard Arneson, G. A. Cohen, Ronald Dworkin,

---

[3] Another way to put that point is to say that the former is better as far as equality is concerned but need not be judged to be better overall.

[4] Rawls, *A Theory of Justice*, 302 and *Political Liberalism* (New York: Columbia University Press, 1993), 291.

[5] Good guides to the literature of contemporary egalitarianism can be found in G. A. Cohen, "On the Currency of Egalitarian Justice," *Ethics* 99, no. 4 (1989): 906–44; Richard J. Arneson, "Equality," in Robert E. Goodin and Philip Pettit, eds., *A Companion to Contemporary Political Philosophy* (Cambridge, MA: Blackwell Publishing, 1995), 489–507; Richard J. Arneson, "Equality," in Robert L. Simon, ed., *The Blackwell Guide to Social and Political Philosophy* (Malden, MA: Blackwell Publishing, 2002), 85–105; and Peter Vallentyne, "Self-Ownership and Equality: Brute Luck, Gifts, Universal Dominance and Leximin," *Ethics* 107, no. 2 (1997): 321–43.

Will Kymlicka, Thomas Nagel, John Roemer, and Peter Vallentyne[6] – is that inequalities or disadvantages that arise through no choice or fault of one's own are unfair and should be rectified or at least minimized in some way. This responsibility or choice condition helps to illuminate the overall structure of egalitarianism. Egalitarians generally divide their theory of justice into two parts. Where people generally make genuine or uncoerced choices, we need – as a matter of respect for persons' capacities to shape their own lives – individual rights that protect the freedom to act on these choices, and fairness requires that people be held responsible for the costs of their choices. Let us call this the *antisubsidization principle*. The other side of the coin of holding individuals responsible for the costs of their choices is that they are entitled to the advantages they gain through their choices, therefore inequalities or advantages resulting from choice are just. However, when unchosen circumstances or luck rather than choice rules, fairness dictates the unlucky or disadvantaged be compensated for their disadvantages, and so such inequalities are unjust.[7]

Many egalitarians use a distinction between option luck and brute luck to further explicate the structure of egalitarianism.[8] Option luck

[6] Richard Arneson, "Equality and Equal Opportunity for Welfare," in Louis P. Pojman and Robert Westmoreland, eds., *Equality: Selected Readings* (New York: Oxford University Press, 1996), 229–41; G. A. Cohen, "On the Currency of Egalitarian Justice," in Ronald Dworkin, *Sovereign Virtue: The Theory and Practice of Equality* (Cambridge, MA: Harvard University Press, 2000); Will Kymlicka, *Contemporary Political Philosophy: An Introduction*, 2nd ed. (New York: Oxford University Press, 2002), ch. 3; Thomas Nagel, *Equality and Partiality* (New York: Oxford University Press, 1991); Eric Rakowski, *Equal Justice* (Oxford: New York University Press, 1991); John Roemer, *Equality of Opportunity* (Cambridge, MA: Harvard University Press, 1998), ch. 3; and Vallentyne, "Self-Ownership and Equality."

   Arneson, however, has recently changed his mind and now favors the priority view. See Richard J. Arneson, "Equality of Opportunity for Welfare Defended and Recanted," *Journal of Political Philosophy* 7, no. 4 (1999): 488–97.

[7] Not all contemporary philosophers who describe themselves as egalitarians believe that the focus should be on correcting for unchosen or involuntary inequalities. They deny that egalitarianism is, at root, a doctrine that is concerned with substantive material equality. I discuss this in section 2.1.3.

[8] The distinction between option and brute luck comes from Ronald Dworkin, who played the crucial role in contemporary egalitarianism's incorporation of a responsibility or choice condition. See "What Is Equality? Part 2: Equality of Resources," *Philosophy and Public Affairs* 10 (Fall 1981): 293. This essay has been reprinted, with slight revisions, in *Sovereign Virtue*, ch. 2. There is, unfortunately, no canonical definition of the brute luck/option luck distinction. Dworkin originally defined it so that option

is the kind of luck or risks one could reasonably have taken into account when making choices, and brute luck is the kind of luck or risks one could not have reasonably avoided having or undertaking. (A slightly different way of making the distinction is in terms of reasonable influence: option luck concerns outcomes that it is reasonable to believe one could influence, while this is not true of brute luck). Because option luck is the kind of luck one can legitimately be said to choose to take into account or to influence, egalitarians view advantages derived from option luck as justly acquired; hence, option luck is placed in the part of the theory having to do with choice and responsibility. Regarding this way of understanding egalitarianism, its primary concern or aim is to extinguish or at least minimize the effects of bad brute luck. Most egalitarians do not see extinguishing or minimizing the effects of *good* brute luck as an essential aim of justice.[9] However, they do think that the beneficiaries of good brute luck are the ones who are supposed to compensate the victims of bad brute luck. Those whose advantages are achieved by choice or option luck are entitled to their advantages, so they cannot justly be compelled to aid the unlucky. Because the point of the transfer from the beneficiaries of good brute luck to the victims of bad brute luck is not to harm the former but to aid the latter, some egalitarians insist that the transfers are justified

---

luck is luck that results from a deliberate or calculated gamble, but later egalitarians have modified this, probably because Dworkin's definition seems too restrictive. The key intuition behind the distinction is whether choices significantly influence one's outcomes, and choices can play a significant role even where one does not deliberate or calculate. My use of the distinction comes from Vallentyne's gloss on Dworkin's distinction; see Vallentyne, "Self-Ownership and Equality," 329, as well as "Brute Luck, Option Luck, and Equality of Initial Opportunities," *Ethics* 112, no. 3 (2002): 531–8. For egalitarian skepticism about the usefulness of the distinction between option and brute luck as a way of tracking responsibility, see Kasper Lippert-Rasmussen, "Egalitarianism, Option Luck, and Responsibility," *Ethics* 111 (April 2001): 548–79.

9 There are at least two reasons for this. First, as Vallentyne notes ("Self-Ownership and Equality," 329–32), to the extent egalitarians endorse some kind of principle of self-ownership, certain ways of attempting to limit persons' brute good luck, such as preventing them from exercising their native talents, are unjust. Second, as G. A. Cohen notes, egalitarians are generally not interested in reducing inequalities among those who are very well off (e.g., between someone who is very rich and someone who is just rich) in part because egalitarianism becomes a very unappealing doctrine if it focuses on leveling down or worsening the position of the better off where this produces no benefit for those who are significantly disadvantaged. Cohen, "Incentives, Inequality and Community," in *Equal Freedom: Selected Tanner Lectures on Human Values*, Stephen Darwall, ed. (Ann Arbor: University of Michigan Press, 1995), 335.

only if the benefits to the latter significantly outweigh the cost to the former or only if the transfers are efficient.[10]

To apply egalitarianism, we need to know which advantages and disadvantages are due to brute luck and which are due to option luck.[11] Although egalitarians do not all speak with one voice on this, there is broad agreement. Paradigm examples of brute luck are advantages and disadvantages stemming from one's genetic or native physical and mental abilities and traits, race or sex, or unproduced natural resources (e.g., the accidental discovery of a mineral deposit). Paradigm examples of option luck are advantages and disadvantages stemming from one's ambitions or conceptions of the good or from one's voluntarily acquired preferences and tastes. We can understand the point of these distinctions by using a thought experiment: if we all began with roughly similar or equal circumstances – similar natural endowments, and similar unproduced resources, and so forth – then any inequality that results would be a matter of choice or option luck and therefore just. In this sense, contemporary egalitarianism is a theory that advocates equal opportunity or equal access, not equal outcomes.[12] Given a fair or suitable starting point, egalitarians say, justice would not require any redistribution.

Of course, we do not begin at such a starting point. In the real world, people find themselves in unchosen circumstances of varying degrees of advantage and disadvantage. Egalitarians see the institutions of the welfare state as, in effect, the equivalent of insurance for bad brute luck. Roughly, the idea is that the welfare state compensates (or should compensate) individuals for whatever bad brute luck they could have insured themselves against if there were a market for such insurance. Of course, sometimes there is a market for insuring oneself against (at

---

[10] Rakowski, *Equal Justice*, 2, 74. Arneson, "Equality," 25, endorses what he calls a weak Pareto norm: principles of distributive justice should not recommend outcomes from which it is feasible to effect a Pareto improvement.

[11] The option luck/brute luck distinction need not be thought of as sharp; as far as I can tell, nothing precludes egalitarians from thinking it is on a continuum. Dworkin, *Sovereign Virtue*, 73–4.

[12] Equal opportunity is not to be understood here in the more restricted sense of people having a fair chance or access to jobs or positions. On the relationship between that more restricted sense of equal opportunity and the more general sense endorsed by contemporary egalitarianism, see Andrew Mason, "Equality of Opportunity, Old and New," *Ethics* 111, no. 4 (2001): 760–81.

least some forms of) brute luck, and when there is – and when it is available on fair terms – we are in the realm of option, not brute luck, and egalitarians would have no objection to private insurance (except perhaps they would want the insurance to be compulsory). However, the qualifier "at fair terms" is crucial here because egalitarians argue that it is unfair when victims of bad brute luck are charged more for being higher than average risks, which is why they favor social insurance as superior to private insurance and why they favor state welfare as providing the kind of compensation that is owed to people whose bad brute luck prevents them from supporting themselves in the marketplace.

Two other features of egalitarianism are worth mentioning. First, egalitarians disagree about the "equality of what?" question: for what kind of unchosen inequalities or disadvantages do egalitarians wish to compensate? Bad brute luck can produce inequalities in resources – for example, income and wealth – but also in welfare, that is, happiness or some psychological state. The main dispute here is whether, in addition to unchosen inequalities in resources, egalitarianism also mandates compensation for unchosen inequalities in welfare.[13] Second, egalitarians disagree about whether their theory applies only to intragenerational inequalities (inequalities between cohorts) or also to intergenerational inequalities (inequalities between different generations).[14]

2.1.2 *The Priority View, an Egalitarian Cousin*
Views that focus on aiding or benefiting the worst off are not, strictly speaking, egalitarian.[15] Both egalitarianism and the priority view focus

---

[13] For good surveys of the "equality of what?" literature, see the references in n. 5. Amartya Sen has proposed that egalitarians should focus on a person's functionings (i.e., one's ability to actually do what one wants), which he thinks of as not reducible to a person's resources or welfare. See his *Inequality Reexamined* (Cambridge, MA: Harvard University Press, 1992). Whether he has proposed a third way to measure equality or whether functionings reduce to resources and/or welfare is a matter of contention. See Dworkin, *Sovereign Virtue,* 299–303 and Andrew Williams, "Dworkin on Capability," *Ethics* 113, no. 1 (2002): 23–39. This dispute is irrelevant for my purposes.

[14] See Larry Temkin, "Justice and Equality: Some Questions about Scope," *Social Philosophy and Policy* 12 (Summer 1995): 73–5.

[15] For some useful and clear discussions, see Derek Parfit, "Equality or Priority," in Andrew Mason, ed., *Ideals of Equality* (Oxford: Blackwell Publishers, 1998), 1–20,

on those who are worse off but in different senses of that term. Being worse off can be understood in a relative or absolute sense: one can be worse off or one's situation can simply be bad in that one's life is miserable, terrible, and lacking in the essential elements for a decent life, and so forth. Egalitarianism, strictly speaking, is a doctrine about relative equality, that is, it aims at reducing the gap between the better off and worse off; whereas the priority view aims at improving the absolute position of the worst off. Because a diminution in the gap between the better and worse off is an improvement from the point of view of equality, egalitarianism seems vulnerable to the charge that it justifies or favors leveling down the better off even if this doesn't improve the situation of the worst off, and even if it harms the worst off. However, that criticism does *not* apply to contemporary egalitarianism. For one thing, contemporary egalitarianism has no objection to someone being advantaged if this was achieved through voluntary means rather than being the result of good brute luck. But apart from that, the aim of the theory is *not* to harm the beneficiaries of good brute luck but to bring about redistributions from those advantaged by good brute luck to those disadvantaged by bad brute luck, which will improve the latter's situation. Nevertheless, although both the priority view and contemporary egalitarianism oppose leveling down, they are still distinct views because the former will favor measures to improve the worst off's situation that have no effect on the gap between the better and worse off and/or that could widen the gap.

Why, despite the differences between these views, are they so often linked and described as "egalitarian?"[16] Perhaps this is because egalitarians often assume that redistribution from the better to the worst off will benefit the situation of the worst off. When that occurs, both views will endorse the same policy. This assumption is debatable, but, in any event, I will only provide a sustained separate discussion of the priority view when the arguments I give vis-à-vis contemporary egalitarianism do not clearly apply to the priority view.

---

in particular, 12–13, and Dennis McKerlie, "Equality and Priority," *Utilitas* 6, no. 1 (1994): 24–42, in particular, 24–7.

[16] See ibid., 14; Richard J. Arneson, "Luck Egalitarianism and Prioritarianism," *Ethics*, 110, no. 2 (January 2000): 340; and Richard J. Arneson, "Why Justice Requires Transfers to Offset Income and Wealth Inequalities," *Social Philosophy and Policy* 19 (Winter 2002): 199–200.

Two final points about the priority view need to be made. First, just as contemporary egalitarianism is concerned with unchosen or involuntary inequalities, so too will the priority view being considered here focus on those who are badly off through no choice or fault of their own. Although some defenders of the priority view are indifferent to the distinction between those who are badly off because of their choices and faults and those who are not – most famously, John Rawls's difference principle is insensitive to that distinction – recent defenders of the priority view insist upon the same emphasis on choice and responsibility that is distinctive of their egalitarian cousins.[17] Second, just as egalitarians disagree about the metric for relative inequality – resources alone or also welfare? – so defenders of the priority view will disagree about whether we should measure one's absolute situation in terms of resources alone or also consider welfare.

2.1.3 An Additional Terminological Complication

Some contemporary philosophers who describe themselves as egalitarians have views that do not fit easily into the frameworks I have described. Elizabeth Anderson, David Miller, and Samuel Scheffler deny that egalitarianism is, at root, a doctrine that is concerned with substantive material equality.[18] Anderson defends a view she calls "democratic equality," Miller defends a view he calls "social equality" or "equality of status," and Scheffler defends a view he calls "a society of equals." Despite the different terminology, these all amount to roughly the same idea, which is that people should be treated as moral equals and live in a society in which people interact based on mutual respect, no one is humiliated because of his or her personal characteristics, and rigid hierarchies and class divisions are absent. Given the way I have defined egalitarianism – as valuing or defending a substantive material equality as such – these views do not count as egalitarian because what they want to equalize is not a certain kind of material equality but a certain form of relationships among human beings. More important, the idea of treating people as moral equals or with mutual respect is

---

[17] See the two articles by Richard Arneson mentioned in n. 16.

[18] See, e.g., Elizabeth Anderson, "What Is the Point of Equality?" *Ethics* 109, no. 2 (1999): 287–337; David Miller, "Equality and Justice," in *Ideals of Equality*, 21–36; and Samuel Scheffler, "What Is Egalitarianism?" *Philosophy and Public Affairs* 31, no. 3 (2003): 5–39.

not particularly controversial or distinctive. It would be hard to think of a contemporary political philosophy that would reject these ideas. Admittedly, all three of these authors think that this equality of status or treating people as moral equals does have distributive material implications that would seem to support the welfare state. The implications, they claim, are that everyone has sufficient access to those goods that enable one to have one's basic needs satisfied and to function as a full-fledged citizen in a democratic society. These authors' way of understanding basic needs does not rest on the importance of the difference between choice and luck. (In the case of Anderson, she says explicitly that these goods would be provided regardless of one's choices or one's responsibility in needing those goods, and Scheffler also registers skepticism that the distinction between choice and luck should be central for egalitarians.) To the extent that these distributive implications focus on having *sufficient* access to *basic* needs, they do not seem to be particularly egalitarian (nor are they the same as the priority view),[19] and I will consider them as an aspect of the view (to be discussed later in the chapter) that there are basic positive rights to health care, social security, and welfare, and so forth on a par with negative liberty rights. To the extent that these ideas stress that one needs these goods in order to be a full-fledged citizen, I will consider them as part of the communitarian idea (to be discussed later in the chapter) that major institutions should sustain a sense of solidarity among citizens.

2.2 Basic Rights, Liberty, and Well-Being

The root idea in egalitarianism is fairness. Another way to evaluate the comparative question of welfare states versus market alternatives is by using the ideas of freedom and well-being. This approach arises in the context of a dispute about whether there are basic positive rights as well as basic negative rights.

Negative rights are rights that require others to refrain from certain kinds of actions. Almost no one doubts that there are basic negative rights: rights over one's mind or body (sometimes described as rights of self-ownership or the right to physical security and integrity), freedom

---

[19] Unless only the worst off lack sufficient access to basic needs but that seems dubious.

of speech, freedom of religion, and privacy.[20] Positive rights, on the other hand, require others to perform certain actions. The classical liberal or libertarian view of rights is that positive and negative rights have a very different status: the only positive rights are special rights, rights that arise from a special relationship between the parties, such as contractual rights or rights between parents and children; whereas negative rights are usually general or universal rights, rights that all persons have.

Welfare-state programs are sometimes justified by arguments that this classical liberal view of basic rights is mistaken, positive and negative rights have the same status because of three important links between the liberty that negative rights protect, and material well-being that positive rights help to provide. One proposed link is that in order for basic negative liberty rights to have value or to be effectively exercised one needs (at least) minimal material resources or well-being that basic positive rights provide. A second proposed link is that in order for one to exercise and/or develop the capacities for agency – the ability to make and reflect upon certain choices, in particular choices about what is valuable or good – one needs both freedom from interference with one's peaceful plans and projects, which negative rights provide, and at least minimal material resources or well-being, which positive rights provide.[21] Yet a third link is that certain negative rights cannot be justified in the first place when one's fellow citizens are deprived of or fail to obtain basic needs. Usually this claim is made with regard to private property rights, the idea being that it is unreasonable to demand that others refrain from taking the private property of the affluent if such appropriation is the only way for these others to avoid severe deprivation or obtain at least minimal

---

[20] Of course, there are disagreements about the grounds of such rights (e.g., do they rest on a deontic or consequentialist moral theory?) but those disagreements are irrelevant for my purposes here.

[21] On the first two links, see Raymond Plant, "Needs, Agency, and Moral Rights," in *Responsibility, Rights and Welfare: The Theory of the Welfare State*, J. Donald Moon, ed. (Boulder, CO: Westview Press, 1988), 55–76; Raymond Plant, *Modern Political Thought* (Cambridge: Basil Blackwell, 1991), 184–213, 253–92; Lesley Jacobs, *Rights and Deprivation* (Oxford: Oxford University Press, 1993), chs. 6, 7; Jeremy Waldron, *Liberal Rights: Collected Papers* (New York: Cambridge University Press, 1993), chs. 1, 10, 13; and Alan Gewirth, *The Community of Rights* (Chicago: The University of Chicago Press, 1996).

basic needs. Establishing basic positive rights are then seen as a way to prevent such deprivation and to help ground the duty not to interfere with private property rights.[22]

Some philosophers who make these arguments about the links between liberty and material well-being have not focused on their institutional ramifications. Their main concern has been to argue that basic positive rights – sometimes called *welfare rights* – and negative liberty rights are "two sides of the same coin,"[23] to use Jeremy Waldron's phrase. But for our purposes these institutional questions are important and once one focuses on these, an obvious problem emerges. All three arguments focus on the need for minimal material resources or well-being; the focus is on deprivation. However, social-insurance programs are not means or needs tested; they apply to all and their benefits go way beyond the provision of goods and services that supply the most urgent needs. As such, none of the arguments I just mentioned seem applicable to them. Because the bulk of the welfare state is social-insurance programs, these arguments seem quite limited as far as justifying the welfare state. They seem designed merely to justify means-tested benefits, the lesser part of the welfare state.

However, some defenders of welfare rights, such as J. Donald Moon, have argued that, contrary to appearances, arguments for welfare rights are actually better at justifying social-insurance programs than means-tested benefits, because the former meet basic needs indirectly.[24] Direct satisfaction of those needs, through means-tested benefits, threatens the idea that self-respecting able-bodied adults will support themselves through productive activity because one can obtain those benefits without working. Therefore they divide the community of able-bodied adults into two classes: those who are responsible moral agents who support themselves through work, and those who depend purely upon others for meeting their needs. (That is why being "on

---

[22] James Sterba, *Justice for Here and Now* (Cambridge: Cambridge University Press, 1998), ch. 3.

[23] Waldron, *Liberal Rights*, ch. 1.

[24] See "The Moral Basis of the Democratic Welfare State," in *Democracy and the Welfare State*, Amy Gutmann, ed. (Princeton: Princeton University Press, 1988), 30–36, 41–6 and "Introduction: Responsibility, Rights and Welfare," in *Responsibility Rights and Welfare: The Theory of the Welfare State*, J. Donald Moon, ed. (Boulder, CO: Westview Press, 1988), 4–8. Also see Jacobs, *Rights and Deprivation*, 196, 198, 200–2.

welfare" is a pejorative phrase and why welfare reform that aimed to make welfare conditional upon work was enacted in the United States in 1996.) Social-insurance programs, by contrast, are universal, so no stigma is attached to being a beneficiary, and because one's benefits are tied to one's ability to produce and contribute to one's benefits, one's right to receive them is compatible with being viewed as an independent person with self-respect, not someone purely dependent upon others for meeting one's needs. In this way, the need for economic security is met without being based upon claims of need.

I will use Moon's argument in Chapters 4 and 5 as a template for my examination of whether social or compulsory private insurance is better at establishing basic positive rights in a way that is compatible with norms linking self-respect, work, and responsibility. (If it seems odd to think of private insurance providing basic positive rights, remember that contracts establish positive rights, and because the insurance is compulsory, virtually everyone will have these rights.) As for the choice between state welfare and private charity, it may seem obvious that because state welfare provides a right to aid, while charity lacks such a right, the former must be superior to the latter from the point of view of an argument that purports to establish the need for positive rights. In Chapter 7 I will also discuss whether this seemingly obvious point is correct.

In addition to discussing whether welfare-state institutions or market-based alternatives are more compatible with the *grounds* of positive-rights arguments, I will also discuss some questions about the *content* of these rights. I will make it clear regarding what it means to say, for example, that citizens have a right to health care or employment security. Then I will discuss whether the legal rights provided by welfare-state institutions, which tend to be broader in scope than the rights market alternatives provide but that tend to be worse in delivering what they promised, are better or worse as far as fulfilling the content of welfare rights.

2.3 Community and Solidarity

Discussion of principles of justice and basic rights used to dominate contemporary political philosophy. Starting in the early 1980s, however, communitarian political philosophers began to change this picture. They argued that contemporary political philosophy and/or liberal society ignored the importance of community for our identity and our individual and social well-being.[25] This importance was such that under today's circumstances in Western democracies some degree of individual liberty may need to be sacrificed to strengthen the bonds of community.[26] It is a bit difficult to nail down what communitarians mean by community, but two ideas seem central. First, a community is an association of individuals who share some common values and interests, in particular a sense of what is public and private, or to put matters somewhat differently, a shared sense of the common good.

[25] For guides to communitarian literature, see my "Liberalism and Communitarianism," *Philosophical Books* 36 (July 1995): 145–55; Chandran Kukathas, "Liberalism, Communitarianism, and Political Community," *Social Philosophy and Policy* 13 (Winter 1996): 80–90; Daniel Bell, *Communitarianism and Its Critics* (Oxford: Oxford University Press, 1993); and Amitai Etzioni's introduction to *The Essential Communitarian Reader* (Lanham, MD: Rowman and Littlefield, 1998), ix–xxiv. The referent of "communitarianism" is a bit ambiguous. The first wave of communitarianism was inaugurated by philosophers such as Alasdair MacIntyre, Michael Sandel, Charles Taylor, and Michael Walzer. Very little of their criticisms of contemporary political philosophy and/or liberal society had specific policy implications and at least some of these criticisms were meant or were understood by others to provide a *contrast* between communitarianism and liberalism (as opposed to a modification of liberalism). The second wave of communitarianism was perhaps inaugurated by the beginning of the journal *The Responsive Community* in 1990 and the publication of the Responsive Community Platform in 1991. That journal and manifesto argued that insufficient attention was paid to the importance of community in American life. Unlike the first wave, however, this wave of communitarianism was less abstract and more policy oriented. Few contributors to *The Responsive Community* and signatories of the Responsive Community Platform were academic philosophers; most were intellectuals and public officials from a variety of fields. Furthermore, these second-wave communitarians often took pains to insist that they were not opposed to liberalism. Their aim, rather, was to modify liberalism so that the need for a balance between individual liberty and one's relationship to one's community took center stage. (Hence, labels such as *liberal communitarianism* or *democratic communitarianism* were adopted.) I shall rely upon both kinds of communitarian writing, although I shall stress the latter because it provides a less speculative basis for making comparative institutional arguments.

[26] Another way, suggested by Bell, *Communitarianism and Its Critics*, 93–4, is that communitarians believe that it is our commitment to the good of constitutive communities – those that partly shape our identity – that we find most valuable. This definition, however, seems to exclude some of the second-wave self-identified communitarians. For many of them believe that a significant number of Americans do not value a commitment to the good of their neighborhoods, families, or nation most of all – that's in part what's wrong with American society in their view, and their emphasis on balancing the values of community and liberty suggests they would be reluctant to insist that the former is more important than the latter.

Second, a community has a shared sense of "we-ness" or solidarity, that is, a sense that one's identity is at least partially constituted by one's membership in this association.

Obviously, we live in many communities. Families, neighborhoods, linguistic and ethnic groups, and cities and nations are or can be communities given the preceding definition. Communitarians would evaluate the choice between welfare-state institutions and market alternatives in terms of which ones have a comparative advantage in sustaining and promoting the common good and sense of solidarity that exists between members of the relevant community. The relevant community varies with the issue in question, although, for most of the institutions discussed in this book, communitarians tend to focus on solidarity among members of the nation.

It will help to list the central features of insurance and welfare systems that are relevant for a communitarian comparative analysis because the communitarian basis for comparative institutional evaluation is rather vague.

1. *Universality.* Communitarians favor a "single-status community." This means that major institutions should treat everyone as a full-fledged member of the community and avoid policies that set some people off from others in their community and thus weaken solidarity.[27] Thus, whenever possible, programs and institutions should be universal. Welfare, it appears, cannot be made universal, but it should be designed in such a way that it sustains solidarity between the donors and recipients.

2. *Shared responsibility.* Major social institutions should express a commitment to the idea that all members of the community are obligated to one another. Individuals need to take responsibility for their own well-being and security, but they should also be responsible for the welfare of other members of the community, particularly those who are unable to provide adequate protection for old age or their health-care needs or are in dire poverty, and so forth. Thus communitarians oppose purely individualistic notions of responsibility whereby each

---

[27] For the importance for communitarians of the idea of a "single-status moral community," see Goodin, *Reasons for Welfare: The Political Theory of the Welfare State* (Princeton: Princeton University Press, 1988), 73–4. For a recent statement, see Philip Selznick, "Social Justice: A Communitarian Perspective," in *The Essential Communitarian Reader,* 69.

person takes responsibility only for protecting him or herself or his or her family from loss of income and other hardships.[28]

3. *Reciprocity.*[29] Communitarians want shared responsibility to be equitable, because this is an essential component of justice and/or because inequities create social division and instability. Communitarian understanding of equity can embrace the priority view, since giving priority to the worst off may sustain solidarity, but it precludes egalitarianism, since equality as such has no independent value if sustaining and promoting the common good of communities is the touchstone for comparative evaluation.

4. *Fidelity.* All insurance schemes promise to provide protection against common risks of a loss of income if and/or when certain events come to pass, such as old-age or illness. In the case of some of these schemes, such as old-age social insurance and NHI, worries about whether these promises can be or are being kept are widespread. Communitarians believe they must be kept because "it is the ethically appropriate thing to do, because if one violates such commitments the social and moral order of a society is diminished."[30] With welfare, the criterion of fidelity is not as salient, but it does apply when welfare systems promise to get able-bodied recipients in the work force.

5. *Responsiveness and Participation.* Communitarians want communities to promote or sustain the common good of its members, but how, in a pluralist society in which individuals have diverse conceptions of the good, can this be done?[31] Many communitarians believe that if communities are to be responsive to members' views and concerns

---

[28] I cannot find an explicit statement of this in communitarian writing, but it seems clearly implied by the communitarian stress on solidarity.

[29] "At the heart of the communitarian understanding of social justice is the idea of reciprocity," states "The Responsive Communitarian Platform," in *The Essential Communitarian Reader*, xxxiv.

[30] Amitai Etzioni and Laura Brodbeck, *The Intergenerational Covenant: Rights and Responsibilities* (Washington, DC: The Communitarian Network, 1995), 3 (author's emphasis).

[31] Some communitarians think pluralism is relevant at a different level, that different goods have different social meanings in different societies and should be distributed in accordance with those meanings. So, e.g., Michael Walzer argues in *Spheres of Justice: A Defense of Pluralism and Equality* (New York: Basic Books, 1983), 84–91, that because citizens in modern democracies think that the purpose of health care is to treat illness and restore physical well-being, health care should be distributed in accordance with need, not the ability to pay. I discuss Walzer's views in Chapter 4.

then there must be democratic participation. Some communitarians believe that there is not just a right but also a duty to participate in institutions that help communities discover or construct a common good. This injunction to participate applies only where the relevant institutions are not so large as to make participation impractical. Thus, for example, it does not apply to pension systems, but does apply to health-care insurance, since local health-care organizations can be structured to allow for citizen input and control.[32]

No welfare-state institution or market alternative embodies all of these criteria, I will argue, so the crucial question becomes which institution embodies more of them or would score higher on a communitarian scale of values.

2.4 Public Justification and Epistemic Accessibility

The perspectives described in this chapter so far and that provide the basis for comparative institutional evaluation in this book cover the main reasons most contemporary political philosophers use to justify the welfare state. Justifications of the welfare state usually appeal to fairness (understood as reducing certain relative inequalities or improving the absolute position of the worst off), well-being (understood as providing for certain basic needs to which all citizens are said to have rights), or community (understood as sustaining a sense of solidarity among people who share a conception of the common good). In addition to these reasons or values that are used to justify the welfare state, many political philosophers maintain that there is a criterion of adequacy for judging any political principle or institution. This is the idea, common to many versions of liberalism, that basic political principles and institutions must be publicly justified.[33] There are two parts to this

---

[32] See Ezekiel J. Emanuel, "A Liberal Communitarian Vision of Health Care," *The Ends of Human Life: Medical Ethics in a Liberal Polity* (Cambridge, MA: Harvard University Press, 1993), 178–244.

[33] For an argument that public justification is central to liberalism, see Stephen Macedo, *Liberal Virtues: Citizenship, Virtue, and Community in Liberal Constitutionalism* (Oxford: Clarendon Press, 1990), 40–8. For helpful surveys of different conceptions of public justification, see Gerald Gaus, *Social Philosophy* (Armonk, NY: M. E. Sharpe, 1999), ch. 2 and Fred D'Agostino "Public Justification," in *The Stanford Encyclopedia of Philosophy*,

idea: the "public" part and the "justification" part. The former means that political institutions and principles must be supported by public reasons, reasons that are widely and openly accessible to citizens with normal reasoning powers. These reasons must be seen by citizens to be good reasons, to offer rationales or arguments that make sense, and provide for them a plausible basis for endorsing (or at least not objecting to) basic political institutions and state programs. This notion of public reasons is based upon or is an outgrowth of a notion of respect for persons. This respect is for what we share in common as persons, namely certain powers of reasoning and judgment; generating public support for political institutions or major social programs in a way that bypasses or subverts such powers manifests disrespect.

As for the justification side of the notion of public justification, an institution supported by public reasons is not thereby publicly justified, because even conscientious and thoughtful people make invalid inferences and accept bad arguments.[34] What links public reasons with public justification, or what counts as a *good* public reason, is quite controversial. However, the following negative requirement is quite plausible. Suppose we are comparing two major institutions or social programs of the same type. One of them (a) blocks or makes it difficult to obtain reasonably accurate or reliable information about the nature or evolution of that institution or program, and/or (b) is so complex and complicated that it is unlikely that anyone but experts can monitor its effects or evolution. Suppose, however, neither (a) nor (b) is true of the other institution or program or these features apply to this other institution or program to a lesser extent. Then the former institution or program is, *ceteris paribus*, unjustified. The rationale for this principle of epistemic accessibility is that if the public is seriously misled or misinformed about the nature of X, then its endorsement

Edward N. Zalta, ed. (Fall 1997 Edition), http://www.seop.leeds.ac.uk/archives/fall1997/entries/justification-public/ (accessed November 2006).

Liberal theorists differ concerning whether the subject matter of public justification is principles of justice, the social order, or basic social and political institutions. I shall assume that state program or institutions like social insurance and means-tested benefits, in virtue of their far-reaching effects and the relevance of questions about its justice and fairness, fall within the subject matter of public justification.

34 Gerald Gaus makes this point, citing much empirical evidence to support it, in *Justificatory Liberalism* (New York: Oxford University Press, 1996), 130–6.

of what it takes to be X may be an endorsement of something different from X, and so we lack grounds for saying in this case that public support implies public justification.

Though this requirement of epistemic accessibility is not a political philosophy or perspective, it is of equal importance with the perspectives of egalitarianism, positive-rights theory, and communitarianism in assessing the welfare state. If an institution fails the test of epistemic accessibility, that is a significant mark against it, and if, in addition, that institution is worse than a feasible alternative institution on egalitarian, positive rights, and communitarian grounds, then we have excellent reasons to believe that the alternative to that institution is the one that is justified and that we should espouse.

What happens, however, if an institution ranks higher according to some of the evaluative frameworks for this book and worse on others? Without some reason to weigh any one perspective or requirement more than others, the default assumption must be that they are of equal weight. Fortunately, for most of the book, we need not be concerned about the weight of different perspectives or requirements because, as I will argue, market-based alternatives to the welfare state are better from the point of view of almost all of the perspectives' requirements and no worse on a few others.

3

Health Insurance, Part I

3.1 The Topic's Importance

The social-insurance programs are the heart of the welfare state, and perhaps the most important of these is government-administered and -financed health insurance. Along with old-age or retirement pensions, spending on government-financed health care and insurance dominates contemporary welfare states' budgets.[1] As I write this, government-administered and -financed health insurance seems politically entrenched: most people cannot even conceive of a (genuine) market alternative to the status quo in health insurance. If an intellectually solid case for market health insurance (MHI) can be established, then supporters of the welfare state should be on the defensive, as social health insurance is an institution central to their vision of the just or good society.

I will make that case in this chapter and Chapter 4. It turns out that what many think of as the strongest argument for social health insurance – that it is more egalitarian than MHI – is the weakest argument. Social health insurance, or NHI, as it is often called, is much more unfair by egalitarian standards because it rations catastrophic care in

---

[1] The U.S. welfare state does not have a national system of government-administered and -financed health insurance, but it does have two large government-financed and -administered health-care insurance programs that, along with other government spending on health care, equal nearly half of the money spent in the United States on health care. Also, the private health insurance in the United States is not genuine market insurance. See section 3.2.2.

favor of the knowledgeable, well-connected and well-motivated middle class, foists the cost of voluntarily assumed health risks upon others, and prevents those with different conceptions of the good from choosing different health plans that match those conceptions. Market health insurance, by contrast, has no government rationing of catastrophic care, gives people the freedom to choose different health plans, and prevents them from foisting their voluntary health choices onto others. Because the kind of MHI defended here incorporates subsidies for the indigent and those with uninsurable risks, it satisfies egalitarian concerns about the poor having adequate access to health care, while avoiding the unfair effects of government rationing. Making the case for these claims will occupy this chapter. In Chapter 4 I discuss whether NHI can be justified in the name of a positive right to health care or by communitarian arguments. I argue that it cannot. I also reject the claim that the popularity of NHI should be used as a reason to defend it.

3.2 The Institutional Alternatives

3.2.1 National Health Insurance

NHI consists of the following key features.[2] First, there is universal or near universal coverage, which is achieved by compulsion.[3] Individuals are forced to pay taxes to cover their own and other people's health care. Governments either provide the insurance (e.g., Canada) or manage a national health service (e.g., Britain, Sweden) or require

---

[2] My information comes from William Glaser, *Health Insurance in Practice: International Variations in Financing, Benefits, and Problems* (San Francisco: Jossey-Bass Publishers, 1991), ch. 1–4, app. A; Joseph White, *Competing Solutions: American Health Care Proposals and International Experience* (Washington, DC: The Brookings Institution, 1995), ch. 4–6; and Anna Dixon and Elias Mossialos, eds., *Health Care Systems in Eight Countries: Trends and Challenges* (London: European Observatory on Health Care Systems, London School of Economics and Political Science Hub, 2002). Glaser discusses Germany, Switzerland, Holland, Belgium, France; White discusses Germany, France, Canada, the United Kingdom, Japan, and Australia; the essays in Dixon and Mossialos discuss Australia, Denmark, France, Germany, Holland, New Zealand, Sweden, and the United Kingdom.

[3] New Zealand is a special case. Government provides universal health insurance for hospital care but not for ambulatory care. The latter is heavily subsidized for most, but not all, users. See Judith Healy, "New Zealand," in *Health Care Systems in Eight Countries*, 76–9.

that one purchase health insurance from a nonprofit sickness fund (e.g., Germany,[4] France, Belgium).

Second, NHI is not market, actuarial insurance. Even in countries with NHI that have nonprofit sickness funds, these companies or funds are forbidden to engage in the *raison d'être* of market insurance, namely risk rating. Premiums are not allowed to vary according to risk, with a few mild exceptions, such as by age. The intent of the premiums or the taxes paid is to redistribute or cross-subsidize: generally, those with low risks of using health services are supposed to subsidize the high risks. Of course, market insurance does involve risk sharing as well as risk rating; one is grouped with a class of people with *similar*, but not identical, risks. In a competitive market, however, significant gains are made by limiting the extent to which different risks are charged the same premium, and whatever "redistribution" is achieved within a class of risks that is charged the same premium is not intentional.

Third, NHI limits the choices of plans. Governments mandate that all plans offer a standardized set of benefits.[5] Choice is somewhat augmented for those who can purchase supplemental insurance that typically provides better benefits than NHI.[6]

The features discussed so far – compulsion, nonactuarial insurance, limited choice of policies or plans – are the typical features of social insurance. But crucial to understanding NHI is a fourth feature: NHI is an example of a comprehensive service plan, not casualty insurance.[7]

---

4 In Germany, close to 25 percent of the population – those above a certain income – is not required to purchase health insurance from nonprofit sickness funds. About two-thirds of this upper-income group chooses to purchase that insurance and most of the other third chooses to purchase private health insurance. Reinhard Busse, "Germany," in *Health Care Systems in Eight Countries*, 49. Except for high-cost treatments, a similar opting-out policy exists in Holland. However, the government has announced plans to require everyone to purchase health insurance. See Reinhard Busse, "Netherlands," in ibid., 62–4; on the recent proposed changes, see T. Sheldon, "Dutch Government Plans to Reform Health Insurance System," *British Medical Journal* 323 (2001): 70.

5 Though as I will discuss in section 3.5.3, this does not mean everyone receives the same kind of treatment or care.

6 In some countries, e.g., Canada, private insurance is only allowed for benefits not covered by NHI (White, *Competing Solutions*, 66). In Australia, private insurance is not allowed for ambulatory care, only for hospital care (Healy, "Australia," in *Health Care Systems in Eight Countries*, 5).

7 For a clear discussion of the differences between these, see John C. Goodman and Gerald L. Musgrave, *Patient Power: Solving America's Health Care Crisis* (Washington,

Service plans provide coverage for the consumption of medical or health-care services, not necessarily for being ill or undergoing an adverse event. This is why coverage is typically comprehensive in the sense that everything from routine doctor visits to hospital care is covered. However, casualty insurance (e.g., auto and homeowners insurance) insures against adverse events, so that one is reimbursed for some identifiable loss one suffers. Typically, a person is insuring against catastrophes or major losses, and payment often goes to the insured (unlike service plans that usually reimburse the providers). Thus, casualty insurance is not comprehensive: auto insurance pays for repairs after an accident, not for tune-ups; homeowner insurance pays for damage due to lightning, not for replacing a worn carpet. Although market insurance could and does involve comprehensive service plans, it is doubtful that these plans would dominate the market.

The difference between casualty-catastrophic insurance[8] and comprehensive service plans is crucial. Because NHI is an example of the latter, this means that the government is directly or indirectly involved in virtually all facets of health-care markets. Casualty insurance, by contrast, does not have that much of a spillover effect in the broader market for services. As it is not comprehensive, and as the insured typically decides how or whether to spend one's payment for losses incurred,[9] casualty insurance's effects on the broader market for services – for

---

DC: The Cato Institute, 1992), 178–82 and Susan Feingenbaum, "Body Shop Economics: What's Good for Our Cars May Be Good for Our Health," *Regulation* 15 (Fall 1992): 25–31.

[8] I combine casualty and catastrophic insurance in this hyphenated expression to emphasize that casualty insurance, because it insures against adverse events and does not reimburse one for services consumed, is usually just insurance against catastrophic or major losses. However, it is important to notice that the connection between casualty insurance and catastrophic insurance does not hold with equal strength in both directions. I.e., although casualty insurance is almost always catastrophic-only insurance, catastrophic-only insurance need not be based on the principles of casualty insurance, i.e., it need not be limited to reimbursement for identifiable losses or illnesses. E.g., one could take out a high-deductible policy that covers all of one's medical expenses above a certain amount, regardless of whether those expenses were incurred for some loss or illness. This would be catastrophic-only insurance in the sense that a high level of medical expenditures often indicates the occurrence of a major medical problem. However, reimbursement for a high level of medical expenditures is not casualty insurance because the reimbursement is for the consumption of medical services, not for some identifiable loss or illness.

[9] Sometimes casualty insurers will place limits on the insured's discretion. Auto insurers, e.g., sometimes place limits on how and when you fix your car after a wreck.

example, automobile insurance's effects on the market for automobile services or products – are necessarily limited. Normal commercial exchanges between buyers and sellers govern those markets. Once insurance is comprehensive, and the government has a role in almost all consumption decisions, then the effects of NHI necessarily dominate and structure all health-care markets.

Once government subsidizes or finances most health-care consumption, it is inevitable that it will play a large role in production decisions. Health-care services in advanced industrial societies require significant expenditures of resources. Because subsidization increases demand, subsidizing those services means that a significant portion of the government budget will be devoted to health-care resources – making it almost inevitable that governments at some point take steps to control those costs. Either governments must then stop subsidizing demand, which would really defeat the purpose of NHI, or they must control supply. Hence we arrive at the fifth feature of NHI, the limited role for competitive market prices. Some countries have a global budget that limits the total yearly amount spent on health care or for hospitals and/or certain procedures. All NHI systems place controls on (private and public) hospitals' capital expenditures, either by global budgets or requirements that they seek permission from a governmental body before making these, or certain types of these, expenditures.[10] Those controls tend to constrict investment in expensive high-tech equipment. As for doctors' fees, they are set by either the government (price controls) or by negotiation between doctor alliances or groups and sickness funds and/or the government (either national or provincial).[11] In most of these negotiations, the funds or governments tend to have the upper hand, and doctors have reluctantly come to accept a yearly expenditure cap, or, more often, a target that can be adjusted downward the following year if spending is above the target for a particular year. Similar situations exist with pharmaceutical prices. Global budgets plus fee regulation and/or expenditure caps/targets are the

[10] They are less likely to be subject to capital controls in countries where there are few private hospitals.
[11] Sometimes, as in Australia, the government sets no fee, but the government forbids private insurance from reimbursing above what Medicare (Australia's ambulatory NHI program) does. Because Medicare pays 85 percent of doctor fees, this amounts to de facto government fee regulation. White, *Competing Solutions*, 96–7.

chief mechanisms by which NHI puts a brake on the consequences of
subsidized demand.

Sixth, all NHI systems engage in nonmarket and nonprice forms
of allocation and cost containment. This is both a consequence and
cause of the absence of genuine market prices. In almost all countries,
this nonmarket and nonprice allocation and cost containment leads to
or involves government rationing, which means there are significant
waits in various sectors of the system.[12] (The prominent exceptions to
this are France and probably Germany.)[13] Sometimes the wait is for a

---

[12] Because some countries do not keep any records of waits, and because there is rarely
a national waiting list (as opposed to a regional or provincial list), it is often hard to
get reliable information about the extent of waits. For an unusually detailed study,
see Nadeem Esmail and Michael Walker, *Waiting Your Turn: Hospital Waiting Lists
in Canada* (Vancouver: The Fraser Institute, 2002). Countries with a national health
service tend to have the worst problems. As Robert Baker notes, the British NHS used
to be dubbed the "British National Health Shortages," given its extensive waits for
many operations and procedures. See "The Inevitability of Health Care Rationing: A
Case Study of Rationing in the British National Health Service," in *Rationing America's
Medical Care: The Oregon Plan and Beyond*, Martin Strossberg, Joshua M. Wiener, Robert
Baker, eds. with I. Alan Fein (Washington, DC: The Brookings Institution, 1992), 208.
Things have improved somewhat in the last decade, but waits are still common. See
Anna Dixon and Ray Robinson, "United Kingdom" in *Health Care Systems in Eight
Countries*, 111. Some countries with national health services, e.g., Sweden and Italy,
have requirements for maximum waiting time. The fact that they fail to work is noted
by Jo Lenaghan, "Health Care Rights in Europe," in *Hard Choices in Health Care*, Jo
Lenaghan, ed. (London: BMJ Publishing Group, 1997) 188–9. For a more recent
account, see Sandra Leon and Ana Rico, "Sweden" in *Health Systems in Eight Countries*
96–100. Glaser, *Health Insurance in Practice*, 250, claims that waits are not a problem
in countries where social health insurance is provided by nonprofit sickness funds.
This was probably true in the 1980s, but as a general statement it is no longer true
today. Waits exist in Holland, e.g. See Busse, "Netherlands," in *Health Care Systems in
Eight Countries*, 70.

[13] As far as I can tell, France has avoided rationing by (a) allowing nonprofit funds
to run deficits and then making them up the next year with tax funds rather than
clamping down on demand, (b) having a thriving market for supplemental insurance
(more than 80 percent of the population), which relieves some of the pressure of
excess demand for government-subsidized services, and (c) using cost containment
primarily in the area of pharmaceuticals, which is somewhat less likely to produce
waits than other forms of cost containment. (The French government's low prices
for drug reimbursement and its tendency to delay or avoid reimbursement for newer
innovative drugs have diminished funds available for drug research and development,
rather than producing a waiting list for drugs.) In Germany, the situation is a bit more
complicated. There have been proposals for government rationing, which have been
(so far) beaten back, and there has been constant concern for the last ten years that
rationing is about to occur. So far, it is not clear that cost-containment measures have
produced any significant waits. The reasons are somewhat similar to what occurs in

doctor, usually a specialist or a hospital-based physician, rather than one's primary-care physician; a place in the hospital; or for equipment needed for a diagnosis or an operation. But wherever the rationing occurs, it is generally true that specific rationing decisions are not made publicly and democratically. They are made, with little public input and awareness, by administrators, local health authorities, and doctors. Although in recent years a variety of governments (the United Kingdom, Denmark, Finland, Norway, Sweden, New Zealand, The Netherlands) have made various attempts to involve or inform the public about the existence and nature of rationing, for reasons I will describe in section 3.5.2, there is little reason to believe that these attempts have had much effect on the nature of rationing or that the public has more than an impressionistic understanding of the process.

Seventh, patients pay little out of pocket and have poor awareness of (monetary) costs. In service plans, the provider usually bills the carrier or insurance fund who then pays the bills. Typically patients pay, at most, relatively small co-payments or have to meet a minimal deductible. Thus there is little incentive for them to know what health-care services cost or for providers to communicate that information to them. This lack of information and incentive to acquire that information extends to the insurance premiums, though this lack of information varies somewhat with the type of system (e.g., patients are more aware of premiums that they pay themselves than those that are paid solely by employers or by taxes). In those countries in which supplemental insurance plays a prominent role (e.g., France) or a certain percentage of the population chooses to or is forced to take private insurance (e.g., Germany and The Netherlands respectively) the awareness of monetary costs is somewhat greater.

Finally, in NHI the patient is not generally treated as a consumer or a paying customer, and he or she generally isn't. It is not the patient who is the direct purchaser or payer of services; given information about

France except that rather than deficits, Germany allows the nonprofit funds to simply raise employer-based premiums when faced with a likely shortfall of revenue, and the market for supplemental insurance is smaller, although, unlike France, a certain percentage of the population is allowed to opt out of the state system altogether. See Heinz Redwood, *Why Ration Health Care? An International Study of the United Kingdom, France, Germany, and the Public Sector Health Care in the USA* (London: Institute for the Study of Civil Society, 2000), ch. 5, 6.

price, quality, or availability;[14] can or is encouraged to shop for better
offers; or directly negotiates with the seller of services. (This is less true
in countries with a variety of nonprofit sickness funds, that engage in
some limited competition, and/or in which a certain percentage of the
public has private insurance.) Of course, in other forms of insurance,
the insurance company is an intermediary between seller and buyer.
The whole point of insurance is that when risky events occur, there is
another party beside oneself and the seller of goods and services to
deal with the adverse event. But what is striking about NHI is the virtual
elimination, from all aspects of the medical system, of the insured's
role in monetary transactions with providers.

To summarize, NHI combines the typical features of social insurance – compulsion, nonactuarial insurance, and limited choice of
plans – with payment for consumption of comprehensive medical care
that characterizes service plans. As a result, NHI requires significant
intervention and domination of the broader market for health-care
services, through fee regulation, expenditure caps/targets, global budgets, and rationing. Not surprisingly, in such a system the patient is not
a consumer and has little awareness of monetary costs.

3.2.2 Market Health Insurance: What It Is Not

The usual contrast with NHI is the private health insurance market in
the United States. However, this is a grave error because it is *not* an
example, nor even an imperfect exemplar, of MHI.

First, the number of insurance mandates has dramatically increased
in the last twenty-five years or so. Insurance companies are increasingly
compelled, usually by state governments, to offer certain benefits (e.g.,
alcoholism and drug treatment programs, mental health benefits, well-
baby care, mammography screening) and to cover certain providers
(e.g., chiropractors, optometrists), which limits consumer choice, in
particular the choice of a cheap "no-frills" purely catastrophic insurance policy that would not cover all of these benefits. Such policies
can't be offered, and the mandates drive up the cost of insurance,

---

[14] An exception is Sweden, which has recently instituted a system whereby patients
can learn about waiting times at different institutions for different procedures. See
Ragnar Lofgren, *Health Care Waiting List Initiatives in Sweden* (Vancouver: The Fraser
Institute, 2002).

making it less affordable.[15] Congress has added mandates of its own, for example, requiring parity between benefits for physical and mental illness and requiring a minimum number of covered hospital days following certain procedures.

Second, risk rating is increasingly restricted or forbidden by law. In 1996, Congress banned insurance companies from excluding pre-existing conditions when people change insurance companies,[16] and state laws prescribing community rating – the same rate for all or most subscribers – are on the rise.[17]

These two points throw serious doubt upon the claim that private health insurance in the United States is genuine MHI, as consumer choice and risk rating, the heart of MHI, have been greatly restricted by government action. Even more damaging to the claim, however, is that the U.S. private health insurance market is dominated by employer-provided and -sponsored service plans, and this was not achieved through market means.

During the 1930s, service plans offered by Blue Cross and Blue Shield – the former a hospital service plan begun by nonprofit hospitals, the latter a physician service plan begun by doctors – achieved market dominance over commercial insurance companies by a number of government-assisted techniques.[18] They achieved exemptions from

---

[15] See Goodman and Musgrave, *Patient Power*, ch. 11 and Gail A. Jensen and Michael A. Morrisey "Employer-Sponsored Health Insurance and Mandated Benefit Laws," *The Milbank Quarterly* 77, no. 4 (1999): 1–21. In 1968, there were five health-care mandates. Now there are more than a thousand. Recently, some states have taken steps to reverse this trend. See Betsy McCaughey, "States Look to Cut Red Tape to Ease Crisis of Uninsured," *Investors' Business Daily* (March 15, 2002).

[16] See Steve Langdon, "Health Insurance Law," *Congressional Quarterly Weekly Report* 54 (September 14, 1996): 2619–23.

[17] Examples are New York, New Jersey, and Florida. For a discussion of these laws, see Richard A. Epstein, *Antidiscrimination in Health Care: Community Rating and Preexisting Conditions* (Oakland, CA: The Independent Institute, 1996), 5–7. Also see Melinda L. Shriver and Grace-Marie Arnett, "Uninsured Rates Rise Dramatically in States with Strictest Health Insurance Regulation," *Heritage Foundation Backgrounder* (August 14, 1998), in particular, app. I and II.

[18] The reason hospitals began offering Blue Cross was because the Great Depression was taking a toll on the hospitals' business. Service plans, with their "first dollar coverage" (i.e., no deductibles but with limits on total expenses covered), were a way of stimulating business. See Terree P. Wasley, *What Has Government Done to Our Health Care?* (Washington, DC: The Cato Institute), 47–50, and Joseph Califano, *America's Health Care Revolution* (New York: Random House, 1986), 41–2. Blue Shield was introduced after commercial insurers introduced plans to compete with Blue Cross.

most taxation that their commercial rivals had to pay. State insurance commissions permitted them to avoid keeping reserves that commercial insurance companies needed to have in order to have adequate funds to pay out benefits (in effect, the Blues were allowed to operate as a pay-as-you-go scheme, and in return they were required to serve the entire community by charging a rate low enough that low-income people could afford). In a number of states, commercial insurers were subject to minimum premium/rate regulations, which the Blues were not. There was an incestuous relationship, as it were, between professional medical associations, hospitals, and the Blues from which commercial rivals were excluded. Hospitals started the Blues and they instituted a cost-plus reimbursement system, that is, they reimbursed the hospitals' cost plus a certain extra amount (for physician services they used the notion of a customary and reasonable amount). Not surprisingly, because cost-plus reimbursement guaranteed the hospitals' survival and produced no incentive to economize, the hospitals were happy to give the Blues some discounts in the early days to attract more customers than their commercial rivals, and doctors and hospitals were encouraged to place American Medical Association (AMA) approved ads for the Blues in their waiting rooms (this during a time when competitive advertising by doctors was forbidden by the AMA).[19]

As a result, by 1940 the dominance of the Blues was already in place: half of those with hospital insurance had the Blues.[20] It was difficult

---

[19] Furthermore, prior to the 1930s the AMA took action to squash *consumer*-based service plans. In the late nineteenth century and early twentieth century, a number of industries, mutual-aid societies, and consumer cooperatives also provided service plans that covered both hospital and physician services for low monthly or annual fees, but these were different from the Blues in one crucial respect. The cooperatives, mutual-aid societies, or industries provided the care without the insurance companies; they hired company or lodge doctors (mutual-aid societies were dues-paying voluntary associations whose social life and provision of services revolved around a lodge) who were paid a fixed salary and/or owned the hospitals or clinics. The AMA eventually eliminated all of these by lobbying successfully for state laws that effectively made all medical service plans fit the AMA's specifications. See Lawrence C. Goldberg and Warren Greenberg, "The Emergence of Physician-Sponsored Health Insurance: A Historical Perspective" in *Competition in the Health Care Sector*, Warren Greenberg, ed. (Germantown: Aspen Systems Corporation, 1978), 288–321, and "The Effect of Physician-Controlled Health Insurance: *US v. Oregon State Medical Society*," *Journal of Health, Politics, Policy and the Law* 2 (Spring 1977): 48–78. I discuss mutual-aid societies in more detail in the appendix to Chapter 6.

[20] However, hospital insurance was still confined to a small group, about 9 percent of the population. Twelve million had hospital insurance; the total population was about 132

for commercial insurers to provide a significant challenge to the Blues, and the former's policies started to take on more of the characteristics of the Blues. In particular, they offered service plans, instead of casualty insurance, and they used cost-plus reimbursement. (However, they continued to use risk rating, not community rating, and make payments to the insured rather than the providers.) At this point service plans dominated but not employer-provided service plans. That was brought about by the second crucial transforming event: tax policy in the early 1940s. The Internal Revenue Service (IRS) declared that fringe benefits up to 5 percent of wages were exempt from wage and price controls during World War II. In addition to excluding employer-provided health insurance from wages, the IRS shortly thereafter ruled that employers could exclude health insurance from taxable business income and that employees getting employer health insurance did not have to include the value of their benefits in calculating taxable income. Thus, there was a double-tax exemption for employer-sponsored health insurance. This, combined with the fact that insurance premiums paid by individuals were not tax deductible (and those by the self-employed only received a small tax deduction), gave a considerable push to employer-sponsored health insurance. When high marginal income tax rates became a permanent feature of American life during and after World War II,[21] the value of the double-tax exemption for employer-sponsored health insurance and the disadvantage to consumer-purchased health insurance became virtually overwhelming.[22] When employers offered health insurance,

million. Blue Cross never held less than 45 percent of the entire health insurance market until the early 1980s. As of 1996, the latest year for which I have been able to obtain data, the Blues held 36 percent of the market. See Health Insurance Association of America, *Sourcebook of Health Insurance Data, 1988* (Washington, DC: Health Insurance Association of America, 1988), tables 1.2, 1.3, and Health Insurance Association of America, *Sourcebook of Health Insurance Data, 1999–2000* (Washington, DC: Health Insurance Association of America, 1999), table 2.10.

[21] See Randall Holcombe, *Public Sector Economics: The Role of Government in The American Economy* (Upper Saddle River, NJ: Pearson Prentice Hall, 2006), 291, table 14.1.

[22] Frank R. Dobbin, "The Origins of Private Social Insurance: Public Policy and Fringe Benefits in America, 1920–1950," *American Journal of Sociology* 97, no. 5 (1992): 1416–50, challenges the importance of tax policy in explaining the growth in employer-sponsored benefits. He argues that starting in the 1920s employers offered private pensions and health insurance as a way to retain or sustain the loyalty of workers and to blunt the appeal of unionization (which in the 1930s and 1940s expanded rapidly). He also points out that there was a sharper rise in employer-sponsored health insurance from 1939 to 1943 (3.5 million to 6.5 million, in surveys taken by

they generally offered the product that was widely available in the market, which was not casualty insurance but service plans. Hence by the end of the 1940s the U.S. market for health insurance was dominated by employer-provided service plan insurance, with cost-plus reimbursement[23] and community rating (most large employers followed the Blues' lead and charged a uniform premium for all workers).

Although the domination of employer-sponsored comprehensive service plans still continues in the United States, in the last twenty-five years that market has changed in an important respect. Explosive rises in health-care costs made cost-plus reimbursement economically unfeasible, and during the 1980s employers required insurers to actively control their health-care costs.[24] This rise in managed care, as it has come to be called, took a variety of forms.[25] No longer did insurance companies passively reimburse claims; instead they conducted utilization reviews to identify unnecessary or wasteful services and procedures, required prior authorization for certain procedures and pharmaceuticals, required second opinions for surgeries and other expensive procedures, provided incentives for patients to participate in

the National Industrial Conference Board, a business association consisting mainly of large publicly held firms) than from 1944 to 1946 (6.5 million to 7 million), yet tax policy didn't take effect until 1944, and so the bulk of the increase occurred before the change in tax policy. However, there are some problems with Dobbin's argument. First, to see the effects of the changes in the tax code, we need to look beyond a three-year period, and the figures cited by the Health Insurance Association of America (see n. 21) show a huge explosion in employer-sponsored health insurance, relative to consumer-purchased health insurance, after World War II. Second, Dobbin's figures don't compare how large the rise was in employer-offered insurance versus consumer-bought insurance from 1939 to 1943, so we can't gauge from his figures the proportional increase of the former. There is no gainsaying Dobbin's point that employers have incentives, apart from tax code, for offering health insurance as a fringe benefit. It's just that it is hard to believe that employer-provided insurance would be so overwhelming dominant without the enormous incentives provided by the tax code.

[23] The cost-plus reimbursement system was reined in during the 1980s.

[24] Some of this pressure occurred by large firms self-insuring. In this way companies established their own rules and procedures; the insurance company's role, if any, was simply limited to processing of claims. Once a significant segment of large employers began to self-insure and engage in cost-control techniques, these techniques rapidly spread through the U.S. health-care market. See Goodman and Musgrave, *Patient Power*, 195–201.

[25] See ibid., 201–8; White, *Competing Solutions*, 180–3; and Richard A. Epstein, *Mortal Peril: Our Inalienable Right to Health Care?* (Reading, MA: Addison-Wesley Publishing Company, 1997), 420–30.

so-called wellness programs that stressed preventive care, and increased employee deductibles and co-payments, and so forth. These measures aimed to make providers and patients more aware of costs and to provide incentives for reducing their use of health-care services. The most important aspect of managed care has been the rise in Health Maintenance Organizations (HMOs). HMOs integrate the financing and delivery of medical care by contracting with selected doctors and hospitals (the former usually paid on a salaried basis, rather than fee-for-service) to provide comprehensive care to members that pay a fixed monthly fee (plus, in some cases, minimal co-payments and deductibles). Members that use doctor and hospital services not part of the HMO network are not covered or must pay a greater amount out of pocket. HMOs provide strong incentives for providers to constantly keep their focus on costs, and the cost savings achieved are supposed to make them attractive to patients despite the restriction of freedom of choice in doctors and procedures. However, although the rise of managed care and the demise of cost-plus reimbursement is obviously an important change in the U.S. health-care market, managed-care plans are still comprehensive employer-sponsored service plans, and the tax policies that favor such plans are still in place. Thus, the dominance of managed care in the private U.S. health insurance market does not affect the fact that this market is dominated by comprehensive service plans and that casualty-catastrophic insurance plays only a small role.

I've argued that employer-provided service plans achieved their domination of the health insurance market through government assistance. The argument, however, doesn't show that such domination is unlikely to have occurred in a genuine free market, and it is that counterfactual claim that is of greater importance here in light of my earlier claim that it is unlikely that service plans, which dominate the U.S. health insurance market, will be the dominant form of health insurance in a free market. Three points support my counterfactual claim:

1. Employer-provided service plans cause significant labor-mobility problems. Many people would prefer to own their own policy, as this makes health insurance portable and eliminates any worry about getting a worse policy at one's new job. Although an employer-sponsored service plan does have its advantages – for example, it reduces the

employee's search costs for the best policy – it is unlikely that these advantages would suffice to result in the almost complete domination of employer-sponsored insurance we see today in the United States (almost 90 percent of all persons with private health insurance purchase it through their workplace) [26] in light of the considerable disadvantages of reduced labor mobility. This point shows why it is unlikely that employer-sponsored plans would dominate a free market, but it does not address the comprehensive versus casualty insurance question, which is discussed in the next two points.

2. In the absence of tax disadvantages and other government obstacles, casualty insurance has a secure place, because of its cost advantage. Comprehensive service plans (which have low deductibles) require higher premiums than casualty-catastrophic insurance (which have higher deductibles), particularly for those in a relatively low-risk pool.[27] Although the higher cost of a service plan may be worth it for some people, others will not be willing to pay that cost. (I discuss this point in more detail in section 3.4.2.)

3. An additional reason why casualty insurance has a secure place in a free market for health insurance concerns a difference between that insurance and service plans. Casualty insurers are liable for damages from the time of the risky or adverse event, even if it takes years for all negative consequences flowing from the adverse event to be

---

[26] Michael A. Morrisey, "State Health Care Reform: Protecting the Provider," in Roger D. Feldman, ed. *American Health Care: Government, Market Processes, and the Public Interest* (Oakland, CA: The Independent Institute, 2000), 231.

[27] Present tax policies encourage people to choose low-deductible rather than high-deductible insurance, even when the cost of the more expensive premiums for the former outweighs the savings achieved by choosing the lower deductible. Because the premiums paid receive the double-tax deduction described in the text, but the money paid out of pocket or for savings for the bills not covered by the deductible is paid for in after-tax dollars, there is a strong incentive to choose the lower deductible. E.g., suppose a $1,000 deductible policy costs $800 a year less in premiums than a $250 deductible (which may be the case, for the middle-aged in a high-cost area). Assuming a standard insurance policy that pays 80 percent of medical bills covered by the policy, the higher deductible policy yields $600 less of health insurance coverage. This is far less than the $800 extra one has to pay in higher premiums. Yet because the premiums are excluded from the employee's gross income, while the money paid for bills not covered by the deductible is fully taxed, for many people choosing the low-deductible policy is more rational (particularly if they are in a high tax bracket). See Goodman and Musgrave, *Patient Power*, 44–6, ch. 8.

revealed. Service plans, however, are liable only so long as the insured pays premiums; if the policy is canceled, the insurer can cease paying benefits even if losses from a risky event are continuing. I did not mention this when I explained how NHI is an example of a service plan, because NHI is not a *market* service plan, and whether one receives services is to a considerable degree independent of whether one has paid or is paying taxes. But this difference is applicable to comparing casualty insurance and service plans that are marketed, and it is that comparison that is relevant right now. Certainly many consumers would prefer a policy that covered damages for the adverse event, even if those losses occurred many years after the event or after one has switched or canceled policies.

Thus, for all these reasons – no job lock, cheaper premiums for low risks, payment of damages for as long as there are losses stemming from the adverse event – it is reasonable to believe that casualty insurance (that is not owned and sponsored by employers) will have a home in a free market.

So far I've argued that private health insurance in the United States bears a remote resemblance to MHI because of state insurance mandates, federal and state restrictions on risk rating, and because that market is dominated by comprehensive service plans, a domination achieved by government policies and unlikely to exist without it. Yet an additional reason why private health insurance in the United States should not be confused with genuine MHI concerns the effects of Medicare and Medicaid, which are the U.S. versions of social insurance, the former a federal government program for seniors, the latter a joint federal and state government program for the indigent. These population groups are large enough that these programs tend to strongly influence and structure the private health insurance market – the amount spent on Medicare and Medicaid and other government-financed and -administered programs is roughly equal to the amount spent in the United States on private health insurance.[28] Particularly with regard to Medicare, which makes up 17 percent of the amount

---

[28] Figures are available at http://www.kff.org/medicare/upload/Medicare-Chart-Book-3rd-Edition-Summer-2005-Section-6.pdf (accessed July 2006).

spent on U.S. health care, the effects are enormous. In 1983, the federal government abandoned its cost-plus procedures for Medicare part A (the part that covers hospital care), for the same reason businesses did (exploding health-care costs), and instituted reimbursement for diagnostic related groups (DRGs). Medicare reimburses hospitals based on its Byzantine system of relative value points assigned to each DRG, and these points are not based on supply or demand but on the government's assessment of the time, complexity, and desirability of the procedure, service, or treatment performed. Thus, much of a hospital's revenue is based on a de facto system of government price controls (as hospitals can't bargain with Medicare). In addition, doctors are also subject to de facto price controls by Medicare, because Medicare sets a payment schedule for them not based on supply and demand. (Doctors can opt out of Medicare's payment schedule, but there are strong incentives not to do so.)[29] Hospitals and doctors try

---

[29] A physician can refuse to accept Medicare's payment schedule in two ways: by being a nonparticipating physician for a certain procedure or by opting out completely. A nonparticipating physician can actually bill approximately 10 percent higher than a participating physician (who accepts "assignment," the Medicare fee schedule) for a certain procedure, but he has to get the entire amount from the patient (whereas if he accepts assignment, Medicare pays him 80 percent of the approved charge directly and he only has to get 20 percent from the patient). However, nonparticipating physicians face a number of obstacles. First, some state laws restrict "balance billing" of patients – billing them above what Medicare allows, and if one is a nonparticipating physician one is excluded from a list of doctors available to senior groups who accept assignment, which may decrease one's patient base among a group of patients (seniors) who see doctors more frequently than the average patient. Finally, nonparticipating physicians have no guarantee they can get the entire amount from the patient, whereas if they accept assignment they have a guarantee of getting 80 percent from the government and only have to get 20 percent from the patient. So in effect, a nonparticipating physician has to gamble that charging more than what Medicare allows will actually bring her more income. But that gamble is often not worth it. There are higher administrative costs for nonparticipating physicians because the physician must process all the claims (unlike participating physicians, who reduce their paperwork by being directly reimbursed by Medicare), the patient base may decrease by seniors who favor doctors that are participating physicians, and there is a distinct possibility that the nonparticipating physician may not get the extra 10 percent anyway (it may depend on the patient's insurance policy, the patient's financial status). Hence, many physicians conclude it is easier to be participating physicians and just accept the fee schedule of Medicare. Notice also that Medicare's price controls plus 10 percent is still price controls, not a market price.

As for opting out, this means the physician decides not to accept Medicare for any and all services performed on Medicare patients (except for emergency and urgent care). In order to do this, a physician must sign a private contract with

to get around this by shifting costs onto non-Medicare patients, so we get something akin to the massive cross-subsidization we see in NHI.[30] The U.S. system also has somewhat of an analogue of capital controls because Medicare is very slow to approve reimbursement schedules for new medical techniques, and its reimbursement of these expensive techniques tends to be stingy, which rations the availability of new technology for seniors, even for those willing to pay for it.[31]

One final respect in which the private health insurance market is radically different from MHI is that hospitals do not charge patients anything that could be called a recognizable price. Hospitals rarely offer to consumers or patients a fixed preadmission price per diem or per procedure. Instead, there are separate items for each provider (e.g., a separate bill for the anesthesiologist, the surgeon, and other specialists), and there are often thousands of items on a hospital bill, many of them not recognizable to an average patient – and the ones that are recognizable are sometimes wildly inflated (e.g., much higher than market prices for over-the-counter medicine and other routine items). The reasons for the incomprehensibility of hospitals bills are due to features of the U.S. healthcare market we have already discussed. First, because most consumers or patients do not pay directly for their health insurance and their health insurance is comprehensive and covers most of patients' expenses, they do not have a strong incentive to press for comprehensible bills. Second, hospitals are mainly responsive to incentives from those who pay their bills, and much of their revenue comes from Medicare and Medicaid, which do not really

each patient and must agree not to accept any payment from Medicare for two years. Given how many seniors have Medicare and the importance of seniors for doctors' income, the incentive not to opt out is very high. For a comprehensible explanation of all this, see The American Academy of Orthopaedic Surgeons, http://www.aaos.org/wordhtml/statesoc/source9.htm (accessed June 2006).

[30] On the DRG system for hospitals and reimbursement for physicians, see White, *Competing Solutions*, 44–5 and Goodman and Musgrave, *Patient Power*, 60–2, 302–15.

[31] Ibid., 60–2, 303–16. Recently, Medicare has taken steps to improve the situation, though I have been unable to find data that indicates whether or not it has succeeded. See Sean R. Tunis and Jeffrey L. Kang, "Improvements in Medicare Coverage of New Technology; How Medicare Responded to the Need to Improve Access to Beneficial Technologies," *Health Affairs* 20, no. 5 (2001): 83–6. In 2001, Secretary of Human Health and Services Tommy Thompson testified that "the Medicare program has not kept pace with modern medicine," which suggests that the problem had not been rectified. See http://www.hhs.gov/asl/testify/t010306.html (accessed June 2006).

pay for their costs, and this means there is a great deal of cost shifting in hospitals – the hospital makes up the differences by charging other payers inflated prices. (Also, managed-care companies often know what hospitals get from Medicare and Medicaid, and in some cases the HMOs are large enough payers to press for similar below-cost discounts, which adds further incentives for the hospitals to inflate prices for those not receiving these below-cost discounts).[32] A third reason is that the DRG system encourages billing for separate procedures, and this Medicare-inspired system of reimbursement has spread to private insurance.[33] In a real market for health insurance, in which most consumers pay directly for their own catastrophic-casualty insurance, there would be enormous incentive to bargain for fixed preadmission prices, perhaps even pressing for a combination of hospital and surgeon fees into one single fixed preadmission price (or for exploratory surgery, a "not to exceed" price).[34] Furthermore, for noncatastrophic expenses or procedures, hospitals would compete for the patients' own money, which would make them far more consumer friendly than they are today, as the need to attract customers would provide a good incentive for attractive services and comprehensible prices. If you doubt that fixed preadmission prices would emerge in a genuine market for health care and health insurance, consider that such prices exist in cosmetic surgery, which is not covered by health insurance in the United States. Somehow, despite the presence of many doctors and a variety of services involved in this surgery, consumers know beforehand what the price will be.[35]

To summarize, U.S. private health insurance deviates significantly from MHI vis-à-vis some restrictions on risk rating, enormous government bias in favor of comprehensive service plans, a noncompetitive pricing system, and, in the case of hospitals, absence of

[32] See White, *Competing Solutions*, 44–5.

[33] Prior to the introduction of the DRG system, hospitals were reimbursed on a cost-plus basis, which also gave hospitals strong financial incentives to inflate costs and bill for numerous separate items. See Goodman and Musgrave, *Patient Power*, 163–9.

[34] Ibid., 53–5.

[35] Ibid., 28–9. The authors point out that package prices are also quoted by hospitals for Canadians seeking care in the United States that they are unable to obtain without a long wait in Canada. I will discuss the way NHI leads to waits in section 3.5.3.

comprehensible prices. Although U.S. private health insurance is not universal, and some aspects of the market do practice risk-rating, this is far from sufficient for it to merit the description of MHI.

3.2.3 What Market Health Insurance Would Look Like

Rather than using the U.S. insurance market as a model, we can elucidate the essential features of genuine MHI by contrasting it with NHI, because in most respects the two are opposites. My analysis stems from a proposal for MHI made by policy analysts John Goodman and Gerald Musgrave in their 1992 book *Patient Power*, which has formed the basis for a variety of subsequent proposals for MHI that are tailored for the United States.[36]

As a form of social insurance, NHI is compulsory, bans most risk rating, and restricts choice of insurance plans; although the form of MHI being defended here is also compulsory, it allows risk rating and a wide choice of plans. In particular, because what gave NHI its special feature among social-insurance programs was that it provided comprehensive service plans, not casualty-catastrophic insurance, MHI would allow casualty-catastrophic insurance to freely compete with comprehensive service plans. Accordingly, the heart of MHI is to alter tax policy so as to end the strong bias toward employer-provided service plans. High-deductible health insurance – that is, catastrophic health insurance – whether purchased by the individual, an employer, or the self-employed, would receive a tax credit. All premiums would be

[36] Ibid., Regina Herzlinger, *Market Driven Health Care* (Reading, Massachusetts: Addison-Wesley Publishing Company, 1997) provides a useful elaboration (and to some degree alteration) of the Goodman-Musgrave proposal. Other modified versions of the original Goodman-Musgrave proposal can be found in Mark V. Pauly and John C. Goodman, "Tax Credits for Health Insurance and Medical Savings Accounts," *Health Affairs* (Spring 1995): 126–39; Gail A. Jensen, "Making Room for Medical Savings Accounts in the U.S. Healthcare System," in Feldman, *American Health Care*, 119–43; and Tom Miller, "Improving Access to Health Care without Comprehensive Health Insurance Coverage: Incentives, Competition, Choice, and Priorities," in *Covering America: Real Remedies for the Uninsured. Volume 2: Proposal Summaries*, Eliot Wicks, ed. (Washington, DC: Economic and Social Research Institute, November 2002). For a discussion in a Canadian context, see Cynthia Ramsay, "Medical Savings Accounts: Universal, Accessible, Portable, Comprehensive Health Care for Canadians," *The Fraser Institute Critical Issues Bulletin* (May 1998) and David Gratzer, "The ABCs of MSAs," in *Better Medicine: Reforming Canadian Health Care*, David Gratzer, ed. (Toronto: ECW Press, 2002), 287–307.

included in the gross income of the insured, who would receive a tax credit for a certain percentage of the premium (or, on some versions of MHI, a tax credit for a fixed dollar amount). For individuals who pay no income tax, this credit would be refundable, and this subsidy would enable them to purchase health insurance. In this way, MHI would be personal and portable; even if purchased by an employer, it would be the insured's property. As for noncatastrophic or routine expenses not covered by the high-deductible insurance, tax-free medical savings accounts (MSAs) would be used. MSAs are accounts into which individuals and families, or employers acting on their behalf, can deposit pretax dollars (on an annual basis, about the amount for an average deductible for a catastrophic-only policy)[37] and then use them to pay for small bills. These accounts are the property of the insured individuals or families (even if the deposits are made by employers), and money withdrawn from them to pay for medical bills (the simplest way is probably with a debit card) will not be taxed, whereas money withdrawn for nonmedical purposes will be fully taxed. Tax-free MSAs, along with the change in the tax code discussed in the preceding text, will provide incentives for many people to self-insure for small bills and choose high-deductible insurance. Furthermore, because MSAs will allow one to accumulate the money deposited each year over a lifetime, they will help one budget for postretirement expenses (unlike flexible savings accounts, the closest analogue to MSAs, offered by many employers, which require forfeiture of any money deposited that is not spent at the end of the year.[38])[39]

---

[37] Goodman and Musgrave leave this matter somewhat open, suggesting at one point that some groups (the young, those living in a low-cost medical area) might be allowed to make larger annual deposits to their MSAs. *Patient Power*, 258.

[38] Since 1996, MSAs have existed in the United States, but they were restricted to a very small group of employees and were hemmed in by fairly rigid rules. See Greg Scandlen, "MSAs Can Be a Windfall for All," *NCPA Policy Backgrounder* (November 2, 2001): 4–5. In December 2003, Congress greatly liberalized the rules for the accounts, which will now be called Health Savings Accounts. For details, see http://www.forbes.com/business/newswire/2004/01/07/rtr1201453.html (accessed January 2004).

[39] What if one prefers a comprehensive service plan with low deductibles? Advocates of MHI disagree about how to structure the U.S. tax code so that the bias against high-deductible catastrophic insurance is ended without going to the opposite extreme of biasing the code against low-deductible insurance. However, we need not go into this dispute, in part because it is at a level of technical detail that is beyond the scope

The other features of MHI follow pretty much straightaway from eliminating the government's role in subsidizing demand for comprehensive service plans. Whereas NHI sharply restricts, if not eliminates, free-market prices and requires nonmarket forms of rationing, MHI does neither. Much of the population will be using their MSAs for noncatastrophic expenses, and so prices will be formed by the normal interaction of buyers and sellers, with a limited role for third parties. For catastrophic and large hospital bills, the absence of one-price-fits-all DRGs plus a significant increase in consumer-purchased casualty insurance will create incentives for hospitals to set genuine preadmission prices for procedures and surgery. Finally, the central role of noncomprehensive private health insurance will increase significantly the amount paid for by savings or out-of-pocket, maximize the insured's awareness of costs, and make patients consumers or customers, in the way that they are in other forms of noncomprehensive private insurance – all the opposite of NHI.[40]

The form of MHI I am defending differs from pure free-market health insurance because it requires purchase of insurance and subsidizes those who pay no taxes. (Though, if the tax code is changed so as to encourage purchase of health insurance, most will do so; therefore, the first deviation does not affect many people.) Besides compulsory purchase and subsidies for the indigent, MHI also differs from pure free-market health insurance in two other respects. First, some specification will have to be given as to what kind of health insurance qualifies for the tax credit-MSA combination. This will have to be rather loose

of our concerns, but also because to some extent the problem has already been solved by a market test. In South Africa the market for private health insurance was deregulated in 1994. Those who wished to go outside the government system had their choice of all sorts of plans, and, within a few years, MSAs acquired the largest market share. The form of MSAs that was the most popular had high deductibles for discretionary expenses (e.g., hospital outpatient care and physician office visits) and low deductibles for nondiscretionary expenses (e.g., hospital inpatient care and treatment of chronic conditions such as asthma, hypertension, and diabetes). See Shaun Matisonn, "Medical Savings Accounts in South Africa," *National Center for Policy Analysis* (June 2000). This suggests that a demand for low-deductible insurance can to some extent be met within the tax credit-MSA framework.

[40] Also, in MHI, Medicare and Medicaid would not exist so their perverse role in setting hospital and doctor prices will be absent. The government will provide subsidies for uninsurable risks and the small percentage of people that are chronically uninsurable, but these subsidies will be from general revenue and will thus not directly interfere with the workings of the market.

in order to avoid reintroducing the problem of mandated benefits – along the lines of "high deductible catastrophic insurance, with a certain limit on total expenses incurred by the insured" – but it is still necessary, particularly on questions such as how high the deductible must be in order to get the tax credit-MSA combination. Second, a small number of people – 1 to 2 percent of the population – are chronically uninsurable,[41] and a somewhat larger group has uninsurable risks.[42] MHI will mitigate the problem of uninsurable risks because some of these risks arise after one has insurance, and, with portable insurance, switching jobs after one acquires the adverse condition will not cause a loss of one's health insurance.[43] Furthermore, to some extent the problem of uninsurable risks is functionally equivalent to a lack of income, because one would not need insurance if one had enough savings to treat the problem. To some extent MSAs would handle this problem, at least for chronic conditions that often require the use of relatively routine medical services (e.g., mild diabetes). However, although MHI would mitigate the problem of uninsurable risks, it does not eliminate them, and for the ineliminable cases, proponents

[41] Mark Pauly and Brad Herring, *Pooling Health Insurance Risks* (Washington, DC: AEI Press, 1999), 88, 90–1.

[42] Why aren't all risks insurable? The reason stems from the economics of insurance. Markets for insurance exist because there are gains from trade from pooling risks. On the demand side, consumers who have some degree of risk aversion gain from paying a certain amount each year to reduce the chance of a loss in any particular year. On the supply side, companies gain because they are reasonably confident that their payouts to insureds who suffer losses in any given year are more than made up by income received from insureds who suffer no loss. However, there are no gains from trade for consumers that will suffer certain losses. Because the losses are certain, insurance companies cannot make money by using income obtained from policyholders in a similar risk class who will not suffer a loss – for there are none. Thus the company will have to offer "insurance" priced at a rate equal to the loss plus the company's profit and overhead, and no rational consumer would want such insurance. Why pay, e.g., $1,500 a year to "insure" against a certain loss of $1,200? Of course, insurance companies could charge consumers who face certain losses the same premium as those with a low probability of facing losses and use the income from the latter to subsidize the former, but this is unlikely to occur in a competitive market where insurers charge different premiums for different degrees of risk.

[43] Goodman and Musgrave, *Patient Power*, 98–9, point out that there is a market for guaranteed annual renewable life insurance, and it seems reasonable to expect something similar with MHI. Even prior to the 1996 law that guaranteed that changing jobs would not lead to loss of health insurance, three-quarters of individual policies (i.e., policies not purchased at work) were issued as guaranteed renewable. See Pauly and Herring, *Pooling Health Insurance Risks*, 18.

of MHI propose subsidizing the premiums of a high-risk pool from general revenue.[44]

One additional feature of MHI needs to be highlighted: the proposal that everyone will get the same tax *credit* for a certain percentage – Goodman and Musgrave suggest 30 percent – of their health-care premiums (or a tax credit for a fixed dollar amount, on some other versions of MHI). The reason for a tax credit rather than a tax *deduction* is because the latter, but not the former, is regressive.[45] One could go further and propose a sliding scale for the credit, thus enabling those with lower incomes to receive a greater percentage of the premiums as a credit, reducing the percentage as income rises. Along the same lines, one could propose that the minimum amount of the deductible in a catastrophic policy that makes one eligible for the tax credit also be on a sliding scale, so that those in lower income brackets could obtain the credit with a somewhat lower-deductible catastrophic policy, while the amount of the deductible that makes one eligible for the credit rises as one's income rises.[46] Although these additions are not essential to the basic idea of MHI, they are compatible with it, and because one of my aims is to show that egalitarians should favor MHI, I will add these features to my comparison of NHI with MHI. Egalitarians may also be concerned that the poor will have nonexistent or inadequate MSAs (as they may not want or be able to save money for

---

44 The reason these subsidies would come from general revenue, not from taxing other insurers, is that if the latter was done, this would be cross-subsidization and incompatible with market insurance. See Miller, "Improving Access to Health Care," 52 and Goodman and Musgrave, *Patient Power*, 98–9.

45 A tax credit for health-care premiums means that one can reduce one's tax bill by the amount of the credit; e.g., if one would otherwise pay $3,500 a year in taxes, and one's health-care premiums are $3,000 a year, a 30 percent tax credit would cut the tax bill from $3,500 to $2,600. A tax credit is not regressive; if two people pay the same amount of health premiums then they get the same reduction in their tax bill. A tax deduction means that a certain percentage of one's gross income is shielded from taxes; e.g., if one is taxed on gross income of $30,000, but one can deduct 30 percent of one's $3,000 health-care premiums, then one would be taxed on $29,100. Tax deductions for health-insurance premiums are regressive, i.e., the value of the exclusion of the premiums from taxable income is more valuable for those in the higher income brackets. Nine hundred dollars excluded from taxation is less valuable to someone who isn't in a very high marginal tax bracket than for someone who is in such a bracket For more details, see Goodman and Musgrave, *Patient Power*, 41–3.

46 This is suggested by Herzlinger, *Market Driven Health Care*, 258.

that purpose). Whether MHI can be modified to mollify such worries will be discussed in section 3.5.2.

3.3 Egalitarianism and NHI

As I noted in Chapter 2, egalitarianism maintains that justice requires reducing unchosen or involuntary inequalities, while its cousin, the priority view, focuses not on inequalities per se, but on improving the situation of the worst off. However, the difference between egalitarianism and its prioritarian cousin will not matter that much, because, as I will argue in section 3.6, the arguments I give regarding the former pretty much carry over to the latter. I also pointed out in Chapter 2 that egalitarians disagree how to answer the question: "equality of what?" Some say the answer is resources, others say it is welfare. A resourcist egalitarian theory, when applied to the topic at hand, would focus on health care, while a welfarist theory would focus on health. Most egalitarian arguments for NHI focus on the former and thus that will be my focus as well.

I will discuss Norman Daniels's and Ronald Dworkin's egalitarian arguments for NHI. One difference between Daniels's and Dworkin's approach should be noted at the outset. Daniels, unlike Dworkin, does not explicitly endorse the view that egalitarianism should focus on unchosen inequalities. His argument for NHI is based upon an application of Rawls's principles of justice, and Rawls's theory does not distinguish between chosen and unchosen inequalities. However, it will turn out that Daniels's arguments for NHI are predicated, at least in part, on the claim that most health-care inequalities are unchosen, which implies that Daniels thinks that if they were chosen, justice would not require their correction. Thus, at least as far as health-care inequalities are concerned, Daniels seems to endorse the view that inequalities are not matters of injustice when they are chosen.

3.3.1 Daniels and Fair Equality of Opportunity

Daniels uses John Rawls's theory of justice to support his view about justice in health care. Rawls defends two principles of justice. One is a principle of equal liberty, which is essentially a list of basic (largely negative) rights.[47] Rawls defends these rights as necessary to give people the

---

[47] Rawls, *A Theory of Justice*, 60–1 and *Political Liberalism*, 291.

freedom to pursue and revise their diverse conceptions of the good life. This is a typical justification of basic rights in contemporary political philosophy, by egalitarians and nonegalitarians.[48] Daniels, however, does not use this principle. Rather he focuses on Rawls's second principle, which contains the difference principle (that social and economic inequalities should be arranged to the greatest benefit for the least advantaged) but also contains the principle that offices and positions should be offered to all under conditions of fair equality of opportunity. Fair equality of opportunity means, roughly, that people with similar talents, skills, and motivation should have the same opportunities.[49] Rawls did not apply his second principle to access to health-care services, but Daniels does by noting that meeting health-care needs is a way of protecting our opportunities, and if we are obligated to protect those opportunities, we are obligated to meet those needs. More specifically, Daniels argues that institutions that affect the allocation of health-care resources should be arranged so that each person enjoys his or her fair share of a normal opportunity range for individuals in his or her society. A normal opportunity range for society is the full set of individual life plans that would be reasonable for individuals in that society to pursue, if they enjoyed "normal species functioning." Daniels does not do much to flesh out this concept; for our purposes what is vital is that disease, illness, and disability reduce this functioning.[50]

From Daniels's view that insuring fair equality of opportunity requires a set of health-care institutions that enable us to function as normally as possible, he derives an argument in favor of universal health insurance with comprehensive benefits. The universality requirement seems obvious – fair equality of opportunity is owed to all – and the comprehensive requirement stems from a variety of services being necessary to restore or maintain full functioning as a human being (routine and preventive care, hospital care, long-term care for the elderly, services designed to maintain and restore our mental as well as physical

[48] For a discussion of the main lines of argument many egalitarians use to defend basic rights, see Daniel Shapiro, "Liberalism, Basic Rights, and Free Exchange," *Journal of Social Philosophy* 26 (Fall 1995): 104–5 and my references therein.

[49] Rawls, *A Theory of Justice*, 73.

[50] Norman Daniels, *Just Health Care* (New York: Cambridge University Press, 1985), ch. 2, 4. Basically the same account is given, in a more compressed manner, in Norman Daniels, Donald W. Light, and Ronald L. Caplan, *Benchmarks of Fairness for Health Care Reform* (New York: Oxford University Press, 1997), 19–22.

health, etc.). Because Daniels's view is that justice requires access to services that restore or maintain, to the extent that this is possible, *normal* functioning (not that we need access to services designed to *enhance* normal functioning), he considers the freedom to buy supplemental insurance that provides benefits above what NHI offers (e.g., private hospital rooms, cosmetic surgery) to be permissible. However, Daniels insists that a two-tiered system of health insurance is acceptable only to the extent that the basic tier provides for those services needed to restore and maintain basic functioning (and only to the extent that the existence of the supplemental tier does not undermine support for the basic tier of the NHI system).[51] He thus rejects the idea that justice only requires that the state provide access to a minimal level of care because that would exclude, he believes, a whole range of services needed to restore normal functioning.

As for actuarial insurance, Daniels condemns it as doubly unjust: it provides barriers to full coverage, and it is unfair to charge people according to expected risk because "most health risks are not affected by choices, and others are so only somewhat and in ways of which we are not aware."[52] (Notice that this implies that if the role of choice in health risks was greater than Daniels thought and if justice requires allowing people the freedom to choose less than comprehensive coverage, then there would be a strong case against NHI, a point to which I will later return.)

Now this account is incomplete as it stands, because the argument so far only focuses on the demand or consumption of health care, and we need to talk about its supply or production. Daniels, and anyone offering a theory of just health-care institutions, must explain how subsidizing health-care needs can avoid being the equivalent of a black hole that sucks out resources devoted to all other goods. This is not just a practical problem but a requirement of justice on Daniels's account, for if excessive resources are devoted to health care, less is left for people to pursue the goals that are part of their life plan, as well as for other government programs that egalitarians view as required by justice. Daniels's account seems particularly vulnerable to this problem because enormous resources could be devoted to certain individuals,

[51] Daniel et al., *Benchmarks of Fairness*, 27–8, 43–4.
[52] Ibid., 46.

yet their illnesses, diseases, or disabilities would not be removed or even significantly lessened.[53] Furthermore, health-care resources compete with other resources and with each other; some criterion for ranking various kinds of health-care needs or medical services is obviously required.

Daniels does attempt to address these issues. He notes that the scope of the right to health care must be constrained by facts about scarcity and technological feasibility within a particular society, and there is no obligation to provide access to services whose chances of being effective are low or speculative. He also says that the most pressing health-care services are those that make the greatest contribution to restoring one's range of opportunities, rather than those that play a relatively minor role in doing so. As Daniels notes, these are vague requirements and do little to blunt the bottomless-pit worry; nor do they show how to make specific choices between different kinds of health services. Daniels's real answer to these problems is government rationing.[54] This constrains demand and a global budget enables us to make explicit tradeoffs with other government programs (ending the bottomless pit problem); furthermore, any rationing procedure implicitly or explicitly provides some ranking of, or some way of making choices between, various kinds of services. Concerning the latter, Daniels maintains, for reasons I will discuss in section 3.5, that the principle of fair equality of opportunity, and principles of distributive justice in general, do not provide any determinate guidance for these choices, and for this reason, as well as to maintain accountability, he argues that this should be a matter for public deliberation.[55] Thus he disapproves of NHI programs whose criteria for rationing, as I will discuss in section 3.5, are generally invisible to the average citizen and applauds some recent trends toward making those criteria more transparent.[56]

---

53 As noted by Allen Buchanan, "Health-Care Delivery and Resource Allocation," in *Medical Ethics*, Robert Veatch, ed. (Sudbury, MA: Jones and Bartlett, 1997), 347–8.

54 Daniels et al., *Benchmarks of Fairness*, 25–6.

55 Ibid., 57–9. Daniels's most recent book is devoted to the topic of fairness and accountability. See Norman Daniels and James E. Sabin, *Setting Limits Fairly: Can We Learn to Share Medical Resources?* (New York: Oxford University Press, 2002), 30–4, ch. 4.

56 Daniels's criticism of proposals in the U.S. Congress for NHI, none of which even mentioned the issue of rationing, as using "doublespeak," implies that he is critical of NHI's secretive criteria for rationing. See Daniels et al., *Benchmarks of Fairness*,

Thus, Daniels's account rationalizes the major features of NHI. The requirement of fair equality of opportunity for access to health-care services is used to support universal provision of comprehensive benefits with little out-of-pocket expenses, and the elimination of most forms of risk rating. The indeterminacy of fair equality of opportunity vis-à-vis the ranking of medical services and the requirement of justice that resources devoted to health care not swallow up resources for other welfare-state institutions are used to support the rationing and global budgets that structure the supply side of NHI. What about the restriction, if not virtual elimination, of the role of patient as a consumer or customer? In one sense, of course, Daniels must approve of this because awareness and negotiation about prices and a wide range of choices of health plans would restrict universal access to the comprehensive level of services he thinks justice requires. But he *also* argues that a system is fairer when it respects autonomous choices and that such choices help to insure the quality and efficiency of care. Thus a requirement of justice is that within the limits necessarily required by NHI, consumer or patient choice of providers and procedures must be maximized.[57] Or to put matters another way: maximize choice wherever it is appropriate. However, choice only has a limited place in health-care policy.

3.3.2 Dworkin and the Results of an Ideal, Fair Market

Dworkin's arguments about justice in health care[58] depend upon his more fundamental theory of justice, in particular, his view about justice

---

116–19. For his discussion of recent trends in NHI away from these secretive criteria, see Daniels and Sabin, *Setting Limits Fairly*, ch. 10.

[57] Daniels does argue that in a mixed system, with both private and public health care, market accountability is important, and this involves choice in health-care plans (and accurate information about these plans). Daniels, *Setting Limits Fairly*, 44–5. However, this discussion occurs in the context of his discussion of what is required for any health system to be accountable to its participants, and nothing in this discussion indicates that Daniels has withdrawn his view that NHI is preferable to a mixed system and to MHI.

[58] See Ronald Dworkin, "Justice in the Distribution of Health Care," *McGill Law Review* 38, no.4 (1993): 883–98, and "Will Clinton's Plan Be Fair?" *New York Review of Books* (January 13, 1994): 1–8, later republished in *Sovereign Virtue* as "Justice and the High Cost of Health," 307–20.

and markets.[59] On the one hand, Dworkin argues markets are essential for justice. To show respect and concern for people with different (peaceful) views of the good life, different ambitions, and preferences, and so forth, justice mandates that individuals have the right to act in accordance with those views and have the freedom to pursue, revise, and realize their ambitions and goals. Furthermore, such respect requires that one be held responsible for one's choices and the costs of those choices. It would be unfair to require those under an obligation to respect individual rights to refrain from interfering with the right holder's choices *and* to subsidize the costs of the right holder's choices. Hence a system that allows one to make choices, gives one information about the costs of the choices so these choices can be informed, and that holds one responsible for these costs is just. Markets do all three. If we lived in a world in which we all began in roughly the same circumstances, then any inequality in wealth and income that resulted would be just, for it would simply reflect people's choices about how to live their lives as revealed by their tradeoffs of work for leisure, tradeoffs of savings and investment for consumption, rates of time preference (i.e., the extent to which they discount the future), and occupational choices, and so forth.

Of course, we don't live in that world. In the real world, people find themselves in unchosen circumstances of varying degrees of unchosen disadvantage or advantage. When markets reflect or compound unchosen disadvantages resulting from one's natural endowments, one's race or sex or social or family background, or other forms of bad brute luck, markets do not embody justice but injustice. Dworkin argues that welfare-state policies that interfere with markets are justified to the extent that they correct for unchosen disadvantages while still allowing people to act on their peaceful ambitions and conception of the good. For the purposes of this chapter, it is not important that I go into detail about what policies he thinks would most closely embody justice; for our purposes what is essential is that he thinks that

---

59 The key pieces are "What Is Equality? Part 1: Equality of Welfare," *Philosophy and Public Affairs* 10 (Summer 1981): 185–246; "What Is Equality? Part 2," 283–345; and "What Is Equality? Part 3: The Place of Liberty," *Iowa Law Review* 73, no. 1 (1987): 1–54. These are reprinted in *Sovereign Virtue*, ch. 1–3.

the present inequalities of income and wealth that exist in the United States are clearly unjust. Although people do voluntarily choose to save or invest different amounts, make different work-leisure tradeoffs, and so forth, compensation for unchosen disadvantages would narrow considerably the range of present-day inequalities in the United States.[60]

Dworkin uses his views about a just distribution of wealth and income to then argue against free-market health insurance, in which there are no subsidies or biases in the tax code distorting people's decisions to purchase or not purchase varying kinds of health insurance. Dworkin says that this policy would be unjust, for one's decision not to purchase such insurance would likely not be a reflection of his or her views of the good life but rather a reflection of his or her inability to afford it, an inability due to background injustice in the distribution of wealth and income. Would a free and unsubsidized market for health insurance be just if there was a more or less just distribution of wealth and income? No, says Dworkin. Patients' information about the value, cost, and side effects of medical procedures – what a good doctor knows – is quite limited and inaccurate, and so decisions to purchase insurance based on such information would not really reflect their views of the good life but instead reflect, in part, brute luck. Dworkin also says that in a free and unsubsidized market with a fair distribution of income and wealth, insurance companies would have information about a person's antecedent risk of being ill or diseased, and because such risks are unchosen,[61] it would be unfair to price premiums in accord with expected risk.

Thus a just market in health insurance would be one in which (1) wealth and income is distributed fairly, (2) patients possess roughly the kind of medical knowledge doctors have, and (3) insurance companies lack information about antecedent health risks. Whatever insurance

---

[60] Dworkin does tend to focus on the United States. It's not clear whether he thinks all present societies have unjust distributions of income. He does say – see ch. 6, n. 18 – that if the world were just we would all be closer to the average income at present, but he doesn't indicate whether any particular society comes close to his ideal.

[61] Dworkin does acknowledge in a note that this is not true of all risks; he mentions that it would seem fair to charge smokers more than nonsmokers. As I argue, this concession helps to undermine Dworkin's defense of NHI. See Dworkin, *Sovereign Virtue*, 491–2, n. 4.

prudent[62] people would purchase in such a market constitutes justice in health care in both a macrosense (whatever level of aggregate resources was devoted to health care would be morally appropriate) and in a distributive sense (however health care was distributed in such a society would be just). Summarizing his views, Dworkin says that 1 through 3 "follow directly from an extremely appealing assumption: that a just distribution is one that well-informed people create for themselves by individual choices, provided the economic system and distribution of wealth in the community in which these choices are made are themselves just."[63]

But because there is and could not be any market that fits Dworkin's version of an egalitarian market, how are we to determine what insurance it would be prudent for, say, the average citizen in contemporary welfare states to purchase? Though Dworkin notes that "what is prudent for someone depends on that person's own individual needs, tastes, personality and preferences,"[64] he thinks that nevertheless we can make some reasonable judgments concerning what the average prudent citizen would purchase in such a market – and it turns out to be functionally equivalent to NHI. He thinks such a person would purchase insurance covering both routine and preventive medical care as well as hospitalization. This corresponds to NHI's being compulsory, universal, comprehensive insurance. On the other hand, Dworkin argues that some health-care decisions would almost certainly be imprudent – for example, insurance coverage for expensive care during dementia or for heroic and expensive treatment that would only prolong life for a few months – and also that at some point our confidence runs out concerning what an average person would purchase, and so justice requires that people have the freedom to buy supplemental insurance. The elimination of risk rating is, of course, equivalent to the lack of information insurers would have in Dworkin's thought experiment about an ideal market. As for NHI's restriction on supply through rationing, global budgets, and the like, Dworkin sees them as the inevitable result of universal coverage combined with

---

[62] It is not entirely clear why Dworkin introduces the concept of prudence at this point. I think it is because he assumes, reasonably, that most people act prudently in a market, and so he applies that assumption to his hypothetical market.

[63] Dworkin, *Sovereign Virtue*, 313.

[64] Ibid.

a prudential commitment to controlling costs. Similar to Daniels, he also believes public input on rationing decisions is required, though he says little about this matter.

Thus although Dworkin, far more than Daniels, stresses that justice in health care flows from a view of equality that is "dynamic and sensitive to people's differing convictions on how to live,"[65] they both end up supporting roughly the same kind of policies. This is because a view that (most) health-care decisions do not reflect genuine choices and a view that they would only reflect them under conditions that could not exist reach the same conclusion that a market under present, actual circumstances compounds and reflects unjust inequalities rather than reflecting the choices of individuals with different preferences, ambitions, or views of the good life.

To summarize, Daniels argues for universal, comprehensive health insurance with no risk rating and limited choice of plans, because he sees justice in health care as requiring the removal of barriers that prevent one from achieving (to the extent that this is possible) normal functioning. His emphasis upon a health-care policy that removes barriers to fair equality of opportunity, rather than one that respects choices that reflect people's different and autonomous choices about how to live their lives, stems from his belief that most health risks are not voluntarily assumed and that most health-care decisions in a market do not reflect genuine choice. Dworkin argues for the same kind of NHI as Daniels because Dworkin believes that (real) markets constitute unfair barriers rather than reflecting individuals' different choices and preferences, though he does not invoke the notion of fair equality of opportunity, and instead uses a thought experiment about an ideal market as a way of showing that NHI would lead to roughly the same result as such a market. As for NHI's global budgets and other constraints on subsidized demand, Daniels and Dworkin justify them in two ways. In part, they are an inevitable result of providing universal coverage joined with a commitment to controlling costs and preventing health-care resources from draining away other resources. In part, they are needed to make tradeoffs between different kinds of medical services, and public input on these tradeoffs is needed to maintain accountability and give some determinate criteria for making these tradeoffs that egalitarian principles cannot provide.

[65] Dworkin, "Justice in the Distribution of Health Care," 898.

3.4 Risks and Choices: Egalitarian Reasons for MHI

As we've seen, NHI differs from MHI vis-à-vis both the consumption or demand for health-care services and the production or supply of such services. In this section, I examine the consumption-side arguments and show why egalitarians should support, not oppose, risk rating and a wide choice of health-care plans. In the next section, I examine the production or supply of health care and argue that egalitarians should support markets over government rationing of health-care services.

Recall that egalitarians argue that risk rating and a widespread choice of health-care plans are unfair because, first, differences in health risks are largely involuntary or, to put matters in a slightly different way, because (real) markets constitute unfair barriers rather than reflecting individuals' different choices and preferences and, second, because choices to forego comprehensive service plans are due to background unjust inequalities. Hence, NHI, which eliminates risk rating and compels everyone to pick similar comprehensive plans (with limited purchase of supplemental insurance), is much fairer than MHI. I first discuss health risks and then proceed to the question of choices to purchase different kinds of health-care policies. One terminological point before I begin: in what follows when I refer to health risks, I am only referring to those health risks that affect one's insurance premiums. Some health risks do not affect it – for example, those about which the customer and the insurer are ignorant – and are excluded from my discussion.

3.4.1 Health Risks

Some health risks are clearly unchosen. Someone who has the gene for Huntington's chorea,[66] for example, has no choice about whether he or she gets the disease; unless he or she dies prematurely from some other cause, he or she will get the disease and then die of it, no matter what is done. (Genetic influence is not normally deterministic, a point I will discuss later.) Similarly, other unalterable or nearly unalterable features of the person, such as age or sex, are not chosen, and so health risks resulting from those features are matters of unchosen

---

[66] Huntington's chorea is a devastating neurological disease characterized by bizarre bodily movements, forgetfulness, and, at its later stages, inability to reason. For information, see "What is Huntington's Chorea?" http://pa.essortment.com/whatishuntingt_rctd.htm (accessed November 20, 2006).

circumstances. There are also features of one's environment that one cannot choose. For example, if one is unknowingly (and nonculpably) exposed to environmental toxins or infectious agents, then the risk of subsequent bad health effects would be bad brute luck.[67] However, many health risks are not matters of unchosen circumstances. An important cause of health risks is "lifestyle" decisions or activities, such as tobacco use, diet and pattern of physical activity, alcohol use, sexual behavior, driving skills (e.g., whether one uses seat belts regularly or drives intoxicated), and the use of illegal drugs.[68] In general, it is not

---

[67] This would probably only affect one's insurance premiums, however, if the exposure was chronic.

[68] See J. Michael McGinnis and William. H. Foege, "Actual Causes of Death in the United States," *JAMA* 270 (November 1993): 2207–12. I thank Robert S. Sade, MD for directing me to this reference. This article surveys and synthesizes articles published between 1977 and 1993 that discuss the causes of death in the United States. The authors estimate that about 40 percent of all such deaths are due to tobacco use, alcohol consumption, sexual activity, motor vehicle accidents, and the use of illegal drugs. J. Michael McGinnis, Pamela Williams-Russo, and James R. Knickman, "The Case for More Active Policy Attention to Health Promotion," *Health Affairs* 21, no. 2 (2002): 82, state that behavior patterns "represent the single most prominent domain of influence over health prospects in the United States." A longitudinal study of 6,928 adult males in Alameda County, California from 1965 to 1974 is also suggestive. It shows that good health practices (not smoking, moderate or no use of alcohol, seven to eight hours regular sleep, regular physical activity, proper weight, eating breakfast, not eating between meals) and not the initial health status of the survey respondents were responsible for significant differences in mortality. See Lester Breslow and James E. Enstrom, "Persistence of Health Habits and Their Relationship to Mortality," *Preventive Medicine* 9, no. 4 (1980): 469–83. I have not located any studies that attempt to quantify the effects of lifestyle choices on mortality in Europe, but because a greater percentage of the population smokes in most European countries than in the United States, it is not unlikely that a higher proportion of deaths in those countries could be attributed to lifestyle choices. See U.S. Congress, Office of Technology Assessment, *International Health Statistics: What the Numbers Mean for the United States* (Washington, DC: U.S. Government Printing Office, November 1993), 70–1, 83–4 and Stephen Platt, Amanda Amos, Wendy Gnich, and Odette Parry, "Smoking Policies," in *Reducing Inequalities in Health: A European Perspective*, Johann Mackenbach and Martijntje Bakker, eds. (London: Routledge, 2002), 125–7.

It is important to stress two limitations of the preceding articles. First, their focus is premature deaths, not morbidity, illness, or injury. The fact that lifestyle risks cause a certain percentage of premature deaths doesn't mean they cause the same percentage of morbidity, illness, or injury. E.g., women generally have greater morbidity than men but tend to live longer. See Mildred Blaxter, "A Comparison of Measures of Inequality in Morbidity," in *Health Inequalities in European Countries*, John Fox, ed. (Aldershot: Gower Publishing, 1989), 199. Second, the first article cited does not discuss how much of the *differences* in premature mortality are due to lifestyle factors.

a matter of bad brute luck if one gets injured, ill, diseased, or dies prematurely from these activities or behaviors. I will now argue that these behaviors should be classified as generally belonging on the voluntary side of the voluntary-involuntary continuum.

Egalitarians believe that choices such as how much work to trade off for leisure, savings to trade off for consumption, and what line of work to pursue, and so forth are, in general, voluntary because they reflect and are constituted by different ambitions and views of the good life (recall Dworkin's argument). However, the same relationship holds for lifestyle risks. Consider the following, all of which reflect and constitute lifestyle risks:

1. Rate of time preference. Those with higher rates of time preference, that is, those who place a high value on present goods over future goods, will engage in more risky behavior, including behavior that might increase one's chances of becoming ill or diseased, or dying prematurely.

2. Choice of occupation. For example, firefighting is a more risky profession than teaching.

Studies that do attempt to determine how much of differential premature mortality was due to lifestyle factors, as opposed to other influences such as years of schooling, relative income, and occupational status have found that lifestyle factors played a role but not the most significant role. The most famous of these are probably longitudinal studies of four occupational classes of British civil servants working in the same office that showed that their occupational status had a stronger correlation with mortality from coronary heart disease than lifestyle factors such as smoking. See Michael Marmot, "Social Inequalities in Mortality: the Social Environment," in *Class and Health*, Richard G. Wilkinson, ed. (London: Tavistock Publishing, 1986), 21–33, and Michael G. Marmot et al. "Health Inequalities among British Civil Servants: The Whitehall II Study," *Lancet* 337 (June 8, 1991): 1387–93. Other longitudinal studies that show a stronger correlation between income and/or education than lifestyle factors are discussed by Mary N. Haan, George A. Kaplan, and S. Leonard Syme, "Socioeconomic Status and Health: Old Observations and New Thoughts," in *Pathways to Health: The Role of Social Factors*, John P. Bunker, Deanna S. Gomby, and Barbara H. Kehrer, eds. (Menlo Park, NJ: Henry J. Kaiser Family Foundation, 1989), 83–6; J. W. Lynch, G. A. Kaplan, and J. T. Salonen, "Why Do Poor People Behave Poorly? Variation in Adult Health Behaviors and Psychosocial Characteristics by Stages of the Socioeconomic Lifecourse," *Social Science and Medicine* 44, no. 6 (1997): 809–19; and Paula M. Lantz et al. "Socioeconomic Disparities in Health Change in a Longitudinal Study of U.S. Adults: The Role of Health-Risk Behaviors," *Social Science and Medicine* 53, no 1 (2001): 29–40. For reasons I discuss in n. 74, however, all of these studies have various methodological and conceptual problems and must be viewed with great caution.

3. Epistemic values. The extent to which I assess and am open to evidence, the value I place on discovering the truth, and the degree to which I desire to hold coherent beliefs, and so forth, will play a role in determining whether I should care about health risks or believe what scientific evidence or scientific methods tell us about the risk of certain behaviors or ways of life. These epistemic values are in part affected by nonepistemic values: given one's aims in life, commitments, and so forth, it can be rational for different people to devote different amounts of time and effort to learning and absorbing information about health risks.

4. Moral and metaphysical views or values. One's views about the meaning and value of life and death, enjoyment and happiness, and suffering and pain will play a role in one's degree of risk aversion. That, in turn, is also reflected and constituted by one through three.

It is clear, then, that one's conception of the good life – which includes one's metaphysical, epistemic, and moral values – influences one's assumption of lifestyle risks (and vice versa) to a significant extent. Because the choices to pursue and revise one's ambitions, conception of the good life, and so forth are considered by egalitarians to be sufficiently voluntary, such that inequalities resulting from such choices are regarded as just, it follows that egalitarians should in general consider lifestyle risks to be sufficiently voluntary.

I anticipate two kinds of objections to this argument. First, an egalitarian might argue that we will only know that lifestyle or behavioral risks are voluntarily assumed when we live in an egalitarian society or, in any event, a society in which the effects of bad brute luck have been minimized. So, for example, we can't conclude that someone who smokes or has a high caloric diet has chosen risky lifestyles. Instead he might do so because he is poor and, because of an unjust distribution of income and wealth, feels trapped and has little motivation to avoid indulging in present pleasures that create a greater risk of future harm to one's health. This reply, however, confuses whether lifestyle or behavior health risks, as a *general* category, should be viewed by egalitarians as voluntarily assumed, as opposed to whether, *for any specific person*, we can know if that risk was voluntarily assumed. My argument concerns the former – just as Dworkin's argument that different work-leisure tradeoffs are voluntary was a general claim, not a claim about any specific person.

Second, it may be objected that even if the initial assumption of such risks is generally voluntary, this diminishes over time, so that subsequent behavior becomes more and more involuntary. This argument might be applied to such risks as the use of legal and illegal drugs. It may be argued that although initial decisions to smoke or use illegal drugs are sufficiently voluntary, after a period of time the user becomes addicted and thus it becomes difficult to quit. The usual basis for this kind of argument is a pharmacological model of addiction – which states that the effects of certain drugs on the brain are so powerful that after a while they overpower an average person's will to quit. However, the pharmacological model does not fit the evidence very well for either legal or illegal drugs, as I argue in the appendix to Chapter 3. In contrast, my explanation of drug addictions (also set out in the appendix) that are hard to break – cigarette smoking being the best example because a smoker's quit rate is much lower than other drug user's quit rate – is that smoking is a central activity for smokers and well integrated into their lives. Central or well-integrated activities are always difficult to alter or eliminate; to do so successfully requires a powerful incentive. However, the incentive is lacking for many people because smoking does not damage one's life but only one's health and the serious damage is, for much of one's life, in the distant future. Egalitarians are precluded from arguing that continued participation in risky central activities is indicative of involuntariness because otherwise much of life – much of what matters in life – would be labeled as involuntary. In particular, because egalitarians, like almost everyone in contemporary political philosophy, defend some basic rights to liberties as necessary to respect persons' capacities to shape their own lives, that respect would be vitiated if not destroyed if central or well-integrated activities were, in virtue of being central or well integrated, to be considered involuntary and to overpower a person's will.

So far I have discussed relatively clear-cut kinds of influences on health risks: lifestyle risks are voluntarily assumed, while risks resulting from fixed features of the person and exposure to environmental harms of which one was nonculpably ignorant are clearly unchosen. Other causes of differential health risks are much harder to classify. Consider, for example, differences in education and income and wealth (in general, the more years of education and the greater one's wealth, the better one's health).[69] Clearly, young children have extremely limited choices concerning what type and how much schooling they receive. However, as they approach adulthood and become adults, they do have such choices (at least in democratic societies, which are our focus here). I will discuss in Chapter 6 what egalitarians should believe about inequalities in income and wealth. For now, note that they cannot take the view that *all* income and wealth inequalities are unchosen,[70] as some of them will be due to differences in

[69] On the relationship between education and mortality, see Tapni Valkonen's longitudinal study of seven European countries, "Adult Mortality and Levels of Education," in *Health Inequalities in European Countries*, 142–72, ch. 7. David Mechanic, "Socioeconomic Status and Health: An Examination of Underlying Processes," in *Pathways to Health*, 19, says that "Education is one of the most consistent predictors of measures of mortality, morbidity and health behavior." Michael Grossman and Theodore J. Joyce, "Socioeconomic Status: A Personal Research Perspective," in ibid., 141, say that education has been shown to be a more important causal determinant than occupational status or income. Leonard A. Sagan also argues that education is a more important causal determinant of morbidity than wealth. See *The Health Of Nations: True Causes of Sickness and Well-Being* (New York: Basic Books, 1987), 176–8. McGinnis et al., "The Case for More Active Policy Attention to Health Promotion," says that for the U.S. population as a whole, "the most consistent predictor of the likelihood of death in any given year is the level of education," 81.

Of course, even if education is a better causal determinant or predictor of mortality and/or morbidity than income, this does not mean income level is unimportant. For some studies that stress the effect of income on health risks, see G. Pappas, S. Queen, W. Adden, and G. Fisher, "The Increasing Disparity in Mortality between Socioeconomic Groups in the United States, 1960 and 1986," in *New England Journal of Medicine* 329 (1993): 103–9, cited in Oliver Fein, "The Influence of Social Class on Health Status: American and British Research on Health Inequalities," in *Journal of General Internal Medicine* 10 (October 1995): 577–86; Mary Haan et al. "Socioeconomic Status and Health," in *Pathways to Health*, 84; and Siegried Geyer and Richard Peter, "Income, Occupational Position, Qualification and Health Inequalities – Competing Risks? (Comparing Indicators of Social Status)," *Journal of Epidemiology and Community Health* 54, no. 4 (2000): 299–305.

[70] There is a recent burgeoning literature that argues that income inequality as such is a cause of differential health risks. This argument makes a stronger claim than that poverty or low income is a significant health risk, as it maintains that the effects of income inequality occur throughout the economic spectrum. For a useful summary of some of this literature see Norman Daniels, Bruce Kennedy, and Ichiro Kawachi, *Is Inequality Bad for Our Health?* (Boston: Beacon Press, 2000), 3–33. Unlike the claim that poverty or low income is a health risk, the claim that inequality as such is a health risk has been vigorously disputed. For criticisms, see Neal Pearce and George Davey Smith, "Is Social Capital the Key to Inequalities in Health?" *American Journal of Public Health* 93, no. 1 (2003): 122–4 and the references cited therein, and Jennifer M. Mellor and Jeffrey Milyo, "Income Inequality and Health Status in the United

ambitions, the tradeoffs one makes between leisure and work, savings and consumption, and time preference.

Similar remarks apply to psychological characteristics of the person, such as a sense of self-efficacy or degree of self-control, ability to cope with stress and adversity, and general outlook on life (e.g., degree of optimism[71] or cheerfulness), which also affect a person's health (in particular, the immune system).[72] To the extent that these characteristics are largely determined in childhood and very difficult to change thereafter, they should be placed on the involuntary side of the spectrum. To the extent that one can, as an adult, develop and/or alter these characteristics, they should be placed on the voluntary side of the spectrum. Some of these characteristics are probably largely determined in childhood (cheerfulness?), and others are more under one's control (a sense of self-efficacy?). So overall it is hard to give a general answer concerning these types of influences.

States: Evidence from the Current Population Survey," *The Journal of Human Resources* 37, no. 3 (2002): 510–39.

[71] Optimism is to some extent a matter of one's metaphysical views about enjoyment, happiness, pain, and suffering, which is a key component of one's conception of the good life. So what we have here is a direct connection between one's conception of the good life and the extent to which one will use and need health-care services and/or make insurance claims.

[72] On self-efficacy, see Albert Bandura, "Self-Efficacy Mechanism in Physiological Activation and Health-Promoting Behavior," in *Neural Biology of Learning, Emotion and Affect*, John Madden IV, ed. (New York: Raven Press, 1991), 229–69; Herzlinger, *Market Driven Health Care*, 60–2, and the references cited therein; and Leonard A. Sagan, *The Health of Nations*, 187–94. On self-control, and its relation to health differentials, see Daniel S. Ballis, Alexander Segall, Michael J. Mahon, Judith G. Chipperfield, and Elaine M. Dunn, "Perceived Control in Relation to Socioeconomic and Behavior Resources for Health," *Social Science and Medicine* 52, no. 11 (2001): 1661–76; and Margie E. Lachman and Suzanne L. Weaver, "The Sense of Control as a Moderator of Social Class Differences in Health and Well-Being," *Journal of Personality and Social Psychology* 74, no. 3 (2001): 763–73. Regarding the way a sense of control affects health habits, see Andrew Steptoe and Jane Wardle, "Locus of Control and Health Behavior Revisited: A Multivariate Analysis of Young Adults from 18 Countries," *British Journal of Psychology* 92, no. 4 (2001): 659–73. On the role of hope and coping skills, see Sagan, *The Health of Nations*, 180–1,184. On the importance of the ability to respond to stress and its affects on the immune system, see the introduction by R. G. Evans and G. L. Stoddart, "Producing Health, Consuming Health Care," in *Why Are Some People Healthy and Others Not? The Determinants of Health of Populations*, Robert G. Evans, Morris L. Barer, and Theodore R. Marmor, eds. (New York: Aldine DeGruyter, 1994), 21–22, 45–7, and Gerid Weidner, "Why Do Men Get More Heart Disease than Women? An International Perspective," *American Journal of College Health* 48, no. 6 (2000): 291–4.

One could elaborate other influences that affect differential health risks; however, the general difficulty is now apparent. Unless it's true that (a) most health risks are due to matters of brute luck, such as the gene for Huntington's chorea, or (b) due to lifestyle choices, such as smoking and excessive alcohol use, egalitarians can provide no determinate answer to the question: "are most health risks voluntarily or involuntarily assumed?" Neither (a) nor (b) is true. Some health risks are merely matters of brute luck. A significant but indeterminate amount is due to lifestyle risks and to the mixed causes. Furthermore, the problem becomes worse when we consider that the causes of health risks interact with each other. For example, the more affluent and more educated tend to follow less risky lifestyles[73] and genetic factors are rarely deterministic but are usually tendencies that may or may not be actualized depending on a variety of behavioral and environmental circumstances. These causal interactions between most of the factors influencing health risks are quite complex and difficult to measure.

Because we can't tell to what extent health risks are due to chosen or unchosen factors and because the various factors interact with each other in complex and difficult to measure ways, it is difficult, if not impossible, to firmly support a conclusion about the extent to which health risks in general are or are not voluntarily assumed.[74]

---

[73] For a discussion of the relationship between education and lifestyle choices, see Sagan, *The Health of Nations*, 179; Raymond Illsley, "Comparative Review of Sources, Methodology and Knowledge [of Health Inequalities]," *Social Science and Medicine* 31, no. 3 (1990): 230; and Mechanic, "Socioeconomic Status and Health," 19. For a discussion that focuses specifically on smoking, see M. Droomers, C. T. Schrijvers, and J. P. Mackenbach, "Why Do Lower Educated People Continue Smoking? Explanations from the Longitudinal GLOBE Study," *Health Psychology* 21, no. 3 (2002): 263–72. There are a number of studies showing a relationship between socioeconomic status and risky lifestyles, some of which I cite in n. 69, but for reasons I discuss in the n. 74, all such studies must be viewed with caution.

[74] Studies that show a correlation between one influence, e.g., lifestyle or income, and another, e.g., mortality or morbidity, or that show differing degrees of correlation between different influences and a certain measure(s) of health are always vulnerable to the third variable problem: correlation isn't proof of causality. Studies that show a correlation between socioeconomic status – defined as a combination of income and/or occupational status and/or education – and health outcomes are particularly problematic, if the correlation between the various factors making up socioeconomic status is not that high, as Victor Fuchs points out in "General Comments of Conference Participants," in *Pathways to Health*, 226. Furthermore, some

What, then, should egalitarians say about the choice between MHI, which has risk rating, and NHI, which does not? First, notice that they *can't* support NHI on the grounds that Daniels and Dworkin provided, which was that most health risks were unchosen. Their argument has been undermined because only *some* indeterminate amount of health risks is unchosen. One possibility would be for egalitarians to say that both MHI and NHI will involve unfairness. MHI will be unfair because differences in insurance premiums will not correspond to differences in voluntarily assumed risks, and NHI will be unfair because some people won't pay more for risks they did voluntarily assume and will be subsidized by people who have chosen less risky behavior. However, we need to recall that although MHI has risk rating, it also subsidizes those with uninsurable risks and provides subsidies for the indigent to purchase health insurance. Thus MHI is structured so that *some* of the people who are victims of bad brute luck will not be required to pay more for risks they did not assume, although *to some extent* people will be charged in accordance with voluntarily assumed risks. Contrast this with NHI in which virtually *no one* bears the cost of risks they voluntarily assumed, and MHI is fairer on egalitarian grounds. MHI has a way of translating into practice the important egalitarian principle that people be held responsible for the costs of their choices, as well as

studies aren't longitudinal, which raises the suspicion that the relationship found is a temporary one. Some studies are only of one country, which is of limited use, and international studies run into problems if countries use different ways of measuring and monitoring morbidity. On the problems in making international comparisons, see U.S. Congress, Office of Technology Assessment, *International Health Statistics*, ch. 2.

Morbidity studies are particularly tricky, because (a) authors often use different notions of morbidity (is it defined in terms of some objective signs of pathology, in terms of self-reported symptoms, or by an inability to perform certain "normal" tasks?), and (b) there is a big gap between actual morbidity and reported morbidity. On different concepts of morbidity, see Blaxter, "A Comparison of Measures of Inequality in Morbidity," 206–21. On the gap between reported and actual morbidity, see Illsley, "Comparative Review of Sources Methodology and Knowledge," 233, and Amartya Sen, "Health Equity: Perspectives, Measurability and Criteria" in *Challenging Inequities in Health: From Ethics to Action*, Timothy Evans, Margaret Whitehead, Finn Diderischen, Abbas Bhuiya, and Meg Wirth, eds. (New York: Oxford University 2001), 70–1.

Finally, even if common measurements are used, some are quite difficult to measure accurately, e.g., diet and physical activity. One reason years of schooling may show up as a better predictor of mortality or morbidity than other factors is simply that years of schooling are relatively easy to measure.

finding a place for the principle that victims of bad brute luck be subsidized. NHI's abolition of risk rating, by contrast, gives *no* weight to the antisubsidization principle. Given that there are *two* sides to egalitarianism – where genuine choices rule, it is fair to hold people responsible for their choices and the cost of their choices, and when bad brute luck rules, it should be compensated or rectified in some way – a system that finds a place for both sides is better from an egalitarian view than a system that finds a place only for one side.[75]

Another objection to my argument that MHI is fairer than NHI because the former has some risk rating and the latter has (virtually) none is that NHI could have the equivalent of selective risk rating; for example, taxes on tobacco products, the repeated use of which increases one health risks. However, taxes in NHI will not really produce the same function as risk rating. Taxes are determined by political considerations, and it's quite doubtful that the level of tax paid would be even roughly proportional to increased risks of mortality or morbidity. The history of so-called sin taxes is hardly encouraging in this regard.[76]

Another consideration strengthens my argument that egalitarians should favor the risk rating that exists in MHI. A health insurance system that has a comparative advantage on communicating effective information about one's health risks and giving incentives to act on that information will be *ceteris paribus* justified on egalitarian grounds, because the degree to which individuals are or can be made cognizant of the various risks they assume (and motivated to act on that information) makes the assumption of those risks more voluntary. Egalitarians believe one should be held responsible for one's choices and the cost of these choices, but responsibility is not just a backward-looking issue, of whether one is or should be held responsible for what one *did*, but a forward-looking issue, that is, how people can be given incentives to *be*

---

[75] Admittedly, Dworkin's views fit more precisely this two-sided view of egalitarianism than do Daniels's views. But, as I mentioned in Chapter 2, this two-sided view is typical of contemporary egalitarianism.

[76] On this topic, see William F. Shughart II, ed., *Taxing Choice: The Predatory Politics of Fiscal Discrimination* (New Brunswick, NJ: Transaction Publishers, 1997). On the effects of recent tobacco litigation in the United States, see Martha Derthick, *Up in Smoke: From Legislation to Litigation in Tobacco Politics* (Washington, DC: Congressional Quarterly Press, 2002), in particular, ch. 9–11.

responsible or to take responsibility in the future. Effective communication of information about one's health risks and incentives to act on that information does this, and so even if health risks are not as voluntary as other kinds of decisions that egalitarians believe are voluntary, a comparative superiority of one kind of system of health insurance in effectively communicating information about one's health risks and providing incentives to act on that information compensates – perhaps more than compensates – for the diminished responsibility in acquiring those risks in the first place. MHI is better than NHI on this score. In MHI, most people pay for their own health insurance and are likely to be directly financially affected by their insurance's risk rating. This is intensified by MSAs for small bills or routine medical expenses, which encourages consumers or customers to budget over time to reap the benefits of healthy lifestyle choices or pay the costs of unhealthy ones.[77] Thus, MSAs will tend to lower people's time preference, that is reduce their tendency to favor present goods over future goods, and thus provide incentives to take preventive health measures. It is interesting to note that in South Africa, the country where MSAs have obtained the greatest foothold, the largest insurance company linked with MSAs stresses preventive medicine and has come up with some innovative financial incentives to encourage healthy lifestyles.[78] By contrast, NHI tends to rely on methods such as public-health campaigns, discussions with or exhortations by physicians and other medical personnel, and taxation of (some) unhealthy products. These, of course, do provide information about health risks and incentives to act on that information, but there are reasons to believe that they are not as effective as the methods MHI would use. Public health campaigns and discussion with medical personnel have the comparative disadvantage that the patient or insured receives no direct financial incentives or direct financial feedback on his or her health risks, and taxation has the

---

[77] Goodman and Musgrave, *Patient Power*, 251.

[78] The Discovery Health network has a program called *Vitality*, which costs about a 5 percent additional premium. Individuals gain points in *Vitality* by participating in wellness-related events such as getting mammograms and pap smears and exercising at a spa. An improvement in health status also earns one points. These points can be used to purchase a variety of benefits; e.g., members with no points can purchase a British Airways round-trip domestic flight for 29 percent of normal fare; members with sixty thousand points or more can purchase the same ticket for 8 percent of the normal fare. Matisonn, "Medical Savings Accounts in South Africa," 11.

comparative disadvantage that it only targets selective (and politically unpopular) health risks and has a tendency to be overly blunt in the message it sends. (Antismoking campaigns in recent years have gone in for overkill, and punitive tobacco taxes can promote black markets and the forbidden fruit phenomena.)[79]

It may be objected that my defense of MHIs depends on an exaggerated or unwarranted faith in the extent to which risk rating can provide incentives for future responsible behavior, because risk rating is based, to some degree, upon unalterable or virtually unalterable characteristics of an individual (e.g., upon age or sex). Because premiums are based in part on such fixed (or nearly fixed) characteristics, risk rating provides no incentive for more responsible behavior, as one is not acting responsibly or irresponsibly by simply having such characteristics.[80] However, recall that the arguments in this book are *comparative* ones. That fact that risk rating is based only *in part* on characteristics or behavior that can be altered is still an improvement vis-à-vis acting responsibly in the future over the absence of risk rating because the former provides more information than the latter concerning the cost of one's (partially) alterable behavior. Furthermore, recall the point I made in the preceding text, that in most cases one's fixed features and alterable behavior interact. If I am a male with a family history of heart disease, and this is reflected in higher insurance premiums than a woman with no family history of heart disease, this does not mean I can do nothing about my health risks. I can try to counteract the influences of sex and family history by eating carefully, exercising, and taking other proactive steps to minimize the effects of my bad biological luck.

An additional reason for an egalitarian (or at any rate his prioritarian cousin) to favor the combination of MSAs and risk-rated catastrophic insurance is that these methods may have a particularly pronounced comparative advantage for the less educated. As noted, the rates of mortality and morbidity drop as education increases, and part of the reason for this is that the more educated engage in less risky

---

[79] See Dwight Filley, "Forbidden Fruit: When Prohibition Increases the Harm It Is Supposed to Reduce," *The Independent Review* 3, no. 3 (1999): 441–51, and Patrick Fleenor, "Cigarette Taxes, Black Markets and Crime: Lessons from New York's 50-Year Losing Battle," *Cato Policy Analysis* (February 6, 2003) and the references cited therein.

[80] I thank economist Robert Sugden for this objection.

lifestyles or behaviors. A system that has a comparative advantage in giving the less educated an obvious and direct way of learning that their actions have a negative effect on their mortality and morbidity and gives them an obvious incentive to act on this information would appear to be close to a necessity on egalitarian or prioritarian grounds, and the MSA and risk-rating combination may very well do this. After all, the more educated and affluent have less need of risk rating and MSAs. They are likely to be informed, have access to information about the effects of various lifestyle choices, and are already more motivated to take responsibility for their health. A system that relies less on patients' or customers' cognitive abilities and prior motivation to care about their health, and that relies more on financial incentives to be aware of health risks and alter one's habits would appear to favor the less educated and be a significant plus for egalitarians (and their prioritarian cousins).

To summarize, egalitarianism should consider MHI's combination of risk rating and some subsidies for uninsurable risks to be fairer than NHI's absence of risk rating for a variety of reasons. First, it gives weight to both the antisubsidization principle (people should be held responsible for the costs of their choices – hence some need for risk rating) and the compensation for bad brute luck principle (by subsidizing uninsurable risks), whereas NHI virtually ignores the antisubsidization principle. Second, the combination of MHI's risk rating and MSAs is more effective than NHI's public-health campaigns and taxes in communicating information about one's health risks and giving incentives to act on that information. This, in turn, offsets any diminished responsibility in acquiring those health risks in the first place. Third, by MHI relying less on patients' or customers' cognitive abilities and prior motivation to care about their health than does NHI and more on financial incentives to be aware of health risks and alter one's habits, MHI has a comparative advantage for the less educated, and this would appear to be another reason for an egalitarian (or at any rate his prioritarian cousin) to favor it.

3.4.2 *Choice in Health Plans*

I now discuss the lesser choice in health plans that NHI allows, in particular its denial of the choice to forego comprehensive coverage. Recall that Daniels's and Dworkin's defense of these restrictions was that present choices to forego comprehensive coverage are due to background unjust inequalities (in wealth and/or opportunities). Strictly speaking, this is a separate issue from risk rating, for even if egalitarian justice requires risk rating, it might require restricting health-care plan choice, in particular the choice to forego comprehensive coverage. However, the arguments that lifestyle health risks are voluntarily assumed carry over to the question of choices in health-care coverage. Individuals' differing ambitions and conceptions of the good life affect the choice of health-care plans. That choice is affected by rate of time preference: people with higher time preferences will prefer a health plan focused more on immediate medical needs and less on long-term and catastrophic care, whereas people with lower time preferences will want a plan that has good catastrophic-care coverage. People who are very risk averse will be willing to spend more for comprehensive plans, whereas less risk-averse people will tend to prefer less expensive casualty insurance. Obviously, occupational choice makes a difference because different jobs affect one's health differently and thus call for different kinds of health insurance and different ways of allocating savings over time. Epistemic values matter because the extent to whether I think I should care about health risks affects what kind of insurance I desire. And moral and metaphysical values play an essential role because questions about the meaning and value of life and death will influence a person's views about the appropriateness of various kinds of life-saving or life-prolonging procedures, contraception, abortion, physician-assisted suicide, and euthanasia, and so forth.

The relationship between one's conception of the good and widespread choice in health-care plans is stronger than in the case of the assumption of lifestyle health risks. The latter are often assumed nondeliberatively and implicitly, while health-care plan choices and health-care budgetary decisions are often made explicitly and deliberately. To the extent that deliberate and explicit decisions are more reflective of a person's conception of the good, the connection between ambitions, conceptions of the good, for example, is even stronger for decisions about what kind of health care to choose throughout the course of life than for the assumption of lifestyle health risks.

Of course, just as lifestyle health risks, which egalitarians should consider to be voluntary, interact with health risks that they consider to be unchosen (e.g., genetic factors, background injustices in the distribution of wealth) so too voluntary factors that influence the choice of health-care plans (e.g., time preference, epistemic values, occupational choices) interact with unchosen factors. For example, those who are very risk averse may be that way because they are in chronically ill health through no fault of their own and thus prefer low-deductible comprehensive plans, while those who are not that risk averse may be that way because they are blessed with good genetic luck and may prefer high-deductible casualty insurance, particularly when they are young. This means that the choice between MHI, which has a wide choice of health-care plans, and NHI, which restricts choice and forbids one to forego comprehensive plans, is similar to the choice between MHI's risk rating and NHI's absence of risk rating: both systems contain injustice. NHI contains injustice because it forces everyone into comprehensive plans and does not allow people with different views of the good life much freedom to pick plans that match their preferences, while MHI contains injustice because it does not subsidize comprehensive care for all who need it through no fault or choice of their own. However, just as I argued that MHI was fairer than NHI because to *some extent* it allowed *some* people to bear the costs of their voluntary choices and subsidized some of those with involuntary health risks (in NHI *no one* bore the costs of their risks), so the same kind of conclusion applies to the comparison of MHI's wide choice in health plans with NHI's elimination of the choice of high-deductible catastrophic health plans. Because the choice side of the mixture of chosen and unchosen factors is stronger with regard to health plan choice than with health risks, then the reasons that give egalitarians grounds for supporting risk rating give them, *a fortiori*, grounds for favoring widespread choice in health-care plans, in particular the choice to forego comprehensive coverage.

So MHI's combination of risk rating, MSAs, and choice in health-care plans are all egalitarian reasons to favor it over NHI, which has no or virtually no risk rating, no MSAs, and a more limited choice in health-care plans.

3.5 Rationing, Visibility, and Egalitarian Outcomes: Why Market Allocation Is Better

In section 3.4 my arguments that egalitarians should favor markets as the chief allocation mechanism for the demand or the consumption of health-care services suffices to show that they should favor markets over government rationing of the supply or production of these services. This is because the main reason egalitarians favored government rationing was to put a brake on the effects of subsidized demand in NHI, but once market forces predominate on the demand side, there is little subsidized demand to brake; there is market demand that can be adjusted to supply by normal market means. However, it is useful to address the production/supply-side issues separately, because it's commonly believed that egalitarians should favor government rationing over market allocation decisions.

In any system in which all wants and preferences cannot be satisfied – that is, any system in the real world – some method or procedure is used to determine which wants or preferences are satisfied (in that sense, both markets and government rationing). However, in certain contexts, rationing also has connotations or implications that make it ill-suited as a description of markets. First, it implies the division of fixed supply with fixed shares. One of the chief virtues of markets is that over time they expand the resources or supply available, which government, strictly speaking, cannot do. (Tax policy, of course, can provide incentives for increasing supply, but strictly speaking it is still individuals producing in the market that increases resources.) Second, and far more relevant to the health-care context, rationing implies limiting, withholding, or denying someone a good that could otherwise be available at a market price. In that sense, of course, market rationing is a contradiction in terms.[81] I will avoid the use of *market rationing* wherever possible and instead speak of *market allocation* or *limiting decisions*.

3.5.1 The Egalitarian Criteria for Fair Rationing
Egalitarians believe that rationing is not just unless it results from a fair process. Daniels has discussed this issue in much more detail than Dworkin, and so I will rely on his account. The most basic feature of a fair rationing process is that it be *visible*. This means that limit setting or rationing should be widely known and acknowledged and

---

[81] The first point I owe to Ellen Frankel Paul; on the second point, see Susanne Hahn "Rationing: Distribution, Limitation or Denial? – Against Conceptual Confusion in the Debate about Health Care Systems," in *Rationing: Ethical, Legal, and Practical Aspects*, F. Breyer, H. Kliemt, and F. Theile, eds., (Berlin: Springer, 2001), 7–20.

that the decisions about limits of coverage and care must be publicly accessible and influenced by some kind of public input or deliberation. In his most recent work, Daniels has added some additional requirements for a fair process of rationing or limit setting.[82] The reasons for rationing or limiting decisions must also be publicly accessible but not just any reasons will do. They must be relevant reasons, that is, reasons that fair-minded people – people disposed to seek terms of fair cooperation – would consider at least relevant for the goal of the health-care organizations that are aiming to find the best value for the money. In addition, there must be both a mechanism for appealing rationing decisions and improving policy in light of new arguments and evidence.[83] Notice that even with Daniels's new additions to the conditions for a fair rationing process, the requirement of visibility is still the essential one. Without visibility, Daniels's other conditions either can't be met or are much harder to meet. If the rationing process or decisions are not visible, then the reasons for limiting care can't be relevant, because in order for a reason for a rationing decision to be relevant, one must be aware of the decision. Lack of visibility makes it difficult to have a mechanism for improving or appealing rationing policy because it is hard to improve or appeal something about which one is not aware or understands rather poorly. Hence, I will stress visible rationing as the *sine qua non* of a fair rationing process.

Egalitarians favor this kind of visible rationing process as essential for fairness for two reasons. First, it is needed as a way to maintain public accountability. Health-care institutions that limit or ration care must be considered legitimate if their decisions are to be judged as fair. Involving the public, making the reasons for rationing available to them so that they can judge their relevancy, and giving them a means to dispute rationing decisions and their rationales, are all ways of maintaining or sustaining legitimacy among the persons affected by the limiting or rationing decisions. Second, egalitarian principles of distributive justice are indeterminate on the question of ranking

---

[82] Daniels and Sabin, *Setting Limits Fairly*, ch. 3, 4. For the earlier account, see Daniels et al., *Benchmarks of Fairness*, 57–9.

[83] He also adds another condition, that there is some scheme of regulation – either voluntary or government – to assure that the other conditions are met. I take that condition to be already present in the other conditions because my arguments all concern comparative institutional justification.

medical services and the proper tradeoffs between health care and
other goods, and making these tradeoffs and rankings is part of the
point of rationing (the other is to limit overall demand). Neither fair
equality of opportunity (Daniels) nor the prudent insurance ideal
(Dworkin) will provide much help in making rationing decisions. Concerning the former, although Daniels at one point argued that we could
rank different health-care schemes in terms of the extent to which they
curtailed a normal opportunity range,[84] he has abandoned this idea.
Even assuming that we could determine the extent to which different
life plans are restricted by different health-care schemes – which is
quite dubious because comparing life plans likely involves comparing
incommensurable activities and goals[85] – we would have to compare
whether it was better that disease and disability greatly restricted a few
life plans as opposed to slightly restricting a large number of them.
There is also the not insignificant matter of deciding to what extent, if
any, we should focus on the worst off, that is, the persons whose disease
and disability are such that they are furthest from the ideal of having
a full set of life plans that are reasonable for them to pursue.[86] As for
Dworkin, his argument depends on determining what most prudent
people or an average prudent person would purchase in a hypothetical market, but, as he recognizes, what is prudent depends upon one's
values, preferences, and tastes, and even if one were to accept his claim
that certain health-care schemes would clearly be imprudent, in many
cases this doesn't tell us what would be prudent. Because egalitarian
principles of distributive justice are unable to yield any determinate,
just rationing decisions, the only reasonable alternative is a procedural one: to use the results of a fair process. Notice that indeterminacy
implies the need to experiment with different limit-setting guidelines,
which is why in Daniels's later work he added the requirement that
a fair process must have mechanisms for improving policy in light of
new arguments and evidence.

Although egalitarians favor a procedural account of fair rationing,
they do not think that fair rationing is an example of pure procedural

---

[84] Daniels, *Just Health Care*, 35.

[85] See Ezekiel J. Emanuel, *The Ends of Human Life*, 130–3, for some cogent arguments
along this line.

[86] Daniels mentions both of these problems, along with some other ones in "Four
Unsolved Rationing Problems: A Challenge," *Hastings Center Report* 24 (July–August
1994): 28.

justice, that is, that *any* result or outcome resulting from a visible rationing process in NHI is just.[87] A second egalitarian criterion, avoiding obviously inegalitarian outcomes, is needed. Suppose the middle class or the relatively healthy received a significantly greater amount of the benefits of rationing than did the poor or relatively unhealthy. This result would clearly be inegalitarian. Almost as regrettable would be a situation in which the poor do use health-care services more than the middle class but not enough to compensate for their greater needs, or if the costs that the poor faced in getting access to health services were significantly higher for the poor than the affluent, which kept the former from receiving the services that they needed.

3.5.2 *Visibility and Rationing*
I will now compare NHI with MHI concerning visibility of rationing or limit setting and avoiding obviously inegalitarian outcomes. MHI, I will argue, wins on both counts.

Rationing or limit setting occurs at three levels. First, a macrolevel, that is, limits on the total amount spent on nonsupplemental health care or the total amount spent for specific services, providers, or geographical areas. Second, a middle level, by which I mean the allocation of resources to particular forms of treatment and services, limits of coverage for different treatment and services, and reimbursement policies. Third, a clinical or microlevel, that is, decisions made by doctors and other health-care personnel concerning treatment and procedures for individual patients – how much should be done for them, who should receive treatment, and so forth.

At the macrolevel, NHI's rationing or limit setting occurs using global budgets and total expenditure caps/targets. These are fairly invisible to the average citizen. Most people are unaware of global budgets, as they are the details of government budgets in general. A budget limit that is not one's own personal budget is not terribly visible. The expenditure caps or targets imposed or negotiated by governments and/or sickness funds are, of course, visible to providers but not to patients.

---

[87] Daniels distinguishes between legitimacy and fairness problems as distinct problems of justice, as a legitimate authority can act unfairly, and an illegitimate one can produce fair decisions. Daniels and Sabin, *Setting Limits Fairly*, 26–7. This means that even the result of a fair process could produce some outcomes that are unfair.

In MHI, by contrast, there are no global budgets, only one's own visible budget (except for those whose health insurance is subsidized). The total amount spent on health care in MHI isn't something intended or under any person's or institution's control; it is whatever emerges from the myriad of spending decisions by numerous individuals and institutions. The closest analogy to intentionally or deliberately set macrolimits in MHI are insurance companies and health-care plans' limits on the total amount of benefits paid (annual or lifetime) or stop-loss provisions, that is, limits on the total amount of out-of-pocket expenses paid for by the insured (annual or lifetime). These limits will be far more visible than global budgets or expenditure caps in NHI. In a competitive market, stop-loss provisions are likely to be big selling points. In any event, a person is much more aware of limits in a policy he or she purchased and owns than global limits over which one has almost no input or choice.

So MHI is far more visible than NHI at the macrolevel. When we proceed to the middle level of limit setting or rationing (e.g., the allocation of resources to particular forms of treatment and services, limitations of coverage, policies on reimbursements) matters become more complicated. In the last few years a few NHI systems – New Zealand, Sweden, Denmark, and Norway – have all had public commissions on limit setting and rationing and have recommended the kind of processes Daniels and presumably Dworkin favor, such as public meetings, focus groups, surveys, citizen juries,[88] and hearings, in an effort to come up with rationing criteria. Although Daniels notes that in most countries these commissions' recommendations have not really succeeded in significantly increasing public involvement and influence,[89] we can ask whether public participation and involvement could be increased significantly and, if it was, whether middle-level rationing in NHI would be more visible than middle-level limit setting in MHI. I will first compare MHI with present-day NHI, in which these steps toward greater public involvement have not yet had that much of an impact, and second with NHI as it might operate if it could be reformed so that

---

[88] A citizen jury is a "trial" where those responsible for health-care allocations decisions are "cross-examined" by experts, after which citizens on the jury deliberate and offer their assessment of those allocation decisions.

[89] Daniels and Sabin, *Setting Limits Fairly*, 156–60.

recent trends toward greater public deliberation and input were expanded and actualized.

When we compare present-day NHI with MHI at the middle level of rationing or limit setting, the same arguments I gave at the macrolevel apply, albeit with a few more qualifications. In countries that have a national health service or where the national or provincial government is the sole source of insurance, allocation of resources to particular forms of treatments or services are almost as invisible as macrodecisions, as they are not made or influenced by patient or consumer choice, but by governments (usually local or provincial), hospital administrators, or local health authorities.[90] In NHI systems with competing sickness funds, decisions about inclusions and exclusions in the basic insurance package are influenced by consumer choice but within strict limits set by the government's requirement that all insurance plans (except for supplemental insurance) have a similar set of benefits and reimbursement policies. Furthermore, the rationing at the macrolevel has an obvious effect at the middle level: if a sickness fund promises to cover a certain treatment or service that is getting pinched because of global budgets and/or expenditure caps, then the insured may be unaware that the promises may be hard to keep.

In MHI, however, consumers choose among different heath-care plans or insurance policies that offer different benefits and have different reimbursement policies, different sets of inclusions, and

[90] Some countries with a national health service, such as the United Kingdom and Sweden, have recently introduced some reforms that made middle-level allocation decisions more sensitive to consumer choice. These reforms are usually described as a purchaser-provider split or the creation of an internal market. The basic idea is that local health authorities purchase care from those hospitals that offer best quality of care (which includes the least waiting time). In that way, hospitals have to compete with each other. Although this does make the hospital sector more competitive, it is still the health authorities, not the consumer, who are making the purchases. A more significant reform is Sweden's abolition of global budgets for hospitals. Revenues for those hospitals now depend on which hospitals patients choose to patronize. However, for this degree of influence to approach what occurs in MHI, two things need to occur: (a) hospitals need to be able to go out of business or be fundamentally restructured if they fail to satisfy customers, and (b) hospitals have to be able to compete on price as well as quality. The first is possible, though very unlikely in a system where decisions to close or restructure a hospital depend on political decisions, and the second seems in contradiction to the idea of NHI. For a description of recent reforms in some NHI systems, see Carl Irvine, Johann Hjertqvist, and David Gratzer, "Health Care Reform Abroad," in Gratzer, *Better Medicine*, 248–68.

exclusions. In so doing, they become more aware of those policies –
and influence them – as plans that provide an unpopular mix of benefits and exclusions are unlikely to stay in business. (Notice also that
visibility of these policies is increased by casualty-catastrophic insurance directly reimbursing the insured.) Furthermore, for routine care
or small bills many people in MHI will use MSAs, which means the
inclusions and exclusions are self-imposed, that is, are a matter of how
they decide to allocate their savings among different forms of care.
Such decisions are obviously quite visible.[91] Admittedly, hospitals will
continue to make their own internal allocation decisions, which are
not that visible to the average customer or consumer, but the issue is
a comparative one. Competition, consumer choice, and an increased
role for savings for routine care or small bills make middle-level allocation decisions more visible than when governments, or sickness funds
with almost identical policies, make these decisions.

It may be objected that in countries where there are significant waiting lists (e.g., United Kingdom and Canada) middle-level rationing is
quite visible because the waits have received considerable publicity.
Thus, for at least some NHI systems, there is no difference between
them and MHI as far as the visibility of middle-level allocation or
rationing. In MHI, competition among different health-care plans
and insurance policies increases awareness of reimbursement policy,
exclusions, and limits of coverage, and so forth; while in NHI systems with extensive waits, publicity about the waits tells citizens that
there has been misallocation to various forms of treatment and services. There are two problems with this objection, however. First, in
most countries where there are waits, accurate information about the
extent of the waits, and a system for comparing waiting lists across the

---

[91] This point about MSAs also provides a basis for responding to an objection that might
arise at this time. One might object that if the competitive process in MHI was rather
sluggish, so that there were only a few health-care plans with similar policies, and
consumers did not actively shop for different plans, then consumer awareness of the
plans' policies might not be terribly different than in those versions of NHI where
there is some limited degree of choice among nonprofit sickness funds. Now we
would need some reason to believe competition for health-care plans in MHI would
be so sluggish, but even if the objection is correct about competition for health-care
plans in MHI, it would be very hard to deny that one's decisions about what kind of
health care to purchase with one's MSAs are much more visible than NHI's allocation
policies that are the outgrowth of a political process.

country (and across procedures and treatments) is absent.[92] Second, and far more important, the objection misses the point. All waits tell you is that something has gone wrong. It doesn't mean patients or citizens have influenced or have had access to the rationing decisions of local health authorities, hospital administrators, or local or provincial governments.

At this point, a critic might point out that even if MHI's middle-level market allocation *decisions* are more visible than NHI's middle-level rationing, this doesn't suffice to show that the former meets all of Daniels's criteria for visible rationing. The rationing process or decisions had to be visible or public, the *reasons* for the rationing had to be ones that fair-minded people would consider relevant, and there had to be some kind of appeals process.[93] The fact that the allocation or rationing *decisions* in MHI are more visible than in NHI doesn't show that the *reasons* for the decisions are more visible, the reasons will be perceived as relevant by fair-minded people, or there will be some kind of appeals process if one disagrees with those policies.[94] There are two problems with this kind of reply, however. First, the key egalitarian criterion for a fair rationing process is visibility of the process or decisions. If the decisions aren't visible, then the reasons aren't either, and so MHI still beats NHI at the middle level because the middle-level allocation or rationing decisions are far more visible. Second, to the extent that not being forthcoming about reasons for limits on coverage, reimbursement policies, and so forth or lacking an appeals process puts one at a competitive disadvantage, then health-care plans that lack one or the other or both will tend to go out of business. This tendency is admittedly counterbalanced by sound business reasons not to reveal to competitors the way in which estimates of profitability impinge upon reimbursement policies and the like, but, to the extent that reimbursement policies, limits on coverage, and

---

[92] An exception is Sweden. See n. 14.

[93] There is also the requirement that there must be a mechanism for improving policies in light of new arguments and evidence. I will discuss that point at the end of this section.

[94] I have adopted this objection from Daniels's discussion of market accountability, which he defines as being informed about the options insurers give us and their record of performance. It is inadequate because it "leaves it to the consumer to infer from the choice available what commitments a health plan has to responsible patient-centered care." *Setting Limits Fairly*, 45.

so forth are driven by clinical judgments, competitive pressures[95] for transparency of reasons and an appeals process will have some degree of effectiveness. Because NHI, at present, is less visible about its decisions than MHI, then even *some* degree of openness in MHI about the reasons for its decisions would reinforce its overall superiority to NHI as far as visibility at the middle level of rationing is concerned.

Let us now discuss whether NHI could significantly increase public involvement at the middle level of rationing decisions, so that public hearings, focus groups, and surveys are used to formulate middle-level rationing criteria concerning inclusions and exclusions and allocation of resources to various forms of treatment. If this is feasible, then NHI at the middle level might become at least equal to MHI as far as visibility is concerned. Realistically, the extent to which the public can really be involved in and influence these middle-level rationing decisions is quite limited. Only some people will be motivated enough to use their leisure time to attend these meetings and stay attentive on the topic at hand. Paying people to attend these focus groups would perhaps lessen some of those problems, but only some of those who attend and stay focused are articulate enough to participate in or influence the discussion and/or are able to understand the scientific and clinical background necessary for an informed discussion. (Hence any such meeting, hearing, or focus group has to include a significant presence of the scientifically and medically informed to make the level of the discussion at least reach scientific and medical literacy.) The problems described worsen because this process must be ongoing if the public is to stay informed about the ever-changing situation in health care. At some point in an iterative process of meetings, Oscar Wilde's witty dismissal of socialism becomes apposite: "it would take too many evenings."[96] It is thus not surprising that in New Zealand, the country that has probably taken the idea of public involvement and influence the most seriously, the best example of public influence on

---

95 It's unclear whether there would be such pressures. In general, when there are a great deal of choices, customers do not really care much why a business makes a decision. What customers or consumers generally want is information about the decisions, not the reasoning process that lies behind them. It is possible that health-care decisions would be different.

96 I have found no reference for this often-cited quote. It may be apocryphal. But whether Wilde uttered it or not, it aptly summarizes the problem.

middle-level allocation decisions one can point to is that public representatives had some influence on the development of guidelines for a *few* select procedures and treatments such as stomach ulcers, hormone replacement therapy, and management of high blood pressure after *many* years of discussion.[97] By contrast, MHI doesn't have to rely on people devoting significant time and energy to become aware of and informed about these criteria. In a competitive market, with health-care plans offering different benefits and types of coverage, companies will have obvious incentives to inform customers and potential customers of the nature of their policies. Of course, some customers will choose to ignore the information. But the point is a comparative one: the cost of obtaining the information is lower, and the time and energy needed to discover or influence a policy's exclusions and inclusions is lower (as the main form of influencing a health plan's policies is to purchase those one most prefers and not purchase less desirable ones).

Another way NHI might be reformed so that it could be more visible at the middle level of rationing decisions is to use public forums to generate a substantive right to a specific set of services. This would mean that anything not on the list would not be covered. No present NHI system actually has such a right to a specific set of services;[98] instead the right is phrased very generally as the right to medically necessary care, a right to certain categories of care to which citizens are entitled (e.g., primary care, emergency care, preventive services), or a right to access whatever the system offers. Proposals for such a right were discussed but rejected in the United Kingdom, Sweden, and New Zealand.[99] The closest approximation that exists is the Medicaid program in the state of Oregon. After a series of highly publicized forums,

---

97 Wendy Edgar, "Rationing in New Zealand – How the Public Has a Say," in *The Global Challenge of Health Care Rationing*, Angela Coulter and Chris Ham, eds. (Buckingham: Open University Press, 2000), 181–2. It is also worth noting that New Zealand is a small country with a small population (about four million); thus even its very limited success in generating some degree of public involvement with middle-level rationing will be harder to replicate in a larger country.

98 See Lenaghan, "Health Care Rights in Europe, 3, 188–9.

99 See C. Ham, "Synthesis: What We Can Learn from International Experience," *British Medical Bulletin* 51 (October 1995): 821–8. In Holland, a government commission proposed something similar to Oregon's rationing system, but so far this has had no effect on public policy. See P. M. M. van de Ven, "Choices in Health Care: A Contribution from the Netherlands," in ibid., 785–8.

meetings, and telephone surveys to determine citizens' views about the criteria that should govern the ranking of health-care services, the publicly appointed Oregon Health Services Commission ranked 709 conditions-treatments pairs (e.g., appendicitis-appendectomy) and presented the list to the Oregon legislature. The legislature was forbidden by statute to alter the list and could only decide the location of the cutoff point for funding (it excluded those below number 587).[100]

It's unclear as to whether such Oregon-style rationing is feasible. To establish a right to a set of specific services means that politicians must go on the record and categorically deny certain kinds of care no matter how pressing the need, which is something that makes them quite nervous. It also threatens to intrude on clinical discretion, something that is resented by physicians and that the public is generally reluctant to do. These obstacles may explain why no present-day NHI system has adopted this kind of rationing. (Oregon was providing an explicit list of services for a small, poor section of the population; the political risks of such a list are much less than an explicit list for the whole population.) Even if we suppose this kind of right could be instantiated, NHI would still be worse than MHI at this level of rationing. A health-care package structured or influenced by consumer choice is still more visible than one that is the outgrowth of a democratic process. An individual is clearly more aware of the shape of a health-care package purchased with one's own funds, than a health-care package produced by collective decisions in which one's input or involvement is probably quite limited.

We turn now to the clinical-microlevel, arguably the most important of these. As Daniels points out, this is the level where patients are most likely to learn about limits or rationing.[101] At first glance, it might seem that there would be little difference between NHI and MHI, because to what extent medical professionals make patients or consumers aware of the basis of their decisions to pursue or not pursue a certain course

---

[100] See Martin Strossberg's introduction to *Rationing America's Health Care*, 3–7 [and J. Kitzhaber and A. M. Kemmy, "On the Oregon Trail," *British Medical Bulletin* 51 (October 1995): 813–17. The number of treatment-condition pairs and the funding cutoff point have changed somewhat but not dramatically since this system was instituted in 1994.

[101] Daniels and Sabin, *Setting Limits Fairly*, 172–3.

of action is a matter of their preferences plus patient input – regardless of the system in which they find themselves. Although there is some truth in that remark, it misses the larger picture. Patients are more likely to spend their own money and have paid for their own insurance policy in MHI than in NHI, and so, in the former, patients have more control and influence over microdecisions. Furthermore, the effects of rationing on the macro- and middle level trickle down to the micro- or clinical level. For example, a primary-care physician's referral to a specialist in an NHI system is not infrequently shaped by assumptions about what volume and type of cases a referral unit can handle, which depends in part on rationing decisions and the extent to which they produce waits at various points in the system. The waiting list acts as a deterrent to a primary-care physician's referrals.[102] Although a primary-care physician can tell a patient that he or she cannot recommend a certain course of treatment because of rationing or political decisions beyond the physician's control, doctors tend to want to make decisions based on their view about what is best for the patient, and thus there is significant potential for self-deception and dissembling. Doctors may tell a patient or give the impression that a decision not to pursue a certain treatment is based on a clinical judgment about the effectiveness of that treatment when the judgment is based on its unavailability. This occurred in the British National Health Service (NHS) when doctors told people over the age of fifty-five with kidney failure that there was nothing that could be done for them and did not mention that age rationing by the NHS made renal dialysis unavailable for those patients.[103] It occurred in New Zealand, when specialists used a "scoring system" to determine eligibility for elective surgery – patients at or above a certain overall score were supposed to be booked a firm surgery date, but medical staff often did not tell patients they

---

[102] As noted by R. J. Maxwell, "Why Rationing Is on the Agenda," *British Medical Bulletin* 51 (October 1995): 765 and S. Harrison, "A Policy Agenda for Health Care Rationing," in ibid., 892.

[103] See Henry J. Aaron and William B. Schwartz, *The Painful Prescription: Rationing Hospital Care* (Washington, DC: The Brookings Institution, 1984), 101–2. That this still occurs in Britain is argued by R. Klein, P. Day, and S. Redmayne, "Rationing in the NHS: The Dance of the Seven Veils – In Reverse," *British Medical Bulletin* 51 (October 1995): 769–70. That most patients in Britain accept the doctor's view that no further treatment is warranted is argued by S. Harrison, "A Policy Agenda for Health Care Rationing," in ibid., 892.

were being scored or, if the patients were sent back to their general practitioners, were not told which components of priority criteria have prevented them from getting enough points to be considered eligible for surgery.[104] Although masking the basis for microdecisions can also occur in MHI in service plans or managed care, it will be far less than in NHI, as service plans or managed care will be unlikely to dominate a genuine market in health care., With fewer waits in the system, clinical decisions will be less likely based upon physician assessment of whether a person will have to wait for care.

However, we need to consider whether it is possible to increase visibility at the microlevel. There are two ways this might occur. First, the public could be involved in helping to create criteria for ranking patients on waiting lists. This happened in New Zealand, where randomly selected members of the public did have some influence in creating the criteria for scoring patients eligibility for elective surgery. In addition to more technical or medical criteria, such as likelihood of the surgery's success, public participation led to adding so-called social factors (e.g., age, ability to work).[105] However, this way of increasing visibility of microrationing seems quite limited because, in general, people are quite reluctant to play a major role in rationing *other* individuals' health care at the microlevel. It's one thing to say in the abstract that, for example, more resources should be devoted to preventive medicine than experimental drugs or surgery; it's another thing to create criteria that could end up denying one's sick neighbor a drug or a certain surgical procedure or that would intrude in the doctor-patient relationship, particularly when one is not the patient in question. However, people do want to know if *their own* health care is rationed, which leads to the second and more promising way to increase visibility at the microlevel of rationing. There is significant *potential* for doctors

---

[104] Robin Gauld and Sarah Derrett, "Solving the Surgical Waiting List Problem? New Zealand's 'Booking System,'" *International Journal of Health Planning and Management* 15 (2000): 266. Another example comes from Ole Frithjof Norheim, "Increasing Demand for Accountability: Is There a Professional Response?" in Coulter and Ham, *The Global Challenge of Health Care Rationing*, 220–7, who suggests that Norwegian doctors, when faced with pharmaceutical limits imposed from above, are likely to tell patients who don't meet them that they are not good candidates for the drugs, rather than that these guidelines prevent the patient from getting the drug subsidized by the NHI system.

[105] Ibid., 262–3.

and clinicians to dissemble or engage in self-deception about ineligibility for a procedure or treatment due to rationing decisions at a higher level, but potentiality is not actuality. Clinicians could simply be blunt about how government rationing influences their decision. They can say: "I'd like to see you get this surgery (drug, procedure, etc.) but given the criteria for access to it (perhaps here the doctor explains these) and the present level of funding, your chances of getting it are slim to none. You'll have to pay for it yourself." (In countries like Canada, where private insurance can only pay for what NHI does not offer, the "you'll have to pay for it yourself" would be "you need to go to another country to get treatment.") This can and does happen.[106] Could it become the general practice? I don't know, but there are reasons to doubt it. Unless the public is extremely docile, widespread visibility and candor about rationing at the microlevel are more likely to lead to protests, appeals, and demands for more funding; the end result being that the protestors get the care they desire. This is particularly so if the persons denied treatment publicize their plight in the media.[107] However, as a general rule, an increase in funding is no solution to the problem. In NHI, attempts to brake subsidized demand are almost inevitable, which means the tendency for supply-side controls to reemerge will be quite strong. If so, as long as NHI exists,[108] the likelihood of dissembling about rationing at the microlevel seems fairly strong, and thus MHI will still beat NHI at this level.

I need to make two additional points before wrapping up this section. First, my arguments about the superiority of MHI over NHI at the clinical-microlevel largely depend on the existence of waits in an NHI system. For those few NHI systems who have (so far) avoided such waits,[109] the argument clearly does not apply. At the microlevel, there may be little to choose from between those systems and MHI as far as visibility is concerned. However, because most of the arguments at the macro- and middle level did not depend on those waits, those NHI

---

[106] For an example, see Gauld and Derrett, "Solving the Surgical Waiting List Problem?" 268.

[107] E.g., see Chris Ham, "Tragic Choices in Health Care: Lessons from the Child B Case," in Coulter and Ham, *The Global Challenge of Health Care Rationing*, 107–11.

[108] Another possibility, of course, is that it leads to a revolt against NHI.

[109] See n. 13 on how Germany and France have so far avoided waits.

systems would still rate as inferior to MHI as far as visibility is concerned. Second, I have not discussed one of Daniels's requirements
for a visible rationing process, that there should be some mechanism
for improving policy in light of new arguments and evidence. However, that criterion does not alter my arguments and may strengthen
them for reasons that Daniels notes. In a chapter discussing how different managed-care organizations in the United States have evolved
policies to handle last-chance therapies – that is, clinically or scientifically unproven procedures and treatments for people at the end
of their lives – he points out that because "of the deep moral disagreement about the underlying issues, it would be wise for society to
experiment with several promising strategies in order to learn more
over time about how well they work and how morally acceptable they
might seem in light of actual practice."[110] Daniels here makes a point
similar to one made by the economist Fredrich Hayek, that competition is a discovery procedure we use when we don't know the best
outcome prior to experimentation or trial-and-error.[111] A health-care
system that has a comparative advantage in effectively experimenting
with different ways of setting limits or rationing care is one that is
decentralized rather than centralized and that has better incentives
to evaluate the results of the experiments. In both regards, MHI is
at least equal to, and is probably better than, NHI. Even a decentralized NHI system will likely not have as much decentralization as
occurs in a market, and a market system adds the incentives of market competition that is lacking or restricted even in a decentralized
NHI system. It is noteworthy that most of the practices that Daniels
applauds as coming close to what he thinks of as a fair process come
from the U.S. healthcare system, which although it is not genuine MHI,
for reasons I discussed in section 3.2.2, nevertheless has considerable
competitive pressures; pressures that would be muted in NHI. To the
extent that we were to apply the criterion of improving policy in light
of the best evidence and argument, this would probably add further

---

[110] Daniels and Sabin, *Setting Limits Fairly*, 68.
[111] F. A. Hayek, "Competition as a Discovery Procedure," in *New Studies in Philosophy,
Politics, Economics, and the History of Ideas* (Chicago: University of Chicago Press,
1978), ch. 12.

support to my argument that MHI is fairer than NHI as far as visibility is concerned.

To summarize section 3.5.2, at the macrolevel of rationing or limit setting MHI is demonstrably more visible than NHI because most people are quite ignorant of global budgets or total caps on expenditures, whereas their own budget is quite visible and limits on their out-of-pocket expenses are likely to be a visible selling point in a competitive health-care insurance market. At the middle level, information about reimbursement policies, limits of coverage, and so forth, emerges in MHI through a competitive process, and so the cost of patients or consumers obtaining that information and influencing those policies is fairly low, whereas in NHI competitive processes are limited. If public forums are used in NHI as a way to provide some degree of public input and influence on middle-level rationing decisions, this influence and input is likely to be less than what occurs in MHI because only a relatively small group of people are interested, motivated, and knowledgeable enough to attend and influence a lengthy series of public forums on middle-level allocation decisions. At the microclinical level, in MHI most people pay for health care with their own money and own their own insurance policy, which gives them a fair amount of control over clinical decisions. In NHI the effects of rationing and waiting lists create the potential for patients not getting the treatments they desire and/or for doctors to dissemble and indicate that a certain treatment is not clinically advisable, even though the reason for the denial or lack of treatment may be one of unavailability. Although nothing prevents doctors or clinicians from telling patients that rationing decisions have intruded on their professional judgment, the extent to which this openness can occur in NHI seems limited. The likely result of such openness is a demand for more funding. In the long-run, subsidized demand tends to outstrip supply leading us back to the problem of waiting lists and denial of care, possibly against a clinician's best judgment.

3.5.3 *Avoiding Inegalitarian Outcomes*

I now examine whether NHI has avoided obviously inegalitarian outcomes and discuss how MHI's outcomes would compare with NHI's outcomes.

Recent studies of the egalitarian effects of present-day NHI have examined the utilization of health-care services by different income groups and have attempted to estimate how this utilization compares with differences in medical needs between the different groups.[112] I will assume, for the sake of the argument, that there are no serious methodological problems with these studies, which have indicated that lower income groups tend to see general practitioners more than specialists, while the reverse is true for the more affluent groups. These studies also suggest that the latter utilization is greater than expected given the level of medical need. This result is one that egalitarians would probably regret.

Even if NHI has outcomes egalitarians would regret, the key issue is whether there are good reasons to believe MHI's outcomes would be less inegalitarian. There are good reasons, and they are hinted at by these studies, because access to specialists is the kind of care for which there tends to be waiting lists. I will argue in the following text that the key problem is that the more affluent will make significantly better and more informed use of services that are rationed by nonmarket means than the poor, and that the gap between the poor and the more affluent is less in a market-based system in which there is no government rationing. I will assume that there is no supplemental health insurance in NHI. I do this because it may be suggested that it is the greater ability of the more affluent to purchase supplemental health insurance that creates unequal access to certain kinds of care. However, I will show that even if there was no supplemental insurance, NHI is more inegalitarian than MHI.

MHI has fewer waits than NHI. The price mechanism quickly eliminates shortages and surpluses, while nonprice mechanisms rely on the sluggish process of waits. (The arguments in this section do not apply to those few NHI systems that have so far avoided significant waits.)

---

[112] Eddy van Doorslaer, Xander Koolman, and Frank Puffer, "Equity in the Use of Physician Visits in OECD Countries: Has Equal Treatment for Equal Need Been Achieved?" in *Organisation for Economic Cooperation and Development* [OECD], *Measuring Up: Improving Health System Performance in OECD Countries* (OECD: Paris, 2002), ch. 11. The authors say their results are similar to those found in other recent studies. Prior to 1994, such studies did not use comparable longitudinal survey data, which meant that cross-European comparisons of levels and patterns of health-care utilization were suspect.

Now getting on a waiting list, and getting to the top of that list, is not a mechanical process. A person has to be motivated enough to go to a doctor and present oneself as sick, press the doctor to move him or her near the top of the list, and seek out information about other hospitals or other specialists where there may be fewer waits; this kind of information may depend upon connections. The prize goes to the motivated, knowledgeable, and connected; in all of these matters, the middle class dominate the indigent. In MHI, with subsidies for the indigent and subsidies for those with uninsurable conditions to purchase catastrophic health insurance, by contrast, most of these barriers are absent. The fact that one must be motivated and knowledgeable enough to seek medical care in the first place, however, is a given in any system.

It might be said that the affluent do not really have a comparative advantage over the poor as far as the issue of wait is concerned. This is because the affluent make more money than the poor, and they give up more by spending time away from work in attempts to jump through hoops or move up in the queues. Thus *ceteris paribus* the affluent have greater opportunity costs in time lost from work, and so their advantage in jumping through the hoops merely counterbalances their disadvantage in bearing these greater costs.

However, it is a mistake, albeit a natural one, to believe that the affluent have greater opportunity costs in this matter.[113] The affluent tend to be salaried, not paid on an hourly basis as is typical with the poor, and so can vary their hours at the margin without loss of pay. Furthermore, the poor have greater travel costs: they own fewer cars than the affluent, and cars have a lower marginal cost and are quicker than the alternatives. Some of the factors that make people poor in the first place, such as disability and single parenthood, raise the travel costs. These higher travel costs of the poor are quite important when considering the issue of waits, for getting a better position in the queues requires the ability and willingness to travel to distant hospitals with a shorter waiting list. Notice, finally, that the poor's greater cost is

---

[113] The following paragraph is much indebted to Robert E. Goodin, Julian Le Grand, and D. M. Gibson, "Distributional Biases in Social Service Delivery Systems," in *Not Only the Poor: The Middle Classes and the Welfare State*, Robert E. Goodin and Julian Le Grand, eds. (London: Allen and Unwin, 1987), 131–2.

independent of distance. If they have to travel a greater distance than the affluent, this will compound the problem. And they may have to in at least some NHI systems that centralize certain types of care in certain locations.[114]

Besides the issue of waits, the arguments I gave earlier about the greater visibility in MHI also provide reasons to believe MHI will be less inegalitarian. At the microlevel, recall that I argued that there is a greater potential for dissembling and self-deception in NHI by clinicians making rationing decisions. The more knowledgeable and motivated middle class are much less likely than the poor to accept a doctor's decision that care is not warranted on clinical grounds, and it is human nature for a doctor to interpret (or reinterpret) those patients' illnesses whose backgrounds are similar to theirs (i.e., affluent) in such a way that these patients are seen as better candidates for treatment than those whose patients are from a dissimilar background.[115] At the macro- and middle level, political decisions about global budgets and the geographical distribution of funding in NHI are likely to benefit the better organized, knowledgeable, and motivated middle class, while MHI will be less subject to such political considerations.[116]

So far I have set out a variety of considerations why nonmarket rationing benefits the more affluent, this being due largely to their superior motivation and knowledge that enables them to work the system, as it were, to their advantage. An egalitarian might respond that the price barriers in MHI more than make up for the disadvantages in NHI, and so NHI ranks higher on avoiding inegalitarian outcomes.

---

[114] Systems with a national health service tend to centralize care within a certain region; while in a market, services are typically dispersed throughout a city or country. See Le Grand et al., "Distributional Biases in Social Service Delivery Systems," 128–30, 133–8. However, this trend has been reversed in recent years.

[115] Julian LeGrand presents evidence that this occurred in the British NHS; i.e., middle-class capture occurred. See *The Strategy of Equality: Redistribution and the Social Services* (London: G. Allen and Unwin, 1982), ch. 3. For an opposing viewpoint, and an argument that LeGrand used inappropriate methodology to measure the extent to which the British NHS allocated resources equitably, see Owen O'Donnell and Carol Propper, "Equity and the Distribution of UK National Health Service Resources," *Journal of Health Economics* 10, no. 2 (1991): 1–19.

[116] Notice that because the better organized, more knowledgeable, and motivated middle and upper class will tend to do better in the distribution of middle-level funding, and in jumping to the top of queues, this limits political disturbances about waits because the middle and upper classes are the ones more likely to protest such waits.

However, MHI incorporates subsidies for the indigent (and those with uninsurable risks) to obtain catastrophic health insurance, thus muting these barriers. MHI clearly has fewer barriers here because NHI mainly rations care that is covered by a catastrophic policy.

Still, the egalitarian may press his point by noting that MHI does not provide subsidies for the indigent to cover noncatastrophic expenses or small bills. Even with a tax credit for health insurance premiums that is completely refundable for the indigent and a subsidy that covers a somewhat lower deductible policy than the tax credit for the affluent, the poor will have to pay for their out-of-pocket expenses prior to meeting the deductible.

I can think of some replies to this objection, although none of them will completely allay the egalitarian's worries. The poor could save some of the tax credit for a catastrophic health insurance and put it in an MSA. However, the most likely way to accrue such savings is by choosing a somewhat higher deductible policy, and this may not occur because the poor tend to have a higher rate of time preference than the affluent and would prefer policies with as low a deductible as possible.[117] One way to avoid that problem would be to increase the size of the refundable tax credit for the poor and mandate that some of the tax credit be deposited in an MSA.[118] Another possibility is to give the poor a refundable tax credit that could be used to purchase comprehensive health insurance. I suspect the proposal of a mandatory MSA for the poor as a way to boost the poor's access to routine care is preferable because the heart of the MHI proposal is to remove the bias in favor of comprehensive health coverage and a subsidy for comprehensive care for the indigent is arguably contrary to the spirit of MHI.[119] In this context, it's also worth noting that when most of the population owns MSAs, prices for routine and noncatastrophic care

---

[117] Paul Menzel, *Strong Medicine: The Ethical Rationing of Health Care* (New York: Oxford University Press, 1990), 143.

[118] This is what is done in China. The fact that China uses MSAs shows that their use is not limited to a private health-care market. See Gratzer, "The ABCs of MSAs." Notice, however, that the administration of such a policy would be tricky, for money withdrawn from a MSA for nonmedical purposes is fully taxed, but many of the poor pay no income taxes. Presumably, some way of insuring that the money in a MSA was used for medical expenses would need to be found.

[119] It is also a reasonable speculation that subsidizing comprehensive care for the indigent will soon lead to subsidizing comprehensive care for those of greater economic means.

will probably decline, making it more affordable for the poor. When people pay out-of-pocket or with savings they are far more price sensitive than when a third party is paying,[120] and this price sensitivity will, in turn, encourage price competition among providers of routine care that is largely absent today.[121]

However, even if the refundable tax credit for the indigent is structured so that some of it is deposited in an MSA and the price of routine care will drop in a competitive market with price-sensitive customers, making it more affordable for the poor, it will still be true that there will be significant inequalities between the MSAs of the affluent and

---

[120] Of course, the poor may not be that price sensitive, as some of their routine and noncatastrophic care will be subsidized if we follow the proposal that they are to have mandatory subsidized MSAs. But the point about price sensitivity and its effects on prices is a point about aggregate effects, not a point about every individual consumer.

[121] Admittedly, this price sensitivity is counterbalanced by what economists call the *wealth effect*, i.e., that unused funds in one's MSA (which will grow over time) will increase's one wealth. Increased wealth would tend to increase demand for health care, which *ceteris paribus* pushes up prices. I owe this point to Ramsay, "Medical Savings Accounts," 15. I'm not aware of any studies that provide evidence as to whether the downward pressure on prices from price-sensitive consumers would outweigh the upward pressure from the wealth effect, but two reasons lead me to believe that the former is more pronounced than the latter. First, MSAs will also be used to save for postretirement expenses, and this mutes the wealth effect. Second, the effect from price-sensitive consumers seems quite large. Eighty percent of people with private health insurance in the United States in 1987 spent less than $2,000 a year on medical expenses. If most of these were paying for those expenses with MSAs rather than with health insurance, it's hard to believe that the aggregate effects of this price sensitivity on routine care wouldn't dominate the wealth effect from having unused money in one's MSAs. The statistics on health insurance expenditures are from the National Medical Expenditure Survey of 1987 (unfortunately, there doesn't seem to be a later survey) and are reported in Jensen, "Medical Savings Accounts in the U.S. Health Care System," in Feldman, *American Health Care*, 121–2.

Having said that, it must be noted that studies that attempt to model the effects of MSAs on total health-care spending are mixed. However, the ones that found that they did not decrease expenditures assumed somewhat of a low deductible for all noncatastrophic expenses, whereas, as I discussed in n. 39, the evidence from South Africa indicates that markets will offer an MSA with high deductibles for certain expenses (physician office visits and hospital outpatient care) and lower deductibles for other expenses (chronic conditions and hospital inpatient care). Furthermore, these are studies of the effects on *total* health-care spending, and my argument is about the *prices* for routine health care. The latter could decline without necessarily having an effect on the former. The studies on the effects of MSAs on total health-care expenditures are summarized in Ramsay, "Medical Savings Accounts," 27–8.

poor that will affect the two groups' relative access to routine and non-catastrophic care. We have arrived at the egalitarian's best argument: MHI provides a barrier to noncatastrophic care (e.g., physician office visits and other small scale expenses), based on price,[122] that does not exist in NHI, as the latter tends to provide ample subsidies in this area and primarily rations expensive and catastrophic care. However, it would be quite a stretch to conclude from this that NHI produces less inegalitarian outcomes than MHI. The bulk of health-care expenses arise from catastrophic care and large bills, rather than from noncatastrophic care and small bills. In MHI, the gap between the poor and affluent's access to catastrophic care will be less than in NHI because of the absence of government rationing and waits as well as subsidies for the poor and uninsurable risks that enable the poor to purchase catastrophic health insurance. If one has to choose whether it is better for there to be less of a gap between the access to catastrophic care of the poor and the affluent or less of a gap between the two groups' access to routine care – and the egalitarian must choose because MHI has the former and NHI the latter – it seems clear that it is better for them to have less inequality in their access to catastrophic care. That gives the poor relatively better access to the kind of care that is the most important and costly. Of course, faced with a choice of how to spend their limited income, the poor may very well prefer to avoid budgeting for long-run problems and catastrophes. In that regard, MHI's policy is definitely paternalistic. But egalitarians cannot use that as an objection because their endorsement of NHI is based upon, to a significant extent, something other than people's present health-care preferences as expressed in a market.

However, perhaps my argument is too hasty. Perhaps an egalitarian might reply that it is more important for the poor to have relatively better access to routine and noncatastrophic care than to have relatively better access to catastrophic care because having the former prevents the need for much of the latter. Under MHI, the poor's access to routine and noncatastrophic care may be lessened, relative to the more

---

[122] Furthermore, the egalitarian could point out that the relative disadvantage for the poor in receiving access to preventive care gets worse over time, as MSAs that are used to pay for such care are tax free over one's lifetime and more valuable for those in a high tax bracket than those in a low or zero tax bracket.

affluent's access to such care, in two cases: illnesses, which are paid for out-of-pocket or by savings in a high-deductible policy, and preventive care, which is not covered by casualty insurance when there is no adverse event or loss.[123]

As for the former, it would be less inegalitarian to provide better access to such kind of care than catastrophic care only if the bulk of catastrophic illnesses or major expenses resulted from such low-cost illnesses. However, this is not the case. Most catastrophic illnesses or expenses result from chronic degenerative conditions that arise in middle and old age. Furthermore, it is worth reiterating a point already made, that, under MHI, the poor will get a (refundable) tax credit for a somewhat lower deductible policy than the tax credit for the nonindigent (and that on some proposals, the subsidy for the poor would include a deposit into an MSA). The issues with preventive care are more complex, but the argument does not hold here either. First, some preventive care involves expensive diagnostic, high-tech equipment, (e.g., CAT scans, MRIs) and so NHI's rationing of high-tech equipment affects access to preventive care and makes it worse in that regard than MHI. Second, the higher rate of time preference of the poor suggests that they will not take great advantage of preventive services in NHI, even if they are available.[124] Whereas, as

---

[123] A third possible case concerns chronic illnesses, which do not fall clearly into the categories of either catastrophic or routine care. Medical expenses that accrue because of such illnesses can be handled in three possible ways in MHI. First, if these illnesses involve only relatively minor annual expenses, they are routine expenses and will likely be handled by MSAs or out-of-pocket expenses. Second, if these illnesses involve major medical expenses and develop after one has taken out a health insurance policy, and the policy is a guaranteed annual renewable – which, as I mentioned in n. 43, tends to be the case in MHI – then it is an adverse event and is covered by the insurance. Third, if the illness involves major medical expenses and occurs before one has taken out a health insurance policy, then it may be an uninsurable risk and would be eligible for a subsidy, at least for the indigent.

[124] The data is somewhat mixed. Studies of the introduction of user fees to groups in the United States and Canada that previously had completely "free" care show a drop in the use of preventive services and care; studies of Medicaid beneficiaries in the United States show that outreach programs to increase preventive care had little effect and introducing Medicaid to preschool children who previously lacked health insurance only increased the use of preventive care by their guardians slightly. For the former studies, see N. Lurie, N. B. Ward, M. F. Shapiro, and R. H. Brook, "Termination from Medi-Cal: Does It Affect Health?" *New England Journal of Medicine* 311, no. 7 (1984): 480–4 and M. I. Roermer, C. E. Hopkins, L. Carr, and F. Gartside, "Copayments for Ambulatory Care: Penny-Wise and Pound Foolish," *Medical Care* 13,

I noted in section 3.4.1, the combination of MSAs and casualty insurance may lower people's time preference, and, to the extent that the poor do have MSAs, this would encourage them to take preventive health measures. (Recall that in South Africa, the MSA-insurance combination has led to innovative financial incentives to encourage people to take preventive health measures.) Third, and most important, even if we were to suppose that the poor will take advantage of subsidized preventive services, and that this will not be rationed by NHI, the logic of the argument is suspect. For an egalitarian to plausibly argue that it is fairer to have relatively better access to preventive care than to catastrophic care, he must argue the following. It is fairer to treat all or almost all of the poor (for preventive care to be effective it must cover all or almost all of the relevant population), most of whom are *healthy* now and only *some* of whom will later acquire the disease or illness that the preventive care is trying to prevent, than it is to inadequately treat a smaller group, who will actually be sick later. There is little in egalitarianism that would support such a conclusion. On the contrary, focusing resources on people who are in acute need seems to be more within the spirit of egalitarianism.[125]

An egalitarian might point out that most people on waiting lists are not emergency cases; if one is about to die or immediately suffer extremely severe medical consequences (e.g., an appendectomy) one will get care, regardless of a waiting list. Waiting lists for surgery, for example, are for *elective* surgery. Hence, the fact that NHI gives better catastrophic care to the affluent is not really that great a problem for egalitarians because if the poor are in a life-threatening situation, they will not be passed over for a person who knows how to game

---

no. 6 (1975): 457–66; for the latter, see Marija Selby-Harrington et al., "Increasing Medicaid Child Health Screenings: The Effectiveness of Mailed Pamphlets, Phone Calls, and Home Visits," *American Journal of Public Health* 85, no. 10 (1995): 1412–17 and U.S. Department of Health and Human Services, Agency for Health Care Policy and Research, "Low Income Children: The Effect of Expanding Medicaid on Well-Child Visits," *Intramural Research Highlights* (June 1994).

[125] If egalitarians are undiluted consequentialists who would only care about aggregate benefit, then perhaps the aggregate benefit of treating a large number of people who now have relatively mild health problems in order to prevent some of them from becoming seriously ill later would outweigh the benefit of treating a smaller group of people who are seriously ill. But because egalitarianism is a theory about fairness, they are not undiluted consequentialists.

the system, so to speak. The problem with this, however, is twofold. First, the existence of a waiting list deters the less assertive (which exist disproportionately in the poor and uneducated) from getting on it in the first place; in so doing some of the sick will get sicker. Second, those on the waiting list for elective surgery will tend not to be better, and some will get worse. Though it's true that those who will die immediately without an operation will tend to get care in NHI, this does not detract from the fact that those on a waiting list suffer serious medical problems. As such, the delays and denials of catastrophic care should not be ignored or downplayed.

Nonmarket rationing (with its attendant waits, at least in most NHI systems) benefits the more affluent and educated due to their superior knowledge of how to game the system, which enables them to get better access to catastrophic care than the less wealthy, educated, and connected. In MHI, the absence of waits makes the barriers the less wealthy, educated, and connected have to catastrophic care less than in NHI. Even if it is true that MHI provides worse access to routine and noncatastrophic care than exists in NHI (and this is not clear, given the way MSAs encourage preventive care), it is more in line with the logic of egalitarianism to focus resources on people who are in acute need right now, which means favoring a system that does not make people suffer from waits for catastrophic care. Thus, contrary to what most egalitarians seem to believe, MHI is better at avoiding obviously inegalitarian outcomes.

Thus, MHI defeats NHI on both egalitarian criteria for a fair system of rationing: visibility and avoiding clearly inegalitarian outcomes. Thus, even apart from the arguments in section 3.4 concerning the demand or consumption side of health insurance, egalitarians should support MHI.

3.6 Why the Priority View Agrees with the Egalitarian Support of MHI

In section 3.3 I said that the arguments that egalitarianism should support MHI over NHI carry over to the priority view. I will now explain why this is so. As with egalitarianism, I start by examining the demand- or consumption-side arguments and progress to the supply- or production-side arguments.

The priority view aims at a health-care system that gives some degree of priority to those who are worst off through no choice of their own. How to define the worst off is a difficult matter, but roughly they would be either those who have the least amount of resources through no fault of their own (i.e., those who are poor for reasons beyond their control) or who are the sickest through no fault of their own (or perhaps some combination of the two).[126] According to the priority view, it is unjust if the involuntarily poor or sick pay more for health care because of their unchosen health risks. At first glance it might appear the priority view would favor NHI's abolition of risk rating because this guarantees that the involuntarily poor or sick will not be charged more for their greater health risks. However, matters are not so simple. The priority view has some similarity to the structure of egalitarianism and must consider it to be some kind of error or injustice that those with voluntarily assumed health risks are subsidized. Giving *priority* to the worst off does not mean failing to count subsidizing voluntarily assumed health risks as an error or injustice; rather, it means that it is considered *less* of an injustice than having some of those with involuntarily assumed risks pay more for those higher risks. If this is right, then what matters is how the numbers affect our overall assessment of the degree of injustice. Suppose those who are the worst off – those who are sickest and/or poorest through no fault of their own – are less numerous than those who are generally responsible for their health risks. Would the injustice of charging the former for their health risks be less or greater than the injustice of subsidizing the former for theirs?[127] I don't know how to answer this question, and

---

[126] How to define the sickest is a difficult matter. Should the priority view focus on those whose overall health is worse or those who have the most urgent need for care right now? How do differences in duration of expected future health impairments matter? These and other unresolved matters are surveyed by Dan W. Brock, "Priority to the Worse Off in Health-Care Resource Prioritization," in *Medicine and Social Justice: Essays on the Distribution of Health Care*, Rosamond Rhodes, Margaret P. Battin, and Anita Silvers, eds. (Oxford: Oxford University Press, 2002), ch. 28.

[127] Of course, those who are the *worst* off are less numerous than those who aren't. But that doesn't mean that the involuntarily sickest and poorest are less numerous than those who are generally responsible for their health status. Given my earlier argument that, in general, health risks are an indeterminate mixture of choice and brute luck, we can't tell how many people there are who are generally responsible for their health status.

I'm not aware of any writings from defenders of the priority view that indicate a clear answer.

Does that mean that regarding the question of risk rating, the prioritarian must be indifferent between NHI and MHI? No, there are other matters to consider. Whether one is involuntarily poor or sick is not necessarily a fixed matter. A person's situation up to a certain point may be such that he or she had little choice as far as economic or health status, but the extent to which he or she is able or encouraged to take responsibility in the future may alter that status. I pointed out that MHI has a comparative advantage on communicating effective information about health risks and giving incentives to act on that information and that this makes the assumption of those risks more voluntary. Although the priority view wants a health-care system to tilt toward those who are worst off through no choice or fault of their own, it also would like the numbers of those to be as low as possible. Providing information and incentives to get people to take responsibility for their health status in the future is a way of reducing those numbers because *ceteris paribus* the extent people take a proactive view toward their health is likely to improve their health status (and their income, as poor health reduces economic opportunity). I pointed out that the combination of risk rating and MSAs provides a distinctive comparative advantage for the poorly educated because it relies less on patients' or customers' cognitive abilities and prior motivation to care about their health, which is what NHI tends to rely on, and more on financial incentives to be aware of health risks and alter one's habits. This argument clearly applies to the prioritarian view because some of the poorly educated fall into the class of the worst off. Of course, in some cases a person's health status is so poor and completely beyond his or her control that there is nothing he or she or anyone else can do about it now and in the future. But this is not always the case, and, for those people who are not permanently stuck in the category of the worst off, the arguments I gave about the comparative superiority of MHI in getting people to take responsibility in the future gives an important reason for the prioritarian to favor the MHI's combination of risk rating and MSAs, which tips the balance of prioritarian reasons in MHI's favor.

I also argued that egalitarians should favor MHI's choice in health-care plans and consider MHI's superiority in reducing moral hazard as another argument in its favor. Both of these arguments also apply to the priority view. It's hard to see how lack of choice in health-care plans would be a plus for the worst off. Given that their being worse off is in part due to their lack of options, increasing options in health-care plans would seem to be something the priority view would have to favor. I suppose the objection here would be to the extent that having choice in health-care plans undermines the possibility of the worst off having access to comprehensive care, which is a bad thing, and so paternalism is in order; that is, we have to restrict the worst off's options so that they are guaranteed the kind of health care they really need. The response to this objection is that the options in MHI that leave the worst off to choose to forego comprehensive care have to do with skimpy or nonexistent MSAs for routine care, and it is access to catastrophic care that is what is most important for the worst off – if by *most important* we mean what is objectively good for them (which is the notion of *most important* being used in the objection). Even apart from the question of choosing whether or how much to fund MSAs, choice in health-care plans involves other matters, which, again, it is hard to see as bad for the worst off (e.g., choice in doctors, hospitals, provider networks, reimbursement policies). NHI has some of these choices as well, but a competitive market will have more of them and will in general be more actively shaped by choices by consumers, including the poorest.

As for MHI's superiority in combating moral hazard, this also seems a plus for the priority view, largely for the reasons I discussed previously: to the extent that the priority view gives some weight to the endorsement of the principle that it is unjust to subsidize people's choices, then to that extent the priority view will favor the system that has a comparative advantage in reducing moral hazard. Admittedly, the weight the prioritarian attaches to that principle may be lower than the weight the egalitarian gives to it. This is because the prioritarian is more concerned with the involuntarily poor or sick not having to pay the cost for decisions over which they had no control rather than the principle that people not slough off the costs of their choices on others. But the prioritarian would give this principle some weight and, as such, would probably favor MHI on moral hazard-reducing grounds as well.

I turn now to the production- or supply-side arguments. Here the arguments I made with regard to egalitarianism apply with even more force to the priority view. Consider visible rationing or decisions about the limits of care: the worse off one is, the more important it is that the health-care system makes this information accessible and gives patients and consumers a way to influence decisions about those limits. Because those who are worse off are that way partly because of limited choices, a health-care system that has a comparative advantage in giving more information about its allocation and limiting decisions, as well as giving patients and consumers some way to influence those decisions, seems extremely important for the prioritarian. In this regard, the political methods of allocation and rationing in NHI come out with a pronounced comparative disadvantage compared with market methods of allocation. Those who are poor and/or ill through influences beyond their control are exceedingly unlikely to be well organized enough to do well in political allocation decisions, and the methods proposed by Daniels to increase public participation in such decisions are likely to work to the advantage of the articulate and the knowledgeable. By contrast, even poor consumers or customers still get access to the information that emerges through a market process and have some ability to influence that process. At the microclinical level, the differences are also likely to be pronounced. Whatever dissembling occurs in NHI when a doctor tells a patient that a treatment is not clinically warranted when it is simply unavailable because of higher-level rationing decisions is likely to be more contested by the more knowledgeable and articulate than by the worst off, and so the lesser potential for dissembling at the clinical level at MHI is particularly helpful for the worst off. As for avoiding inegalitarian outcomes, the arguments are virtually identical, because the outcomes I focused on were the effects in NHI of rationing catastrophic care for the poor as compared with the lesser access to routine care that would exist in MHI. The arguments apply to those who are extremely ill as well because the type of care they tend to need is not routine care but catastrophic care.

So, overall, the prioritarian ends up with the same endorsement of MHI as does his egalitarian cousin. The arguments on the demand or consumption side are slightly weaker perhaps because the prioritarian considers shielding the involuntarily poor and sick from being charged for their health risks as more important than preventing those whose risks are more voluntarily assumed from dumping their costs on others. On the supply or production side, the prioritarian arguments in favor of MHI are at least as strong, if not stronger, than the egalitarian arguments, and so overall both the priority view and egalitarianism end up at the same place.

Appendix A

Addiction, Health Risks, and Voluntariness[128]

The concept of drug addiction is rather imprecise, but the rough idea is that a drug addict is one who uses drugs heavily, repeatedly, perhaps compulsively and would like to stop or cut back but finds it difficult to do so. The usual basis for believing that drug addictions are involuntary is a pharmacological model of addiction. The idea is that after a while a user of certain drugs experiences cravings (strong and persistent desires) to continue to take the drug; achieves tolerance, that is, requires more of the drug than in the earlier days of his or her drug use to experience the same effects; and suffers very disagreeable effects (withdrawal symptoms) if he or she tries to stop. Only someone with "an extraordinary act of will," to quote Robert Goodin,[129] a defender of this pharmacological model, can overcome this cravings-tolerance-withdrawal-symptoms combination. However, if we look at each aspect of the combination, none explains addiction. Cravings are simply strong and sometimes persistent desires for something; people – ordinary people – don't have to act on their desires. Tolerance

---

[128] For a fuller version of these arguments, see Daniel Shapiro, "Smoking Tobacco: Irrationality, Addiction and Paternalism," *Public Affairs Quarterly* 8 (April 1994): 187–203, and "Addiction and Drug Policy," in *Morality and Moral Controversies*, 7th ed., John Arthur, ed. (Upper Saddle River, NJ: Prentice Hall, 2002), 515–21. Douglas Husak, "Liberal Neutrality, Autonomy, and Drug Prohibitions," *Philosophy and Public Affairs* 29, no. 1 (2000): 70–8, defends views very similar to mine.

[129] Robert E. Goodin, *No Smoking: The Ethical Issues* (Chicago: University of Chicago Press, 1989), 26.

just means one needs more of the drug than one previously needed to get the effect one wants, but this doesn't explain why one wants that effect. That leaves withdrawal symptoms, but for these to explain continued use of a drug that is causing one harm, the effects one experiences upon cessation of the drug must be truly awful. However, they aren't *that* bad. Heroin is usually considered the drug with the worst withdrawal symptoms, yet pharmacologists describe those symptoms as like having a bad flu for a week.[130] Although no one desires to have fever and chills, muscle aches, vomit, or diarrhea for a week, this is not the end of the world, particularly if the benefits achieved by going through withdrawal are great. There is no correlation between relapse and withdrawal symptoms – most of those who quit and then relapse do so after withdrawal symptoms are gone. Nor is the argument improved if instead of analyzing each part of the standard explanatory triumvirate – cravings, tolerance, withdrawal symptoms – separately, we do so together. The fact that a person desires to take a drug, needs more than he or she used to need to get a certain effect from it, and will suffer some bad, temporary effects if he or she stops taking the drug, hardly shows that the drug has overpowered a person's will, especially if, to repeat, the expected benefits from stopping are much greater than the costs of cessation.

Perhaps the most devastating problem with the pharmacological explanation of addiction is that the drug habit that has the lowest quit rate is cigarette smoking (in the United States only half of all smokers successfully quit), yet what is striking about nicotine's pharmacology is that it is a *mild*, subtle drug. That is part of the reason why smoking is so well integrated into smokers' lives. Smokers smoke to relax, concentrate, as a way of taking a break during the day, as a social lubricant; the list could be extended as there are a large variety of situations, moods, and activities into which smoking is woven. Other drug addictions – cocaine, alcohol, and heroin – are also means to or parts of many situations, moods, and activities, but most users of these drugs are occasional or moderate users, not lifelong addicts or heavy users, because these drugs are not as mild, and heavy use has a stronger tendency over time to disrupt people's lives. Hence the

---

[130] John Kaplan, *The Hardest Drug: Heroin and Public Policy* (Chicago: University of Chicago Press, 1983), 15, 19, 35.

addiction rate is much lower for these drugs and the quit rate much higher.

The fact that smoking is well integrated into smokers' lives isn't the only reason smokers find it hard to quit. Also important is that the harms of smoking are slow to occur, cumulative, and largely affect a person's health, not the ability to perform normal activities (at least prior to getting seriously or terminally ill). Furthermore, to eliminate these harms requires complete smoking cessation, cutting back rarely suffices (even light smokers have significantly elevated odds of getting lung cancer, emphysema, and heart disease). Quitting smoking requires very strong motivation because its bad effects are not immediate, and it does not disrupt one's life. By contrast, the motivation to stop a drug addiction that is disrupting and harming life right now is much greater.

None of the factors that make an addiction hard to break suffice to show, using the standards that egalitarians use to distinguish choices from unchosen circumstances, that continued addictive use of a drug is involuntary. If one lacks motivation to quit because harms are in the future, then that shows high time preference. The difficulty in changing a nondisruptive activity because it is well integrated into one's life is simply a reflection of the way humans lead their lives – with settled patterns of activity that make up the structure of a life. Thus elevated or differential health risks that result from unhealthy habits or addictions cannot be judged as involuntary. One might argue that the risks are not voluntarily assumed because of ignorance, but the evidence for that, at least in the case of smoking, is lacking as well.[131]

---

[131] On this point, see V. Kip Viscusi, *Smoking: Making the Risky Decision* (New York: Oxford University Press, 1992), 68–9, 77–8.

4

Health Insurance, Part II

In this chapter I will argue that the positive-rights view and the communitarian view should prefer MHI to NHI and that the popularity of NHI is no reason to think it is preferable to MHI.

4.1 Basic Rights and the Right to Health Care

It may seem obvious that NHI is better than MHI in providing citizens with a positive right to health care. NHI entitles all citizens to health care, while MHI entitles one only to services purchased using insurance or savings. Although everyone is required to purchase health insurance in a MHI system, MSAs are optional (except perhaps for the poor, depending on some proposals for MHI). Though the changes in the tax code will provide strong incentives for those with significant disposable income to have adequate MSAs, the poor will tend to have skimpy MSAs to purchase routine and noncatastrophic care. Thus, this issue seems settled.

But this argument moves too quickly. When we take a closer look, it turns out that if one thinks that there is a positive right to health care, one should not oppose MHI and may have some reasons to favor it.

4.1.1 The Content of the Right

To evaluate whether the arguments for a positive right to health care support NHI or MHI, we need to get clear about the content of this right. However, before we begin this discussion about the content of the right, we need to clear up an important matter: is the right in question best analyzed as a right to health care, as I have assumed, or is it a right to health? The latter seems absurd because it would seem to imply a duty to make others healthy, which is an impossible duty to meet because some people will never be healthy no matter what one does (and others can be made healthy only at staggering and bankruptcy-inducing cost).[1] However, despite this problem, two arguments seem to support a focus on the right to health, rather than health care, or at least suggest that we should not dismiss the viability of the former.[2] First, international documents that list positive rights as human or basic rights (e.g., the International Covenant on Economic, Social, and Cultural Rights) assert a right to health, not health care, and those constitutions in affluent democratic societies that broach this topic usually affirm a right to health, not health care. If one is interested in specifying the content of a positive right, ignoring the vocabulary of documents that assert a right to health seems like an error. Second, because clearly factors other than access to health care significantly affect one's health, a right to health care might seem too narrow. It doesn't cover, for example, factors such as good sanitation facilities or healthy environmental conditions (factors that often fall under the rubric of "public health"). Thus we should think of the right to health as including the right to health care but as broader than that (though presumably not so broad as to lead to the absurd conclusion that others are obligated to make one healthy).

Both points are legitimate, but for my purposes, the focus should be on the right to health care because I am concerned with the choice between private and social insurance in affluent democracies, and threats to public health are pretty much irrelevant for those concerns. The gross threats to public health are a thing of the past in affluent democracies and the more subtle threats (e.g., air and water pollution) are not dealt with by insurance but by other institutions. As for the documents that refer to a right to health, presumably their point is to

---

[1] Furthermore, one might worry that the concept of being healthy is so vague and indeterminate that it is useless as a basis for assigning obligations.

[2] E.g., Kristin Hessler and Allen Buchanan, "Specifying the Content of the Human Right to Health Care," in Rhodes et al., *Medicine and Social Justice*, 85–6, and Brigit C. A. Toebes, *The Right to Health as a Human Right in International Law* (Antwerp, Belgium: Intersentia, 1999), 17–19.

incorporate both a right to at least minimally healthy environmental conditions and a right to health care, so our focus on the latter will coincide with some of the concerns of those documents.

Let us now turn our attention to the content of the legal right to health care. A number of interpretations of that right are possible, but, for our purposes, two issues are salient. First, how should *health care* be understood? When discussing egalitarianism, I noted that one could measure equality in terms of resources or welfare, and a related kind of division applies here. A right to health care might mean a right to certain *health services*, that is, a right to an insurance package of benefits, or it might mean a right to a certain *standard of care* that these services should provide.[3] (The latter comes closer to the idea of a right to health because the point is that health care is valuable largely insofar as the care we receive positively affects our health.) A second issue is the scope of the right. Most writers on this topic insist that it only covers a "decent minimum" or an "adequate minimum" of health care.[4] It would be absurd, they point out, to think that all citizens have a right to any technologically feasible or available form of health care. That's a prescription for bankruptcy. However, beyond ruling out *all* health-care services or the highest standard of care money could buy, what does a "decent minimum" mean? Although "minimum" certainly sounds very restrictive, most writers who endorse the right to a

---

3 For the former, see Lenaghan, "Health Care Rights in Europe," 188–92, and Janet Weiner, "Towards a Uniform Health Benefit Package," in Health Care Reform: *A Human Rights Approach*, Audrey Chapman, ed. (Washington, DC: Georgetown University Press, 1994), 197–207; for the latter, see Mary Ann Baily, "Defining the Decent Minimum," 167–169, in ibid.

4 Allen Buchanan "The Right to a Decent Minimum of Health Care," *Philosophy and Public Affairs* 13 (Winter 1984): 57–9, argued or implied that the decent minimum is fairly restrictive but acknowledged in "Health Care Delivery and Resource Allocation," in *Medical Ethics*, 352–3, that the vagueness of the concept could easily make it far more expansive. Baily, "Defining the Decent Minimum," in Chapman, *Health Care Reform*, 181, confirms Buchanan's point because she believes NHI comprehensive services provide the decent minimum. See also Tom L. Beauchamp and James F. Childress, *Principles of Biomedical Ethics*, 5th ed. (New York: Oxford University Press, 2001), 244, where a decent minimum is equated with "basic and catastrophic health needs." Beachamp and Childress's discussion is a bit confusing, however, because when they list what would be covered by the decent minimum they seem to omit catastrophic health care. If that is not included in the decent minimum then their conception of a decent minimum is fairly minimal, along the lines of David Ozar's proposal, which I discuss later in this section.

decent minimum of health care interpret that phrase in a fairly expansive manner: either everyone has the right to a set of comprehensive healthcare services or the right to a "cost-conscious standard of care to which a well-informed person of average [or middle class] income is willing to pay to ensure access."[5] In what follows I will generally understand the right to health-care services and the right to a certain standard of care in this fairly expansive way. Occasionally, a writer will define the right to health care in a very austere manner, and I will turn my attention to that proposal toward the end of this section.

A legal right to health-care services is either a right to a specific set or list of services or a right to some general or generic set. As I noted in section 3.5.2, no NHI system has the former, such as exists in Oregon's Medicaid program, which funds only a specific list of morbidity-treatment conditions. All seem to have the latter, in the sense that laws regulating health insurance promise that a comprehensive set of services such as primary care, preventive care, hospital care, nursing home care, and diagnostic procedures will be covered. Some NHI systems – particularly those in which insurance is provided by nonprofit sickness funds – combine this general list with some specific list of inclusions or exclusions (e.g., a list of drugs not covered). How well protected is this legal right? In general, a legal right is well protected if it is enforceable, in particular if it can be used successfully to support a legal claim when one believes the right is violated or not respected. We can answer that question by seeing what occurs when, because of government rationing, some service is denied, access to it delayed, or the amount diminished and the quality diluted. The right is well protected to the extent that one can use the right to health care as a sound legal basis to win a case in such situations.

Until recently, such a right in almost all countries with NHI was generally useless in prevailing against a decision to limit or delay care. Provided one's right to privacy, informed consent, and access to one's medical records, and so forth had not been violated, judges were quite reluctant to interfere with allocation or treatment decisions in NHI.[6]

---

[5] Baily, "Defining the Decent Minimum," in Chapman, *Health Care Reform*, 177. On 179, "average person" becomes "middle class person."

[6] Jo Lenaghan, summarizing the situation vis-à-vis the right to health care in NHI in the mid 1990s said, "[A]ttempts to enforce a right through the courts have tended to fail,

In the last five years or so, however, courts in some countries have become somewhat less willing to defer to a local health authority's decision that denial or delay of treatment is justified because resources are scarce. In some countries, claimants who raise objections to denial or delay of treatment win their case if the judges find that the rationing authority has not given an adequate justification for its decision. So, for example, in the United Kingdom, the court reversed a denial of the drug Interferon for multiple sclerosis patients because it found that the health authority's rationale for the denial – that it didn't have money to pay for everyone in this condition and so some deserving cases would not receive the drug – irrational. The court held that this would be a reason for refusing any expensive treatment in virtually all circumstances, and that clinicians should consider such factors as the likelihood of the benefit of the treatment and the needs of the patient. In another United Kingdom case, in which the NHS held that trans-sexual surgery was not an important enough priority to be funded, the court overruled, not because they overruled the NHS's judgment about priorities but because they found that the denial of treatment was not made on an objective and proper review of the clinical evidence. The court held that the NHS had closed its mind to the evidence and simply adopted a blanket ban on funding the surgery.[7] In Italy (whose constitution asserts a right to health and promises free care for the indigent) the courts have at times been quite assertive. For example, they have ruled that patients could seek care outside Italy even if the Italian health authorities considered a treatment ineffective. They have also ruled that a cancer drug, rejected by the ministry of health on the grounds that its scientific effectiveness was never demonstrated, should be made free of charge to a patient who requested it for a trial period until clinical testing was completed. (However, in other cases the Italian courts have been more willing to defer to health authorities,

because judges have ruled that they cannot interfere with the distribution of finite resources." "Health Care Rights in Europe,"188. Lenaghan noted that Germany was an exception, which I discuss in the following text.

7 For information about these decisions and the recent change of attitude in U.K. courts, see Christopher Newdick, "Judicial Supervision of Health Resource Allocation – The U.K. Experience," in *Readings in Comparative Health Law and Bioethics*, Timothy Stoltzfus Jost, ed. (Durham, NC: Carolina Academic Press, 2001), 66–9.

and authorization for foreign care has recently become harder to obtain.)[8]

What we see emerging in some countries with NHI is something roughly like the following: the right to health care means, or entails, that rationing decisions cannot be arbitrary and that the rationing authorities must present at least a plausible rationale for their decisions when they are challenged. The courts are more willing to accept a denial of care if it appears to be based on clinical judgments rather than simply on a desire to reduce expenditures. In other countries with NHI, however, the right to health care remains basically unenforceable; judges defer to local health authorities and decline to overrule or criticize allocation decisions.[9]

How far could this recent trend toward judicial assertiveness go in upholding a legal right to health care? Not much further, because there are inherent limits in an NHI system in claiming such a right. First, in most NHI systems one does not purchase an insurance policy or health-care plan, and so one lacks a contractual right to any set of services or benefits. What one has, instead, is a statutory right to those benefits. Contractual rights have an advantage over statutory rights in this context because in the former each insured has exchanged money with a company in return for an explicit agreement to provide certain services, whereas each taxpayer has not made an explicit agreement with the legislature for these services. Admittedly, this advantage of contractual over statutory rights to health care can be overcome if strong legal remedies to combat denial or delay of care could be built into the law – which leads to the second built-in limit in NHI.

---

[8] On the assertiveness of Italian courts, see George France, "The Changing Nature of the Right to Health Care in Italy," in *The Right to Health Care in Several European Countries: Expert Meeting Held in Rotterdam, the Netherlands, April 27–29, 1998*, Andre den Exter and Herbert Hermans, eds. (The Hague: Kluwer Law International, 1999), 50–3. On recent shifts away from this assertiveness, see George France and Francesco Taroni, "Evolution of Health Care Reform in Italy," presented at European Health Care Discussion Group at London School of Economics, available at http://healthpolicy.stanford.edu/GHP/GeorgeFrancepaper.pdf (accessed March 2003).

[9] E.g., in Canada and the Scandinavian countries. For the former, see Louise R. Sweatman and Diane Wollard, "Resource Allocation Decisions in Canada's Health Care System: Can These Decisions Be Challenged in a Court of Law?" *Health Policy* 62, no. 3 (2002): 275–90; for the latter, see Tuija Takala, "Justice for All? The Scandinavian Approach," in Rhodes et al., *Medicine and Social Justice*, 185.

Legislatures and local rationing authorities' supply-side controls (which produce waiting lists in almost all NHI countries) will become ineffective if judges frequently overrule or question their decisions. As long as these supply-side controls exist, judges' abilities to rule that these controls produce rights violation are necessarily circumscribed. These two considerations are mitigated in NHI systems in which one can choose one's nonprofit sickness fund and supply-side controls have (yet) to be firmly established. Germany, for example, has some degree of competition among nonprofit sickness funds and supply-side controls have yet to be firmly established. Not surprisingly, those who challenge limits to care have a good chance of succeeding in German courts.[10]

How, by contrast, does a right to health care fare in MHI? Everyone has a health insurance policy that covers catastrophic care and is entitled to whatever is covered by that policy. Of course, disagreements will arise about coverage here as with all insurance, and a court may not rule in the insured's favor, but the two built-in limits in NHI that restrict the enforceability of a right to health care are (virtually) absent in MHI. First, the person who has purchased the policy has a contractual right to what is promised by the policy. Second, there are no governmental health authorities that are imposing supply-side controls to limit expenditures, and so judges do not have to consider these government controls in their decisions. Admittedly, political interference will occur through the legal specification of what counts as a minimally acceptable catastrophic policy – particularly for those whose health insurance is subsidized – but compared with NHI, there is much less interference, because there are no national or local health authorities imposing price controls, global budgets, and expenditure caps, and so forth that produce waiting lists.[11] Besides having a stronger legal

---

[10] See Timothy Stolftzfus Jost, "Health Care Rationing in the Courts: A Comparative Study," *Hastings International and Comparative Law Review* 21 (Spring 1998): 653–81, and "The Role of the Courts in Health Care Rationing: The German Model," *Journal of Contemporary Health Law and Policy* 18 (2002): 613–18.

[11] In addition, in Anglo-American law, courts follow the doctrine of *contra proferentum*, which means that when there is an ambiguity in the contract, it is to be interpreted against the interests of the person who drafted the contract. This is typically the insurer; this means, of course, that courts will typically resolve ambiguities in favor of the insured. This might add a further reason why, at least as things stand today in Anglo-American courts, a contractual entitlement to (catastrophic) health care

obligation to deliver care that is promised, competing insurance companies or health-care plans have a stronger motivation to do so. Being inattentive to consumer or patient desires or breaking agreements is a money-losing proposition in MHI. Whereas in NHI the motivation is weaker because the ability to exit the government system and choose a competitor ranges from very limited to nonexistent: the former in countries with a limited degree of competition between nonprofit sickness funds; the latter in countries where there are no private insurers for nonsupplemental care.[12]

Of course, catastrophic care is not the same as comprehensive care, and MHI does not provide everyone with a legal right to comprehensive health care. Not everyone will have well-funded MSAs. To what extent the MSA high-deductible health insurance combination provides comprehensive care is up to the individual (as is the choice to forego that combination and purchase a comprehensive service plan). Thus the choice is between an NHI system whose laws provide expectations of comprehensive health-care services to all but is sharply limited in the remedies it can provide when catastrophic or nonroutine care is rationed, versus an MHI system that lacks such a law but provides better remedies when care or reimbursement promised by an insurance company or a provider is denied or "rationed." It's not obvious as to which one is better, but MHI is not clearly worse.

gives a person more of an enforceable right than exists in NHI. It is worth noting that it is not obvious that the doctrine of *contra proferentum* actually helps the insured. Interpreting ambiguities according to the intent of the parties may be the most reasonable policy and better for the insured. For criticisms of the doctrine, see Michael B. Rappaport, "The Ambiguity Rule and Insurance Law: Why Insurance Contracts Should Not Be Construed against the Drafter," *Georgia Law Review* 30 (1995): 171–257. I thank G. Marcus Cole and Michael Rappaport for their help in explaining *contra proferentum* to me.

At this point, it is also worth noting Timothy Jost's view about contract law and health insurance. He argues in "Health Care Rationing in the Courts," 707–8, that courts in the United States are and should be rejecting the view that health insurance coverage disputes should be resolved by contract law, because in many cases the insured didn't negotiate the contract with the insurer; the contract is between the employer and the insurance company. Jost thinks that these cases "resemble more judicial review of the reasonableness of regulatory actions imposed upon beneficiaries" (ibid., 708) rather than contract disputes. However, even if Jost is right, his point would not have much application in MHI because its health insurance agreements would be more likely between the insured and the insurance company.

[12] Recall that these funds must offer a fairly standard set of benefits and cannot engage in risk rating.

It might be argued, however, that because casualty-catastrophic insurance provides reimbursement for adverse health events, rather than reimbursement of health-care expenses, it does not provide a right to health-care services. In casualty insurance, reimbursement often goes to the insured, who can then spend the money as he or she likes – on cheap care, expensive care, or no care at all. The same point applies to MSAs – having a medical savings account does not force one to spend the money on health services. (One will face a tax penalty for using MSA funds for nonmedical expenses, but that won't prevent such occurrences.) However, a right to health-care services does not require that one use health-care services. (The right is probably more precisely phrased as the right to have access to such services.) This is true in NHI as well because the patient need not seek care. The difference is that in MHI the right holder has more of a choice concerning how or whether to trade off money allocated to health for other goods, while this choice is much more diluted in NHI. That hardly counts against MHI; on some understandings of the concept of a right, it might count in favor of MHI's way of upholding that right because rights are supposed to provide the right holder with a significant range of choices.[13]

Let us turn to the other interpretation of the right to health care: the right to a cost-conscious standard of care to which a middle-class person is willing to pay to ensure access. To be cost *conscious*, one must be aware of costs. And the best way to determine what a person is willing to pay is to see what he or she pays with his or her own funds. In NHI, the patient or consumer has virtually no awareness of monetary costs and at best partially funds his or her own health care. Thus even if NHI actually provided this standard of care, no one would know if it was met. In MHI, many people will own and control their own MSAs and catastrophic insurance policy, and so will be far more aware of costs. Not all will, of course; poor people in MHI are less likely to get

---

[13] See, e.g., the theory of rights defended by Carl Wellman, *A Theory of Rights: Persons under Laws, Institutions, and Morals* (Lanham: Rowman and Allenheld, 1985). Of course, one could define a right to health-care services so that it means one is entitled to receive health care without purchasing it. See Mark Kelman, "Health Care Rights: Distinct Claims, Distinct Justifications," *Stanford Law and Policy Review* 3 (1991): 90. By this definition, MHI can't provide a right to health-care services. But for purposes of this book, this definition begs the question in favor of NHI and so must be rejected.

a middle-class standard of care because they won't have middle-class MSAs. But at least we would know that most, though not all, people got the kind of care that the middle class get when they fund their own health care, so in that regard MHI may get closer to protecting such a right.[14]

So far I've argued that if we understand the legal right to health care in a fairly expansive way, as a right to comprehensive health-care services or a right to a middle-class, cost-conscious standard of care, MHI is no worse than NHI and might be somewhat better in protecting such a right. What if we interpret the right to health care in a more bare-bones sense? David Ozar says that the kind of health care to which one has a right is that which satisfies those needs that are necessary to provide minimal security.[15] By *minimal security* he means that one has resources to survive some period into the future so that it is reasonable and possible for that person to devote some of his or her time and energy to ends other than survival. On Ozar's view, basic health care would include services such as emergency medical care, some degree of preventive care to prevent illnesses from becoming life threatening, and some services for conditions that aren't life threatening (e.g., physical therapy and pain relief). (It might include other services, but as he says this is uncertain, I will limit the discussion to the core set.) If we understand Ozar's view of the right to basic health care in terms of the services required by the right, then both systems are equally justified. Because the services Ozar mentions cut across the routine–catastrophic care distinction, it is hard to see how either MHI or NHI would be better in providing access to these services. By rationing catastrophic care, NHI runs the risk of turning a condition that is not immediately life threatening into one that is, which is a mark against it; some of the services that Ozar mentions, such as relief of pain, might be considered routine care and it would thus be a mark

[14] One could drop the idea that the right to health care is a right to a *cost-conscious*, middle-class standard of care, but if one does, neither system is superior. Neither system provides all with a middle-class standard of care: NHI falls short because of the way government rationing denies the poor and uneducated the kind of catastrophic care the middle class obtains, and MHI falls short because the poor's access to routine care is less than the middle class obtains because of skimpier MSAs.

[15] David T. Ozar, "What Should Count as Basic Health Care?" in *Philosophical Issues in Human Rights*, Patricia Werhane, A. R. Gini, and David T. Ozar, eds. (New York: Random House, 1986), 298–310.

against MHI that the poor's access to routine care is not as subsidized as it is in NHI. If we focus on the standard of care needed to provide minimal security, again both systems are roughly on a par. In both systems some people will not have sufficient resources to survive some period of time into the future because there are people who will die immediately or almost immediately unless they receive prohibitively expensive health care. So shifting the discussion to a more minimal understanding of the right to health care does not do much to alter the conclusions I've drawn about neither MHI nor NHI clearly providing better protection for the right to health care.

4.1.2 The Grounds of the Right to Health Care

Neither system is better in protecting a legal right to health care, though MHI gets closer to protecting a right to catastrophic and non-routine health-care services and provides more evidence that it is providing a middle-class, cost-conscious standard of care. Perhaps examining the *grounds* of the right to health care will establish a firm basis for preferring one of the systems. Or to put it another way, instead of focusing upon the legal rights in the two health insurance systems, let us consider the moral right, that is, the arguments why that legal right should exist.

Arguments for the right to health care come in two varieties: as implications or applications of more general arguments for basic positive rights, or as arguments specifically about that right.

As I noted in Chapter 2, the former typically proceeds in two steps. The first step of the argument is that persons need a certain level of material well-being to give negative rights value or to enable them to exercise and/or develop their capacities for moral agency. The second step of the argument is that social insurance, not means-tested benefits, is the preferred institutional form of meeting those needs. It's the second step that is the crucial one for our purposes. The first step, even if plausible, would seem to support means or needs-tested benefits. That's because it focuses on those who lack minimal or adequate material well-being. Social insurance is provided to all citizens and its provision of benefits (in the case of health insurance, comprehensive insurance) would seem to go way beyond what is needed to give negative rights value or enable one to exercise and/or develop moral agency.

Many defenders of positive rights stop at the first step,[16] and so their arguments are not relevant for my purposes. Instead, I will focus on J. Donald Moon's rationale for step two, as it seems to be most thorough.[17] He argues that a necessary condition for the justification of basic rights is that their legal instantiation does not undermine self-respect, by which he means the belief that one is a person of worth who lives up to certain standards, who is entitled to respect. In a society in which markets are the predominant form of producing and allocating goods and services, people are expected to be able to support themselves through productive activity, and positive rights based purely upon need run the serious risk of undermining self-respect. This problem is avoided by delivering state services on the basis of universal provision and social insurance. Universal provision means that these services are provided to every citizen, so no stigma is attached to receiving them, and social insurance means that one's positive rights are based upon having contributed to their provision. Because an individual's contributions help to fund his or her benefits,[18] that individual is viewed as an independent person, not someone purely dependent upon others for meeting needs, or "on welfare" as it is often pejoratively put, at least in the United States. Another way Moon puts his argument is that these social-insurance programs help to balance welfare rights with the notion of responsibility, which is inherent in the notion of a moral agent. The principle of individual responsibility implies that relations among adults will be based on reciprocity, not asymmetrical relations of dependence; that one's right to certain benefits is based on contribution means that it is no threat to this norm of reciprocity.

The upshot of this argument is that the best way in a market society to meet needs is *indirectly* through a program that is not exclusively or

---

[16] E.g., Plant, "Needs, Agency, and Moral Rights," 55–76; Plant, *Modern Political Thought*, 184–213, 253–92; and Waldron, *Liberal Rights*, ch. 1, 10, 13.

[17] See "The Moral Basis of the Democratic Welfare State," 30–6, 41–6, and "Introduction: Responsibility, Rights and Welfare," 4–8. Also see Jacobs, *Rights and Deprivation*, 196, 198, 200–2.

[18] In "The Moral Basis of the Welfare State," 46, Moon says that recipients of social-insurance benefits have contributed their fair share, but in the introduction to *Responsibility, Rights and Welfare*, 7, he merely says that "at least in theory" the recipients have contributed the resources that make the benefits possible. Hence, it is unclear to what extent Moon really believes that social insurance is funded by one's own contributions.

primarily needs based. Of course, this is not always possible, given the inability of some people to work, which is why, Moon says, some purely needs-based or means-tested programs are necessary. But they should be avoided as much as possible.

I will not challenge Moon's argument that social insurance is better than pure means-tested programs as a way of protecting positive rights without threatening self-respect or the idea of a responsible moral agent. However, applying his argument to the choice between NHI and MHI reveals the superiority of the latter in two respects.

First, in MHI, everyone except the indigent and those with uninsurable risks funds his or her own health benefits, while in NHI there is a rather insubstantial connection between one's taxes or premiums and benefits. In NHI systems with a national health service, the connection is quite tenuous because there is nothing even resembling an insurance package, but even in systems with earmarked taxes and/or nonprofit sickness funds, the subsidizing of high health risks within the funds plus government rationing weakens any significant link between taxes and benefits. Second, it is MHI, not NHI, that stresses responsibility for one's voluntarily assumed health risks, responsibility for budgeting for routine and noncatastrophic care (through the use of MSAs), and choosing one's own health plan. NHI systems provide more limited incentives for patients to take responsibility for their own health care because they are not really treated as consumers, have little financial incentive to moderate or minimize their health risks, and do not budget for health care over time.

Moon might reply that his argument is only meant to show why social insurance is better than means-tested benefits and provides no basis for choosing among alternative insurance systems. To *some* extent both fund benefits by contributions, unlike means-tested benefits, where beneficiaries may not fund them at all, and to *some* extent both stress responsibility and reciprocity because benefits flow from being a productive, income-earning member of society. By passing these tests, both systems are not a *threat* to self-respect. If the concern was regarding which system helped one *promote* or *sustain* self-respect, then one could compare the degree to which these systems achieved that end, but that is not at issue because there is no relationship between different systems of health insurance and promoting or sustaining self-respect.

However, this reply misses the point. Moon argued that a *necessary* condition for justifying positive rights is that their legal instantiation not undermine self-respect, but clearly a *sufficient* condition is the existence of a solid rationale for these rights.[19] Moon had ruled out need as a sufficient rationale. Because the only other rationale he mentions is moral agency and its concomitant notion of responsibility – which is why he thinks there must be some link between contributions to insurance and benefits received – then it is legitimate to defend MHI as providing a better grounding of positive rights based on these ideas of moral agency and responsibility compared to NHI.

Perhaps it might be argued that Moon's objection to using need as a sufficient rationale for grounding positive rights does not apply to the right to health care. That is because health care needs are so unpredictable, and health-care expenses so potentially ruinous, that concerns about self-respect are simply irrelevant in establishing a right to health care based upon the way health-care needs can be a threat to moral agency. If one is vulnerable to having one's plans and life disrupted and devastated by lacking resources to handle health-care needs, self-respect is unaffected by relying on others to fund health insurance. Thus, Moon's view that social insurance must provide an indirect way of meeting needs and balance the notion of responsibility with positive rights is not applicable to the need for health care and health insurance. No such balancing or indirect way of meeting needs is necessary because, other than the very rich, everyone's ability to exercise and/or develop his or her capacity for moral agency is at risk without positive rights to health care.

This objection overlooks the arguments I made in Chapter 3 about health risks being partially voluntary and the ability of many people to

---

[19] Or, more precisely, that there be a solid rationale that does not, in turn, undermine self-respect. It is possible that the best rationale for a program, if made public, would undermine self-respect. E.g., suppose that the best rationale for hallway monitors in schools might be that some children are incapable of defending their honor against mild challenges to it made by school bullies, but if that rationale was made public it would undermine children's self-respect, so some other rationale is offered, e.g., that they are necessary to pick up the trash or something similar. (N. Scott Arnold offered me this example.) However, it would be difficult for Moon to say that public rationales for positive rights based on agency arguments would undermine self-respect because he has argued that rationales based on need undermine self-respect, and if both rationales undermine self-respect, then all the rationales for positive rights that Moon discussed would have to be rejected by him.

budget over time for at least some health-care needs. It treats health-care needs as something that simply happens to a person and, once this is rejected, Moon's point that an argument for positive rights must have some kind of link with contribution makes a great deal of sense. In any event, even if we suppose the objection succeeds, it will provide no basis for choosing between MHI and NHI because all the argument shows is that there should be some institutions that provide health insurance to all, and both systems do that. The objection is not fine grained enough to pick out a particular system of health insurance because all it shows, if it is successful, is that without some way of meeting health-care needs, the capacity for moral agency is at risk.

Another argument that attempts to show that negative and positive rights have the same status is Henry Shue's argument that a right to health care is a basic right. Shue has a very distinctive notion of a basic right: by this he means that one must enjoy or exercise that right in order to enjoy or exercise *any* right as a right. By enjoying a right as a right Shue means that one is entitled to it, as opposed to having it by favor, gift, request, and so forth; one can legitimately demand that something one enjoys as a right be respected or provided.[20] Shue's argument can be best grasped by examining his argument about the right to physical security that along with the right to subsistence and right to certain liberties (freedom of movement, political participation) comprise his list of basic rights. I will then discuss how Shue's arguments apply to the right to health care, which he believes is part of the basic right to subsistence.

Shue's argument that the right to physical security – which includes the rights not to be assaulted, murdered, raped, tortured, and subjected to mayhem – is basic goes as follows: if one cannot demand that others not subject one to these harms, one will not be able to exercise or enjoy nonbasic rights (e.g., the right to assemble). This is because one won't be able to legitimately demand that others not assault, murder, and rape, and so forth while one is exercising or enjoying these nonbasic rights. I can't be said to attend a rally or meeting as a matter of right if I can't demand that others not stop me from attending by subjecting me to severe harms.[21]

---

[20] Henry Shue, *Basic Rights: Subsistence, Affluence and U.S. Foreign Policy*, 2nd ed. (Princeton: Princeton University Press, 1996), 14–15, 19–20.
[21] Ibid., 20–2.

Trying to plug health care into this argument schema, however, causes some interpretative problems. Because Shue says that the right to health care is part of the basic right to *subsistence*, this implies that it justifies only a right to fairly minimal health care, something very much like the kind of health care Ozar maintained was the kind to which one had a basic right.[22] However, when we look at why Shue includes the right to political participation (that is also on his view a basic right) as part of the right to liberty, this suggests that he thinks that the content of basic rights is far more expansive. Shue thinks the right to political participation is a basic right in part because if there are no channels of communication to convey one's demands that rights be respected and protected, then one's enjoyment or exercise of one's rights, as rights, are damaged.[23] But he also says that participation must involve open channels of communication and some influence *over the outcomes*.[24] That is quite an extensive requirement; having a right to free speech need not produce such influence.[25] If we apply this expansive interpretation of a basic right to health care, then this implies that Shue thinks the basic right to health care covers a great deal more than minimal health care; perhaps it covers something approaching comprehensive health care. One hesitates to attribute this view to Shue because it is utterly implausible that one needs a right to comprehensive health care to enjoy *any* right as a right; however, whichever interpretation of Shue is correct, on neither understanding is a basic right to health care (in the way Shue defines a basic right) something that can be used to support NHI or MHI. If we understand the right to health care as requiring minimal subsistence-maintaining health care, then both NHI and MHI provide that. If we understand it to be something akin to a right to comprehensive care, then neither system provides such a right for all.

One other general argument for positive rights that can be applied to the right to health care deserves some attention. In Chapter 2, I noted that some contemporary political philosophers argue that in

---

[22] Ibid., 23, 25. In the former he refers to "preventive public health care"; in the latter, he says "elementary health care."

[23] Ibid., 75.

[24] Ibid., 71.

[25] Buchanan and Hessler, "Specifying the Content of the Human Right to Health Care," in Rhodes et al., *Medicine and Social Justice*, 90–1, make this point.

order for everyone to be treated as a moral equal or live in a society in which everyone is treated with mutual respect, no one should be humiliated because of his or her personal characteristics and rigid hierarchies, and class divisions should be absent. Although these philosophers (Samuel Scheffler, Elizabeth Anderson, David Miller) call themselves egalitarian, they fit uneasily with the way I have defined *egalitarianism* – as valuing or defending a substantive material equality as such – because what they want to equalize is not a certain kind of material equality but a certain form of relationships among human beings. Because these writers say that the distributive implication of their views is that everyone should have sufficient access to those goods that enable them to have their basic needs satisfied, which sounds like an argument for basic positive rights, we can ask how their views can be applied to a comparison of NHI and MHI vis-à-vis the grounds they give for basic rights. To answer that question we need to know which is less humiliating and a less rigid hierarchy: the kind of differential access to the need for catastrophic care that exists in NHI or the differential access to the need for routine care that exists in MHI? MHI seems preferable because having to wait for surgery or other forms of catastrophic care because one cannot jump through queues as well as more educated, wealthier persons seems more humiliating and a worse kind of hierarchy than having worse access to routine care than a wealthier person. Furthermore, notice that differential access based on connections, motivation, and education in NHI is access based on personal characteristics far more than differential access in MHI based on income. Money is fungible, impersonal; connections, motivation, and education are not.

I turn now to arguments for a right to health care that are not part of or implications of more general arguments for positive rights. (As arguments based on egalitarian premises were discussed Chapter 3, I set those aside.)[26] One such argument is a kind of civil rights argument that differentiates between discriminatory versus nondiscriminatory bases of denying or providing access to health care. MHI provides

---

[26] It would not be that difficult to use Daniels's and Dworkin's arguments to support some kind of right to health care. Daniels has done so: "Is There a Right to Health Care, and, if So, What Does It Encompass?" in *A Companion to Bioethics*, Helga Huhse and Peter Singer, eds. (New York: Blackwell Publishers, 1998), 316–25.

access in part on the basis of expected risk, which may seem like illegitimate discrimination.[27] My arguments in section 3.4.1 that at least some health risks are voluntarily assumed throw doubt on that claim. For the sake of the discussion, I will set aside those arguments and suppose that pricing health insurance according to expected risk is illegitimate discrimination. The problem with the argument is that NHI also discriminates: the better informed, motivated middle class beat out the poor in getting access to rationed care. So it seems like the civil rights approach provides no basis for preferring NHI to MHI.

It might be argued, however, that NHI is superior to MHI because differential access to health care in the former is a matter of manipulating the system, while the whole *raison d'être* of MHI is discrimination based on expected risk. There is something to this distinction, in the sense that discrimination based on expected risk wouldn't even be considered in a MHI system as the basis for a claim that one's rights had been violated, while discrimination based on differential access to health care that is unrelated to need might be considered to be a rights violation in an NHI system. Still, both are rights violations according to the assumptions of this civil-rights approach to the right to health care, and it's hard to see why one should be considered worse than another.

Two other prominent nonegalitarian arguments for the right to health care deserve a brief mention. Allen Buchanan argues that voluntary coordination of some kinds of health-care provision is a kind of public good, and on standard analyses of a public-goods problem, the rational thing to do is not contribute. State coercion is needed to overcome this problem.[28] We need not go into details of this argument for it provides no basis for distinguishing NHI from MHI because both employ the use of state coercion for the provision of health care, although NHI relies on coercion much more than does MHI. Tom

---

[27] See Audrey R. Chapman, "A Human Rights Approach to Health Care Reform," in Chapman, *Health Care Reform*, 149–63.

[28] Buchanan, "The Right to a Decent Minimum of Health Care," 68–72. Recently, Buchanan has proposed a different argument, that the interest people have in their health justifies a right to health care. See Buchanan and Hessler, "Specifying the Content of the Human Right to Health Care," 91–2. However, as Buchanan recognizes, that argument provides no clear basis for determining what health care one is entitled to receive. Thus it is of no use in favoring either system.

Beauchamp and James Childress attempt to derive a right to health care by seeing it as a return on the social investment made in funding for physicians' education, biomedical research, and other parts of the system that pertain dominantly to public health care.[29] Again, the details of this argument are unimportant because the argument cannot provide a preference for NHI over MHI as the favored form of this "return."

If we turn to the grounds of the right to health care to resolve the standoff regarding which system is better at providing a right to health care, we find that neither NHI nor MHI is a clear winner. Moral agency and mutual respect arguments favor the latter, while Shue's basic-rights argument, nondiscrimination, public goods, and social investments arguments provide no basis for preferring either system. Because neither NHI nor MHI was a clear winner vis-à-vis the content of the right to health care, then those who believe that there is such a right have no sound basis for preferring either system.

4.2 Health Care and Communitarianism

There is no univocal communitarian argument about health insurance. Michael Walzer provides a brief argument for NHI on the grounds that it is necessary to avoid treating health care as a commodity.[30] Ezekiel Emanuel provides a more comprehensive communitarian examination of health care and health insurance.[31] As we shall see, he argues for a health-care system that allows for far more choice and decentralization than is compatible with NHI, yet is not MHI either, because each individual gets a health voucher from the federal government. In addition to Walzer and Emanuel's arguments, I will also examine the communitarian criteria for evaluating market versus social insurance that I discussed in Chapter 2.

I will argue that Walzer's attempt to support NHI fails, in part because it ignores that there are a plurality of reasonable views about the best way to understand the nature of health care and the way to

---

[29] Beauchamp and Childress, *Principles of Biomedical Ethics*, 242–3.
[30] Walzer, *Spheres of Justice*.
[31] Ezekiel J. Emanuel, *The Ends of Life: Medical Ethics in a Liberal Polity* (Cambridge, MA: Harvard University Press, 1991).

allocate health-care resources. Emanuel's argument is an interesting attempt to have a much decentralized pluralistic health-care system without having MHI, but I argue that it is difficult to accept this pluralism without sliding all the way into MHI. As for the general communitarian criteria that are relevant for evaluating the choice between social and private insurance, although no one system can meet all of them, the balance of communitarian reasons turns out to favor MHI.

4.2.1 *Walzer's Argument*

Walzer's argument is part of his own particular version of communitarianism that says that different goods should be distributed in accordance with the social meaning of those goods in a particular society.[32] Because we (citizens of modern democracies) understand that the primary purpose of health care is to treat illness and restore physical well-being, health care should be distributed primarily in accordance with need, not the ability to pay.[33] Or to put it another way, the purpose or meaning of health care implies that we should reject or drastically limit the extent to which it is treated as a commodity, as something that can be bought or sold. Because MHI obviously treats health care as a commodity, it should be rejected in favor of NHI, which has at most a market for supplemental health insurance.

This argument, however, has two serious problems.

1. It fails the test of comparative institutional evaluation. NHI's restrictions of health-care markets do not thereby produce a need-based distribution. In a world of scarcity and voracious medical needs – the real world – not all needs can be met and some process of allocation or rationing is necessary. Government rationing of health care enables the well-connected, well-motivated, and knowledgeable middle and upper class to obtain superior access to nonroutine and catastrophic care – the kind of care that is often the most desperately needed. To use Walzer's argument from need to support NHI, it has to be less bad that access to the most needed kind of health care depends on superior connections, motivation, and knowledge, rather than income, which is a tough argument to make, particularly because the gap between

---

[32] Walzer, *Spheres of Justice*, ch. 1,13.
[33] Ibid., 86–91.

the poor's and the affluent's access to such care is more pronounced in a system of government rationing than in one in which that kind of rationing is absent.

To some extent Walzer recognizes the necessity of political decisions in an NHI system or any system that allocates using nonmarket methods.[34] Perhaps he would say that as long as the health-care system recognizes the pull of medical needs at some basic level, it is all right if some non-need-based principle is used. But that concession would ruin his argument. For at some level, need is recognized in an MHI system. Patients' and health-care providers' perceptions of patients' medical needs obviously play a role in determining what health-care patients seek and obtain. (Furthermore, the indigent and those with uninsurable risks are subsidized in MHI.) One's own budget constraint is often a very effective device for focusing attention on what one considers the most needed care, while the lack of that constraint can encourage people to go to doctors for not very weighty reasons. Because Walzer stresses that the social meaning of health care is incompatible with market distribution, perhaps he would say that the symbolism of MHI makes it objectionable because even if needs are recognized indirectly, the aim of the system is (for the most part) not to distribute by need. However, the symbolism of care denied, diluted, or delayed through government rationing seems equally at odds with need-based distribution.

Thus, Walzer's anticommodification argument produces no solid preference for NHI over MHI.

2. Although virtually everyone will grant that health care is not *simply* a commodity, in a pluralist society there is considerable disagreement about whether or not the significance of the provider-patient relationship drastically limits the legitimate role of markets for health care and health insurance. Some people think that because we can be so vulnerable when we need health care that it is unseemly to introduce financial considerations into the provider-patient relationship and are suspicious of the use of markets in health care. Like Walzer, they may want the doctor or clinician to be a professional devoted to the patient's needs without other considerations intruding. Others, who are more concerned with autonomy and think that this means they should be

---

[34] Ibid., 94.

in charge of their budgetary decisions, may view the doctor-patient
relationship as not radically different from other relationships with the
professionals one hires and are more likely to be sympathetic to the
role of markets in health care. Similar differences arise on the tradeoff
between resources devoted to health care versus other goods. Those
who are more risk averse will likely devote more resources and time
to health care and their relationship with their health-care providers;
those who are less risk averse are less likely to do so.[35] All of these
differences would seem to imply a role for widespread choice in the
health-care system, for as Walzer notes, "when people disagree about
the meaning of social goods, when understandings are controversial,
then justice requires that society be faithful to the disagreement."[36]
Because communitarianism's fundamental concern is with the promotion and sustenance of the good of the various communities, different
attitudes toward health risks and different views of the provider-patient
relationships mean that we have in effect different health-care communities that should be allowed to go their own way.

This point has been insisted upon by Ezekiel Emanuel, and to his
account we now turn.

4.2.2 Emanuel's Argument

Emanuel describes his view as liberal communitarianism.[37] It is liberal
in two senses. First, he stresses that there is a plurality of reasonable,
contested views about the conception of the good, or the best way to
lead one's life. Second, he also stresses the importance of basic negative
rights. What makes it communitarian is that he believes a particular
conception of the good is essential for justifying laws and policies, and
he rejects the idea, endorsed by liberals such as Rawls and Dworkin,
that a theory of justice can be justified without bringing in such a
conception. Emanuel argues that because conceptions of the good
enter into politics, democratic deliberation is necessary. The liberal
communitarian vision sees such deliberation as essential to leading a
good life because it enables one to live a life in common with others,

---

[35] In effect, this is an application of the argument I made in section 3.4.1 about one's
   conception of the good constituting one's lifestyle risks.
[36] Walzer, *Spheres of Justice*, 313.
[37] Emanuel, *The Ends of Life*, ch. 5–6.

gives one control over one's institutions, and enables one to develop capacities for empathy and reflection that would not be engaged by other kinds of social or communal interaction.

Because deliberative communities are necessary, but there are a variety of good deliberative communities, Emanuel is drawn to a decentralized kind of politics. There will be a variety of deliberative communities embedded within a liberal state. Emanuel considers pluralism not as an inevitable fact but as a positive good – as affirming diversity of human goods and worthy lives that realize various possibilities of human existence. Similarly, Emanuel does not see negative liberty rights as merely providing protection against tyranny and allowing a wide variety of conceptions of the good to flourish; rather, he stresses that these rights are required as a way to foment and protect democratic deliberation.

Emanuel applies his views to health care in the following manner. Each citizen gets a health-care voucher from the federal government, good for five years of payments. Vouchers are used at community health plans (CHPs) that receive payments for each voucher received. CHP's policies are set by democratic deliberation. To make democratic deliberation feasible, Emanuel proposes that membership in each CHP be limited to no more than approximately twenty-five thousand. CHPs would hire physicians, contract with others for more specialized care, and run and organize facilities. (CHPs sound a great deal like small-scale managed-care organizations with democratic participation; in other writings, Emanuel puts forth a modified version of his proposal based upon the dominance of managed-care organizations in the United States.)

Emmanuel stresses that his scheme would encourage pluralism by the sheer number of CHPs in a country the size of the United States and because each CHP can formulate and revise policies based on a shared conception of the good. Similar to arguments I made in section 3.4.2, Emanuel stresses how different health-care schemes depend crucially on a conception of the good.[38] Those, for instance, who favor a conception of the good life that emphasizes the opportunities provided by longevity (e.g., opportunities to have new experiences and role changes, continue relationships, have the chance to have children or

[38] Ibid., 126–44.

grandchildren) may favor a CHP that emphasizes high-tech innova-
tion, new and exotic life-extending procedures, and so forth.[39] Those
who stress the value of autonomy and mental capacities to formulate life plans and fulfill long-term goals would favor health care that
could play a real role in maintaining these capacities but might not
place much importance on health care that extended life for those
with no such capacities. Those who had a utilitarian view might favor
a scheme that refused to provide expensive health care for the elderly
when the chance of success was dim. Because people may become dis-
satisfied with their CHP, or change their conception of the good, the
five-year vouchers are only cashed out yearly by the CHP, and if someone changes his or her mind before the year is up, he or she can obtain
a refund and use the voucher elsewhere. Also, people can spend their
own money for additional care not covered by their CHP.

CHPs will make different funding decisions because they will have
different lists of priorities. They may require less or more than the value
of the voucher from each participant. If they require less, citizens-
participants, as Emanuel calls them, can receive a refund. If they
require more, they can be "taxed" by their CHP. (Emanuel has a plan
so that these extra taxes are equitable, but the details are unimportant
for our purposes.) As far as I can tell, Emanuel does not think CHPs
can charge on the basis of expected risk; however, they are allowed to
restrict their membership based on their conception of the good and
the way this applies to health and health care. (E.g., some CHPs that
fund abortion may deny membership to those who think abortion is
murder; religious-based CHPs may deny membership to secular individuals, etc.)[40]

Because the value of the vouchers is fixed by the government, we
have in effect a global budget akin to NHI. However, the presence of
many CHPs with different benefit packages, and the fact that CHPs live
or die depending on their demand, makes the system too dissimilar to
NHI to call it an NHI system. Furthermore, rationing at the level of the
CHP is self-imposed because if one disagrees with a CHP's allocation

---

[39] Emanuel proposes that the federal government require that a certain amount of
CHP funds go to research, and that each CHP can supplement that amount with
their own funds. Ibid., 186.
[40] Emanuel concedes that this could involve discrimination based on gender and race.
See ibid., 238–40.

system, you can take your voucher and go elsewhere.[41] Yet the system is not MHI either, because most demand for health care is subsidized, and all CHPs must be run on democratic participatory lines.

However, perhaps that conclusion is too hasty. What happens to citizens who don't want to participate in collective deliberation about a CHP's policy? Emanuel does not require that they participate and realistically acknowledges that most people won't, but the real sticking point occurs when one doesn't want to belong to a CHP governed by democratic deliberation. Emanuel acknowledges that there could be "Adam Smith" CHPs that would just turn over their vouchers to individual members who would then cash them out and spend the money for whatever health care they prefer.[42] If there were many of these, then the whole system would probably collapse both institutionally and as a matter of principle. Institutionally, it would collapse because if people are allowed to cash in their vouchers, then the number of CHPs run along democratic lines would shrink, and there would be a flourishing market in private non-CHP care. (Emanuel proposes subsidies to help CHPs if they are threatened,[43] but this may not help if the demand for market health care is strong.) As a matter of principle, the system collapses because if people are allowed to cash in their vouchers, why not just let them spend their money in the first place and allow those who want a democratic CHP to form one?

The root of the problem is Emanuel's inconsistency regarding pluralism and health care.[44] On the one hand, he wants to allow a variety of health-care communities to flourish. On the other hand, the liberal communitarian vision rejects market health care. On what basis can any form of liberalism try to eliminate or severely restrict market health care? There seem to be two answers. Market health care might be so unjust that the role of market should be minimal. Although Emanuel has some sympathy with the view that health-care markets undermine

---

[41] However, as I argued in section 3.5.2, rationing at the global or the macrolevel trickles down to the middle level (the CHP in this system) that blunts the extent to which rationing is self-imposed.

[42] Emanuel, *The Ends of Life*, 238–9. Emanuel does not discuss any institutional mechanism that would prevent them from cashing out their vouchers and spending it on goods other than health care.

[43] Ibid., 221, 231.

[44] For a similar criticism, see Baruch Brody, "Liberalism, Communitarianism, and Medical Ethics," *Law and Social Inquiry* 18 (Spring 1993): 403–6.

justice, he does not make that argument.[45] Or there might have been
a nationwide deliberative decision that market health care reflects an
unacceptable conception of health care. That seems unlikely given the
pluralism that Emanuel rightly stresses as a feature of contemporary
democracies. It does not seem that his theory can provide a privileged
place for CHPs. Because MHI provides a place for CHPs, but not a
privileged place, it is preferable on Emanuel's own premises to his
system.

The same point applies to Emanuel's later writings in which his
vision of liberal communitarianism is applied to managed-care organizations, whose dominance in the U.S. market Emanuel sees as continuing and expanding in the future. He proposes that legislation should
be adopted to limit the ability of such organizations to use financial
incentives for physicians to limit care (Emanuel believes these incentives undermine professional autonomy) as well as requiring these
organizations to have member-controlled boards of trustees and public forums (as a way of increasing public involvement and control).[46]
The problem with this model is pretty much the problem with the
model of competing CHPs. Emanuel wants legislation to make all
managed-care organizations conform to a certain structure, but given
his pluralism about conceptions of the good, such one-size-fits-all legislation is unjustified. MHI would allow Emanuel's favorite version of
a patient-controlled managed-care organization to exist,[47] but the legislation he proposes would not allow a market-oriented managed-care
organization to exist. A view that stresses pluralism about conceptions
of the good should favor the former.

---

[45] Emanuel does believe that the majority of Americans endorse the view that having
market health care "would undermine the value of justice" (and here he cites Norman
Daniels), but he also says that a key component of American values is "celebration of
the market." Ezekiel J. Emanuel and Linda L. Emanuel, "Preserving Community in
Health Care," *Journal of Health Politics, Policy, and Law* 22, no. 1 (1997): 166 and 164,
respectively. More to the point, given that Emanuel acknowledges disagreements
among Americans about the role of the market in health care, it will be difficult
for him to argue that the promarket views are so unreasonable that justice requires
that citizens who hold those views not be allowed to use their resources to create or
sustain market health-care institutions.

[46] Ibid., 175–9.

[47] Emanuel thinks the kind of managed-care organizations he proposes will have advantages in the competitive marketplace, ibid., 178. If so, the need for legislation to
eliminate competitors becomes mysterious.

4.2.3 Why Communitarians Should Favor MHI

Because Walzer and Emanuel both adopt different versions of communitarianism, there may be flaws in my arguments that their premises do not support NHI (Walzer) or support MHI (Emanuel). To remove that suspicion, I will use the criteria I mentioned in Chapter 2 that communitarians use to evaluate the choice between social and market insurance: universality, shared responsibility, reciprocity, fidelity, and participation and responsiveness. For health insurance, an additional criterion is needed: preserving or protecting the noncommodity or personal nature of the health-care relationship.

Both systems are universal, though in different senses. NHI forces everyone to have comprehensive insurance; although as I already observed, this does not mean it provides comprehensive care to all. MHI requires that everyone have at least catastrophic insurance, and requires on some proposals that the poor have MSAs. Furthermore, most people will also choose to have MSAs, giving many of them access to comprehensive care.

The shared responsibility and reciprocity criteria concern the way health insurance systems divide the responsibility for one's own health and the extent to which others are obligated to relieve illness, disease, and so forth. MHI and NHI draw the divide quite differently. In MHI, risk rating and MSAs mean that one will tend to bear the cost of one's own health risks and reap the rewards of careful behavior, except for those with uninsurable risks and the indigent, whose health care is subsidized. Furthermore, a wide range of choice in health-care plans will be available. In NHI, risk rating and choice of plans are quite limited. This enables one to shift the cost of risky health behavior to others, although cost-control measures limit this to some extent. Choice in plans is limited, although there is choice of providers. Which ways of sharing responsibility do or should communitarians favor?

I suspect that there is no clear answer to this question.[48] A key communitarian motif is that citizens in contemporary democracies are too assertive in demanding their rights and too reticent in assuming or

---

[48] Clare Andre, Manual Velasquez, and Tim Mazur, "Voluntary Health Risks: Who Should Pay?" *The Responsive Community* 4 (Spring 1994): 73–7, present both sides of the issue as part of the case studies section in their journal. These studies are meant to illuminate both sides of the issue without taking a position. The presence

living up to their responsibilities. This suggests at least uneasiness with the absence of costs for those who behave irresponsibly, which suggests NHI would rank lower on this communitarian criterion. However, communitarians may find that MHI's risk rating goes too far in the other direction because it is for the most part a system of individual responsibility that may imply to them a shirking of any community-wide sense of collective responsibility for health care. Perhaps what they would favor is something in the middle, a system that forbids most risk rating but allows it for a few select risky habits (e.g., smoking, excessive drinking). As I mentioned in section 3.4.1, this may not be a viable alternative.[49]

What about fidelity? To what extent do both systems keep their promises or commitments? If the promise made by NHI is that it will protect a legal right to comprehensive health care, I already argued in section 4.1.1 that this promise is not kept in most NHI systems; whereas MHI, being based on contract, can at least keep its promises to provide catastrophic care for all. If the promise is that all citizens get fair access to health care (where fairness is interpreted in an egalitarian sense), then the arguments in section 3.5.3 show that MHI fulfills this promise better. Most likely, it is probably not clear as to just what NHI promises. The invisibility of government rationing and the lack of a guarantee of specific health services make it hard for the average person to know what is or is not covered by NHI. In MHI, by contrast, because citizens own their own policies and most fund their own health care, it is somewhat easier to understand what is promised and what is and is not covered by that policy.

So overall it seems that MHI has an edge. It is clearer what is promised, and it is more likely to keep those promises. It is less clear what NHI promises, and if it does promise a legal right to health care or egalitarian access to all forms of health care, then these promises are not kept.

---

of this case study may indicate that the matter remains unsettled within communitarian thought. Also, Gavin Mooney, "'Communitarian Claims' as an Ethical Basis for Allocating Health Care Resources," *Social Science and Medicine* 47 (November 1998): 1178, says that it is appropriate to make health-care allocation decisions based on people's responsibility for their health status, but he does not say how much weight to assign that principle.

[49] Something like this seems to be favored by Christine Cassell et al., *Core Values in Heath-Care Reform: A Communitarian Approach* (Washington, DC: The Communitarian Network, 1993), 11–14.

It may be argued, however, that if NHI's promises are vague or unspecific then the difficulty of knowing what NHI has promised or what services are covered may not matter much. After all, we don't accuse someone of breaking a promise if we are unsure that a promise was made. There is something to this objection, but I don't think it can succeed in getting NHI off the hook. NHI, like all health insurance systems, makes a commitment to some kind of protection against the risks of illness, disease, and disability, and NHI promises some kind of comprehensive protection because it covers all kind of health services. That it is less clear what this entails doesn't show that it's unclear that NHI makes promises; rather, it shows only that it is unclear what kind of promises NHI makes. Although we may not literally accuse someone of breaking his or her promises if it's unclear what kind of promise he or she makes, we would, I think, find his or her fidelity lacking when compared to someone who made a clear promise and then kept it.

The criterion of participation and responsiveness is meant to capture the important communitarian point that in a pluralist society with widespread reasonable disagreement about the good life, promoting the good of the relevant community requires participation and responsiveness to the members' views and concerns. If one stresses the idea that responsiveness requires that all sorts of different health communities be allowed to form, then, for reasons I noted in my discussion of Emanuel, this requires MHI. Perhaps some communitarians would interpret responsiveness in a different way. They might argue that those whose conception of the good requires market health care do not form a community and/or have such pernicious effects on more democratic health communities that such "individualist" understandings of health care must not be allowed to flourish. I suspect that this is tantamount to an elimination of the criterion of responsiveness, not an interpretation of it, but even if we accept this viewpoint, it would seem to be just as strong an argument against NHI as it is against MHI. NHI makes its important rationing decisions without democratic participation, and, for reasons I discussed in section 3.5.2, it's doubtful this can change to any significant extent. As Emanuel rightly stresses, genuine democratic control over health-care allocation decisions is probably only effective in a very decentralized system. If the system allows that decentralization, then it is allowing different communities to provide different sets of benefits. Because the relevant community here is not geographical, but one based on a person's beliefs about health care, then free exit and entry are allowed – in which case the kind of choice that is available is incompatible with NHI.

So, either this criterion favors MHI, or it rejects both MHI and NHI and proposes a kind of decentralized system such as that proposed by Emanuel.

Turning to the final criterion of preserving or protecting the personal or noncommodity nature of health care, I already argued against Walzer that if one understands this to mean that health care should be distributed according to need, then this does not favor NHI. A different interpretation of this idea focuses on the provider-patient relationship and stresses that it is a moral, not a financial one. It involves trust between providers and patients and compassion on the part of those dispensing care. Health care reminds us of our common vulnerability and frailty and helps remind us of our connectedness to one another. Buying and selling of health-care services alters the focus of this relationship for the worse.

However, financial relationships are perfectly compatible with relations of trust and compassion. Many personal services involve just such a relationship (e.g., psychologists, lawyers [consider discussions about one's will], social workers). The seller of services in fiduciary relationships is supposed to act in her client's best interest, but that doesn't mean she has no financial relationship with her client.

Perhaps the worry is that MHI makes the doctor-patient relationship too impersonal, too bureaucratic. Rather than simply the doctor and the patient, the insurance company is also a silent or not-so-silent partner, which can and sometimes does interfere with the doctor's and/or patient's assessment of what is best. Ironically, this objection may support MHI. In MHI, most people will use MSAs and not use insurance for noncatastrophic care. At this level, there is no intermediary in MHI, although there is in NHI because it provides comprehensive insurance. (The lack of rationing of nonroutine care in NHI makes the difference between the two systems at this level perhaps not that important.) For nonroutine and catastrophic care, insurance is an intermediary in both systems. However, there are *more* intermediaries in NHI. Government rationing occurs at a variety of levels, and thus a variety of political considerations intrude upon the

provider-patient[50] relationship; in MHI the only additional intermediary is the insurance company.

I conclude that preserving the personal or noncommodity nature of
health care provides some support for MHI. This may, at first glance,
seem somewhat surprising, but once we realize that when the consumer or patient has more control over how to allocate his or her
income to health care, then there are fewer intermediaries between
the patient and health-care providers than if government or third parties dominate this relationship.

Where does this all leave us? Overall, communitarian criteria support MHI. Although there is no clear communitarian argument for
preferring either system's division of responsibility, MHI allows for a
variety of health-care communities to peacefully coexist and does a
better job in protecting the personal nature of health care and keeping its promises than does NHI. A somewhat different way to put my
arguments is that communitarianism provides no case for NHI and
provides some basis for preferring MHI. Although there is not a decisive communitarian argument for NHI, the balance of communitarian
reasons favors MHI.

4.3 Public Justification, Information, and Rationing

NHI appears to be quite popular, and this fact might seem to provide a
strong counterweight to its failure to meet egalitarian, positive rights,
and communitarian requirements. However, in Chapter 2 I discussed
a principle of epistemic accessibility, which is accepted by most contemporary liberals. The principle lists two conditions: (a) does the
institution or program block or make it difficult to obtain reasonably accurate or reliable information about the nature or evolution of
that institution or program? and (b) is the institution or program so
complex and complicated that it is unlikely that anyone but experts
can monitor its effects or evolution? To the extent that the institution
or program is worse on (a) and/or (b) then the public's support or
endorsement of that program fails to provide justification for it.

---

[50] The contrast is less stark in countries with nonprofit sickness funds that have so far
avoided government rationing. In those countries, the intermediaries between the
doctor and the patient may be roughly equivalent to what would exist in MHI.

NHI is worse than MHI, according to (a), for two reasons. First, the relative invisibility of costs in NHI systems counts against it. Most citizens pay little of the monetary costs of their health insurance or medical bills, even in systems that have nonprofit sickness funds. Furthermore, as I argued in section 3.5.2, the main nonmonetary costs of NHI – the rationing of catastrophic care and the resulting waits – tend to be not terribly visible and not accessible to the average citizen. (E.g., in most NHI countries with waits, publicly accessible national waiting lists are not available, and it requires digging on the part of academics and other experts to get some kind of accurate information about the extent and nature of the waits for catastrophic care.) Because the average person will have considerable difficulty obtaining information about the costs or harms of the system, although the benefits will be apparent (e.g., subsidized or "free" health care), it is likely that the public is misinformed or misled about the nature of NHI. By contrast, more people in MHI pay their own health bills with MSAs and fund their own catastrophic health insurance, and so "rationing" is more self-imposed, based on the choice of one's health insurance plan and budgetary constraints. The average person is likely to have a better understanding of the benefits and costs for him or her because choices based on one's own budget and values are more visible than politically imposed costs and subsidized care.

This contrast should not be overdrawn. Sheer inertia may lead some people to stick with an employer-sponsored comprehensive health plan, in which case the rationing in MHI is less actively chosen, and some people won't pay directly for their own health care, which reduces the accessibility of information about MHI. To the extent that NHI publicizes facts about rationing and responds to public objections to rationing, then the costs of NHI are somewhat easier to obtain. However, the contrast between the systems would still remain because it will still be true that more people will pay their own health-care bills and fund their own health insurance in MHI than in NHI, and rationing will be more self-imposed in the former.

A second advantage for MHI is the presence of individual property rights to one's health insurance policy and nontaxable income. When patients pay the bills and own their own policy, the incentive of the health insurance company and health-care providers to provide reasonably accurate information about costs and benefits of the policy or health-care services increases, as does the incentive of the policy-holder or patient to ask and search for such information. Furthermore, health insurance companies have an enforceable obligation to provide, and policyholders and patients an enforceable right to demand, such information. These obligations are considerably weaker in an NHI system in which individuals do not own their own policy and do not pay most of their medical bills.

One could imagine reforms of NHI that might increase public awareness of its costs as well as reduce its costs. Supplemental health insurance might be expanded to include more people. Countries with a national health service might replace it with competing nonprofit sickness funds and allow them to compete on price. Instead of premiums or taxes being split between employer and employee, the latter might pay all the tax. Publicly accessible national waiting lists could be mandated, and transportation to countries without waiting lists might be encouraged (as Canada has transported people to the United States when waiting lists became too long).[51] However, any such reforms make NHI more like MHI and thus concede the point in issue.

A more promising response is that many people don't want to know or be reminded of the costs to them of their health insurance policy or health-care services. That's why, it might be claimed, NHI is popular. There is something to this objection. Anecdotally, some people like the idea of never seeing a medical bill and not knowing the true costs of their care. And although I have argued that service plans that provide comprehensive care would not dominate in MHI, I have not denied that there would be some market demand for it, which implies that NHI's disguised information about costs is to some extent not imposed but a genuine reflection of citizens' preferences. However, the objection fails nonetheless. We cannot know that the reason NHI is popular is because it masks information about costs because voters and citizens do not have a genuine MHI to which they can

---

[51] Goodman and Musgrave, *Patient Power*, 514–15 and the references cited there and Theodore Marmor, "Global Health Policy Reform," in *Health Policy Reform, National Variations, and Globalization*, Christina Altenstetter and James Warner Bjorkman, eds. (New York: St. Martin's Press, 1997), 353.

compare it. More important, clearly not all citizens want costs to be disguised, their health care to be paid by others, and so forth. MHI, rather than NHI, responds to the diversity of preferences concerning shielding information about costs of care because it allows a place for service plans (which does some shielding of the costs of care) yet allows those who want to know the costs to have MSAs and have the freedom to have a catastrophic-only health insurance plan. By contrast, NHI imposes comprehensive care upon all and makes it difficult for citizens to be aware of the monetary and nonmonetary costs of the system.

As for (b), the question about whether the system is so complex only experts can understand it or follow its evolution, the existence of MSAs in MHI for routine care and small bills mean that the role of insurance is less, which simplifies the system greatly. So even if catastrophic health insurance in MHI is as complex as the way catastrophic care is handled in NHI, overall MHI is less complex and more comprehensible to the average citizen.

Thus, according to both the criterion of visibility of costs and complexity, MHI is more epistemically accessible, which means that the popularity of NHI is no reason to favor it and to override the egalitarian, positive-rights theory and communitarian arguments against it.

4.4 Conclusion: The Reasons for MHI's Superiority

Why does MHI do better, or at least no worse, than NHI on all the criteria I have examined? Rather than summarizing the chapters on health insurance, I conclude by explaining the main reasons for MHI's superiority.

One reason is that a person's health is like many important goods that are crucial in leading or having a good life; it depends on a complex mixture of choices and unchosen circumstances. This means that a health-care system that is attuned to that complexity, by pricing insurance based on expected risk but subsidizing the most obvious cases of involuntary risks, is fairer than a system that simply is permeated with subsidization of voluntary choices. In addition, encouraging people to budget for their health-care needs and expenses over time allows them to take increased responsibility for their health status, which is fairer than a system that doesn't have as direct a way of encouraging such responsibility.

Another reason concerns not just choice but pluralism. People's views about the best or most suitable kind of health care and of the nature of the health-care relationship depend on their conception of the good life, even if they are also influenced by background injustices. Most contemporary political philosophies stress the importance of freedom so that people with differing reasonable views of the good life can go their own way. This is another basis for MHI's superiority because it allows for a wide choice in health-care plans and allows different health-care communities to form, rather than trying to shoehorn nonsupplemental health care into a one-size-fits-all model as does NHI.

A third reason is that government rationing generally favors the knowledgeable, connected, and well-motivated middle class. Because catastrophic and nonroutine health care is rationed in NHI, this source of unfairness is a strike against NHI, when compared with an MHI system that avoids government rationing and mutes barriers to access by subsidies for the poor to purchase their own health insurance policy.

A fourth reason is that MHI is a decentralized system in which most individuals own their own health insurance and savings that they use to pay for health care. This gives MHI some crucial advantages over NHI in which individual ownership of nonsupplemental insurance is absent. Budgetary or allocation decisions become more visible when it's one's own budget and policy, than when these decisions are made politically. It makes it easier to get reasonably accurate information about the costs and benefits of health care. And when insurance benefits are based on contract rather than legislative discretion and weak judicial enforcement, a person's right to promised benefits is more secure.

Notice that the first two reasons, with their stress on the role of choice and pluralism in health and health-care decisions, refer to reasons that many contemporary political philosophers cite for the need for markets and protection for basic negative rights. The other two reasons point to advantages that markets have over government means of producing and allocating goods and services. I've used the libertarian elements of contemporary political philosophy and applied these to the choice of health insurance systems and reminded egalitarian, positive-rights theorists, and communitarians that there are advantages of markets (from their own perspectives) that are not easily duplicated when health-care markets are abolished or drastically limited.

5

Old-Age or Retirement Pensions

5.1 Introduction

Although old-age insurance is one of the oldest social-insurance programs – it first began in Germany in 1889, and by the start of World War II it was in place in most industrialized countries[1] – today a wide variety of welfare states have partially privatized the program. Still, except for Chile, no government has replaced it completely with a private-pension system.

I will come to the same conclusion about a Chilean-type private-pension alternative to old-age social insurance that I did about a market-based alternative to NHI in the previous chapters. In certain respects, the case against government provision and financing of retirement pensions is even stronger than the case against NHI.

Because the term "old-age social insurance" is awkward, I will henceforth use "Social Security" or SS for short. Not all countries use the label of *Social Security* to refer to government-financed and -administered pensions, but some do.[2] The reader should keep in mind that SS will refer to old-age social-insurance programs, regardless of whether or not they are called SS. The market alternative to SS are compulsory private pensions (CPPs). Systems that are neither pure SS nor pure CPP will be called *mixed systems*.

---

[1] World Bank Policy Research Report, *Averting the Old-Age Crisis: Policies to Protect the Old and Promote Growth* (New York: Oxford University Press, 1994), 104.

[2] Some countries use the term to refer to all or almost all social-insurance programs.

5.2 The Institutional Alternatives

5.2.1 The Central Features of SS

SS has two central features: first, it is a pay-as-you-go scheme (PAYGO), rather than being fully funded, and second, in many cases the management and financing of the system reflect both insurance and welfare (i.e., needs-based) principles.

In a fully funded pension,[3] a certain percentage of the recipient's wages or the recipient's contributions are invested, and the contributions plus the interest finance the retirement pension. In PAYGO systems, the source of the retirement pensions is not investment in the capital market but the power to tax. Taxes on the present generation of workers fund pensions, rather than the pensioners' contributions or their past taxes. In a particular year, the total taxes collected from workers may be more than the amount needed to fund pensions for that year, and what happens to that surplus of taxes indicates whether we have a pure (or nearly pure) PAYGO or one with some degree of advanced funding.[4] In a pure (or nearly pure) PAYGO system, any surplus of taxes over outlays in a particular year is used (almost always) to fund other government programs and so none of the surplus taxes are invested. Therefore, (as I will explain in more detail shortly) in such a system there are no (or virtually no) reserves in the SS system to handle years when promised pension outlays outstrip tax receipts. In a PAYGO system with some degree of advanced funding, some of the surplus is invested, and so a portion of the money paid out to pensioners is accumulated from interest. However, the reserves accumulated in a PAYGO system with some advance funding does not make the system fully funded, for the taxes invested plus the accumulation of interest falls *far* short of the amount needed to fund all the benefits that have been promised to existing workers and beneficiaries. One way to appreciate this point is that the analogy of a trust fund, which is sometimes used to describe these reserves, is quite misleading.

---

[3] A fully funded pension is usually, but not always, a private pension. A few countries do have government-managed, fully funded pensions, rather than PAYGO systems. See my discussion in section 5.2.6.

[4] See World Bank, *Averting the Old-Age Crisis*, 110–12, and Carolyn L. Weaver, "Controlling the Risks Posed by Advance Funding – Prospects for Reform," in *Social Security's Looming Surpluses: Prospects and Implications*, Carolyn L. Weaver, ed. (Washington, DC: American Enterprise Institute, 1990), 167–84.

A *genuine* trust fund that promises to pay benefits over a specified number of years keeps its promise by using the assets in the fund plus the interest accumulated, that is, it should not need any infusion of assets or subsidization from another source to keep its promises. (In addition, in a trust fund the beneficiaries have legal rights to their benefits, which, as I will explain later, one lacks in SS.)[5] For an SS system to function in this way, its "trust fund" would need to be large enough that, were the program to end today and no future taxes collected and, therefore, no future entitlements accumulated, the assets in the funds (the portion of the taxes on present workers that were not paid out immediately) plus the interest could pay all the benefits to which existing workers and beneficiaries were entitled.[6] In *no* case of SS is this true or even close to being true; even in a PAYGO with some degree of advance funding and thus some genuine surpluses at present, such as Sweden, the implicit public-pension debt – the liability for future expected or promised benefits – is as large as and often larger than the gross domestic product (GDP), which, in turn, is *considerably* greater than the reserves in these "trust funds."[7] Furthermore, in some countries, such as the United States, the term *trust fund* covers up the fact

---

5 John Attarian, *Social Security: False Consciousness and Crisis* (New Brunswick, NJ: Transaction Publishers, 2001), 131–2.

6 See Peter J. Ferrara, *Social Security: The Inherent Contradiction* (Washington, DC: The Cato Institute, 1980), 49–51.

7 In the OECD countries, the implicit public-pension debt in 1990 ranged from 90 percent of the GDP (United States) to almost 250 percent of the GDP (Italy). Sweden at that time was the country with the greatest degree of advance funding, with a "trust fund" of about 30 percent of the GDP. In 1999, this rose to 40 percent of the GDP. Some of this trust fund contains government bonds, which when redeemed will require tax revenues to redeem, but a considerable amount of the reserves do contain real assets. On the implicit public-pension debt, see World Bank, *Averting the Old-Age Crisis*, 139–40. On Sweden's reserves, see Gorman Normann and Daniel J. Mitchell, "Pension Reform in Sweden: Lessons for American Policymakers," *Heritage Foundation Backgrounder* (June 29, 2000), in particular 3 and 7.

It's worth noting that economists disagree about how to measure the implicit public debt. However, no matter what method is used by economists, the implicit public debt in OECD countries is as large as and often much larger than the GDP – according to studies that were done from 1993 to 1996 – and it's doubtful that any of the reforms I will discuss later in the chapter have shrunk the level of this debt. On different ways of measuring the implicit public-pension debt, see Robert Holzmann, Robert Palacios, and Asta Zviniene, "On the Economics and Scope of Implicit Pension Debt: An in International Perspective," *Empirica* 28, no. 1 (2001): 97–129. See table IV, 111, for their summary of different studies of the implicit public-pension debt in selected OECD countries.

that the system is a nearly pure PAYGO system; the "surpluses" in the U.S. trust fund are only an accounting device that does not reduce the liability of the government for future expected benefits. To put it another way, in the United States, a nearly pure PAYGO system, all the surpluses in the trust fund have already been spent by the government.[8]

I need to address an important claim made by the economist Nicholas Barr, that fully funded and PAYGO systems are basically similar because in both systems the consumption of a group of pensioners is produced by the next generation of workers. "From an *aggregate* viewpoint, the economic function of pension schemes is to divide total output between workers and pensioners, i.e., to reduce the consumption of workers so that sufficient output remains for pensioners."[9] However, all Barr is examining is the relationship between the two classes (workers and pensioners) and *ignoring* what happens to the income or assets the pensioners previously surrendered. In a fully funded scheme, all of the income the workers save – their foregone consumption – to provide for their pensions is *invested*; this does not happen in a PAYGO scheme. This investment in a fully funded scheme expands the productive capacity of the economy and provides for the future consumption

---

[8] In the United States excess payroll tax revenue not needed to meet current benefits is "invested" in new special-issue government bonds. The trust funds are credited with a bond – an IOU from one part of government to another – and the U.S. Treasury gets the cash. This cash is being used to finance the general operations of the federal government. Another way to put this is that the figures given for the surpluses supposedly in the trust fund are merely records of transfers from one part of government to another. (The only years in which this was not true were in the atypical years of 1998–2000, when the non-SS part of the budget also ran a surplus. Therefore, there was no deficit in general revenues for the SS payroll tax surplus to finance; during those years the excess of payroll taxes paid some of the national debt owned by private individuals). When SS's cash outflow exceeds the cash inflow from taxes (probably around 2018), the government will not find any money to pay promised benefits, only U.S. Treasury obligations. When the government then calls in the IOUs, it will have to do what it would do were there no trust fund: raise taxes, and/or cut benefits, and/or borrow money, and/or monetize the debt (unless the system has been privatized or partially privatized by then). For an excellent account of why the *U.S. trust fund* is an utterly misleading term, see June O' Neill, "The Trust Fund, the Surplus, and the Real Social Security Problem," *Cato Project on Social Security Privatization* (April 9, 2002): 2–3.

[9] Nicholas Barr, *The Economics of the Welfare State* (Stanford: Stanford University Press, 1993), 220, his emphasis.

of the pensioners.[10] Barr's aggregate analysis looks at retirement pensions the way he would look at a black or opaque box: he looks only at the income in (reduction in workers' wages) and the income out (pensions) without looking at what happens to the former in order to transform it into the latter (what happens inside the black or opaque box). It is true, however, that a long-term economic disaster could prevent a significant amount of savings from workers' paychecks from being invested and then retrieved to pay for pensioners' later consumption. If it were true that markets are subject to systematic and significantly long-term discoordination, then the extent to which the savings for pensions would fund pensioners' future consumption would be significantly lessened. But that is a separate issue, and, in any event, modern economies are not repeatedly subject to semipermanent economic depressions.[11]

SS frequently incorporates aspects of both an insurance and welfare system; this second feature is reflected in the method of financing and the payout of benefits. Virtually all SS systems are financed, at least in part, by a payroll tax, and in many systems the more taxes paid, the more benefits received: both of these are appropriate for an insurance scheme. They are, however, inappropriate for a welfare scheme because payroll taxes are a regressive method of finance (as they are a flat tax on earnings and typically there is a ceiling on the earnings taxed) and because need, not taxes paid, should determine benefits in a welfare scheme. However, some SS systems have progressive

---

[10] I have been aided here by Norman P. Barry's remarks, "The State, Pensions, and the Philosophy of Welfare," *Journal of Social Policy* 14 (1985): 479–80.

[11] That modern economies are not subject to repeated depressions is a fact; the explanation for this fact is a matter of controversy, which revolves around the extent to which various government policies are or are not responsible for the depression-free record of modern economies. It might seem that this controversy is relevant for the evaluation of SS versus CPP, for if CPP were to threaten the ability of modern economies to prevent long-term depressions, then that would be an excellent argument against CPP. However, the government policies that are often claimed to be the defense against economic depressions, such as preventing bank failures and the shrinkage of the money supply, keeping world trade reasonably free, the existence of automatic "stabilizers" (programs that transfer income to the unemployed during economic downturns), etc., have no necessary connection with a CPP system, as will become clear from the description of CPP that is given within the text.

benefit formulas so that those with low earnings histories get a higher percentage of their past incomes in benefits than those with high earning histories; some systems have a means-tested component that awards benefits completely independently of one's earning history (and that is sometimes financed out of general revenues and not a payroll tax); and some SS systems withhold benefits to pensioners who work after reaching the official retirement age. All of this reflects the idea of awarding or denying benefits based on need but is incompatible with an insurance scheme.

The connection between old-age SS's PAYGO feature and the way it combines insurance and welfare elements is historical-empirical, not logical or conceptual. These systems began by paying out benefits to current retirees who had put nothing or very little into the system, but who were considered entitled to considerable benefits. That justification had to be based on need, not earnings history or the amount of taxes paid, and guaranteed that the system would have to be financed on a PAYGO basis. Many old-age SS systems did not begin with an earnings-related component at all but paid a flat rate and/or a means-based benefit: the earnings component, with benefits based in part on a person's earnings' history, came later. It would have been *possible* for a PAYGO system to begin by paying no benefits to current retirees and delay paying benefits until workers had a certain degree of earnings history or paid at least a certain amount of payroll taxes, but the system never would have acquired support or been instituted under such circumstances.[12]

5.2.2 *The Early Stage of PAYGO*

PAYGO has a typical, virtually universal, lifecycle.[13] The early stage of PAYGO is marked by high benefits for retirees – much higher than they would have received had they invested their contributions in the market – and low costs or taxes for the workers. This is due to three reasons or causes: (1) those inherent in a PAYGO system, (2) those due to contingencies that were present during PAYGO's early stages, and

---

[12] World Bank, *Averting the Old-Age Crisis*, 102–5 and Ferrara, *Social Security: The Inherent Contradiction*, 5–7, 53–5.

[13] World Bank, *Averting the Old-Age Crisis*, 315–16. They use a more fine-grained analysis, dividing PAYGO into three, not two stages, but for my purposes such detail is not necessary.

(3) those that are in all likelihood necessary for the introduction and development of PAYGO to receive support. (As I note in the following text, the second and third factors overlap.)

1. The essence of PAYGO is that pensions are funded by taxes on present workers. Retirees who receive pensions during the early years of the system haven't paid into the system for very long, certainly not their whole working lives, and thus they get a great "rate of return."[14]

2. A lower life expectancy than exists today, plus a period of high population growth helps to produce a high support or dependency ratio – the ratio of workers to pensioners – in the range of fifteen-to-one to eight-to-one. Lower life expectancy reduces the number of beneficiaries (and the total cost of the benefits), although high population growth increases the stream of workers and taxpayers, which reduces the cost per taxpayer. In many cases, the system's early phase also coincided with high wage growth, which, although not affecting the support ratio, made the collection of payroll taxes more painless and increased the total amount of benefits.

3. Major political programs or policy changes are usually introduced gradually, and in this case, PAYGO's gradual emergence kept costs low and the support ratio high. Costs were kept low because the full range of benefits was not eligible to the first retirees,[15] which is why the biggest winners in a PAYGO system are not the first retirees but the cohort who were thirty to fifty years old at the time the system was founded. The support ratio was high because as benefits were expanded, so was coverage (e.g., agricultural workers and members of small firms who were originally excluded are added to the system). Point number three overlaps with point number two because benefits and coverage typically had their greatest expansion shortly after World

---

[14] I put this phrase in quotes, because in as much as SS taxes are not invested, the notion of a rate of return for SS is strictly speaking inaccurate. Strictly speaking, only market investments bring rates of return. However, the term has become commonplace for comparing the ratio of one's SS taxes paid in to benefits one receives and is useful for comparing how different generations fare during the life cycle of SS, so I will continue to use it.

[15] E.g., disability and survivors benefits are often added later. That SS schemes combine retirement pensions with these benefits is a complication that for the most part I shall ignore in this chapter, as it does not affect my central arguments.

War II through the 1960s, when population and/or wage growth were quite robust.[16]

Because the rate of return was high, and taxes were still relatively low, it is not surprising that the system is enormously popular at this stage. Few people pay attention to the implicit public-pension debt – the liability for the present value of the future stream of expected benefits – that is quietly building up.

5.2.3 The Later or Mature Stage of PAYGO

At this stage, typically when the system is more than forty years old, all the conditions that lead to the rate of return being high and costs being low have been reversed.

At this point, almost all people receiving benefits have paid into the system for most or all of their working lives, and so the terrific rates of return that PAYGO gives in its early stages cannot be replicated.[17]

The support or dependency ratio has dropped significantly: it is less than six-to-one and falling. (Today in most of the affluent democracies, when the system has been existence much more than forty years, it is less than four-to-one and in some countries less than two-to-one.)[18] This is due to the ageing of the population, which increases

---

[16] Ibid., 105.

[17] That later retirees cannot get the windfall that early retirees receive is a separate matter from whether the former can get a greater-than-market "rate of return," an issue I shall discuss in the following text.

[18] Sometimes this point about a worsening dependency ratio is disputed. E.g., Theodore Marmor, "Social Security Politics and the Conflict between Generations: Are We Asking the Right Questions?" in *Social Security in the 21st Century*, Eric R. Kingson and James H. Schulz, eds. (New York: Oxford University Press, 1997), 201, 206, n. 13, argues that the relevant dependency ratio is not the ratio of workers to retirees but the overall dependency ratio, between the working-age population and the sum of dependent young population and the elderly. That overall dependency ratio has been falling and is not expected to rise for many decades. This is because while the number of elderly is rising, the number of infants and school-age children are falling even faster, and the dependent young are projected to fall as a share of total population. Thus we could reallocate resources from the dependent young to the dependent old. Marmor's analysis, however, is confused. First, most children are supported by their parents, and most of this support is private, so it is irrelevant as far as the burden on the taxpaying public. Second, most programs supporting young children are funded on an annual basis by taxes allocated for that purpose (e.g., state schooling), so these program do not burden future taxpayers over time. Third, in the United States (Marmor's main focus) programs for the elderly run about seven to

the number of retirees, and the slowing of population growth, which lessens the flow of new workers to support the burgeoning retiree population. Thus, the level of taxes increases significantly. In many cases, wage growth also slows (which may be due in part to the increased burden of payroll taxes), and so the increased cost of the system becomes more noticeable.

Because the system is obviously no longer being phased in, virtually everyone is covered and entitled to full benefits. In the beginning of the mature phase, benefit levels are likely to increase due to the increased political clout of retirees (e.g., early retirement is allowed, benefits are indexed to wage growth and/or price increases). However, as the mature phase continues, the recognition that the implicit public-pension debt is as large as, and in many countries larger than, the annual GDP, and that expenditures are climbing up to 10 percent of GDP may lead to a scaling back of benefits (e.g., raising the retirement age, taxing benefits, reducing indexing). The increased expenditures and rising public-pension debt also leads to deficits in the trust fund and a dipping into general revenues to cover them or a further increase in payroll taxes, which in some cases is used to create some advance funding.[19] However, these measures only postpone the problems, as the demographics of a worsening support or dependency ratio mean that these surpluses will lead to deficits unless taxes are sharply increased and/or benefits are sharply reduced.

The result of these increased taxes for people who will be paying most or all of their lives for the system in its mature phase is that their long-run rate of return is worse than what they would get in the private capital market. (How much worse depends on the country and the time period.) Things promise to look even worse down the road as people who are just entering the system can only look forward – if the system remains as a SS system – to further reduction of benefits and increased

eight times what is spent on children so the diminishing amount spent on the former doesn't matter very much. Finally, even the overall dependency ratio is expected to rise after 2040. For criticisms of Marmor's argument, see Attarian, *Social Security: False Consciousness and Crisis*, 7–8.

[19] If the payroll tax increase is sizeable, and the taxes are actually invested and not used to cover other government spending, the surpluses created at this point can be considerable, but they still don't come even close to eliminating the public-pension debt, as I discussed in n. 7.

taxes, as the trends in the mature phase of slow population growth and increase in life expectancy do not seem reversible and reduction in the number of retirees covered seems politically unimaginable.

Because some of the reasons PAYGO moves from its early phase to its mature phase are due to contingent factors, it is not strictly speaking *necessary* that PAYGO go from an early phase to a mature phase, in the sense that it could continue to have a greater rate of return than investing in the private capital market, as the economist Paul Samuelson proved.[20] Suppose population growth is zero and the rate of growth of real wages on covered employment is greater than the rate of return on capital. If there is a constant payroll tax, then the total taxes collected and benefits paid would increase by the rate of growth in payrolls, which is greater than what the individual would have gotten on his own if he invested the taxes and received the average rate of return on capital. Or suppose there is zero growth in real wages, but population growth is greater than the return on capital investment. The increase in population will cause a similar increase in workers, and, with a fixed tax on payrolls, total taxes collected will also increase at this rate. Therefore, the individual is again better off than if he had invested his contribution. Thus, if population growth plus the growth in real wages is greater than the return on capital investments, then PAYGO can continually provide a rate of return greater than one could obtain by investing the money oneself.

However, Samuelson's proof is of little relevance for comparisons of real institutions. The contingent conditions required to sustain a rate of return above market returns are not sustained over the long run. Except during periods of unanticipated inflation, interest rates and the return on capital investments are usually significantly higher than the growth in wages,[21] and population growth drops as living standards

[20] Paul Samuelson, "An Exact Consumption Loan Model with or without the Social Contrivance of Money," in *The Collected Scientific Papers of Paul Samuelson, volume 1*, Joseph Stiglitz, ed. (Cambridge, MA: MIT Press, 1966), 219–34. Samuelson's argument is explained, minus the complex mathematics, by Ferrara, *Social Security: The Inherent Contradiction*, 293–4, and Gordon Tullock, *The Economics of Income Redistribution* (Boston: Kluwer-Nijhoff Publishing, 1983), 111–22.

[21] Data from World Bank, *Averting the Old-Age Crisis*, 299–302, 355, for selected OECD countries from 1971–90, indicates that the average annual rate of return for a portfolio containing half stocks and bonds was about 3 percent above the growth in real

increase. Because the existence of high population and wage growth that produces a greater than market rate of return will not last long (if they exist at all), and the other conditions that keep the rate of return high in the early stage (i.e., the phasing in of benefits and coverage, the high ratio of workers to retirees, the windfall present to retirees who have paid nothing or almost nothing into the system) will also disappear with time. In the real world, the early stage of PAYGO leads, almost inevitably, to the later or mature stage.

5.2.4 Redistributive Effects of SS

The progress, or perhaps one should say regress, from the early to the late stage of PAYGO entails a significant redistribution of wealth from the later generations to the earlier generations. This intergenerational effect is clear and needs little elaboration; its normative significance will be the heart of my argument in sections 5.3 through 5.6. What may be less obvious is that the intragenerational effects, that is, the transfers of expected lifetime income among those born at about the same time may very well not be progressive.[22] Although some SS systems, such as those in the United States, United Kingdom, the Netherlands, Switzerland, and Sweden, have progressive benefit formulas (i.e., those with

wages, and for a portfolio with only stocks, the difference is considerably greater, ranging from 5.5 percent to 8 percent. Data from the OECD's *Database of Main Economic Indicators, 2001*, also indicates that the average equity return in countries composing the European Union during the last few decades (the time period varies across countries, due to incomplete data) is also considerably greater than growth in real wages. That data is reported in William G. Shipman, *Retirement Finance Reform Issues Facing the European Union* (Washington, DC: The Cato Social Security Policy Studies, January 2, 2003). Notice also that with capital becoming more mobile, an international portfolio is likely to do better than a national one, and provide advantages to those living in countries with sluggish economies, which should give an additional advantage to equities over PAYGO in the future.

The point about unanticipated inflation comes from Gordon Tullock, *Welfare for the Well-To-Do* (Dallas: The Fisher Institute, 1983), 54. He provides no data, but the point is an obvious one.

[22] World Bank, *Averting the Old-Age Crisis*, 131–4. Strictly speaking, the phrase "intragenerational redistribution" is a bit misleading in this context because the source of the transfer of income to retirees is workers, many of whom are from a different generation than retirees. However, because the usage is standard, I will adopt it, and it should cause no problem, provided the reader keeps in mind that "intragenerational redistribution" means comparing how different income groups, who were born close to the same time fare as far taxes/benefit ratios are concerned.

lower earning histories get a somewhat higher proportion of their past income in benefits than do higher income recipients), there are other features of SS that mitigate or may eliminate this influence. Upper-income people tend to enter the work force later than the poor and live longer after retirement. (The poor have much higher death rates before age sixty-five than do the affluent, and this gap has been increasing.) Hence there are a number of years in which the more affluent will not pay SS taxes while poorer people are paying those taxes, and the former will receive benefits for many more years than the poor. Furthermore, the method of financing PAYGO systems, which relies largely upon a payroll tax, is usually regressive;[23] typically, there is a ceiling on taxable earnings in systems with payroll taxes. Studies of the intragenerational effects of SS in the United States have disagreed about whether the affluent's longer life expectancy, later entrance in the work force, and SS's regressive funding suffice to cancel out the effect of the progressive benefit formula so that the system as a whole is regressive in its intragenerational effects. Some have found that to be so, although others have found that the system is very slightly progressive.[24] However, it's possible that an egalitarian may find studies like this that focus on groups defined by their lifetime income to be incomplete because they do not focus on some important groups that are often considered to be among the most disadvantaged. For example, blacks do worse than whites,[25] and black males born in the early

---

[23] An exception is Switzerland, which has no cap on the payroll tax. Estelle James, *Social Security Reform around the World: Lessons from Other Countries* (Dallas: National Center For Policy Analysis, August 2002), 24.

[24] See Julia Lynn Coronado, Don Fullerton, and Thomas Glass, "The Progressivity of Social Security," *National Bureau of Economic Research Working Paper No. 7520*, available at http://www.nber.org/papers/w7520 (accessed March 2003) and "Distributional Impacts of Proposed Changes to Social Security," in *Tax Policy and the Economy*, James M. Poterba, ed. (Boston: MIT Press, 1999), 149–86; Jeffrey Liebman, "Redistribution in the Current U.S. Social Security System," in *The Distributional Aspects of Social Security and Social Security Reform*, Martin Feldstein and Jeffrey B. Liebman, eds. (Chicago: University of Chicago Press, 2002), ch. 1.

[25] Michael Tanner, *Disparate Impact: Social Security and African Americans* (Washington, DC: Cato Institute Briefing Papers, February 5, 2001) and General Accounting Office, "Social Security and Minorities," available at http://www.gao.gov/new.items/do3387.pdf (accessed March 2003). The General Accounting Office report found that black Americans receive lower net lifetime benefits than whites of the same income. Admittedly, it also found that, in the aggregate, blacks have higher disability rates and that this means that as a group they tend to receive greater

1970s that make close to half the average wage will get a negative return from SS.[26] And women as a whole fare less well than men.[27] There are plausible grounds to doubt that even SS systems with progressive benefit formulas have overall progressive intragenerational effects.

5.2.5 *Private Pensions*

Private pensions are either defined benefit or defined contribution. In the former, the sponsor promises to pay a pension related to career earnings (e.g., a certain percentage of final or average salary) or a flat rate (per years of service). Recipients thus trade a portion of their wages for pensions, while sponsors (usually employers) bear the investment risk. (SS pensions might seem to be defined benefit, and it is not uncommon for them to be described as such; however, as the level of benefits is frequently redefined by the vagaries of the political process, no set benefit is promised.)[28] In the latter, contributions are fixed and benefits vary with market returns; the risk is borne by the recipient, not the provider. The former runs a risk of not being fully funded, as employers may not invest sufficiently to guarantee the benefit, while the latter does not run this risk, as no benefit is guaranteed.[29] In many countries, tax laws and regulations have skewed the growth in pensions toward occupational pensions,[30] many of which are defined benefit,

---

benefits relative to taxes than whites. However, it is not clear whether disability benefits should be aggregated with the other SS benefits, and the study did not address whether whites of the same income level receive less or more disability benefits than blacks.

[26] William W. Beach and Gareth E. Davis, *Social Security's Rate of Return* (Washington DC: The Heritage Foundation, January 15, 1998), 2, 7.

[27] See Peter J. Ferrara and Michael Tanner, *A New Deal for Social Security* (Washington, DC: The Cato Institute, 1998), 102–4 and the references cited therein.

[28] On the spotty record of SS keeping its promises, see World Bank, *Averting the Old-Age Crisis*, 112–13.

[29] It was the belief that a significant number of defined-benefit occupational pensions were not being fully funded by U.S. employers that helped to produce the Employment Retirement Income Security Act (ERISA) in 1974. The act provided both tax incentives and legal penalties for failure to fund pensions adequately and created a set of regulations governing employee participation and the vesting of benefits (i.e., the conditions under which employees could leave the company without losing their pension). For further information, see Barbara J. Coleman, *Primer on ERISA* (Washington DC: Bureau of National Affairs, 1985). Laws similar to ERISA exist in many of the OECD countries. See World Bank, *Averting the Old-Age Crisis*, 193–7.

[30] Ibid., 167–9, 182–3.

but it is probably safe to say that given the problems with labor mobility inherent in occupational defined benefit pensions, in a free market defined contribution pensions would play a very large if not dominant role.[31] Both types of pensions can be converted at retirement age to annuities and/or can be received in a lump sum or in phased withdrawals.

In a CPP system the government requires that a person save for retirement, but the management and financing of these pensions are left largely to the free market. A CPP system can be either a defined contribution system – it if requires that one set aside a certain percentage of one's wages – or a defined benefit system – if it requires that the pension at retirement must be a certain amount. I will use Chile[32] as my model for a CPP system that combines elements of both defined contribution and benefit. Employees are required to contribute at least 10 percent of their wages and invest them in an individual pension savings account managed by private investment companies. In addition, workers must purchase private disability and life insurance. After retirement, workers must either purchase annuities (indexed to inflation) or make phased withdrawals from their pension savings account. However, if one's pension (or disability and life insurance) does not meet a certain minimum benefit at retirement, the government makes up the difference. The government provides pensions funded by general revenues or those not covered by pensions (e.g.,

---

[31] Partly for these reasons, and partly because some employers consider the ERISA regulations burdensome, occupational pensions plans in the United States have been shifting from defined benefit to defined contribution. That trend also exists in some other OECD countries, such as Australia and Switzerland. For the United States, see Karen Fergenson and Karen Blackwell, *Pensions in Crisis* (New York: Arcade Publishing Company, 1995), 168–9, 173; for the OECD countries, see World Bank, *Averting the Old-Age Crisis*, 198–200. Also, see the discussion of mixed systems in section 5.2.6. Some of those systems owe their origin to defined-benefit occupational pensions being changed into defined-contribution pensions.

[32] My information about the Chilean system was obtained from World Bank, *Averting the Old-Age Crisis*, ch. 6; L. Jacobo Rodriguez, *Chile's Private Pension at 18: Its Current State and Future Challenges* (Washington, DC: Cato Project of Social Security Privatization, July 30, 1999); Sebastian Edwards, "The Chilean Pension Reform: A Pioneering Program," in *Privatizing Social Security*, Martin Feldstein, ed. (Chicago: University of Chicago Press, 1998), ch. 1; and H. Fred Mittelstaedt and John C. Olsen, "An Empirical Analysis of the Investment Performance of the Chilean Pension System," *Journal of Pension Economics and Finance* 2, no. 1 (2003): 7–24.

those who have never been in the job market). The Chilean system has two aims: to force retirement savings and to provide a safety net for those whose pensions do not meet a certain minimum. Of course, one can voluntarily save more than the CPP system requires.

Although I use the Chilean system as my model for CPP, I do not include all features of that system. The pension system in Chile is tightly regulated. There is a minimum age of retirement; the investment companies that manage the pension savings accounts must provide a minimal annual return; workers are allowed to invest in only one of these companies at a time (though they may switch their accounts between the companies every six months); these companies, whose sole function is to manage pension savings accounts, were until recently required to hold a portfolio that contained a significant percent of government securities; until recently foreign investment was not allowed; and so forth. As these features reduce the sense that there is a free market in pensions and are not essential to the aims of forced savings and the provision of a safety net, I will not include these features in my comparison of SS and CPP. This raises an important question: besides mandating a certain minimum contribution toward one's retirement and providing a safety net for those whose pensions at retirement are below a certain minimum, what other features should be added to a CPP system? First, the safety net should probably be at least equivalent to the minimum provided by a typical SS system (e.g., a replacement rate of a certain percentage of the average wage) so that poor outcomes under CPP would be no worse than poor outcomes under SS. Second, the aim of providing a safety net may require that on retirement one can't receive a lump sum payment but must purchase annuities or make phased withdrawals, so that could probably be included as a feature of CPP as well. Third, the aim of providing a safety net also provides some indirect support for regulations that forbid firms managing pension funds from making excessively risky investments. Although there will be a variety of portfolio options, they will tend to be ones that will involve wide diversification (e.g., a mixture of stock and bond index funds). (Similar rules prevail for voluntary, occupation-based, defined contribution pensions, and when pensions are compulsory the political need for ruling out the very risky investments is likely to be overwhelming.) Finally, it is plausible to impose informational requirements on pension fund managers, so that information about expected rates of return, different portfolio options, administrative costs, and the like are relatively easy for an average person to understand. (The first three features are part of the Chilean system; the last is not.)[33]

Because CPP systems are fully funded, they lack the significant intergenerational transfers of SS. As a result, early generations do not do well at the expense of later ones, and the poor returns that later generations get in the mature stage of a PAYGO system are generally absent in CPP, which has a much higher rate of return than PAYGO's mature-stage rate of return. (The issues involved in assessing the comparative superiority of CPP's rate of return over PAYGO's rate of return in its later stage are a bit complex and are discussed in the appendix to Chapter 5.) Fully funded pensions do not redistribute across persons but only across different portions of a person's life.[34] However, CPP's

---

[33] It might be argued that because Chile is the only country (at present) that has a (full-blown) CPP system and my aim here is to compare real welfare-state institutions with real market-based alternatives, I should include all the features of the Chilean system in my analysis of CPP. However, when there is only one instance of a system in existence, reproducing all the features of that system in one's model or analysis of that system runs the risk of including features that are idiosyncratic. The opposite risk, of course, is that by not reproducing all the features in one's model one creates an ideal version of a system that is likely never to exist anywhere, which would violate the methodological strictures I set out in Chapter 1. I suspect that all one can do here is to make a judgment call and include those features that seem clearly linked to the aims of the system and that do not seem unfeasible because of political and other institutional constraints. It's worth noting, in this context, that some governments that have partially privatized SS do not regulate investments as much as the Chilean government does (e.g., Australia) and that greater transparency of information about administrative costs, portfolio options, etc. is available in other countries that have partially privatized SS. Hence, the features I am including in my analysis of CPP do have an empirical basis. On Australia, see Malcolm Edey and John Simon, "Australia's Retirement System," in Feldstein, *Privatizing Social Security*, ch. 2, in particular p. 86. On transparency of information in a CPP system and a partially privatized SS system, see Salvador Valdés-Prieto, "Comments," in *New Ideas about Social Security*, Robert Holzmann and Joseph E. Stiglitz, eds. (Washington, DC: The World Bank, 2001), 84–8.

[34] Note that if one views these different stages as different selves, in the manner of Derek Parfit's theory of personal identity, then the distinction between transfers between different parts of a person's life and different persons is not metaphysically significant. For purposes of this book, however, Parfit's views are not relevant because whether or not they are true, they are not *politically* significant, as people generally

safety net involves redistribution. Because it goes only to the elderly poor and is financed out of general revenues, it is likely to be more progressive in its income effects than the intragenerational redistribution in SS, which is either regressive or just barely progressive.

5.2.6 Mixed Systems

SS and CPP do not exhaust the institutional alternatives. Two mixed or hybrid systems exist in a variety of countries.[35] There is a system called *provident savings*. Employees and/or employers are required to save, but the savings must be deposited in a government-managed system that invests primarily in government securities. One has a property right in one's account, and when the system works the way it is supposed to, without government corruption or mismanagement, it is fully funded – one gets back one's contribution plus interest, although the rates of return are much lower than in a CPP system. Because the government manages the system, it would be too large a stretch to place this in the category of *private* pensions. The number of provident systems is declining, and they exist in few of the affluent democracies,[36] which are my concern in this book, but it remains an option to consider, as it shows it is possible to have a fully funded system with individual accounts that is not privately managed. The other system is *partial privatization*, which has been expanding and

view redistribution across different stages of a life as in a vastly different category than redistribution across different persons. For Parfit's views, see *Reasons and Persons* (New York: Oxford University Press, 1985), 199–347.

[35] I rely here on the following: Louise Fox and Edward Palmer, "New Approaches to Multipillar Pension System: What in the World is Going On?" in Holzmann and Stiglitz, *New Ideas About Old-Age Security*, 90–100; Estelle James, "Reforming Social Security in the U.S.: An International Perspective," *Business Economics* 36, no. 1 (2001): 20–6; James, "Social Security Reform around the World," in Feldstein, *Privatizing Social Security*, ch. 2–3; and Martin Feldstein, "The Future of Social Security Pensions in Europe," *National Bureau of Economics Research Working Paper 8487*, available at http://www.nber.org/papers/w8487 (accessed March 2003).

[36] They exist in a few Sub-Saharan African countries (Gambia, Kenya, Swaziland, and Uganda) and some East Asian countries (Hong Kong, Indonesia, Singapore, Papua New Guinea, Sri Lanka, and Singapore). See Robert Holzmann, Richard P. Hinz et al., *Old-Age Income Support in the 21st Century: An International Perspective on Pension Systems and Reform* (Washington, DC: The World Bank, 2005), 159–63, 168 and https://www.socialsecurity.gov/policy/docs/progdesc/ssptw/2004-2005/africa/guide.html (accessed June 2006).

is now found in a variety of the affluent democracies (plus in some less affluent countries). In Switzerland, the Netherlands, Australia, Denmark, and Sweden, a system of CPPs has been either carved out of or added onto the SS system; in the United Kingdom the carving out is optional (and benefits have been cut in part[37] of the SS system to increase the incentive to exit). By *carved out*, I mean that SS taxes are reduced roughly by the amount one is required to contribute to private pensions; by *added on*, I mean that there is no reduction. These systems differ in their details: some are like Chile's system, funded by employee contributions (e.g., Sweden's system); most others are occupational based and contributions are made by employers and employees or employers alone. Most are pure defined-contribution systems with no minimum pension guarantee because the SS system provides the guaranteed minimum; others (e.g., Switzerland's system) have a minimum guarantee within the private system and are thus a mixture of defined contribution and defined benefit. Some have minimal regulations about investments (e.g., Australia's system); others are extremely regulated, even more so than Chile's (e.g., Switzerland's system). However, most of the differences will not be important for our concerns.

In many cases, these systems of partial privatization have been introduced along with reforms in the SS system. Most of the reforms are simply a continuation of trends in the late stage of PAYGO (e.g., reducing benefits, increasing the retirement age, eliminating or reducing indexing, attempts to start or increase advance funding), but one new reform found in Italy and Sweden is worth a mention. This is the introduction of a notional defined-contribution system. In that system, each person has a personal account to which she (or her employer) pays the prescribed amount. These funds are not invested – it's still a PAYGO system – but unlike standard SS systems, each individual's "account" is directly credited with an amount the individual or her employers paid into the system. The account also receives a rate of return equal

---

[37] The U.K. SS system has a flat-rate benefit in which everyone gets the same amount (plus a means-tested addition for the poor) and an earnings-related component that assigns benefits based on earning history. The privatized component of the system is carved out from the latter.

to a notional rate of "interest" equal to rate of growth in the aggregate payroll tax base. For our purposes, the significance of this is that at retirement, a notional defined-contribution system makes it possible for an individual to claim the amount in the account and cash it in for a private annuity, thus adding another element of privatization to a PAYGO system.

5.3 Egalitarianism, Fairness, and Retirement Pensions

Should egalitarians – and their prioritarian cousins – favor SS or CPP or a mixed system? First, I will compare SS with CPP and then I will discuss mixed systems. Recall that egalitarians' main concern is to reduce unchosen inequalities while prioritarians' main concern is to raise the absolute position of those who are worse off through no choice or fault of their own and that both egalitarians and prioritarians measure well-being in terms of either resources or welfare. One additional point is needed: egalitarians and prioritarians disagree amongst themselves about whether or not there are obligations to future generations. But even those who deny that there are obligations to future generations admit special obligations to their children as well as a concern for their descendants, even if they are not yet born.[38]

An egalitarian/prioritarian argument for the superiority of CPP over SS is straightforward and is based on the intergenerational and intragenerational differences between the two systems. First, the effects of a PAYGO system compared to a funded one make SS far worse. SS places significant burdens upon later generations that the earlier generations did not have – a low rate of return, a high level of taxes, and implicit public-pension debt – therefore reducing the later generations' resources and most likely their welfare compared with what would exist if CPP were in place. These burdens and inequalities, of course, could hardly be said to be due to the later generations' fault or choices. Second, CPP has more progressive intragenerational redistribution than SS. Third, the absolute position of the poor and

---

[38] Another way to put this is that those who reject obligations to future generations, i.e., who relativize justice to time, are primarily rejecting such obligations for strangers.

disadvantaged[39] will greatly improve under a private system.[40] The rates of return in a private system are much greater than in SS and most of the poor's postretirement income comes from SS, whereas the more affluent are more likely to have private pensions in addition to SS. Notice also that the people burdened and made worse off are the children and descendants of the earlier generations, and so the argument applies also to those who reject obligations to future generations because they admit special obligations to their children and a concern for their descendants. I can think of three egalitarian/prioritarian replies to this argument.

1. Some egalitarians believe that natural as well as social inequalities are an injustice that should, subject to tradeoffs with other values, be rectified. Because being old in many ways makes one worse off than being young, SS's redistribution from young to old makes it a positive feature, not a negative one.[41] This response, however, ignores the fact

---

[39] My equation of poverty and disadvantage, or being poor and being worse off, is only meant in a rough sense. It is not true that necessarily or by definition the worst off are the poorest. First, as I noted earlier, some egalitarians are concerned with inequalities in welfare, and there is no necessary connection between being unhappy or lacking satisfaction and poverty (though extreme poverty, over the long run, considerably reduces happiness and satisfaction). Second, some people who are temporarily poor (e.g., college and graduate students) are often well off. Third, measuring poverty simply in terms of low income, as is often done, omits some important considerations that affect the quality of people's lives. E.g., two people can have equal incomes (at one time or over a period of time) but not be equally well off because of different capabilities of converting that income into resources (e.g., someone with a high metabolic rate, a large body size, or a parasitic disease that wastes nutrients may have a much harder time meeting minimal nutritional norms with her income than someone who does not have these characteristics). See Sen, *Inequality Reexamined*, ch. 7, for more discussion of this point.

  Thus, although there are obvious connections between the poor and the worst off, egalitarians cannot and do not equate them. The best one can say here is that when concerned with policy or institutional choices, long-term poverty is a plausible but not always reliable marker for being badly off.

[40] To what extent egalitarians and prioritarians believe that poverty is involuntarily produced will be the subject of Chapter 6, but clearly they believe that some of it is. Thus, the fact that SS has less progressive intragenerational distribution than CPP and that it worsens the absolute position of the poor compared with CPP are injustices according to egalitarianism/prioritarianism.

[41] Temkin makes this argument about the justifiability of transfers from the young to the old in "Justice and Equality," 96–7, although he makes no mention of SS. The prioritarian version of this objection is that some kind of priority should be given to the old because being old is in many ways worse than any other stage of life. Dennis

that CPP also "redistributes" from young to old in that income is saved for old age and a safety net is provided for the elderly poor, and more important, the reply doesn't justify SS making those who are young during the early stage of SS worse off when they become old during the mature stage as compared with those who are old during the early stage of SS.

2. My response to (1) may produce the following counterargument: even though later generations do worse vis-à-vis SS than earlier generations, all things considered later generations will be better off (due to the effects of economic growth, science, and technology, etc.) than earlier generations.[42] This inequality between generations is *prima facie* objectionable (at least when it occurs in societies that are already affluent),[43] because it is due largely to circumstances that no one chose (i.e., when one was born). Accordingly, the redistribution within SS, but not within CPP, from later to earlier generations is not an objection against SS but, on the contrary, is exactly what egalitarians want: to mitigate the extent to which the later generations' lives will be better than the earlier generations. This argument will be made by egalitarians who object to inequality as such, rather than by prioritarians who are concerned with the absolute position of the worst off. For the latter, the fact that later generations are better off than earlier ones is probably a plus, not a minus, at least to the extent that the increase in living standards or quality of life makes the worst off of the later generations better off than they otherwise would be and does not occur at the expense of the worst off of earlier generations.

However, even if egalitarians should favor redistribution from later to earlier generations, the way this redistribution occurs with SS is objectionable on egalitarian grounds. Even though in a growing economy the average member of a younger cohort will have a higher

---

McKerlie defends this time-specific priority view in "Justice between the Young and the Old," *Philosophy and Public Affairs* 30, no. 2 (2002): 152–77.

[42] Loren E. Lomasky raised this objection (which he does not, incidentally, endorse). After Lomasky raised this objection, I discovered that Temkin in "Justice and Equality," 93–4, makes a similar point, although he does not do so in the context of a discussion of SS, and Andrew Levine, "Just Social Security," *Public Affairs Quarterly* 12, no. 3 (1998): 327, also raises a similar objection (which he does not endorse).

[43] I add this because it is inconceivable to me that any egalitarian would object to later generations being better off than earlier ones in situations where grinding poverty is the norm.

lifetime income than the average member of an older cohort, people who survive to old age are not a random sample of their cohorts. They generally come from higher socioeconomic groups, whose expected longevity is higher. A larger proportion of people who are young will have shorter lifetimes and lower lifetime annual income than people who are old.[44] Thus the redistribution from later to earlier generations is not really from those who are better off to those who are worse off; in a significant respect, the redistribution goes the other way. What an egalitarian should favor, perhaps, is a system that redistributes from the better off members of later generations to the worse off members of earlier generations, However, because neither SS nor CPP does this, while CPP avoids the perverse redistribution from the worst off members of the later generations to the better off members of the earlier generations, then CPP is, in that respect, preferable to SS on egalitarian grounds.

3. Egalitarians who believe that there are no obligations of justice to those not yet born but acknowledge obligations to their children (and grandchildren) might argue that they can mitigate the negative effects of SS by gifts and bequests. (It's worth stressing, in this context, that one cannot bequeath the money one paid into SS to one's children.)[45] However, if one believes that the negative effects of SS on one's children (and grandchildren) should, as a matter of fulfilling one's parental obligations, be mitigated by gifts and bequests, it would make more sense to avoid these negative effects in the first place by having a system of CPP instead of SS, especially because SS by its coercive transfers guarantees these effects, while gifts or bequests, which are voluntary transfers, do not necessarily mitigate them, as some parents will not and/or cannot provide substantial gifts or bequests.

Thus none of the egalitarian counterarguments I've discussed come to grips with the antiegalitarian effects of SS (as compared with CPP) and/or show how the problems can be remedied (without having a

---

[44] World Bank, *Averting the Old-Age Crisis*, 78–80.

[45] Minor children and spouses are entitled to survivor benefits, but that is not the same as bequests. The survivor benefits are limited by a set formula to a certain percentage of taxes paid, and adult children get nothing. There is no accumulated wealth one can bequeath, because, as I will discuss in the next section, one has no retirement account that one owns.

CPP system). Argument (1) focused on the egalitarian virtues of transfers from young to old, but ignored the fact that the old of later generations do much worse vis-à-vis SS than the old of the earlier generations. Argument (2) tried to make a virtue of the fact that later generations do worse than earlier ones on the grounds that this mitigated the extent to which later generations are (involuntarily) better off than earlier ones but ignored the fact that transfers go from the worse off members of the later generation to the better off members of the earlier generations. Argument (3) at least acknowledged the redistributive problems with SS, but its solution of parental gifts and bequests was a weak remedy for the problem, as compared with having a CPP system that avoided these effects.

Let us now compare CPP to mixed systems. Recall that there were two types of mixed systems: provident systems, which are fully funded by government rather than by private firms, and a system of partial privatization. The former, even when they work well (no government corruption and mismanagement), invest mostly in government bonds that give a lower rate of return than in a CPP system. Although there is not necessarily a problem of intergenerational unfairness here,[46] the lower rate of returns mean that prioritarians should favor a CPP system that gives higher rates of return (because this provides a big boost to the worse off's retirement income), and faced with a choice of two intergenerationally fair systems, contemporary egalitarians, at least those who reject leveling down, should prefer the system with the higher rate of return.[47] As for a system of partial privatization, it is still

---

[46] However, to the extent that a provident system leads to an explosion of government debt, then issues of intergenerational unfairness can arise.

[47] This point also applies to another possible argument for SS. One might argue that while CPP is a sufficient solution to the problem of intergenerational inequalities, it is not a necessary one. Instead, we could treat bygones as bygones, not worry about the differences between the early and mature stages of a PAYGO system, raise SS taxes substantially, and invest some of these taxes. While this would further lower the rate of return, it would insure the financial sustainability of SS in the future, so that those who are young would not face an even worse rate of return in the future (which they will if SS persists and SS taxes are not raised). (I believe that Robert E. Goodin makes an argument of this sort in "Treating Likes Alike, Intergenerationally and Internationally," *Policy Sciences* 32, no. 2 (1999): 195–8, though I am not sure I understand his argument, so my attribution may be incorrect.) However, even assuming such a tax raise is feasible, this argument amounts to saying that we should avoid intergenerational inequality by making sure that all future generations have a

a PAYGO system and thus the arguments I gave for the superiority of a fully funded system still apply to it.

It might be suggested that government management of pension funds could avoid the low rate of return that provident funds have experienced. Government managers could be directed to invest all the SS taxes in the stock market, or in a mixture of stocks and bonds, the way that a private insurance company or pension fund manager would do, so as to maximize long-term returns. However, government management of pension funds is likely to produce poorer returns than private management because government managers' employment and compensation is unlikely to be linked with performance, and without a choice of different managers or pension funds, citizens will have limited ability to discipline inefficient managers. It will also be difficult in a democracy, when such a large amount of assets are at stake, to avoid politicizing the investment process and directing investment to projects favored by special interest groups, rather than to what gives the best rate of return. This worry about politicized and inefficient investments may be why no democratic country has adopted such a system. At most what we see is that some countries, such as Sweden and Canada, have invested some of their SS taxes in the stock market.[48] However, what I want to stress here is that even apart from the lower rate of return and the dangers of politicizing investment decisions, there are other reasons for egalitarians to favor private ownership and management of pension savings accounts.

Individual ownership and control over one's pension savings account means that individuals are taking responsibility, or are at least in a better position to take responsibility, for planning for their retirement, whereas that is significantly lessened when governments control and manage pension accounts. As I pointed out in Chapter 3, egalitarian views about responsibility apply not just to one's past choices but also concern how people can be given incentives to be responsible or

---

very low rate of return. This just seems like another version of leveling down. Surely it is less perverse to avoid intergenerational inequality by raising all future generations' rate of return.

[48] On Canada, see M. Townson, "Strengthening Public Pensions with Private Investment – Canada's Approach to Privatization Pressures," in *Building Social Security: The Challenge of Privatization*, Xenia Scheil-Adulung, ed. (New Brunswick, NJ: Transaction Publishers, 2001), ch. 6. On Sweden, see n. 7.

to take responsibility in the future. Clearly, owning and having control over one's own pension saving account increases these incentives vis-à-vis retirement decisions, and so egalitarians should favor the individual ownership and control of pension accounts that is present in CPP, lacking in SS, and less prominent in mixed systems. What is crucial to notice here is that many of the more affluent members in today's welfare states now have this kind of individual ownership and control because many of them have a private-pension or retirement account to complement their PAYGO "account." CPP enables the poor and the less affluent to enter and participate in this system of individual ownership and control by making them all investors in their retirement, all owners of capital. Egalitarians and prioritarians ought to be wildly enthusiastic about this: the poor and less affluent would own a significant chunk of capital, they would have accumulated significant assets that they could pass on to their children, and the gap between those who own capital and those who don't would be eliminated. What could be better, if one thinks justice requires minimizing unchosen inequalities or tilting toward aiding the worse off?[49]

It may be objected, however, that this argument about the benefits of individual ownership and control for the poor and less affluent members of society overlooks the problem of economic risk. Although the poor and less affluent get individual ownership and control, and a greater rate of return, they become subject to the ups and downs of the market.[50] This at least cancels out the benefits of individual ownership and control and a greater rate of return, particularly for those egalitarians and prioritarians who do not define one's relative or absolute standing only in terms of one's resources but also think considerations of welfare, that is, of happiness or some other desirable psychological state, are relevant for assessing a person's overall situation.

However, this objection is flawed at a number of levels. First, let us recall that CPP has a minimum pension guarantee, which reduces

---

[49] Perhaps one might argue that egalitarians would favor eliminating the legal right to bequeath wealth, i.e., favor a 100 percent inheritance tax. I doubt this; it's hard to see why they would oppose those who are less affluent having wealth that they could bequeath. Most likely, egalitarians would favor a progressive tax on bequests. This is Dworkin's position; see *Sovereign Virtue*, 348–9.

[50] Norman Daniels, *Am I My Parents' Keeper?* (New York: Oxford University Press, 1988), 134–5, raises this as a reason not to get rid of SS.

economic risk to some extent. Even with a period of poor stock-market returns, such as in the United States from 2000–2, the chances that the value of one's pension at retirement will be above the minimum guarantee is quite high, given the long-term performance of the stock market.[51] If the worry is about economic risk after retirement (e.g., outliving one's annuity; see n. 53), there are also ways to handle this, and it is compatible with CPP to require some kind of regulation to minimize this risk.[52] Second, and more important, the objection fails to make a comparative argument by just focusing on the risks involved in CPP and ignoring the risks involved in SS (or in mixed systems). SS and mixed systems subject everyone to political risks: benefits may be reduced or the benefit formula recalculated, taxes may be increased, government investment of SS taxes may be mismanaged or used to fund other government programs, and indexing may be readjusted or suspended, and so forth. (These are very close to certainties for

[51] Feldstein, "The Future of Social Security Pensions in Europe," table 1. Feldstein uses figures from the U.S. stock market, and so the probability would be somewhat elevated for worse-performing markets, but the general point still holds. Andrew Biggs, "Personal Accounts in a Down Market: How Recent Stock Market Declines Affect the Social Security Reform Debate," in *Social Security and Its Discontents: Perspectives on Choice*, Michael D. Tanner, ed. (Washington, DC: The Cato Institute, 2005), 333–47. Biggs compares the return from a private account invested in diversified stocks and one invested in 60 percent stocks and 40 percent bonds with the average PAYGO "returns" (i.e., the ratio of taxes paid to benefits received) and notes that the data show that over almost any forty-year period dating from 1927, the pure stock portfolio would always do better than a PAYGO system, and a mixed portfolio system would do better in almost all forty-year periods. He also provides data that show that the existence of a few bad years makes very little difference to the long-run rate of return. Feldstein, using figures from 1945 to 1995, examines the probability that a mixed portfolio would receive a return worse than the average return in a PAYGO system and concludes that the probability is low. Admittedly, Feldstein didn't include data that incorporated the very poor returns in 2000–2 (he wrote the paper in 2001), but given Biggs's point that these kind of years don't affect long-run rate of return very much, this omission doesn't matter much. Of course, Feldstein and Biggs's data concerns the U.S. stock market, and many other countries have worse-performing markets, but given the considerably higher rate of return in private accounts, the general point still holds.

[52] The best strategy seems to be to annuitize about one-half of one's pension and take the rest in phased withdrawals. See Max Alier and Dimitri Vittas, "Personal Pension Plans and Stock Market Volatility," in Holzman and Stiglitz, *New Ideas about Old Age Security*, ch. 11. For a discussion of possible regulations for the retirement phase, see Jan Walliser, "Regulation of Withdrawals in Individual Account Systems," in ibid., 382–9. Also see n. 82 for a suggestion of a market-based mechanism that might obviate the perceived need for such regulation.

SS given the problems with the late stage of a PAYGO system.) CPP subjects one to economic risks, but to a considerable extent one is allowed to choose one's level of risk. For example, a person can pick a less risky portfolio that will probably have lower returns or pick a riskier portfolio that will likely have higher but more volatile returns. Comparing the two kinds of risks, it is clear that CPP is preferable because there is some degree of escape from or control over the risk (as well as a minimum pension guarantee), whereas in SS, there is only escape for those who have complementary private pensions. So even granting the point that economic risk may lower the value of owning and controlling one's pension saving account and receiving a greater rate of return, the kind of risk in CPP is preferable.

I conclude that the egalitarian and prioritarian case for CPP is quite strong. Because it is fully funded, it avoids the intergenerational inequalities of a PAYGO system; because it has a minimum pension guarantee funded by progressive taxation, it has more progressive intragenerational redistribution than a PAYGO system; and because it is privately managed, it has a higher rate of return than any government-managed system. Furthermore, it enables the poor and less affluent to take responsibility for planning their retirement by giving them the kind of individual ownership and control over their retirement income and assets that right now only the more affluent have.

5.4 Positive Rights and Security

In a CPP system, people own their pensions and have a right to it based upon contract.[53] In SS, by contrast, there are no individual accounts, and people do not own their pensions. In some countries, this lack of a contractually based right to a pension in SS has led the courts to rule that there is no legal right to a pension – as in the United States, where the Supreme Court reasoned that because SS is not based on contract and is not akin to a private annuity or insurance, the government has

---

53 What about the minimum pension guarantee? Is there an explicit legal right to that minimum? I have found no discussion of this in the writings on the Chilean system, which suggests that the issue has not been litigated. Notice, however, that even if that minimum was not guaranteed, CPP would still be better than a SS system where there is no firm legal right to a pension, because most people don't end up needing CPP's guarantee and rely upon their market pension to which they do have a right.

the right to alter benefits if it so chooses.[54] In other countries with SS, courts have made decisions that appear to be quite different. In Italy, a constitutional court did hold that the government must make up the difference between the benefits it promised and the reduced benefits it paid.[55] However, the nature of a PAYGO system necessarily limits the enforceability of such promises. Because the system is (largely or completely) unfunded and very sensitive to demographic changes, changes in taxes and benefits must be frequent. After the court's ruling, Italy continued to reduce its benefits (not surprisingly, because it spends more on government pensions than any other country).[56] This point about the limits on enforceability of promises in SS is also illustrated by court decisions in Germany. In Germany, SS benefits are considered to be property, and constitutional protections for property rights or prohibitions against retroactive legislation might seem to provide a basis for a legal right to a pension. However, the courts have generally allowed governments to make changes in promised benefits, on the grounds of financial necessity or making the system more efficient, provided the changes aren't too sudden, drastic, or don't impoverish the recipients.[57] Overall, there is no legal right to a pension in

---

[54] *Helvering v. Davis*, 301 US 619 [1937] and *Fleming v. Nestor*, 363 US 603 [1960].

[55] World Bank, *Averting the Old-Age Crisis*, 113.

[56] Daniele Franco, "Italy: A Never Ending Pension Reform," in *Social Security Pension Reform in Europe*, Martin Feldstein and Horst Siebert, eds. (Chicago: University of Chicago Press, 2002), 211–22. In addition, there are some special features of the Italian political system and the nature of the 1994 ruling that make it unsurprising that this ruling did not alter the difficulty of enforcing promises made in the Italian SS system. First, the ruling required that individual claimants would have to go to court to get their increased pension, which is a time-consuming and difficult process. Second, the ruling may very well have conflicted with the Italian constitution, which specifically states that new state expenses must be authorized by a new law, which implies that courts cannot mandate new expenses. I am grateful to Professor Stefania Ninnatti of the Public Law Institute, School of Law, Milan, for explaining these points to me (e-mail, February 2004).

[57] Nils Eliasson, *Protection of Accrued Pension Rights: An Inquiry into Reforms of Statutory and Occupational Pension Schemes in a German, Norwegian and Swedish Context* (Lund, Sweden: Akademibokhandeln, 2001), 88–95. Norway has even weaker judicial protection of SS pension rights than does Germany because the protection is based only on a constitutional prohibition against retroactive legislation, and courts have ruled that legislatures are only prohibited from making manifestly unreasonable or unjust decisions. In Sweden, there is no constitutional protection for pension rights in the SS system, although legislatures have proceeded very cautiously in making any changes. For Norway, see 104–6; for Sweden, see 121,183–6.

SS, or if there is some judicial protection given to promises made to beneficiaries, it is not terribly strong protection, and so clearly one's right to a pension is far more protected in the contractually based CPP system.

As for CPP versus mixed systems, the contrast is less dramatic. A government-managed system with individual accounts does provide a right to one's pension and so does the private account in a system of partial privatization. However, CPP is still somewhat superior. In a government-managed system the right is more restricted, as one is unable to direct the course of one's investments or choose one's pension fund; in a partially privatized system one has only a right to a certain percent of one's pension because much of the pension remains in SS.

Will things look different if we examine the grounds of arguments for positive rights? I am not aware of any arguments whose specific aim is to show that there is a moral right to a state pension, so we must focus on general arguments for basic positive rights and see how they apply to the choice between SS and CPP. As I discussed in Chapter 4, the key argument is J. Donald Moon's, which says that state services should be universal and provided as social insurance, rather than as means-tested benefits, in order to justify positive rights without undermining self-respect. Universal provision means that these services are provided to every citizen, so no stigma is attached to receiving them, and social insurance means that one's positive rights are based upon having contributed to their provision. Because one's contributions help to fund one's benefits, one is viewed as an independent person, not someone purely dependent upon others for meeting one's needs, or on welfare. Another way Moon puts his argument is that these social-insurance programs help to balance welfare rights with the notion of responsibility, which is inherent in the notion of a moral agent. The principle of individual responsibility implies that relations among adults will be based on reciprocity, not on asymmetrical relations of dependence. The fact that one's right to a pension is based on contributions means that it is no threat to this norm of reciprocity.

Moon's argument is meant to show why social insurance is better than means-tested benefits. If, however, we use his argument to compare SS with CPP, then CPP wins decisively on three counts. First, in SS a person does not get the result of his or her contribution, while in CPP everyone except those needing a safety net gets the result of his or her contribution (plus interest). Second, SS is a serious threat to the norm of reciprocity because of its severe intergenerational transfers, while in CPP there is little if any harmful transfer between generations. Third, the indirect way SS meets needs is quite harmful for the poor of later generations, while CPP does not have this feature. Thus, rather than indirectly meeting needs in a way that does not violate the norm of reciprocity, SS is a significant threat to that norm and is a poor way of meeting needs, while CPP does not violate the norm of reciprocity and is a comparatively better way of meeting needs. (These arguments also apply to the comparison between a system of partial privatization and CPP because the former still has the same features of not being fully funded, intergenerational transfers, and so forth. They do not, however, apply to a fully funded system with individual accounts that is managed by the government. In what follows, Moon's argument will be understood to be neutral between that system and CPP.)

I will assume that Moon would have to concede the points mentioned previously. I can think of two strategies he could employ to reply to my argument despite admitting these facts. One strategy is to argue that although SS is objectionable on the grounds that it violates a norm of reciprocity or contribution, CPP is objectionable because of its paternalism: by forcing a person to save for his or her own retirement, CPP treats sane adults as if they were children who must be protected from harming themselves, thus undermining their self-respect. On the other hand, SS forces workers to save for others' retirement and so does not face this problem of paternalism. Thus CPP and SS are on par as far as balancing positive rights with self-respect, which, after all, was Moon's main concern. CPP has a comparative advantage because it is no threat to a norm of reciprocity or contribution, while SS has a comparative advantage on the issue of paternalism.

Now as Joel Feinberg has pointed out,[58] whether a law or policy is paternalistic is a matter of its (predominant) justification. Because the issue here is the citizens' sense of self-respect, we have to ask how the citizens understand the justification of CPP and SS. However, there are often multiple justifications for a law or policy, and this muddies the waters. CPP clearly can be justified nonpaternalistically: I've already

[58] Joel Feinberg, *Harm to Self* (New York: Oxford University Press, 1986), 16–17.

argued that it is a fairer system than SS. SS can be justified on paternalist grounds: you might wonder why workers must save for other people's retirement, and the answer is that these others can't be trusted to save for their own pensions.[59] Furthermore, in a number of respects CPP involves greater trust of the citizenry than SS: citizens have much more freedom within the system to choose their own particular type of retirement plan, how much to invest (provided it's not below a minimum), where to invest, and when to retire.[60] I conclude that an argument that CPP is more paternalistic than SS and, in that regard, more potentially destructive of self-respect, is speculative at best. If one wants to avoid all taint of paternalism, the best way to do so is to avoid any system of forced savings.

A different strategy that Moon might employ is to argue that my criticisms of SS are irrelevant for his main concern. That concern is that the legal protection of positive rights not undermine self-respect, and because self-respect depends on one's beliefs, not on whether these beliefs are true, then whether recipients of SS get the result of their contributions or SS is a threat to a norm of reciprocity is not of crucial importance. What is of crucial importance is that the system be widely perceived as embodying or being compatible with the principle of contribution or reciprocity and not be viewed pejoratively as "welfare." In this regard, Moon might continue, SS has generally been a resounding success. The point of this rebuttal on behalf of Moon is not to show that SS is better than CPP but to show that it is no worse as regards embodying positive rights to a pension without undermining self-respect.

This rebuttal, however, has three problems. First, one may wonder how long the belief that SS is compatible with a norm of contribution

---

[59] One might argue that this can't be a paternalist argument because the persons who can't be trusted to save are not the persons being required to save. However, as Feinberg notes, paternalism is a matter of the justification of a law or policy, and if the justification for forcing A to save for B is that otherwise B will harm B (rather than, say, that B will harm A), then the rationale for the law is paternalistic. Although this is a rather indirect way of meeting a paternalist objective, it is paternalist nonetheless so long as the aim is to prevent B from harming B. Furthermore, as I argue later, PAYGO systems are not infrequently misunderstood and workers come to think that their taxes are being invested for their own retirement, in which case they may view the justification of SS as paternalist in the more obvious sense.

[60] This argument also applies to a comparison of mixed systems with CPP.

or reciprocity will last or even whether it is still widespread anymore; recent developments in the United States throw doubt on this claim.[61] It would hardly be surprising to see this belief collapse because it is based upon an illusion. And as I shall discuss in the section on public justification, there is something very troubling with a program whose support depends crucially upon illusions.

Second, the value of self-respect is diminished if it is based upon illusions. After all, presumably the reason why Moon thought it important to argue that the legal instantiation of positive rights does not undermine self-respect was that self-respect is supposed to be an extremely important value, and if there is a threat that its value will be diminished by SS then this is a reason to favor CPP. (But this is not true for CPPs because the latter are founded on a genuine insurance principle of getting one's contribution back plus interest.)[62]

---

[61] It is not entirely clear what Americans really believe about SS. Americans consistently express support for SS in the abstract, but majorities or near-majorities express low confidence in the program. Majorities support partial privatization and all candidates who ran on a platform of partial privatization won in the 2002 elections. Furthermore, more people think that SS is riskier than partial privatization because SS cannot pay all the benefits it has promised. The latter would seem to imply that many Americans no longer believe SS embodies reciprocity between generations. However, how many people make that inference is unclear because, as I noted in Chapter 2, many people are prone to illogical reasoning. Still, support for partial privatization and a recognition that SS may not pay what it has promised certainly throws doubt on the claim that in general Americans think SS embodies reciprocity between generations.

For the data on Americans' attitudes toward SS see John Zogby et al., "Public Opinion and Private Accounts: Measuring Risk and Confidence in Rethinking Social Security," Cato Project on Social Security Choice (Washington, DC: The Cato Institute, January 6, 2003) and Fay Lomax Cook and Lawrence R. Jacobs, "Assessing Assumptions about Attitudes towards Social Security: Popular Claims Meet Hard Data," in *The Future of Social Insurance: Incremental Action or Fundamental Reform*, Peter Edelman, Dalls L. Salisbury, and Pamela J. Larson, eds. (Washington, DC: Brookings Institution, 2002), ch. 5. Fox and Jacobs and Zogby et al. disagree about majorities' support for partial privatization. Zogby affirms it, while Fox and Jacobs deny it, arguing that the support only exists in the abstract, but that when questions about the risks posed by private accounts are added to the question, support drops. However, Zogby points out that a question that just mentions risk of private accounts without mentioning risks of SS is biased in SS's favor. As I noted in the preceding text, when questions are asked about which is a greater risk, SS failing to keep its promises or people losing money in private accounts, more people choose the former.

[62] The strength of this reason is unclear. It's difficult to say to what extent the value of self-respect is diminished if it is based on illusions. Furthermore, the sources of

Third, and perhaps most important, Moon's point was that a necessary condition for the justification of positive rights is that their legal instantiation not undermine self-respect, but clearly a sufficient condition is that there be a solid basis or rationale for these rights. Recall that in Chapter 2 I pointed out that need would seem the most promising way to ground positive rights, but that Moon argued that grounding these rights by contribution was preferable because it would not threaten the notion that one was an independent person worthy of self-respect, and it would not divide society into two classes: one needy and dependent and the other providing the support for the needy. Because contribution is a suspect way of grounding rights to one's pension in SS, and if need as a basis for supporting positive rights is tainted because of its threat to self-respect, there seems to be no plausible way to ground SS within the realm of positive-rights arguments. Because CPP does have a legitimate ground in that realm, that is, contribution, then conceding that SS may lack such a ground is relevant, to put it mildly.

Closely related to the question of positive rights is the value or importance of security. SS is often justified in terms of creating economic security for the elderly or, more realistically, in terms of minimizing economic insecurity during retirement. One's security is a function of (1) a guarantee or high probability of an income and (2) the amount of income guaranteed. Now in the early stage of PAYGO, present retirees and workers who will retire within fifteen to thirty-five years have a greater degree of security than they would have under any private alternative. SS in that stage has a higher degree of (2) than CPP, although it is no worse on (1) because at this stage, the redefinition of benefits is to the retirees' favor and the changes in tax rates is only mildly to the workers' disadvantage. However, in the later stages retirees and workers have a lower degree of (1) and (2) than in CPP. The rate of return is lower, worries about whether promises will be kept are widespread, and redefinition of benefits to the retirees and workers' disfavor is common.

self-respect are multiple, and it's unclear to what extent the self-respect of SS recipients is linked with a view that they are entitled to their pensions or are not harming later generations.

Another way to put this comparison is that SS redistributes security over time. The early generations are made more secure at the price of reducing security for later ones. On the other hand, CPP keeps all generations at an even keel of at least moderately high security.[63] I assume that the value of security lessens if it is achieved at the expense of others, and so I conclude that CPP is better than SS on this score. The same conclusion would be reached if one were concerned with overall security over time; although there is no way to even semiprecisely aggregate this, a fairly high level over time seems to beat a very high level followed by a decreasing level.

These arguments about security also show that CPP is better than mixed systems. A partially privatized system has roughly the same problem of redistributing security over time, and although this is avoided in a fully funded system with government management, that system's low rate of return means that it provides less security than CPP.

Overall, the results of this section are that those who believe there are basic positive rights should favor CPP. First, only CPP gives one a full-fledged legal right to one's pension. Second, Moon's argument about justifying positive rights without undermining self-respect by basing such rights on contribution, not asymmetric relations of dependence or need, supports CPP (and a fully funded government-managed system), not SS. Third, CPP is better at providing security than SS or mixed systems.

5.5 Community, Solidarity, and Pension Systems

The prospect of privatizing SS in the United States has prompted some communitarian discussion of SS,[64] and I will rely upon that along with the communitarian criteria I discussed in prior chapters for evaluating social insurance versus market alternatives. Four of those criteria seem relevant to the choice of pension systems: universality, shared

---

[63] It might be objected that this is false, because in the beginning of a CPP system those who hadn't saved much on their own voluntarily, or who invested imprudently, will have little security when they retire. All this means is that in the beginning of a CPP system, the safety net may have to be larger than in the later stages. It doesn't negate the point that a CPP system does not redistribute security through time.

[64] See Etzioni and Brodbeck, *The Intergenerational Covenant.*

responsibility, reciprocity, and fidelity.[65] Both systems are universal. However, it appears that SS expresses a deeper sense of shared responsibility. A CPP system establishes a property right to a pension and is basically a system of individual responsibility plus a residual safety net for the indigent. Although SS does have traces of a notion of individual responsibility (a person's earning history helps determines her benefit level), its lack of individual property rights to a pension and its PAYGO financing mean that it is primarily others (in one's generations and later generations) that assume responsibility for one's retirement. As the U.S. Social Security Advisory Commission report put it, "Social Security is based on the premise that we're all in this together, with everyone sharing responsibility not only for contributing to their own and their family's security, but also the security of everyone else, present and future."[66]

However, this more collectivized sense of responsibility is achieved at a substantial cost, namely huge intergenerational inequities. Defending SS because it embodies a deeper sense of shared responsibility than a privatized system comes at the price of admitting that SS is worse than a private system vis-à-vis minimizing intergenerational inequities. Furthermore, SS is far worse than CPP on the criterion of fidelity. Virtually all SS systems are steeped with deceptive rhetoric and misleading terminology. Calling SS "social insurance," the payroll taxes "contributions,"[67] government IOUs a "trust fund,"[68] all give the distinct impression that SS is a funded pension plan, rather than a PAYGO system. In the United States at least, the illusion that SS was akin to funded pensions may very well have been crucial for obtaining

---

[65] No communitarian, to my knowledge, discusses democratic participation or responsiveness as a value for pension systems. I am not entirely sure why this is so. Perhaps it is because it would be unfeasible. Perhaps it is because while retirement choices reflect and constitute one's conception of the good, this is clearly a matter of individual, not collective, decision.

[66] Social Security Administration, *Report of the 1994–1996 Advisory Council on Social Security Volume 1: Findings and Recommendations* (Washington, DC: Government Printing Office, 1997) 89, their emphasis.

[67] Furthermore, that the payroll tax is split between employee and employer may give the impression that the employee only pays half of the tax, which is almost certainly false. Employers usually lower wages to compensate for the imposition of the payroll tax.

[68] Even PAYGO systems with some degree of advance funding do not have a trust fund, for reasons I noted in section 5.2.1.

the high level of support that it has enjoyed[69] (or has enjoyed until very recently). And even if citizens believe that they are not being promised a market rate of return and understand that SS cannot promise such a return, PAYGO systems make it very difficult for them to understand the system and determine just what is being promised. The relationship between taxes paid and benefits received is opaque: frequent changes are made in the taxation and benefit rates and schedules, its actuarial status is heavily dependent upon population trends and growth in wages, and in general the system is subject to frequent political maneuvering. It is unsurprising that accurate information about the way the system is being run, its likely future performance, and so forth is hard to come by because the absence of individual property rights in a PAYGO system means there is no incentive to provide such information (and makes it harder to enforce any obligation to provide such information).[70]

CPP is pellucid compared to SS and its promises are not difficult to keep. CPP, except for the minimum pension guarantee, is a defined contribution system: the value of one's pension at retirement depends upon market returns. Unless fraud is present, defined contribution systems generally deliver market rates of return, which is what they are supposed to do. It is easy to understand the relationship between premiums and benefits. Private-pension plans have both the incentive and the obligation to provide information about their actuarial status and

[69] See Carolyn L. Weaver, *The Crisis in Social Security* (Durham, NC: Duke University Press, 1982), 80–6, 123–4; Martha Derthick, *Policymaking for Social Security* (Washington, DC: Brookings Institution, 1979), 199–201, 204; and John Attarian, *Social Security: False Consciousness and Crisis*, ch. 4–10. Virginia P. Reno and Robert B. Friedland, "Strong Support but Low Confidence: What Explains the Contradiction?" in *Social Security in the 21st Century*, 183, maintain that data since the mid-1970s show that the public has a good understanding of the basic features of SS. However, the surveys they cite do not explicitly ask questions about the PAYGO nature of the system. Recent surveys show that the public has more confidence in private pensions than in SS (ibid., 186), which may indicate that the public now understands how SS works.

[70] E.g., not until 1990 was a law passed in the United States requiring the Social Security Administration to provide personal benefit earnings and benefit estimates to everyone for whom a current address can be determined. This began in October 1999; statements to those under age fifty are not required to include estimates of monthly retirement benefits. Reno and Friedland, "Strong Support but Low Confidence," 194, n. 8. In many countries, even such minimal measures are lacking. See Axel Borsch-Supen, "Comments," in Holzman and Stiglitz, *New Ideas about Old Age Security*, 74.

their expected rate of return, so as a result the investor or participant has a good basis for understanding the system.[71] With the exception of the definition of the minimum contribution and minimum retirement pension, CPP is not inherently subject to political manipulation, and one has a genuine property right in the system, which adds further incentive to follow and monitor the progress of one's investment or contribution.

It might be said in reply that the comparison offered here is unfair: of course defined contribution systems can keep their promises because the whole point of a defined contribution system is that no specific return is promised and the recipient bears the investment risk. Defined benefit systems remove this risk from the recipient but in so doing make it harder to keep a promise to maintain a certain benefit level. However, this reply fails. To ask whether SS or CPP is better at keeping its promises or commitments is a separate matter from whether or not their promises or commitments were easy or difficult to keep. More to the point, given the long-run performance of the capital market, CPP's promise of a market rate of return is a promise that one's return will be above most other forms of investment (e.g., government securities, CDs, etc.), and therefore even people with modest incomes can look forward to an adequate retirement. SS cannot, in its later stage, make or keep such a promise. As I noted earlier, SS in both the late and the early stage is not really a defined benefit system, given the frequent changes in its benefit formulas. Defined benefit systems that tend to keep their promises, such as well-managed occupational pensions,[72] are fully funded or nearly so, unlike SS. It is this lack of funding, rather than it being a defined benefit system, that makes SS unable to keep its promises.

Thus communitarians should favor CPP, not SS. CPP lacks intergenerational inequities, keeps its promises, and expresses a sense of

---

[71] This point is overlooked by Peter Diamond, who argues that in a defined-contribution system it is very difficult to determine one's future benefits that depend on the particular pattern of investments and on the pricing of annuities. In the abstract, Diamond is probably right. But given individual ownership of one's retirement account, and competition among funds, the incentives to provide that information (and the obligation to provide it) make defined contributions considerably less opaque than in SS where those incentives and obligation are much less. See ibid., 76–7.

[72] World Bank, *Averting the Old-Age Crisis*, ch. 5 provides a detailed analysis.

shared responsibility using its safety net for the elderly poor. Admittedly, the kind of shared responsibility involved in CPP is more individualistic than communitarians would like. However, the more collectivized sense of shared responsibility in SS is achieved at the price of creating enormous intergenerational inequities and making misleading promises that it cannot keep. This is too high a price for communitarians to pay, as such inequities and the failure to keep promises present a real threat of creating social division and undermining solidarity between the old and the young. Furthermore, we would do well to remind ourselves of the limits of intergenerational sharing of responsibility. The living cannot share responsibility with the dead. Shared responsibility between completely removed generations – those whose lifetimes never overlap with those of the present generation[73] – exists only in a symbolic sense. Although there may be value to SS's expression of symbolic bonds between generations, it's dubious that this value outweighs its actual unfairness to later generations.

Let us now turn to comparing CPP to mixed systems. The arguments I made about intergenerational inequities and fidelity also apply to partially privatized systems because they still remain, fundamentally, as PAYGO systems. However, it might seem that a fully funded system that is government managed would fit communitarian criteria the best. Because they are fully funded, they avoid intergenerational inequities and keep their promises. And if communitarians think of government investment as a sort of proximate stand-in for a kind of collective, shared responsibility, then perhaps this system is better than CPP in meeting the communitarian criterion of shared responsibility.

The problem with this argument is that it completely ignores the political strife that would result from such a system, a point I alluded to in section 5.3. Communitarians presumably want to avoid the fierce and unresolvable political struggle that divides citizens, undermining a common set of interests and sense of solidarity, yet that is what almost certainly would occur if, in a democratic society, governments managed the investment of SS taxes, assuming, as I think is likely, that

---

[73] I adopt the terminology from Peter Laslett and James S. Fishkin, "Introduction: Processional Justice," in *Justice between Age Groups and Generations*, Peter Laslett and James S. Fishkin, eds. (New Haven: Yale University Press, 1992), 6.

there will be pressures to invest at least some of these in the stock market to get a good rate of return. Disputes about the right way for the government to invest involve complex problems: we usually rely on experts for investment advice because sound investing involves skills and information most of us lack. When investment becomes collective and political, it's hard to see what commonly accepted principles would be used to solve disputes concerning how to invest payroll taxes. There will be disagreements about investment strategies, and these will be intertwined with fierce moral disagreements about the appropriateness of certain investments. (E.g., should we invest in companies that do a substantial business in authoritarian or dictatorial regimes? In tobacco stocks? Liquor companies? Companies that provide benefits to unmarried couples and gays? Gun manufacturers?) Although there is perhaps a practical solution to these problems – a politically insulated agency that invests passively in index funds – the pot of money available is so great (trillions of dollars) that the temptation for meddling may well be irresistible, offering no alternative to fierce and endless disputes about investment decisions.

It might be said, in reply, that CPP also will have its share of political disputes because decisions about where to set the safety net are political decisions and can be expected to divide the public into two groups: those who have private pensions and those who rely on the minimum pension guarantee. However, disputes about a minimum pension level are unlikely to be as fierce or as unresolvable. For one thing, the amount of money involved is much less, which tends to dampen political disputes. A more important point is that disputes about a safety net in a CPP system involve a relatively simple problem: at what level should the minimum pension guarantee be set? Certain commonly accepted principles could be used to solve the problem: the guarantee should be set high enough to eliminate significant elderly poverty but not so high as to create a moral hazard problem, that is, tempt people to engage in excessively risky investments, knowing that if they fail, the government will bail them out.[74] This solution to the problem of where to set the minimum pension guarantee is not merely a theoretical point but a practical one. If the minimum pension guarantee is set at close to today's average benefit of SS, that eliminates

---

[74] Furthermore, as I noted in section 5.2.5, CPP prohibits extremely risky investments.

any severe problem of elderly poverty, but the benefits from long-term investment are so much greater than today's average SS benefit, that there is little risk of moral hazard.[75] By contrast, disputes about the right way for the government to invest involve complex problems and the chances of a solution to these problems (e.g., a politically insulated board that passively invests in index funds) are unlikely to come about.

CPP is superior to SS on communitarian grounds, and it is also superior to mixed systems. Although a fully funded system managed by government may look like the most promising system from a communitarian viewpoint, this is only so if we abstract away from political realities about the type of disputes such management would engender.

5.6 Public Justification, Epistemic Accessibility, and the Superiority of Private Pensions

Until very recently, SS was quite popular, and even now its popularity has only diminished somewhat. However, the principle of epistemic accessibility means that this popularity fails to provide justification for a program to the extent that this support was due to the public being misled and/or being misinformed. I already pointed out that this is true of SS's popularity, although it is not that difficult for an ordinary person to obtain reasonably accurate or reliable information about CPP.

What about mixed systems? Clearly partial privatization will help. By creating some direct competition between SS and a carved out or added on private-pension component, citizens will probably become somewhat more aware of how SS operates. Furthermore, one can imagine some reforms to the SS part of the system that would also help:[76]

1. SS could be placed in a separate budget, rules could be established to prevent it from being influenced by the normal budgetary maneuvering, changes in tax rates and benefits could be subject to

---

[75] Ferrara and Tanner, *A New Deal for Social Security*, 160–1, 211–12. Their argument seems plausible for countries like the United States whose long-term history of stock returns is quite good. However, in countries where the long range of performance of the stock market has been less robust, the minimum pension guarantee may need to be set somewhat lower; otherwise the moral hazard problem may become significant.

[76] Some of these changes are suggested by Etzioni and Brodbeck, *The Intergenerational Covenant*, 24–7.

a supermajority rule, and so forth. In some countries, some of these reforms are already in place.

2. SS could be financed exclusively by an employee payroll tax in order to avoid disguising its costs to present workers.

3. Advance funding could be increased to limit the PAYGO nature of the system, with the taxes invested in whatever would lessen the implicit public-pension debt with the least risk (e.g., some combination of private and government securities). This already exists in some countries.

4. Though genuine private property rights are incompatible with SS, the government could provide individuals with the equivalent of accurate quarterly or annual reports and make widely available accurate information about SS's actuarial status, expected rates of return, and so forth. Doing so would probably compel governments to make the benefit schedules simpler and easier to follow. To some extent this has been introduced in countries that have adopted notional defined-contribution accounts in their SS systems.

However, even if we suppose that all of these reforms could happen, a reformed SS with a private component still remains a PAYGO system. This means that the ratio of taxes paid to benefits payed out is heavily influenced by such factors as demographics, which, in turn, implies that there will be no set contribution or benefit, that determining one's rate of return, the actuarial status of the system, and so forth will necessarily remain difficult compared with CPP. Even if the reforms were enacted, CPP would still be superior to SS as far as epistemic accessibility is concerned.

The other mixed system, a fully funded but government-managed system, avoids the problems inherent in understanding a PAYGO system. However, because one will not be able to direct the flow or course of investments, choose one's pension fund and the like, then the incentive as well as obligation to communicate clear information to the account holders is limited, and therefore CPP is also more epistemically accessible than this system.

There is another way of trying to make SS more epistemically accessible that does not involve adopting a mixed system and is worth a mention. One could actually increase the PAYGO nature of the system and make this explicit. The SS system could be redescribed as "old-age assistance" programs or something to that effect, and advance funding and references to trust funds could be abandoned. The system could be financed largely or completely by general taxation, thus helping to eliminate confusion between a tax and a genuine investment. Adding a healthy dose of means testing to the system (e.g., prohibiting those in the top quintile of income from obtaining public pensions) could also facilitate breaking the comparison of social to market insurance.

However, although in one sense these suggested reforms would make SS more easily comprehended by the average citizen, by making it clear that SS has nothing to do with market insurance, in other respects they would make it less epistemically accessible. That is because if SS (now called old-age assistance under these proposed reforms) becomes completely integrated into other government programs by being financed by general revenues, abandoning analogies to market insurance, and so forth, it becomes even more subject to political maneuvering. As such, changes in benefits paid and taxes required might become more, not less, frequent, and the cost of the system would become harder, not easier, to comprehend.

There is, perhaps, an even deeper problem with trying to make the PAYGO nature of SS more explicit. Recall that the problem at hand is that public support does not translate into public justification if the public is misled or misinformed about the institution it supports. Many of the reforms we have discussed are designed to make it easier to obtain accurate information about SS. But if making that information available would eliminate or drastically reduce public support for SS, then the issue of the relationship between public support and justification wouldn't arise in the first place for SS. Were governments to advertise loudly, clearly, and persistently that the system is PAYGO, this would mean letting citizens know that there are significant intergenerational transfers that harm later generations, that one's taxes are not being invested in a genuine trust fund, and that it should not be confused with market insurance (for even with partial funding the analogy is strained). In the United States there is evidence that equating SS with a fully funded pension system (or viewing them as closely analogous) was and has been crucial to its support, and although one cannot rule out the possibility that in different political cultures such a system would be supported by a public knowledgeable of the nature of SS, it does seem unlikely in light of its distributive unfairness, redistribution of security, and restrictions on freedom. Because CPP does not have these problems (or has them to a lesser degree) accurate information about its nature does not seem an obstacle to it obtaining public support.

5.7 Conclusion

The case for replacing the PAYGO system of SS with CPP is quite strong. For egalitarians and prioritarians, CPP is far better because it eliminates SS's intergenerational unfairness, has more progressive redistribution, provides higher rates of return, and makes virtually everyone an investor in their own retirement. For positive-rights theorists, CPP is obviously better because it gives everyone a right to their pension and creates real security for all generations rather than making early generations more secure at the price of making later ones less secure. For communitarians, the intergenerational inequities of a PAYGO system and its failure to keep its promises overshadow whatever (mostly symbolic) advantages SS has in its system of collective responsibility, and so a CPP that keeps its promises and eliminates these inequities is far better. Perhaps the easiest case for CPP is based on the requirement of epistemic accessibility. SS is incredibly complicated, full of misleading and deceptive rhetoric, whereas a system of private pensions is a relatively simple matter easily handled by market institutions that have the incentives and the obligations to provide accurate information.

Mixed systems are to some extent an improvement over SS but not as good as CPP. Partial privatization is still a PAYGO system and thus still has PAYGO's problems: it is intergenerationally unfair, won't give the less affluent the same kind of wealth and ability to be an investor in one's retirement as in a CPP system, is still fairly opaque and reliant on misleading rhetoric about trust funds, and one only has a right to a certain portion of one's pension. As for provident systems, even when they work the way they are supposed to – without government corruption and mismanagement – their rates of return are lower than in a privately managed system, the ability to control and direct the course of one's investment is less than in CPP, and if we imagine them in a democratic context with debates about how to invest the SS taxes, the political strife would likely be enormous.

Appendix B

Comparing PAYGO's Rate of Return with a CPP System

PAYGO systems in their mature stage provide a very slight positive rate of return, close to 2 percent. But that is an average, and, for many groups, the rate of return is close to zero and may be negative. (Furthermore, in countries where population growth is below the replacement rate, the average of return is near or below zero.) The actual rate of return depends on a variety of circumstances: the degree of maturity of the system, whether it is a pure PAYGO or one with some degree of advance funding, how long one paid taxes into the system, age of retirement, the benefit formula used to determine payouts, and life-span, and so forth, but the demographics of a low ratio of workers to retirees guarantees that the days of substantial rates of return in the early stages are over. How then, does CPP compare? The most general answer is that it will pay better because the long run rate of return for equities or a mixture of stocks and bonds is higher. How much better depends on a variety of factors listed in the following text:

1. The time period under consideration. Obviously, stocks provide no guaranteed return, but in exchange for the greater risk they will, over the long run, do better than any other investment. The relevant time period to compare investment in stocks, or a mixture of stocks and bonds, with the rate of return in the mature phase of PAYGO is probably forty to forty-five years because that is roughly how long an average person in a CPP system will be invested in the market (although after retirement, part of the money may remain invested,

unless one converts all of one's investment into a fixed annuity upon retirement). With increasing life-span and delayed retirements, we could probably increase this figure to fifty years. However, we need to look also at one half of these time periods because arguably it is close to the time when people become middle-aged that they really focus on their retirement and also because in a CPP system without a fixed retirement age, one needs to consider that some of those who do quite well in the market may desire an early retirement. Hence, two time periods seem particularly salient: forty to fifty years and twenty to twenty-five years.

2. The portfolio mix. Stocks do better than bonds in the long run, but the former are riskier. It's probably reasonable to assume that as people get nearer to retirement more of their portfolio will shift toward bonds (particularly for those who are more risk averse). Hence, it probably makes sense to compare some kind of time-sensitive mix of stocks and bonds, at least for the forty- to fifty-year period.

3. The country in question. Work by Elroy Dimson, Paul Marsh, and Mike Staunton, who studied twenty-one of the world's largest stock markets' returns over the past 101 years, indicates that rates of return and the volatility of stock markets vary significantly.[77] In Canada, Australia, and the United States, over any twenty-year period the rate of return is positive and for virtually all of the twenty-year periods significantly above what a PAYGO system pays in its mature phase. For other countries, however, one has to go to a longer time period to get these results. In the case of the two worst stock markets – Belgium and Italy – only over any seventy- to eighty-year period would the rate of return be positive, and for four others – Japan, France, German, and Spain – the time period is fifty to sixty years. (There is a direct correlation between volatility and poor returns; the countries with the worst returns were much more volatile than the countries with the best returns.) However, for all the stock markets they studied, the probability of having a positive return during any twenty-year period was quite considerable, and if one extends the period to the forty- to fifty-year period the probability increases. Furthermore, most of the countries with periods of poor performance were countries with considerable

[77] Elroy Dimson, Paul Marsh, and Mike Staunton, *Triumph of the Optimists*, (Princeton: Princeton University Press, 2002), ch. 18–33.

political instability and rather terrible economic policies. If one examines the period in the last thirty years, rates of return are far better in almost every country, well above the PAYGO rate of return.[78]

Unfortunately, Elroy et al. have not investigated the long-term rates of return for a stock-bond mixture, so we don't know how these results would differ for such a mixture.

4. International investing. Countries that have had poor rates of return in their stock markets would, of course, benefit from a diversified international portfolio, thus increasing both their rate of return and the probability of positive returns over the twenty- to twenty-five-year period and certainly over the forty- to fifty-year period.

5. Administrative costs. Because SS is a centralized government monopoly that does not have to compete for customers, it can keep its administrative costs low (as there are low selling and advertising costs), but because pension funds compete for customers in CPP, it may have higher administrative costs. If these costs are high enough, it could narrow the difference between CPP's rate of return and SS's rate of return. Administrative costs in the United Kingdom, which has partially privatized SS, are quite high.[79] However, Chile's administrative costs are less than the costs found in the average U.S. mutual fund, and other countries are experimenting with methods that may lower administrative costs further,[80] so the worry about administrative costs in CPP being so high that they significantly reduce the difference between its rate of return and SS's rate of return seems overblown.

6. Plausible connections between instituting CPP (in which virtually everyone becomes an investor) and improving rates of return. (a) If everyone is an investor, stock markets in the long run are likely to be less volatile, and less volatile markets tend to have greater rates of return. (b) If everyone is an investor, growth rates will tend to increase,[81] and

[78] See Shipman, *Retirement Finance Reform Issues Facing the European Union*, 4, table 1.

[79] Manta Murthi, J. Michael Orszag, and Peter R. Orszag, "Administrative Costs under a Decentralized Approach to Individual Accounts: Lessons from the United Kingdom," in Holzman and Stiglitz, *New Ideas on Old Age Security*, ch. 8.

[80] Estelle James, James Smalhout, and Dimitri Vittas, "Administrative Costs and the Organization of Individual Account Systems: A Comparative Perspective," in *ibid.*, ch. 7.

[81] If the increased investment was simply taken from savings, then this would not be true. But it is unlikely that if one moves from a system where most people don't invest, to one where almost everyone does, that all of the increased investment would come from present savings.

increased growth tends to increase the rate of return. (c) If everyone is an investor, then democratic governments are much more inhibited in their ability to pursue economic policies that can harm economic growth and the stock market.[82]

Thus, the upshot of (1) through (5) is that the probability that the market rate of return over a twenty- to twenty-five-year period, and particularly over a forty- to fifty-year period, will be higher than the PAYGO's rate of return in its mature phase is quite high, and instituting a CPP system would make the probability even higher. Of course, this is not a certainty. However, we need to remember that CPP also has a minimum pension guarantee, and so even under the most pessimistic scenario it will not do worse than a PAYGO system.[83]

---

[82] On the second point, see Gregorio Impavido, Alberto R. Musalem, and Thierry Tressel, "The Impact of Contractual Savings Institutions on Securities Markets," *World Bank Policy Research Working Paper 2948*, January 2003, available at http://wbln0018.worldbank.org/html/FinancialSectorWeb.nsf/(attachmentweb)/2948/$FILE/2948.pdf and Klaus Schmidt-Hebbel, "Does Pension Reform Really Spur Productivity, Saving and Growth?" Central Bank of Chile Working Papers 33, available at http://econpapers.hhs.se/paper/chbbcchwp/33.htm (both accessed March 2003). The third point seems almost self-evident: if everyone's retirement depends on the stock market, democratic governments will be very careful to avoid policies that will have deleterious long-term effects on rates of return. I find the first point to be obvious because the larger the number of people in a market, the more likely it is that individual idiosyncrasies cancel each other out, but it's the kind of claim about which one would like empirical confirmation. For an argument that mutual funds with greater depth of ownership are less volatile, see Joseph Chen, Harrison Hong, and Jeremy C. Stein, "Breadth of Ownership and Stock Returns," *Journal of Financial Economics* 66 (November 2002): 171–205. Admittedly, Chen, Long, and Stein's results do not necessarily apply to the stock market as a whole.

[83] In a CPP system, investors could contractually guarantee themselves a baseline minimum return, even without a government safety net. The basic idea is that financial markets would offer a contract whereby the investor would reduce his risk of retiring with a low annuity by foregoing some or all of the annuity payments above a certain level. See Martin Feldstein and Elena Ranguelova, "Accumulated Pension Collars: A Market Approach to Reducing the Risk of Investment-Based Social Security Reform," National Bureau for Economic Research Paper No. w7861, available at http://papers.nber.org/papers/w7861 (accessed March 2003).

6

Welfare or Means-Tested Benefits, Part I

6.1 Introduction

Having completed our examination of the two major social-insurance programs, NHI and SS, and having found MHI and CPP to be superior on the basis of four central viewpoints in contemporary political philosophy (egalitarianism and its prioritarian cousin, positive-rights theory, communitarianism, and the requirement of epistemic accessibility common to many forms of liberalism), we turn our attention to the other major part of the welfare state, namely social assistance or pure welfare programs. Unlike social-insurance programs, which are based (for the most part) on contribution, social assistance or pure welfare programs are based on financial need. The *means* in *means-tested programs* usually refers to income, but sometimes income and assets are considered. Examples of social assistance or pure welfare programs are cash benefits for heads of households who have children, housing subsidies, and medical care for the poor or for immigrants, even those who have paid no taxes.[1]

As I noted in previous chapters, the distinction between social insurance and welfare is not sharp. As the example of "free" medical care for those who paid no taxes indicates, virtually all social-insurance programs are supplemented by or contain within them benefits for those who have never contributed. My concern in this chapter is with

[1] I rely on Barr's cataloguing, "Economic Theory and the Welfare State, 742–5, 755.

welfare programs that are relatively independent of social-insurance programs, and thus the main focus here will be on cash benefits for heads of households.

As a general rule, state welfare is a great deal more controversial than social insurance and probably gets more negative attention than the latter. Ironically, it will turn out to be more justified than social insurance, which is really the heart of the welfare state, at least in a budgetary sense.

6.2 Different Kinds of State Welfare

State welfare can be conditional or unconditional. Strictly speaking, virtually all government programs are conditional, in that one must meet *some* condition(s) to receive a certain benefit,[2] but by conditional welfare I mean a welfare program or policy that requires that one must act or behave in a certain way in order to receive aid or a certain level of aid and take credible steps to ensure that this requirement is met. With regard to aid for able-bodied or nondisabled adults, which is the main concern of this chapter, the condition is that one must work or take active steps to enter the work force (e.g., learn new skills, change destructive behaviors), and that condition is enforced by withdrawing or significantly reducing aid if the recipient does not enter the work force after a certain period of time. Unconditional aid, by contrast, does not enforce such a behavioral requirement, or its enforcement is rather weak or half-hearted. The most permissive forms of unconditional state welfare simply give aid to those below a certain income. A somewhat less permissive form of unconditional aid will provide financial and other inducements to work or enter the work force but does not withdraw or significantly lessen aid for those who don't work or take steps to enter the work force. Only if the state makes a credible claim that it will at least *significantly* lower benefits for recipients if they do not, after a certain period of time, enter the work force, do we clearly enter the realm of conditional aid. Thus, I am treating the distinction between unconditional and conditional aid as on a continuum. The

---

[2] The only exception to this would be a policy of a basic income, which would give a cash stipend for every person or citizen living in a certain jurisdiction. I briefly discuss this proposal in Chapter 7.

larger the gap between the aid given if one enters or takes clear steps to enter the work force after a certain time and the aid given if one does not, and the more credible the state's claim that it will enforce the gap, the more conditional the form of aid.

All welfare states in recent years have abandoned the most permissive forms of unconditional aid and have instituted policies that have getting able-bodied recipients into the work force as their ostensive aim.[3] However, in most, if not all, European welfare states these attempts still don't seem serious enough, or their enforcement sufficiently credible, that we can describe these as systems of conditional aid.[4] Only in United States, New Zealand, and some Canadian provinces are there systems that clearly fall on the conditional side of the spectrum. I will discuss the details of the U.S. system later in the chapter. For now it is worth noting that even in those systems, conditional aid is embedded within programs of unconditional aid. Nondisabled adults who violate the rules and fail to enter the work force lose cash assistance but remain eligible for in-kind food and medical aid and subsidized housing.

---

[3] For a thorough summary of these changes, see Neil Gilbert, *Transformation of the Welfare State: The Silent Surrender of Public Responsibility* (New York: Oxford University Press, 2002), ch. 3, and Neil Gilbert and Rebecca A. Van Voorhis, eds. *Activating the Unemployed: A Comparative Analysis of Work-Oriented Policies* (New Brunswick, NJ: Transaction Publishers, 2001). The latter has separate chapters devoted to welfare policies in the United Kingdom, Italy, Holland, France, the United States, Switzerland, Sweden, and Norway.

[4] Although some European welfare states do have financial penalties for recipients who fail to enter the work force, they are rarely enforced, and in most of those states the ethos or cultural expectation of getting recipients into the work force (into real, not temporary or make-work jobs) does not yet seem to me strong enough to convincingly maintain that these are systems of conditional aid. See Gilbert, *Transformation of the Welfare State*, 83–6, for a discussion of the lax and somewhat erratic enforcement of financial penalties for failure to enter the work force into real, rather than make-shift or temporary work. Aside from a cultural resistance to requiring work in exchange for welfare, part of the problem is that labor policies in many European countries (e.g., France, Italy, and Germany) have created high unemployment rates, and absent a change in those labor policies, it is simply not feasible to require welfare recipients to enter the work force when unemployment is so high. Accordingly, those governments tend to focus on creating temporary government jobs, make-shift work, or subsidized private-sector jobs. On persistently high unemployment in many European countries, see Constance Sorrentino and Joyanna May, "U.S. Labor Market in International Perspective," *Monthly Labor Review* 125 (June 2002): 15–35, in particular table 1 and charts 1 and 2.

6.3 Nongovernmental Aid

The usual description of the alternative to state welfare is charitable institutions. This is correct, but it is an incomplete description because it doesn't tell us how these charities would function. Today's charities are not necessarily a model. Charities that exist today in the shadow of state welfare are not the same as charities that would exist when it is absent. Numerous charities today receive subsidies from the state[5] and view themselves as adjuncts to the welfare state.[6]

Charities that would exist absent state welfare would tend to have two central features. First, at least for able-bodied adults, aid would be conditional. Because conditional aid is usually premised on the idea that some recipients are deserving of aid and others are not, another way to put this point is that charities would generally make a serious attempt to distinguish deserving from undeserving claimants. Second, there would tend to be more emphasis on personal involvement by the donors. For many donors today, charity involves writing a check and perhaps reading a report from the recipient institution. In the

---

[5] In the United States, in 1998, 31 percent of nonprofit organizations' revenue was from tax revenues. The figures were similar for Britain. For the former figure, see *The New Nonprofit Almanac and Desk Reference* (San Francisco: Jossey-Bass, 2002), a summary of which is available at http://www.independentsector.org/PDFs/inbrief.pdf (accessed March 2003). For the latter, see Robert Whelan, *Involuntary Action* (London: Institute for Economic Affairs, 1999), 3, 23. A study of twenty-two countries, most of which were affluent democracies (including the United States and the United Kingdom), found that in 1995 40 percent of the revenue of the nonprofit sector was from taxes. See Lester M. Salamon et al., *Global Civil Society: Dimensions of the Nonprofit Sector* (Baltimore: The John Hopkins Center for Civil Society Studies, 1999), 24–5. In a number of European countries (e.g., Ireland, Belgium, Netherlands, Germany, and France), the figure was way above 50 percent.

Nonprofit organizations or the nonprofit sector include more than charities. E.g., they include cultural and educational organizations. However, if we exclude such organizations, it is likely that the average percentage of revenues from taxes would be higher, not lower, than the figures I cited in the preceding text. The Salamon et al. study found that 55 percent and 45 percent of revenues for nonprofit organizations whose main focus was "health" or "social services," respectively, was from taxation, and it is those kinds of organizations who are most likely to be providing the kind of aid to the poor that is the subject of this chapter.

[6] For the common view among charities that they are merely a supplement to the welfare state, see Laurie Goodstein, "Churches May Not Be Able to Patch Welfare Cuts," *Washington Post* (February 22, 1995); Karen Arenson, "Gingrich's Welfare Vision Ignores Reality," *The New York Times* (June 4, 1995) and "Weak Foundations," *The Economist* (September 18, 1993), 64–5.

absence of state welfare, charities would place a greater emphasis on giving time rather than money.

Why think that charities will have these features in the absence of state welfare? One reason is that a significant percentage of donors are unlikely to give aid with no strings attached. Although some donors may be indifferent as to how their money is spent or view conditional aid as objectionable as the size of their donations rise, the incentive to give to a charity that engages in monitoring increases. Another reason is that because the state will not be forcing people to provide welfare for the disadvantaged, the assumption that others will take care of this problem is gone. Once it is gone, the incentive to get personally involved increases. Of course, not everyone, and not even most people, wants to get involved with others' problems. But it seems reasonable to assume that this increased incentive will make some kind of difference.[7]

It is also worth noting that when state welfare, particularly by the federal or national government, was at a very low level, namely in nineteenth- and early twentieth-century Britain and the United States, charities also made a deserving/undeserving distinction and personal involvement by the donors was stressed.[8] Deserving recipients were considered those who were poor due to no fault of their own and who were unlikely to change their situation quickly without assistance (or those who were poor due to their own fault but were willing to seize opportunities offered to change their situation), while the undeserving were considered to be those who were poor because of their own faults and who were unlikely to change their lives even with assistance. (This distinction is very close to contemporary egalitarians' distinction between those who are disadvantaged because of their choices or faults, and those who are disadvantaged through no choice or fault

---

[7] A counterargument is that people will not contribute because they believe their contribution will be ineffective. I discuss this in section 6.5.

[8] For some helpful accounts, see Kathleen Woodroofe, *From Charity to Social Work in England and the United States* (London: Routledge, Kegan, and Paul, 1962); Gertrude Himmelfarb, *The De-Moralization of Society* (New York: Alfred Knopf, 1994), 125–69, ch. 4–5; Marvin Olasky, *The Tragedy of American Compassion* (Washington, DC: Regnery Gateway, 1992); and Michael B. Katz, *In the Shadow of the Poorhouse: A Social History of Welfare in America*, 10th anniv. ed. (New York: Basic Books, 1996). Himmelfarb and Olasky favor private charity, Katz opposes it, and Woodroofe is relatively neutral, but they all agree that charities prior to the welfare state made the undeserving/deserving distinction and stressed personal involvement.

of their own.) Charities generally used two kinds of tests to divide
potential recipients: investigation of a person's situation or circumstances and, for able-bodied adults, a work test. If the potential aid
recipients were orphans, elderly, incurably ill, children who could
not be supported by their one-parent families, disabled, or suffering
from an accident, no investigation was needed: clearly these people
deserved aid. Investigation generally occurred for able-bodied adults.
It was generally done by affluent or middle-class volunteers (usually
from a church or synagogue, for many charities were faith based)
who attempted to determine if fraud was present or if the person's
problems stemmed from what were viewed as faults – too much drink,
laziness, or thriftlessness.[9] Even if the person's problems were considered his own doing, the work test was considered a good indicator
of whether or not the person was willing to help himself, and thus
be deserving of aid. Men were generally asked to chop wood, and
women were asked to sew; the chopped wood and clothing were given
to other needy persons. Besides helping to reveal whether the recipient had good work habits, the provision of goods that other needy
people needed was meant to instill some sense of reciprocity – a sense
that the recipients were contributing, not just taking. As for personal
involvement by donors, this was considered essential, particularly for
those aid recipients whose problems were not temporary and who
needed more than just material aid (e.g., food, clothing, shelter, and
help finding employment). For those whose problems ran deeper, aid
meant restoring family ties if possible; in those cases in which it was
not, volunteers tried to bond with the recipient. Volunteers had a narrow but deep responsibility: to become, in effect, part of the family (or
a newly created family). Sometimes the recipient's problem was the
neighborhood, and so some volunteers literally lived with the disadvantaged, as occurred with the mission movement in the United States
and the settlement houses in the United States and England.[10] This

---

9 Sometimes charities worked with government authorities, even visiting homes of
potential recipients with them, which meant that the latter did not clearly perceive
a difference between private charity and government welfare. To the extent that this
occurred, charities took on a coercive character. See Stephen T. Ziliak, "The End of
Welfare and the Contradiction of Compassion," *Independent Review* 1, no. 1 (1996):
63–4.

10 Missions, begun by Jerry McAuely, an ex-convict and alcoholic, were meeting halls in
the worst parts of cities, where locals were invited for cheap, hot food and stories of
depravity, with follow-up stories of how others had changed their lives through God's

intense personal involvement was an attempt to break down the barrier between donor and recipient, a problem inherent in any charitable enterprise in which donors are from a different class or milieu than the recipients.

One final point needs to be noted. Historically, charities were not the only alternative to state welfare; there were also mutual-aid or fraternal societies or, as they were known in England, friendly societies. These societies were at least as important, if not more important, than charities in the voluntary provision of welfare services, but because I am not sure they are viable today, I discuss them in the appendix to Chapter 6.

6.4 Egalitarianism and Welfare-State Redistribution

The salient features of egalitarianism and its cousin, the priority view, were discussed in the previous chapters. What I will do now is to examine whether egalitarians are correct that their view mandates government redistribution of income and wealth from the more affluent to the less affluent. I begin with the "donor" side of the relationship and will go on to discuss the recipient side, which for this topic are those that receive welfare. As in the previous chapters, the intramural dispute between resourcist and welfarist egalitarians will be generally unimportant. In a later section, I will show why the priority view ends up with the same conclusions as egalitarianism.

6.4.1 Coercive Versus Voluntary Transfers: The "Donors"

A necessary condition for a justly imposed government redistribution is that the taxable income and wealth of the donor must be due (mainly) to brute luck. A two-part procedure is necessary to determine whether someone's income or wealth is or is not mainly a product of choice

help and acceptance of personal responsibility. The settlement houses were houses that were built in poor areas and populated by both local residents and middle-class volunteers; the latter viewed themselves as "settlers" who would both teach and learn from the locals. The homes fulfilled the role of a residential and civic club with the aim of social and moral improvement in the neighborhood. The settlers taught classes in a variety of subjects, such as literature, languages (e.g., teaching immigrants English), and science. They also helped the local residents with child care and assisted them in handling many of the daily problems of life. See the references cited in n. 8.

rather than circumstance. First, one must categorize the voluntariness of different factors involved in obtaining income and wealth. Second, a causal account of individuals' income and wealth is necessary. This account would seek to explain the various factors that interacted with each other and to explain which factors did and did not play a primary role in producing someone's or a group's income and wealth over a certain time period. The first part was to some extent discussed in Chapter 3, so I will go through this quickly and emphasize only some new points.

Egalitarians view differences in income and wealth resulting from effort, different tradeoffs between leisure and work, and different tradeoffs between income and consumption as voluntary[11] because they are manifestations of different ambitions and life goals. The same is true for differences in income resulting from different occupational choices. Business losses and profits are, according to at least some egalitarians, to a considerable extent due to option luck – gambles and risks knowingly taken or assumed, and opportunities seized or ignored, and so forth – and thus fall on the side of voluntary inequalities.[12] In general, the results of deliberate gambles (e.g., fairly run lotteries) are also treated as voluntary inequalities for the same reason.

On the unchosen side are income and wealth inequalities resulting from genetic or native endowments and race, sex, or national origin. Those business losses and gains that one could not insure against and that it would be unreasonable to take into one's calculations (e.g., a

---

[11] Dworkin, "What Is Equality? Part 2," 303–6; Rakowski, *Equal Justice*, 107–12; and Nagel, *Equality and Partiality*, 108.

[12] Rakowski, *Equal Justice*, 83. Dworkin might disagree with Rakowski, in as much as he says that luck is the most important factor in what he calls "wealth-talent." He doesn't explicitly say whether this is brute or option luck; but he seems to mean the former because he defines "wealth-talent" as one's "innate capacity to produce goods or services that others will pay to have," and also says that the biggest factor in "wealth-talent" is being in the right place at the right time (*Sovereign Virtue*, 323, 327). However, Rakowski's views seem to cohere much better with egalitarianism's view about luck. First, it is very hard to see why business decisions would be different than any other voluntarily assumed gamble. Second, Dworkin insists that a person's ambitions, as well as his judgment and courage, energy, doggedness, and persistence (see n. 14) belong on the chosen side of the chosen-unchosen continuum. Entrepreneurial profit depends on being alert to and taking advantage of opportunities, and that depends to a considerable extent on the very characteristics that Dworkin says are a matter of choice, not circumstance. On entrepreneurship and profits, see Israel Kirzner, *Competition and Entrepreneurship* (Chicago: University of Chicago Press, 1973).

completely accidental or freakish gain or loss) are matters of brute luck
as well. Because one does not choose one's parents or family, inequalities due to one's initial start in life are also unjust (e.g., inequalities
resulting from inherited wealth).

One's psychological characteristics, such as cheerfulness or grumpi-
ness,[13] ability to cope with adversity, sense of self-efficacy, and character
traits (e.g., diligence and persistence) also affect one's ability to succeed. As I noted in Chapter 3, egalitarians find these rather difficult
to classify and they are probably best viewed as mixed cases,[14] and the
same holds for education and schooling.

Though this is not a complete cataloguing of all the factors that
influence a person's income and wealth, the problem egalitarians
face is that most, if not all, of the uncontroversial cases of choice
and brute luck reciprocally influence each other, so that almost *everything* becomes a mixed – and hence hard case. Although genetically
based or native abilities and traits differ, people choose to develop
(or not develop) these abilities and traits, and so differences in these
things are partly a matter of choice and partly a matter of brute luck.
One's ambitions and preferences in part depend upon one's talents
and background, so different conceptions of the good life and different ambitions are partly chosen and partly unchosen. Egalitarians are
aware of this.[15] How could they not be? Yet the main way they have
dealt with this problem is through intramural disputes about whether
or not *certain* factors are correctly classified as belonging on the voluntary or the nonvoluntary side of the spectrum. So, for example, there
is a great deal of discussion regarding the problem of expensive tastes:
to what extent is the costliness of a person's preferences his responsibility if it was formed in a social or economic background for which
he is not responsible?[16] But the problem is global not local. Without
a causal theory that shows how much of an individual's or groups of
individuals' situation is due to choice and how much is due to brute

---

[13] Cohen, "On the Currency of Egalitarian Justice," 930–1.

[14] However, in Dworkin's most recent thoughts on this subject, he considers "energy,
industry, doggedness, and ability to work now for distant rewards" as part of one's
character, which he places on the side of choices, not circumstances. *Sovereign Virtue*,
322.

[15] See, e.g., Dworkin, "What Is Equality? Part 2," 313–14, and Nagel, *Equality and Partiality*, 110–21.

[16] See, e.g., Arneson, "Equality and Equal Opportunity for Welfare," 230–1.

luck, egalitarians are in the dark about whether or not or to what extent the income and wealth that is used to fund redistribution is or is not justly acquired. But egalitarians have no such theory. Instead, they (or some of them) offer a theory about a different subject: about how much one would insure against the risk of being disadvantaged in a hypothetical insurance market in which one did not know one's social and natural disadvantages and everyone had equal purchasing power.[17] However, even if we knew how much and what kind of insurance persons ignorant of their own vulnerabilities would purchase in a hypothetical insurance market, that would be irrelevant to the point at hand: how much of one's wealth and income, in the real world, is due to one's own choice and how much is due to brute luck? Although some egalitarians make *claims* about this matter, I have been unable to locate anything that amounts to a sustained argument about this important question.[18]

Egalitarians may object that they need no argument or causal theory to justify redistribution. They may point out that some portion of virtually everyone's income and wealth is due to brute luck (e.g., one's family background and genetic inheritance) and that whatever is infected with brute luck is brute luck, period.[19] We are justified in redistributing from the affluent to the less affluent because it is redistribution from the lucky to the unlucky.

However, this attempt to avoid determining how much of one's income and wealth is caused by brute luck is a dead end, for two reasons. First, the claim that whatever is infected with brute luck is brute luck, period, seems clearly false: normally, when X is partially due to Y

---

[17] This is developed in considerable detail by Dworkin, "Equality of Resources," 293–334, and Rakowski, *Equal Justice*, 97–106, 120–48.

[18] Nagel says that egalitarianism would require more redistribution and less inequality of wealth and income than exists at present in contemporary welfare states (although he worries that such redistribution will harm the incentives necessary for the talented to produce wealth). See *Equality and Partiality*, 74–5, 93, 123–5. Dworkin makes a similar claim about the United States; see "Why Liberals Should Care about Equality," in his *A Matter of Principle* (Cambridge, MA: Harvard University Press, 1983), 208, and also says in *Sovereign Virtue*, 312, that if wealth were fairly distributed, most people would be closer to the average income than is true at present. However, because egalitarians do not object to inequalities per se, but only to unchosen ones, Nagel and Dworkin's confidence that more redistribution is required would need to be based on an argument that bad brute luck produces a significant amount of present-day inequalities of wealth and income. They provide no such argument.

[19] Nagel, *Equality and Partiality*, 112–13, may be suggesting something like this.

we don't infer that it is completely due to Y. Second, were egalitarians to accept that whatever is infected with brute luck is brute luck, period, the point or motivation for their theory of justice would be mysterious. It's odd to spend time explaining that justice requires compensation only for inequalities due to bad brute luck, not simply inequalities per se, when it turns out that one's theory is practically equivalent to those that claim that inequalities per se require correction or compensation.

Now that egalitarians apparently lack a theory or argument that gives us at least a rough idea as to how much of one's income and wealth is due to choice and how much is due to bad brute luck does not mean that one does not exist. Perhaps social scientists that specialize in these matters can help them out.

If longitudinal studies showed that there is very limited income and wealth mobility, it might be reasonable to conclude that one's income and wealth is largely a matter of brute luck. After all, because most people want to improve their situation, if they are blocked in their attempt to do so, then circumstances, not choice, rules. Some egalitarians hold something like this view, seeing family background, particularly the economic holdings of one's family, as virtually determining one's lot in life in contemporary America.[20] However, that view is false. Although there are a range of views among economists about how much income and wealth mobility there has been in recent decades in the United States, the consensus seems to be that it is alive and well in general.[21]

---

[20] Ibid., 93, says that capitalism gives rise to "large and inheritable inequalities in the conditions of life." G. A. Cohen thinks that the condition of the proletariat in capitalism can be understood by the following thought experiment: A group of people are locked in a room. A key exists, but it works only for the first person who uses it. Although each is free to seize the key and leave, his freedom depends on others not getting the key. "The Structure of Proletarian Unfreedom," *Philosophy and Public Affairs* 12 (Winter 1983): 11. Thus both Nagel and Cohen see capitalism as very close to a kind of caste system.

[21] Stephen Rose, "Is Mobility in the United States Still Alive? Tracking Career Opportunities and Income Growth," *International Review of Applied Economics* 13 (September 1999): 417–37, surveys the views of economists on this question and finds the differences to be largely due to methodological differences concerning how to measure income mobility, but the fact that the extreme view that mobility has largely vanished for most of the population is erroneous. For an optimistic account, see W. Michael Cox and Richard Alm, *Myths of Rich and Poor: Why We're Better Off than We Think* (New York: Basic Books, 1999), 72–87. For somewhat less sanguine accounts, see Richard Freeman, *When Earnings Diverge: Causes, Consequences and Cures for the New Inequality in the U.S.* (Washington, DC: National Policy Association, 1997), 28–30, and Isabel

There are some specific groups for whom mobility does seem to be a problem and/or for whom it may have lessened in recent decades: poor, single parents find it difficult to escape from poverty, and the growth of earnings of men with a high school education or less has been sluggish or perhaps has diminished in real terms.[22] However, that certain population groups may be experiencing mobility problems is irrelevant to the issue at hand, which is whether the vast majority of the population's income and wealth that will be the source of the funds for transfers is due to good brute luck. It's also worth noting that the mobility problems for these groups do not seem causally related to the mobility experienced by the vast majority of the population. Those with a college or professional degree in the United States (and elsewhere)

V. Sawhill, "Still the Land of Opportunity?" *Public Interest* 135 (Spring 1999): 3–18. Studies of wealth mobility are scarcer then studies of income mobility, but see Erik Hurst, Ming Ching Luoh, and Frank P. Stafford, "The Wealth Dynamics of American Families, 1984–1994," in *Brookings Papers on Economic Activity 1998, No. 1*, William C. Brainard and George L. Perry, eds. (Washington, DC: Brookings Institution, 1998): 267–337, which argues on p. 285 that there is rising wealth mobility in the United States. Nancy A. Jianokopolos and Paul L. Menchik "Wealth Mobility," *Review of Economics and Statistics* 79 (February 1997): 18–32, found somewhat less mobility than did the Brookings paper in their study of mature American men from 1966 to 1981. However, one would expect their study to find more limited mobility because the men in their survey (ages 45 to 59) may have already achieved a significant amount of mobility as they went from being young adults to being middle-aged.

One complication worth noting is that studies of individual mobility tend to show more mobility than studies of household mobility. This is not surprising. When a household becomes wealthy enough that one of its wage-earning members can leave and set up his or her own household, then the resulting drop in income to that household can make it appear that household mobility has slowed, when the truth is that the exit of that wage earner is a sign that everyone is better off. I owe this point to David Schmidtz, "Equal Respect and Equal Shares," *Social Philosophy and Policy* 19 (Winter 2002): 267–8.

[22] Regarding single parents and poverty, see Peter Gottschalk and Sheldon Danziger, "Income Mobility and Exits from Poverty of American Children, 1970–1992," in *The Dynamics of Child Poverty in Industrialized Countries*, Bruce Bradbury, Stephen P. Jenkins, and John Micklewright, eds. (Cambridge: Cambridge University Press, 2001), 135–53. Regarding men with a high school diploma or less, see Freeman, *When Earnings Diverge*, 10–11; Sawhill, "Still the Land of Opportunity?" 11–12; and Rose, "Is Mobility in the United States Still Alive?" table 2.

Gottschalk and Danziger's work was misinterpreted by Michael Weinstein, "America's Rags to Riches Myth," *New York Times* (February 18, 2000), as showing that it is difficult to escape from poverty in today's America. As Schmidtz points out in "Equal Respect and Equal Shares," 268–71, their work shows a great difference between poor two-parent households and poor one-parent households. The former's ability to exit from poverty during the 1970s and 1980s was substantial.

are not causing the decline in mobility among men with a high school degree or less, and two-parent families are not the ones that cause the fact that single parenthood makes it harder to get out of poverty.[23]

Now, strictly speaking, the presence of significant income and wealth mobility doesn't show that the mobility that does exist is due to choices or a mixture of choices and unchosen circumstances. Thus another way social-science studies might help the egalitarian case is if it were true that most middle-class and rich people's income and wealth, or their rise into the middle class or affluence, were due largely to good brute luck. However, if we look at the usual explanations for income and wealth inequalities we find that the usual causes listed either fall clearly on the chosen side of the chosen-unchosen spectrum or are one of the mixed cases:

1. Inheritance does not play a large role in the fortunes of the very rich.

2. Entrepreneurship does play a large role in the fortunes of the very rich.[24]

3. Forming a family, working full time all year round, sticking with a job long enough to get skills and training, completing college, and moving to areas with high-paying jobs all help maintain or propel one into the middle class.[25]

---

[23] Although I presume it is relatively obvious that the existence of two-parent families is not among the reasons that single parenthood makes it harder to get out of poverty, the situation of the sluggish or perhaps declining earnings of men with a high school diploma or less may be not so obvious. It might seem when an economy increasingly rewards jobs that require greater skills and education that *therefore* those with average or below average education and skills will suffer diminished income and wealth mobility. However, that is a fallacious inference. Setting aside the fact that the sluggishness and perhaps real loss of earnings of those with high school diplomas or less has occurred mainly among men, not among all who earned a high school diploma or less, an increasing economic return to the well educated doesn't mean that the less educated's mobility must decrease. Both groups could experience significant mobility, although the increasing return to the college-educated group means its income will rise faster than the less educated group.

[24] On these first two points, see Young Bak Choi, "On the Rich Getting Richer and the Poor Getting Poorer," *Kyklos* 52 (June 1999): 239–58; Rudolph C. Blitz and John J. Siegfried, "How Did the Wealthiest Americans Get So Rich?" *Quarterly Review of Business and Economics* 32 (Spring 1992): 5–26; and James Smith, "Inheritances and Bequests," in *Wealth, Work, and Health: Innovations in Measurement in the Social Sciences*, James P. Smith and Robert J. Willis, ed. (Ann Arbor: University of Michigan Press, 1999), 137.

[25] Cox and Alm, *Myths of Rich and Poor*, 85–7.

4. Character traits such as diligence, reliability, and persistence are valued by employers: people with those traits are more likely to be hired, stay hired, and be promoted, thus increasing their chance of improving their situation.[26]

As we've seen, (1) is good brute luck, (2) is option luck,[27] and (3) and (4) are mixed cases. Thus, these four points falsify any claim that the middle class and the rich got where they are purely or largely by brute luck.

So the real problem for egalitarians is not that they lack – and have not done – the social-science research they need in order to demonstrate that government transfers are justified. The real problem is that such literature does nothing to remove the problem we began with: the situation of the "donors" is some indeterminate mix of choice and brute luck.

Because we have no basis for determining the extent to which people's advantages are or are not the product of brute luck, then any coercive transfer[28] will involve injustice because it will take some income and wealth from some or perhaps many of those who earned it by their choices or by option luck and therefore have a right to it. If there is no coercive redistribution, and transfers to the unfortunate or the poor are purely voluntary, then some injustice will also occur. Although it is not unjust (according to egalitarians) to voluntarily transfer some of one's income or wealth to the unfortunate or poor, it is unjust to refrain from transferring income or wealth derived from good brute luck because one is not entitled to that income or wealth. Although we cannot predict to what extent these transfers to the poor and unfortunate

---

[26] Susan Mayer, *What Money Can't Buy* (Cambridge, MA: Harvard University Press, 1997), examines to what extent parental income affects children's outcomes. She finds that once basic minimal material needs have been met, parental income per se does not make that much difference. Rather, the characteristics that employers value and are willing to pay for, i.e., skills, diligence, honesty, reliability, etc., also improve children's life chances, independent of the effects of parents' income. Children of parents with these attributes do well even when their parents do not have much income.

[27] But see n. 12 for Dworkin's dissent on this point.

[28] A coercive transfer (or redistribution) is a transfer of income and wealth that is not voluntary. A voluntary transfer (or redistribution) is transfer of income and wealth that occurs with the donor's consent and that is not an ordinary market exchange (e.g., the recipient receives the income and wealth without necessarily providing some good or service in return).

would occur if they were purely voluntary, it is quite safe to predict that some transfers would occur, and thus that a system based on voluntary transfers, like one based on coercive transfers, will involve some injustice.[29]

Thus, for egalitarians the choice between coercive and voluntary transfers is a choice between different kinds of injustice. Either alternative involves some indeterminate amount of injustice, and egalitarians are in the dark about the degree of injustice involved in each alternative and as to which injustice is worse. Thus voluntary transfers, that is, abolishing state welfare and relying on private alternatives, are no worse than coercive welfare-state transfers, if we focus just on the side of the donors.

I discussed a similar problem about health risks in Chapter 3; they are an indeterminate mixture of chosen and unchosen factors. But there is a crucial difference between, on the one hand, the choice between MHI and NHI and, on the other hand, the choice between coerced and voluntary transfers of income and wealth. In the case of health risks and the choice between MHI and NHI, it was clear that MHI was better. *Some* of the people who are victims of bad brute luck in MHI are not required to pay more for risks they did not assume, while *to some extent* people are charged in accordance with voluntarily assumed risks, whereas in NHI virtually *no one* bears the cost of risks he voluntarily assumed. Thus, although both systems had elements of injustice, MHI was clearly more just or less unjust. Or to put the point in a somewhat different way in terms of weight of reasons, MHI had stronger reasons on its side because it gave weight to the principle of holding people responsible for their choices and the cost of their

---

[29] Perhaps it might be thought that there is a causal difference between the two kinds of injustice. Coercive transfers will definitely *cause* or produce some acts of injustice, as some individuals' rights to their justly acquired income and wealth are violated, while if voluntary transfers are relied upon, injustice will be *allowed*, as some individuals refrain from transferring the income and wealth to which they are not entitled. If this was a correct way of characterizing the egalitarian choice between coercive and voluntary transfers, then we could settle the question of which choice is worse by settling the question of whether it is worse to do injustice or refrain from doing justice. However, this way of characterizing the egalitarian choice is probably mistaken. When one has a positive obligation (in this case, the positive obligation of those whose income and wealth is derived from good brute luck to transfer it to those with bad brute luck), failing to do what one is obligated to do is not a mere refraining. It is an act of injustice. Thus both choices involve acts of injustice. I thank Eric Mack for setting me straight on this point.

choices (the antisubsidization principle) and the principle of subsidizing victims of bad brute luck, whereas NHI ignored the former principle completely. However, in the choice between coercive versus voluntary transfers all an egalitarian can say is that both have reasons against them or that both involve injustice.

One additional objection should be discussed. Recently, Liam Murphy and Thomas Nagel have argued that all property rights are conventional, and so there is no right to any pretax income that can be used as a touchstone to criticize redistributive taxation.[30] It might seem this conventionalism can be used to block my argument that welfare-state redistribution involves some injustice because it takes income and wealth from those who acquired it by voluntary means. If so, then welfare-state redistribution is superior to voluntary aid when we focus on the side of the "donors," because the latter involves some injustice, in as much as some people who are obligated to give aid won't, and the former does not, as least insofar as the focus is on whether redistribution per se involves injustice.

However, Nagel and Murphy also defend, more or less, contemporary egalitarianism's view about justice and markets.[31] This means that they hold to the view that markets embody justice to the extent that income and wealth reflect choices, and thus that to the extent that redistribution takes away that income and wealth it embodies injustice. Thus, it seems that either Nagel and Murphy's conventionalism about property rights is incompatible with their endorsement of the egalitarian view about markets, or that they maintain that evaluating the justice or injustice of markets and government redistribution need not depend on any views about a nonconventional right to pretax income. In either case, however, the denial of the nonconventional right to pretax income right need not entail the denial that redistribution embodies injustice to the extent that it coercively takes income and wealth from persons who achieved it through voluntary processes.

6.4.2 Coercive Versus Voluntary Transfers: The Recipients

At first glance, it appears as if the argument made in the previous section applies to the recipients of transfers as well. If we cannot tell to

---

[30] See Liam Murphy and Thomas Nagel, *The Myth of Ownership: Taxes and Justice* (New York: Oxford University Press, 2002), 8–9, 34–6, 74.

[31] See ibid., 67–8.

what extent a person's advantages are due to choice as opposed to brute luck, then we cannot tell to what extent a person's disadvantages are due to choice as opposed to brute luck. However, things are different when we look at the recipients of transfers because a new matter arises here that does not arise with the "donors," namely *changing* the recipient's situation so that his or her lot in life is more influenced by genuine choices rather than bad brute luck. I mentioned the difference between a backward- and forward-looking view of responsibility in Chapter 3, and for welfare policy, this distinction takes on crucial importance. Even if a person's disadvantages up to the present were due primarily to bad brute luck, he might *now* be in a position to do something about it or could be placed in a situation in which his future lot in life could be due more to choices than brute luck. Notice, however, that this distinction between the cause of a person's present situation and what he might now be able to do was irrelevant for the egalitarian rationale for taking some of the donor's income and wealth. That rationale did not center on the idea that we should change the donor's situation so that in the future he or she could make genuine choices.[32] The rationale, you will recall, was that justice requires compensating the involuntarily disadvantaged and that those with good brute luck cannot claim that it is unjust for them to be forced to redistribute some of their income or wealth. Furthermore, except perhaps in extraordinary cases, no one doubts that those blessed with good brute luck will, after redistribution, be able to lead a life in which their lot in life is to a significant extent determined by their choices. However, this is in doubt with the victims of bad brute luck because merely giving them monetary compensation for their bad luck may not thereby make them able to change their situation, if the problem is an *internal* one having to do with their character traits, abilities,

---

[32] Which is not to say egalitarians wouldn't view it as *desirable* if redistribution results in the situation of the beneficiaries of brute good luck being altered so that it was closer to what life would be like if they hadn't been so lucky. However, as I noted in Chapter 2, egalitarians generally do not view the existence of good brute luck as an *injustice*. It's *bad* brute luck that is an injustice.

It's also worth noting that egalitarians need not be indifferent to the incentive effects of redistribution. I noted in Chapter 2 that some egalitarians will reject redistributions that do not produce any improvements for the worst off. I thank Ralph W. Clark for reminding me of this.

skills, or uncorrectable severe disabilities. (I return to this point in the following text.)

Given that the point of taking the donor's money was not to change their situation so that in the future their lot in life could be to a considerable extent determined by their choices, why should egalitarians be interested in changing the recipient's situation in this way? To explain why, let us expand upon the backward-versus forward-looking perspectives on responsibility I discussed in Chapters 3 and 5 and call the former holding someone responsible and the latter taking responsibility.[33] Holding someone responsible for his actions is a matter of assessing his past behavior and making judgments of blame and praise. Taking responsibility, by contrast, is forward looking: it means that individuals will regard their welfare, future, and the consequences of their actions as their responsibility, not anyone else's. Though it is wrong to hold those harmed by bad brute luck as responsible for their situation, there are two reasons why egalitarians want or should want recipients to take responsibility for their future. First, the egalitarian vision involves, in part, a world in which individuals are able to make their choices and have their fate determined, to a significant extent, by their choices. This means that justice requires changing the situation of those dominated by bad brute luck so that their lives are more under the control of their choices, which will not occur unless they can take responsibility. A person's life is not under his or her control if he or she is unwilling or unable to regard one's future as one's responsibility. Second, as I noted in the preceding text, monetary compensation is not always sufficient to fundamentally change the situation of those whose lives have been harmed by bad brute luck. It may not significantly raise their welfare or their resources when their problems are internal ones, having to do with their character traits, skills, abilities, or disabilities.

6.4.3 Conditional Versus Unconditional Aid

Because there is an asymmetry in egalitarianism between the donors and recipients as far as the point or aim of redistribution, the next

---

[33] David Schmidtz, "Taking Responsibility," in *Social Welfare and Individual Responsibility*, David Schmidtz and Robert E. Goodin, eds. (New York: Cambridge University Press, 1998), 8–10.

question to consider is if discovering whether recipients will take responsibility for their future is any easier than discovering whether or not the donors' advantages were chosen. It is easier because there are some common sense tests that can be used: Is the person willing to work if work is made available? Does the person accept offers to change his life by grasping or taking advantage of opportunities to learn new skills, develop talents, or change behavior and thus alter his character traits?[34] If a disadvantaged person refuses offers of work when options are made available or offers of help to develop skills, talents, or change behavior that would help improve his situation, then this shows that the person is not taking responsibility for his future and welfare.

Conditional aid is far better at employing these tests than unconditional aid. The most permissive form of unconditional aid – simply giving aid to claimants who fall below a certain income – employs no such tests and thus provides no way to discover whether the recipients will take responsibility for their future. But even the less permissive forms of unconditional aid, which provide some incentives to get recipients to change their behavior, learn new skills, and enter the work force, don't do as good a job as conditional aid. Even in the less permissive systems of unconditional aid, the difference between the benefits from learning new skills and entering the work force, and refusing to take advantage of these opportunities is not as large as in conditional aid. Furthermore, unconditional aid makes no serious attempt to see if the person will change his life in as much as it does not substantially reduce aid if the person fails to respond to the offers, whereas conditional aid provides less or no aid for nondisabled recipients who, after a period of time, refuse the opportunities to improve their situation.

It may be argued, however, that because conditional aid provides a combination of rewards and sanctions, it goes beyond *discovering* whether or not a person will take responsibility for her future and *coerces*, or comes uncomfortably close to coercing, the recipient. Robert Goodin argues that conditional welfare is not a pure offer but a "throffer," that is, a combination of a threat and an offer.[35] The offer is the

---

34 These are the kinds of tests charities used prior to the rise of the welfare state, and, as I discuss later in this subsection, to some extent recent welfare reform incorporates these tests also. See also n. 43.

35 Robert Goodin, "Social Welfare as a Collective Social Responsibility," in Schmidtz and Goodin, *Social Welfare and Individual Responsibility*, 180–3. Threats and offers are typically defined in terms of whether they improve or worsen the situation of the

benefits one receives if one learns new skills, gets a job, alters destructive behaviors and the like; the threat is the elimination or reduction of aid, if the person does not, after a certain period of time, accept the offer. Declining a pure offer leaves one no worse off than one was before the offer, but a throffer does not; if one rejects the offer one is worse off than one was prior to the throffer. Evaluating to what extent, if any, a throffer is coercive is a tricky matter. Unlike pure threats (e.g., "your money or your life"), which really leave you with no viable option, a throffer does present an alternative – the offer – that will make you better off than the status quo. But if the threatened alternative is bad enough, the person is not really voluntarily accepting the offer; if so, then inferences from the acceptance of the offer to a conclusion about the recipient taking responsibility for his future become quite suspect.

I have two responses to this objection. First, the threatened option in a system of conditional welfare is not so dire that it's legitimate to label conditional welfare as coercing the recipients. The choice is not "accept these offers or starve," or something to that effect, because in a system of state conditional welfare, as I noted in section 6.2, not all aid is eliminated, only cash assistance, and in a system of private conditional welfare, there are a variety of competing charities, so being denied by one charity does not mean being denied all aid, period. Furthermore, even apart from welfare or charity, recipients have the option of relying on family and friends and later seeking work.[36]

person to whom they are addressed relative to some status quo. If the status quo is unconditional aid, then conditional aid is a throffer; if the status quo is no aid at all, then conditional aid is a pure offer. It's not clear to me why one should consider unconditional aid as the status quo, but for the sake of the argument I will grant Goodin's analysis and consider conditional aid to be a throffer.

[36] The data on welfare reform in the United States to some extent supports my point. Ron Haskins, "Reform, Family Income and Poverty," in *The New World of Welfare*, Rebecca M. Blank and Ron Haskins, eds. (Washington DC: The Brookings Institution, 2001), 110–11, summarizing studies of those who left welfare, says that at any one time 60 percent are working and 40 percent are not working, but after ten months the latter figure falls to 20 percent, indicating that many leavers later find work. Admittedly, at least 15 percent of leavers seem to have no connection to the (official) labor market. See Sheila Zedlewski and Pamela Loprest, "Will TANF Work for the Most Disadvantaged Families?" in ibid., 319. Although studies do not indicate how these people are getting by, one assumes they are relying on family and friends and getting unconditional aid that does not require work (e.g., Medicaid, food stamps). As Douglas Bersharov notes, "The Past and Future of Welfare Reform," *The Public Interest* 150 (Winter 2003): 11–12, few of the families who leave welfare and have

Second, and more important, Goodin's argument gets matters backward: unless conditional welfare has sanctions, it fails to replicate the way in which ordinary working people take responsibility for their lives. If one doesn't work at any job, then those that don't have some source of guaranteed income or savings eventually have their economic situation worsened. Were state welfare to be unconditional and have no sanctions, it would not reflect the way in which most people take responsibility for their lives, by realizing it is up to them to work, learn whatever skills are needed, or alter whatever behavior is keeping them from working. Instead, it would be closer to the situation of the person who, even if he declines to work, is not financially worse off for that decision. It is only when welfare replicates the process of taking responsibility in the real world that it is reasonable to use the decisions people make under it as providing evidence for whether the recipients are willing to take responsibility. If welfare were unconditional, it would be less like the real world, and it would then be suspect as a source of evidence about recipients' attitudes toward responsibility.

Richard Arneson provides a different objection to my argument that conditional aid provides good evidence regarding whether or not the recipient is willing to take responsibility. Unlike Goodin who focuses on the recipient's (alleged) lack of alternatives, Arneson focuses on the psychological state of the recipient. He argues that a refusal of a healthy, nondisabled person to work may be due to such terrible or discouraging circumstances that his refusal is excusable in the sense that it would have been exceedingly difficult for the person to accept the offer.[37] Or to put matters in a slightly different way, his character

---

no adult engaged in (official) work have ended up on the streets or in homeless shelters, so while their lives, as he says, may be "grim," they are not starving or near starvation. Supporting Bersharov's point is that only a very small number of families in the bottom quintile have shown a decline in income since welfare reform began. See Rebecca Blank and Robert F. Schoeni, "Changes in the Distribution of Children's Family Income over the 1990s," *American Economic Review* 93, no. 2 (2003): 304–8. (Admittedly, Blank and Schoeni also acknowledge [n. 1, 304] that reports of family incomes at the very bottom of income distributions may have more errors than reports of other income groups, so it may be that we don't have that clear a picture of how the poorest of the poor have fared under welfare reform.) The effects of welfare reform are discussed in more detail later in this section.

[37] Richard J. Arneson, "Egalitarianism and the Deserving Poor," *The Journal of Political Philosophy* 5 (December 1997): 331–2.

traits may have been so warped by bad brute luck that he is simply so discouraged that it is not reasonable for him to accept the offer. In this case, it is not simply that the person is unwilling to take responsibility; the deeper problem is that taking such responsibility is too difficult for him.

In one sense, Arneson's epistemic objection is sound. The tests I described do not necessarily reveal *why* someone failed to take responsibility and so the person may not be culpable. My point, though, was that conditional aid at least provides a plausible way of determining *whether* a person is willing to take responsibility,[38] which is what egalitarians should want the disadvantaged to do, while unconditional aid provides a worse way or no way of determining this.[39] My response, however, raises a moral objection to a system of conditional aid: because some of those who refuse to take responsibility will be nonculpable, then any system of conditional aid will produce significant injustice to those who nonculpably fail to take responsibility. If the refuser is not at fault for refusing, then a denial of aid is unjust and a lesser amount of aid for the refusal to take responsibility may also be unjust. A system of unconditional aid avoids this injustice, even if it does create injustice by giving unconditional aid to those who are simply unwilling to take responsibility and by failing to attempt or making rather half-hearted attempts to determine whether someone is willing to take responsibility. Given this, one could argue that a system of unconditional aid is at least as just, on egalitarian principles, as a system of conditional aid.

I suspect that this moral objection to a system of conditional aid fails. Most adults are willing to respond to offers of conditional aid.[40]

---

[38] Notice that in a competitive charities market different charities will specialize in aiding different groups and, as such, will be able to use specific tests for determining whether a recipient is capable of taking responsibility. This is another reason why conditional aid would have more reliable tests for determining whether someone is capable of taking responsibility because unconditional aid will have less of this specialization.

[39] True, the person who receives unconditional aid may later take responsibility by earning a living and removing himself from state welfare. But the point is that the acceptance of unconditional aid by itself doesn't tell us that the person is willing to take responsibility.

[40] I presume that this is common sense. It is also supported by some (admittedly incomplete) evidence from surveys conducted by organized charities in the nineteenth century. See Olasky, *Tragedy of American Compassion*, 105–7. It is also supported by the evidence from welfare reform (see n. 36 and n. 49). In addition, surveys of

Furthermore, egalitarians should presume that unwillingness by an able-bodied adult to take responsibility is culpable. After all, we are talking about making an effort – about a willingness to respond to a challenge, incur an obligation, and contribute rather than just taking. Because egalitarians find income and wealth derived from effort to be among the least suspect sources of income and wealth, it seems that they should presume that a failure to take responsibility is culpable. Even if this presumption can be overcome, the only way the objection could succeed is if the injustice done in a system of conditional aid to the number of people who are nonculpably failing to take responsibility outweighs the injustice done in a system of unconditional aid by giving aid to people who are not entitled to it. If both of these injustices are of the same type, then the issue becomes a purely quantitative one. Because most adults are culpable if they fail to take responsibility, it seems clear that fewer people are unjustly harmed by a system of conditional aid than are unjustly benefited by a system of unconditional aid. As there is no basis in egalitarian writing for assuming that failing to give aid to nonculpable refusers is worse than giving aid to those who are not entitled to it, the fact that the system of unconditional aid unjustly affects more lives means that it creates more injustice. Therefore, the moral objection fails and egalitarians should favor conditional aid.

Conditional aid does not entail private aid. As I mentioned in section 6.2, state welfare can be conditional as well. In the United States,

---

welfare recipients show a high degree of approval of linking welfare benefits with a work requirement. See Robert Solow, "Who Likes Workfare?" in *Work and Welfare*, Amy Gutmann, ed. (Princeton: Princeton University Press, 1998), 11–13, and Ellen K. Scott, Kathryn Edin, Andrew S. London, and Joan May Mazelis, "My Children Come First: Welfare-Reliant Women's Post-TANF Views of Work-Family Tradeoffs and Marriage," in *For Better and for Worse: Welfare Reform and the Well-Being of Children and Families*, Greg J. Duncan and P. Lindsay Chase-Lansdale, eds. (New York: Russell Sage Foundation, 2001), 132–53. The former was a survey done from states that, prior to the national change in welfare policy, had experimented with programs linking work and welfare. The latter is a survey of welfare-reliant women in Philadelphia and Cleveland in 1997 and 1998. Also worth noting, although it involves a somewhat different group, is a survey of those who left Wisconsin's welfare program from January to March 1998 and did not return during the next six to nine months; the overwhelming majority thought getting a job was easier than being on welfare. See Wisconsin Department of Workforce Development, "Survey of Those Leaving AFDC or W-2 January to March 1998, Preliminary Report," available at http://www.dwd.state.wi.us/dws/w2/pdf/leavers1.pdf (accessed March 2003).

which I will use as the paradigm for state conditional welfare, the federal entitlement to Aid to Families with Dependent Children (AFDC), which provided cash benefits mainly to unmarried mothers, ended in 1996 and was replaced by capped block grants to the states. Under this system, called Temporary Assistance to Needy Families (TANF), the federal government gives the states a fixed amount of money for cash assistance (based on AFDC spending in the mid-1990s) to needy families, but the states get to keep any money they do not use. In addition, states are penalized if they do not get an increasing percentage of recipients into the work force (by 2002, 50 percent of caseloads were supposed to be working thirty hours per week) and are expected to impose sanctions on families that fail to work after a certain period of time. Furthermore, states are forbidden to use TANF money for families who have been on welfare for more than five years (although they are allowed to exempt 20 percent of caseloads from this requirement on grounds of special hardship and can use their own funds as they wish).[41] Since TANF was instituted, the ethos of welfare has changed: instead of welfare offices being places whose aim is to verify eligibility and to ensure that recipients receive their benefits, many states turned their welfare offices into job centers, emphasizing as soon as recipients walked in the door (often before they were approved for benefits) that work was expected very soon. (A sign stenciled in pencil in a New York City office summarized it well: "Be prepared to work, or be prepared to leave.")[42] Do egalitarians have some basis for preferring this kind of conditional aid to the conditional aid provided by charities? I now turn to this question.[43]

---

[41] For a thorough description of the 1996 law that reformed welfare in the United States, see Rebecca M. Blank and Ron Haskins, "An Agenda for Reauthorization," in Blank and Haskins, *The New World of Welfare*, 9–15.

[42] For accounts of how welfare reform changed the behavior of welfare offices, see Thomas L. Gais, Richard P. Nathan, Irene Lurie, and Thomas Kaplan, "Implementation of the Personal Responsibility Act of 1996," in Blank and Haskins, *The New World of Welfare*, 35–52, and Douglas Bersharov, "The Past and Present of Welfare Reform," *The Public Interest* (Winter 2003): 6–7.

[43] I originally wrote this chapter in spring 2003. Since then there has been some new data on the effects of welfare reform and TANF has been reauthorized. As my discussion in the text indicates, this new data and the reauthorization does not fundamentally alter my views vis-à-vis what egalitarians should believe about the relative merits of state versus conditional private aid.

6.4.4 Conditional Aid: Comparing the Alternatives

A system of conditional aid should be a flexible system, because although common sense tests can help reveal whether someone is willing to take responsibility, there are a variety of ways of implementing or instantiating these tests, and given the diversity of human nature, different methods will be needed for different kinds of people. In order to change their lives or fates, some people just need to work, others need skills, others need to alter their attitudes, habits, and character, and some need a combination of these. For each of these situations, numerous particulars need to be answered: does that person need to learn how to budget his income or write a resume? Does that person need transportation to work? Does that person need help with child care? Does that person need to learn how to be a good parent, remain in a marriage, or stay sober? One size most certainly does not fit all. Thus, decentralized solutions are better than centralized ones.

State welfare can be decentralized. In the United States, the welfare reform of 1996 gave states significant autonomy to design their own rules. Some states emphasized making work pay by increasing the amount of benefits welfare recipients can keep while at work, others focused on diverting welfare recipients from applying in the first place, others emphasized training programs, a few instituted a mandatory work program for those who couldn't find work in the job market, and so forth.[44] However, even when state welfare is decentralized,[45] it's unlikely it can be as flexible as a private one. Part of the reason for this is sheer numbers. Unless the political system is extremely decentralized with every locality designing its own type of system, it's unlikely that the number of different types of programs or approaches in a political system can rival the pluralism of a competitive system of private charities. (So, in the United States, for instance, while states differed *among* themselves in the way they instituted welfare reform, *within* each state, localities or municipalities were not free to alter the states' rules; their discretion was generally limited to the way they instituted or applied

---

[44] See Gais et al., "Implementation of the Personal Responsibility Act of 1996," in Blank and Haskins, *The New World of Welfare*, 52–9.

[45] Besides the United States, welfare programs in the United Kingdom, Canada, Australia, and The Netherlands have become more decentralized. See Organisation for Economic Co-operation and Development, *The Local Dimension of Welfare-to-Work: An International Survey* (OECD, 1999).

those rules.)[46] Private institutions have more freedom to treat those receiving aid as individuals or to target their aid to specific groups with very specific problems. More important, flexibility also involves the ability to quickly change policies if need be, and private institutions need to jump through fewer hoops or go through fewer intermediaries than a political system to get approval or permission to try a new approach or alter their policies.

Of course, the reasonableness of an institution changing policies or approaches depends on its ability to obtain and evaluate information about whether or not it is reaching or making progress toward reaching its goals, and here private institutions also have a comparative advantage. It's easier to determine how a policy for a small specific group is working than for a larger, heterogeneous group. Furthermore, private institutions tend to be more effective monitors because those doing the monitoring have a greater incentive to do a better job. The ultimate monitors of state welfare are the voters, and this runs headlong into the problem of rational ignorance. In modern democracies, particularly when governments take on an enormous range of functions, it is perfectly rational for the voters to be ignorant of and not take a terribly strong interest in the workings of or effectiveness of the government. The time and energy needed to become knowledgeable on the wide range of areas that governments regulate and control is enormous, the extent to which one can actually make a serious difference is fairly limited. These points, combined with the obvious fact that time and energy are scarce resources in the first place, mean that it is unsurprising and perfectly appropriate that most voters rely on a kind of impressionistic approach to make political decisions. The political

[46] An exception is North Carolina, which allows counties to opt out of the state welfare program (provided the state legislature approves). Jack Tweedie, "Building a Foundation for Change in Welfare," *State Legislatures Magazine* January 1998, available at http://www.ncsl.org/statefed/welfare/foundtn.htm (accessed March 2003). In general, states set policies for benefit levels, eligibility, work requirements, time limits, and sanctions. Counties and localities are given considerable discretion on how they administer the program and somewhat less discretion on how they meet the work requirements and apply the sanctions. Michael Tanner, *The Poverty of Welfare: Helping Others in Civil Society* (Washington, DC: The Cato Institute, 2003), 86, and references cited therein. Gais et al., "Implementation of the Personal Responsibility Act of 1996," in Blank and Haskins, *The New World of Welfare*, 52–9, reports that only a few states allow caseworkers to design individualized solutions depending on their assessment of what their clients needed.

process is thus not an impressive mechanism for generating interest in detailed monitoring about the best way to relieve involuntary disadvantage or in evaluating whether programs have been effective in achieving their purported aims. Private charities have an advantage here because they are more likely to be supported by people who have an incentive to closely monitor and evaluate whether their approach is succeeding, namely those who voluntarily supply the funds. This is not to say that private donors can't be as uninterested as voters generally are in figuring out how well their money is spent. The point is that when one's own money is being used, one's incentive to evaluate the relevant programs increases, particularly when one selects the charity and is personally involved with it.

It may be objected that the problem of rational ignorance means that the bureaucracies administering the aid have a great deal of autonomy, and given the right kind of professional ethos, bureaucrats will carefully monitor the progress of their program or perhaps hire consultants to do the evaluating. Political scientist Lawrence Mead argues that something like this occurred in the state of Wisconsin in the United States.[47] Even if Mead is right, however, this does not overcome the rational ignorance problem. Wisconsin may be a special case. Mead cites the unusually high quality of the Wisconsin welfare bureaucracy, and if overcoming rational ignorance requires unusual circumstances, then it will as a general rule not be overcome.[48]

Another way to see if state or private conditional aid is better at reducing involuntary disadvantage is to see which is better at reducing moral hazard. In the context of welfare policy, moral hazard means that payment for disadvantage tends to bring about more disadvantaged people. Because egalitarians oppose subsidizing people's choices, they must view a reduction of moral hazard as an important criterion for evaluating welfare policies. Moral hazard is a far worse problem for unconditional aid than conditional aid because the attachment of

[47] Lawrence Mead, "The Twilight of Liberal Welfare Reform," *The Public Interest* 139 (Spring 2000): 35.

[48] Ladonna Pavetti and Dan Bloom, "State Sanctions and Time Limits," in Blank and Haskins, *The New World of Welfare*, 251, report that "Some welfare offices [in the United States] have problems with the most basic tasks, such as informing recipients about sanctions and time limits and explaining how they work." This does not exactly inspire confidence in their ability to monitor their programs.

conditions to aid reduces the incentives to be eligible for welfare or remain on welfare for extended, uninterrupted periods of time. Still, it's a problem for both kinds of aid because even conditional aid may at times loosen its conditions and have sporadic enforcement of those conditions, which worsens moral hazard. In order to combat moral hazard, one needs a credible threat to significantly reduce or cut off aid for those not meeting the requirements for aid. However, it seems that for two reasons, government agencies are in a worse position to make this kind of credible threat.[49]

First, to make a credible threat involves a willingness to tolerate the hardship that might occur if the threat is carried out. If governments (national or state) are providing most of the aid, then they will very likely be *the* agency held accountable for virtually any hardship that results from a cutoff of aid. But if any particular private agency cuts off aid, this will not be so because there are other agencies; hence any particular charitable society can credibly threaten to cut off aid. Second, the arguments I gave earlier that those who donate to charities have a greater incentive than the voters to see how well their money is spent applies here as well: bureaucrats are likely to face fewer negative consequences, if conditions for receiving aid are not strictly enforced, than employees of private institutions. Furthermore, government officials are rarely subject to the bottom line; they are typically paid regardless of how well they do their job.

An objection to the first point is that if private charities are efficient then they will communicate information to one another about those who are refusing to take responsibility. If so, then private charities will all adopt the same policies and the system of private charities as a whole will be held responsible were they to cut off aid, in just the way that state welfare agencies are held responsible. Hence, the objection goes, there is no real difference between state welfare and private charity as far as the credibility of making threats to cut off aid is concerned; both will not be credible because both will be held responsible for the misery they cause, and so they will not, in the final analysis, carry out their threats. However, private charities (in the absence of state welfare) will

---

[49] I have been influenced here by Richard Wagner, *To Promote the General Welfare: Market Processes Versus Political Transfers* (San Francisco: Pacific Research Institute for Public Policy, 1989), 164–76.

differ in their willingness to cut off aid as a way of enforcing their policies. Indeed, some charities may give aid unconditionally if some donors favor unconditional aid. In general, there will be a tendency in a system of private charities for a kind of a match between donors and recipients: the donors who are more willing to put up with some moral hazard will in effect pay for that by tending to donate to those charities that give unconditional aid or aid with rather loose conditions, while those who are not willing, or are less willing, to put up with moral hazard, will tend to donate to charities that give conditional aid or aid with strict conditions. Thus the differences between private charities regarding their moral hazard policies means that any particular charity can make credible threats to cut off aid, whereas this is less likely when there are a small number of government agencies responsible for providing most of the aid.

However, this leads to a different objection, which is that the success of welfare reform in the United States, which has sharply reduced caseloads and sharply increased labor force participation by former recipients,[50] shows that there are institutional mechanisms for state conditional aid to overcome or mitigate moral hazard problems. I already noted that the system of capped block grants to the states gave states an incentive to cut caseloads (the states keep the unspent funds). This, plus the TANF rules that required cutting (or eliminating) benefits to those who refuse to take serious steps to enter the work force, as well as rules setting time limits for receiving welfare, shows, it might

---

[50] Welfare caseloads dropped 60 percent from 1994 to mid-2001. (In 1994, the Department of Health and Human Services began giving a variety of states waivers to drop AFDC rules and employ their own rules. Those states adopted the kinds of rules that were later incorporated into the 1996 act.) Labor force participation for single mothers – the largest group receiving welfare – rose almost 10 percent from 1996 to 2000. For a good summary, see Bersharov, "The Past and Future of Welfare Reform," 5–6, 10–12; for more detailed analyses, see Rebecca M. Blank, "Work, Wages and Welfare," in Blank and Haskins, *The New World of Welfare*, 71–5; and Demetra Smith Nightingale, "Work Opportunities for People Leaving Welfare," in *Welfare Reform: The Next Act*, Alan Weil and Kenneth Feingold, eds. (Washington, DC: The Urban Institute Press, 2002), 103–7. For data on single-mother labor force participation since 2000, see http://www.urban.org/publications/311128.html (accessed January 2007). Also see n. 36.

Although the drop in caseloads is quite impressive – by the end of 2001 the caseload amount was the lowest in had been in forty years – in a sense the numbers are a bit misleading because some state governments (e.g., California and New York) continued to spend their own money on welfare recipients who remained on the rolls. Tanner, *The Poverty of Welfare*, 176, n. 44 and n. 45.

be said, that state conditional aid can make credible threats to cut off aid and thus reduce moral hazard.

However, when one looks more closely at the success of welfare reform in the United States, it is unclear whether the moral hazard problems faced by state welfare have really been significantly mitigated, for two reasons. First, from 1996 to mid-2001, welfare reform in the United States had the good fortune to coexist with a booming economy with rising wages for low-wage earners, which, along with increased subsidies for low-income working families (using a refundable tax credit called the Earned Income Tax Credit), made leaving welfare and working a powerful draw for many welfare mothers.[51] Second, we have not really had a chance to see whether the changed ethos at welfare offices that emphasized work and getting off welfare really was supported by a credible threat of sanctions. That is because a little-known feature of the welfare reform act obviated, for the most part, the need to invoke sanctions. This feature was that states did not have to place an increasing percentage of welfare recipients into work if their caseloads were dropping; in effect a drop in caseloads gave them a credit against the requirement to get welfare recipients into the work force. Because caseloads were dropping fast (in part because of the booming economy and subsidies for low-income working families), welfare officers rarely had to threaten sanctions for recipients who were not actively getting into the work force. In addition, the issue of time limits was irrelevant during the earlier years of welfare reform because no one was receiving TANF funds for five years straight.[52]

---

[51] On the effects of the booming economy and subsidies to low-income working families, see Blank, "Work, Wages and Welfare," in Blank and Haskins, *The New World of Welfare*, 75–86, 93–4, and Haskins, "Reform, Family Income and Poverty," in ibid., 111–16. Bersharov, "The Past and Future of Welfare Reform," 11, gives perhaps the best indication of how the improved job market and subsidies for working families combined to produce dramatic incentives to leave welfare. An average mother who left welfare made about $7 an hour. That equals $14,000 for full-time work. In 2001, an EITC refund added $3,800. If you add subsidized child care and transportation, which most states provided, the difference between welfare and work would be substantial. The working mother, if she was a U.S. citizen, would also be eligible for food stamps, Medicaid, and subsidized lunches for her children, although that is not terribly significant in this context because she would get those benefits while on welfare as well.

[52] On the caseload credit and work requirements, see Lawrence Mead, "The Politics of Conservative Welfare Reform," in *The New World of Welfare*, 217; Jason A. Turner and Thomas Main, "Work Experience under Welfare Reform," in ibid., 296; and Tanner, *The Poverty of Welfare*, 97. Regarding the different policies of states on sanctions and

We can only tell if welfare reform will really make credible threats to reduce or cut off aid for noncompliance when the draw of a booming economy is lessened; caseloads are no longer declining and so the caseload credit is disappearing, and recipients are approaching the time limits for being on welfare. To some extent this has occurred since mid-2001, when the U.S. economy slowed and went into a mild recession (from which it slowly recovered in 2002 and early 2003)[53] and some TANF recipients began hitting the five-year time limit. The overall picture since mid-2001 is mixed. On the one hand, caseloads have still dropped even during the recession (whereas in previous recessions when welfare was unconditional, they stayed flat or rose). On the other hand, they have dropped much more slowly than the rapid drop from 1994 to 2000;[54] in some states they rose, and some policy analysts believe that in many states sanctions and time limits have become bluffs. Welfare officers are increasingly becoming very lenient on what counts as work or looking for work in order to avoid imposing sanctions, and states are trying to avoid punishing five-year welfare recipients into work by declaring such people special hardships (recall that TANF allows a 20 percent exemption on the time limit) and/or by using its own programs to fund such recipients.[55] Thus, the positive outcomes produced by welfare reform in

time limits, see Pavetti and Bloom, "State Sanctions and Time Limits," in *The New World of Welfare*, 246–50; regarding different estimates of the frequency of sanctions, see ibid., 259.

[53] The recovery was sustained through the end of 2006. See http://bea.gov/bea/ARTICLES/2006/08August/NIPA_annualUPDATE.pdf (accessed January 2007).

[54] After 1998, the caseload drop began leveling off. From mid-2001 to late 2004, the drop in caseloads was very gradual. See Nightingale, "Work Opportunities for People Leaving Welfare," in Weil and Feingold, *Welfare Reform: The Next Act*; http://www.acf.dhhs.gov/news/stats/2002tanffamilies.htm (accessed March 2003); and http://www.ncsl.org/statefed/welfare/caseloadwatch.htm (accessed January 2007). For the figures from 1980 to 2001, see http://www.census.gov/prod/2003pubs/02statab/socinsur.pdf (accessed March 2003).

[55] See Bersharov, "The Past and Present of Welfare Reform," 16. Though Bersharov says that this trend is *increasing*, TANF was never very strict about what counted as work or work activities. Almost all states count vocational education and training, community service jobs, and attending job-assistance programs as work activities. See Nightingale, "Work Opportunities for People Leaving Welfare," in Weil and Feingold, *Welfare Reform: The Next Act*, 112. Tanner, *The Poverty of Welfare*, 180, n. 129, based on his analysis of the Department of Human Health and Services' "2001 Annual TANF Report to Congress," tables 3.4a, 3.4b, and 3.4c point out that only 31 percent of people receiving welfare are in jobs, either private employment or subsidized

the United States do not refute the point that state conditional aid will find it difficult to credibly threaten to cut off or reduce benefits when this might cause hardship; the evidence is still somewhat cloudy.[56]

There is, however, one qualification I need to make. When I originally wrote this chapter in the spring of 2003, the debate about reauthorizing TANF had not been settled. In late 2006, it was reauthorized until 2010,[57] and the reauthorization and the subsequent issuing of rules by the Department of Health and Human Services (DHHS) may, in the future, produce some significant changes in welfare reform in the United States. Although the reauthorization did not abandon the caseload credit, a state's participation rate (the percent of recipients that it must get into the work force to receive TANF funds) is now based upon caseload declines after 2005, rather than declines from the mid-1990s. Because the large drop in caseloads from the booming economy and the EITC (from 1998 to 2001) has already occurred, this means the states must now take actions to reduce caseloads by

community-service jobs. The report is available at http://www.acf.dhhs.gov/ programs/ofa/annualreport5/chap03.htm (accessed January 2007). There has been only one further annual report since Tanner wrote his book, and the data from it are very close to the data yielded by the 2001 report. See http://www.acf.dhhs.gov/ programs/ofa/annualreport6/chapter03/chap03.htm (accessed January 2007). These reports are further evidence that the decline in caseloads had little to do with sanctions for violating work requirements. As for time limits, Tanner also points out, 180, n. 135, that the 20 percent exemption for special hardship cases actually makes the time limits look more stringent than they are. The time limits (and sanctions) don't apply to child-only cases – where children are eligible for benefits but the parents are not – yet in calculating the 20 percent, all recipients, including child-only cases, are counted. Thus, in some states, the majority of adults are exempt from the time limits.

[56] This suggests that Dworkin's condemnation of the 1996 welfare reform law, *Sovereign Virtue*, 331–8, is off the mark. He condemns it because he thinks that in a hypothetical market where wealth was fairly distributed and everyone had the same antecedent probability of losing one's job, one would not purchase unemployment insurance that had sanctions of the sort found in that law. Dworkin makes two mistakes here. First, the policy Dworkin thinks we would purchase, one that requires the insured to pursue job training and take any job the insurer finds or lose one's benefits if one refuses a certain number of such offers, is very close to the welfare reform act – particularly in light of the various measures that I described in the text, which weaken the bite of its sanctions. Second, he ignores the moral hazard problem, which suggests that the problem with state conditional welfare is likely to be that it is too lenient about cutting off aid, rather than too strict.

[57] For a clear summary of the changes, see http://www.clasp.org/publications/tanf. guide.pdf, ch. 1 (accessed January 2007).

making it harder to stay on welfare or must place larger number of welfare recipients into the work force than have hitherto taken place. (See notes 50, 51, 54, and 55 on the leveling off of the initial fast drop in caseloads and the small percentage of welfare recipients doing genuine work.) In addition, TANF reauthorization and subsequent DHHS interpretations of the language of the statute appear to have tightened up the definition of what counts as "work" a bit.[58] And a new penalty of up to 5 percent of a state's block grant was added to TANF if a state fails to implement the procedures described in the new DHHS regulations.

Having said all that, the caseload credit still exists, and the definition of work and work-related activities hasn't changed that much; furthermore, it has taken over a decade to take steps to add further bite to welfare reform to reduce moral hazard so as to produce further caseload declines and increased labor force participation of single mothers beyond the dramatic effect of the first 3–5 years of welfare reform. Also, it remains quite possible that future administrations or rulings could interpret or enforce the statute differently (so that the definition of *work* is more like the 1996 law and penalties are not applied to the states for violating the rules). This implies it takes a lot of pushing against the grain, so to speak, to take steps to reduce moral hazard that would be natural tendencies within private conditional aid. No doubt welfare reform is an evolving institution, and perhaps some day the caseload credit will be abandoned, and perhaps welfare reform will one day employ significant incentives to make welfare officers more willing to impose sanctions for noncompliance. (For example, government officials' pay could be tied to performance, and performance could be defined in terms of reducing clientele. Bonuses could be paid in accordance with how many people government welfare officials removed from the welfare rolls for an extended period of time.)[59]

---

[58] For the Department of Health and Human Services "final interim rules," see http://peerta.acf.hhs.gov/ppts/Discussion_Tour_TANF_Interim_Final_RuleGC.ppt and http://peerta.acf.hhs.gov/ppts/Afternoon_SessionGC.ppt (both accessed January 2007).

[59] Some states have given financial incentives to localities that reduce their caseloads or place recipients into the work force. See Jack Tweedie et al., *Meeting the Challenge of Welfare Reform: Programs with Promise* (Denver, CO: National Council of Legislatures, 1998), 88–9. The practice does not appear to be that common, however. See Gais et al., "Implementation of the Personal Responsibility Act of 1996," in Blank and Haskins, *The New World of Welfare*, 60–1.

So the point remains that state conditional welfare has built-in tendencies that make it hard for it to seriously mitigate the moral hazard problem; its usual *modus operandi* is not to want to be responsible for threatening to impose hardship on clients or to tie pay to performance or reward bureaucracies for shrinking their clientele. For conditional state welfare to be as effective as private charities in reducing moral hazard it must push against the grain, so to speak; this does not seem to be true of private charities. So it still appears that the latter have an edge on this matter.

Overall, private charities seem more effective in reducing involuntary disadvantage: they will be more flexible in designing policies, in monitoring their effects, and in reducing moral hazard. Because I argued in the previous section that egalitarians have no basis for preferring coerced to voluntary donors and because private charities seem more effective in achieving the egalitarian goal of reducing involuntary disadvantage among the recipients, should egalitarians favor private charities? It depends, to some extent, on the kind of egalitarian in question. I mentioned in Chapter 2 that some egalitarians believe that transfers are justified only if they are efficient. These egalitarians hold this view, I noted, because they saw it as connected to the important egalitarian dictum that the aim of coercive redistribution is not to harm the beneficiaries of brute good luck but to help those victimized by bad brute luck. Furthermore, some egalitarians measure equality in terms of well-being, not resources. Because private charities' superiority in getting recipients to take responsibility and have their lives determined more by their choices than bad brute luck means charity is better at promoting recipients' well-being than conditional state welfare, such egalitarians may have special reasons for favoring private charity. However, although some egalitarians do have reasons to consider private conditional aid to be superior to state conditional aid, it would be too strong to conclude that egalitarians must view conditional state welfare as unjust. That conclusion would require the premise that egalitarian justice requires the most efficient system, and egalitarians don't seem to subscribe to such a premise. So although there are some weighty reasons for (some) egalitarians to favor private charities over state welfare, they are not decisive ones, and we remain with the somewhat weaker, although still quite significant, conclusion that egalitarians should view private charities as more just than state unconditional aid, at least as just as state conditional aid, and perhaps as somewhat superior to any system of state welfare.

6.5 Why Prioritarianism Agrees with Egalitarianism about Welfare Policy

Let us see whether egalitarianism's cousin, the priority view, ends up with different conclusions. Notice that prioritarianism does not have any distinctive view about the donors. Because it believes public policy should tilt toward the involuntarily worst off, which in this case are the welfare recipients, its view about whether or not the donors have a right to their income or wealth, or under what circumstances they have such a right, is purely instrumental. To the extent that income and wealth inequalities help the worst off, then it applauds them; to the extent that they do not, it condemns them. This is a very large topic that I will not be able to discuss in this book. Let us then focus on the recipients. I will now show why prioritarianism replicates, with some small changes, the arguments I gave concerning egalitarianism regarding the recipients.

First, like egalitarianism, prioritarianism favors a system that is superior at discovering who is involuntarily worse off. Unconditional aid gives no way of doing this, so prioritarianism favors conditional aid. However, a possible objection I discussed, which an egalitarian might raise against conditional aid but which I argued failed, might seem to succeed on prioritarian grounds. That objection was that because some of those who refuse to take responsibility will be nonculpable, then any system of conditional aid will produce significant injustice to those who nonculpably fail to take responsibility, an injustice that is at least as bad as the injustice of giving unconditional aid to those who are simply unwilling to take responsibility. Recall that I concluded that this objection failed because most people are able and willing to respond to offers of conditional aid, and therefore fewer people are unjustly harmed by a system of conditional aid than are unjustly benefited by a system of unconditional aid. However, it appears that because prioritarianism tilts toward the worst off, it would have to count the harm or injustice of failing to give aid to nonculpable refusers (in conditional aid) as *worse* than the injustice of giving aid to culpable refusers (in unconditional aid) because the former is a harm to the worst off. Thus, even if there are fewer numbers of people who are unjustly harmed by a system of conditional aid than unjustly benefited by a system of unconditional aid, the overall injustice in conditional aid might be greater than the overall injustice in a system of unconditional aid on prioritarian grounds.

There is something to this possible prioritarian objection, but it is less strong than it appears to be. That is because even though the prioritarian would count the harm or injustice to nonculpable refusers as worse than the harm or injustice to culpable refusers, it would not consider the injustice to culpable refusers to be trivial or insignificant. After all, to give aid to those who are able and, given the right incentives, to be willing to take responsibility for their welfare and future can induce such people to stay on state welfare and fail to absorb or adopt the attitude of taking responsibility. This seems as if it is not accurately described as an unjust benefit; it could be harmful to them, it could make them join the ranks of the worst off. So even if the harm or injustice to nonculpable refusers (in a system of conditional aid) is a somewhat worse harm that the harm or injustice to culpable refusers (in a system of unconditional aid), the larger numbers affected by the latter (most adults who refuse offers of aid are culpable) means that the overall harm or injustice in the latter is greater than the former.

As for the choice of state versus private conditional aid, the same arguments apply because the greater effectiveness of the latter in helping the involuntarily disadvantaged applies whether or not we understand disadvantage in a relative or absolute sense. Thus, I conclude that egalitarianism and prioritarianism should maintain that private charities are no worse than conditional state welfare.

However, my arguments about egalitarianism and prioritarianism will look suspect unless we address a common argument against private charities – that they won't provide sufficient aid. To that topic I now turn.

6.6 Will Private Charity Be Enough?

One of the most common reactions to any proposal to replace state welfare with private charity is that voluntary provision of aid will be insufficient. How should we understand this claim? One way to understand is that private charity will fail to equal spending for state welfare.

One could support this claim by arguing that people are more likely to vote for welfare than to give aid voluntarily because they will perceive the former as cheaper.[60] However, even if it is true that the quantity of aid produced by political means will outweigh the amount produced by voluntary means, it is irrelevant because private aid does not have to match exactly the level of state welfare. As I argued in the last section, private charity will likely be more efficient and discriminating in its choice of recipients than state welfare is, and thus, if state welfare were abolished, the need to have a sufficient amount of private charity would not entail that the amount of aid provided be equal to that provided under state welfare.[61] In the context of egalitarianism, it seems more reasonable to understand the claim of insufficiency as meaning that the quantity of voluntary aid provided, were state welfare abolished, would be so small that it would cancel out the virtues of private aid – that it avoids doing injustice by not forcing those entitled to their income and wealth to surrender part of it, that it is more effective than state welfare in reducing involuntary disadvantage, and so forth. At the extreme, "insufficient" would also mean that voluntary aid is stingy to the point that enormous suffering is tolerated (e.g., widespread malnutrition, large numbers of people without shelter). If these things

---

[60] I thank Tyler Cowen for this point. His argument rests on the idea that voting involves expressive preferences, and that it is cheaper to express a preference that an outcome occur than to bring it about oneself. That idea is elaborated in Geoffrey Brennan and Loren E. Lomasky, *Democracy and Decision: The Pure Theory of Electoral Preference* (New York: Cambridge University Press, 1993).

[61] I will not discuss here two other factors that affect how much private charity would be needed were state welfare abolished. First, arguably certain government regulatory programs increase the need for state welfare. If these programs are abolished along with state welfare, that would provide an additional reason as to why private charity need not equal state welfare to be sufficient. E.g., rent control and zoning increase the cost of housing, and minimum wage and licensing laws worsen the employment situation for those with minimal skills. Thus these regulatory programs increase the need for state welfare because they reduce the disposable income of the poor and those with below-average income. I thank Richard Epstein for reminding me of this point. Second, a consideration pointing in the opposite direction is that recessions tend to decrease donations to private charity. If these cycles continue or worsen after state welfare is abolished, this might, all other things being equal, make it somewhat more difficult for private charity to be sufficient. I thank Edward Wolff for reminding me of this point. To the extent that one thinks that certain government policies and programs, such as government control of the money supply, cause business cycles, then one might argue that it is wrong to eliminate state welfare until the policies and programs that cause business cycles are abolished. I cannot consider that argument, proposed by Jeffrey Paul, in this book.

really would occur, then regardless of whether or not one was an egalitarian, support for state welfare would be quite plausible.

Is there any empirical evidence for this claim of insufficiency? At first glance, it is hard to see how there could be because there was never a period, even in the United States or England, when state welfare was completely absent or abolished at all levels of government. However, the late nineteenth century in the United States provides something very close to a natural experiment for testing the claim that private charity would be insufficient absent state welfare, because from the mid-1870s until the turn of the century unconditional aid to able-bodied needy people (outdoor relief, as it was called) was either abolished or curtailed drastically in large and some medium-sized cities.[62] Because organized charities kept fairly detailed records of their activities, we can see whether the claim that charity will be insufficient is historically accurate. It does not appear to be. In almost all of these cities, private giving rose to the occasion, and the amount contributed per household was roughly comparable to the amount given by outdoor relief.[63]

---

[62] I say that this is *very close* to a natural experiment, because although unconditional government aid was abolished in these cities, not all forms of government welfare were abolished. Prior to the rise of an extensive welfare state at a national level, government aid in England and the United States was of two types: poorhouses (indoor relief as it was called) and outdoor relief or unconditional aid (cash and in-kind aid such as food or fuel for the winter). Poorhouses were workhouses that had rather harsh conditions: long hours were mandatory, and whipping and other punishments for infractions of the rules were common. The harshness was designed to deter people who were thought capable of working from applying for government aid. See Tanner, *The End of Welfare*, 34–5. Poorhouses were not abolished in the cities that abolished outdoor relief during this period. Still, examining whether or not private giving made up for absence of outdoor relief is relevant for the issue at hand: a major form of government welfare was abolished or drastically reduced for a quarter century, and thus these cities relied on private aid for a substantial portion of the provision of aid to the needy and unfortunate.

[63] Ziliak, "The End of Welfare and the Contradiction of Compassion," 56–8, 61–2, shows this occurred in Indianapolis. In 1899, Frederic Almy, secretary of the Buffalo Charity Organization, gathered data on unconditional government welfare – outdoor relief – and private charity in forty cities and found that the cities with the lowest level of the former had the highest level of the latter, and vice versa. See his "The Relation between Private and Public Outdoor Relief – I," and "The Relation between Private and Public Outdoor Relief – II," *Charities Review* 9, no. 1 (1899): 22–33 and 65–71, respectively. Almy's study does have some drawbacks. The relationship he found did not hold very well for cities in the middle category, where the main observable relationship was that northern cities provided more total aid (public and private) than southern cities. (Almy thought that the explanation for the regional difference

Of course, that individuals seem to have risen to the occasion a century ago doesn't prove this would occur today. However, there is a more general argument that explains why these results of the late-nineteenth-century United States should not be too surprising. Economists frequently discuss the crowding-out effect of government welfare, by which they mean that when government provides aid, individuals react by giving less than they otherwise would. However, if crowding *out* occurs when there is government welfare then we should expect crowding *in* when there is not.[64] If people react to government welfare by decreasing their donations to charity, then it is plausible that they will react to its absence by increasing their donations.[65]

---

was the harsher winters in the former.) Also, Almy's study only measured private giving by regularly organized charitable societies and omitted charity provided by individual churches, mutual-aid societies, and the Salvation Army, so it may be that the amount of private charity is systematically underestimated. Still, Almy's study seems to refute the claim that when state welfare is abolished or drastically cut back, enormous harm must result because private charity will not pick up the slack.

As with any correlation, of course, Almy's study by itself cannot prove causation. Katz, *In the Shadow of the Poorhouse*, 44–5, speculates that other factors may explain why those cities that abolished outdoor relief had large amounts of private charity, namely whether or not a large proportion of women worked outside the home. If that occurred, local officials could safely vote to abolish outdoor relief, knowing it would not bring about great hardship even if the man of the house became unemployed. I find Katz's argument unconvincing because he only mentions two cities of the ten listed by Almy and his explanation would seem to show less need for aid period, not just less need for government aid, yet the total amount of aid in the cities where public relief was abolished remained high.

[64] Ziliak, "The End of Welfare and the Contradiction of Compassion," 60–2. It's worth noting that Ziliak believes that along with crowding-in comes what he calls futility, by which he means that private charity will produce roughly the same negative effects as government welfare as far as promoting moral hazard is concerned. He argues that if private charity's funding matches government welfare, then private charity will be no more effective in getting people into the work force (ibid., 62–4). He thinks that the empirical evidence supports this claim because the average duration of a spell on private charity in Indianapolis from the mid-1870s to 1900 was not that much different from the average spell on government welfare in recent times (pre–welfare reform). Ziliak's argument for futility, however, seems flawed, because comparing Indianapolis from 1870–1900 with recent times proves little, as obviously other factors could account for the lack of difference. To support his point, one would need, at the very least, a before-and-after study of the same city, such as what Ziliak and Almy (see n. 63) did to support the crowding-in thesis.

[65] Notice also that the abolition of state welfare means, all other things being equal, that the tax burden is lessened, which means that more money is available for donations to charity. Admittedly, specifying what counts as "all other things equal" is not an easy matter. It could be, e.g., that abolition of state welfare leads to more spending on the safety-net features of private compulsory insurance.

A natural response to this argument is that we can't rely on crowding-in. Even if it is plausible that the abolition of state welfare would increase donations, the increase may not be sufficient in today's circumstances. It may not be. The question is, though, if history does not support a claim of insufficiency, and if crowding-out with state welfare suggests some crowding-in when it is absent, why think charity will be insufficient? Because so far no decisive reason has been found for egalitarians to favor state welfare over private charity; some kind of argument for insufficiency is needed if one wishes to tip the balance of reasons in favor of state welfare. The most likely argument at this point is that voluntary provision of charity is a public good and, as such, will tend to be underproduced.

A standard argument that public goods will be underproduced if supplied voluntarily goes roughly as follows. A public good is nonexcludable – it is impossible or exceedingly costly to exclude nonpayers or nonusers – and is jointly consumed – one person's consumption or enjoyment of the good does not diminish others' consumption or enjoyment. Faced with the decision to contribute to a public good, a rational person will reason in this manner: If I believe that some amount of the good will be provided by others' contributions, then because I can get the benefits of the good without paying for it, I will "free ride" and not contribute. If I think that some amount of the good will not be provided by others' contributions, then I still won't contribute because my contribution will be wasted if it is insufficient to bring about the public good or bring about enough of the public good so that the benefit I receive will outweigh the cost of my contribution. Thus noncontribution is a dominant strategy: I won't contribute regardless of what others do.

But is provision of charity a public good? At first glance, it appears not to be, because it is excludable. Those who don't contribute to charity are excluded from the good, if what they value or what is a good for them is their own contribution to charity. By not contributing, people with these values or views are, by definition, excluded from its benefits because the good for them is simply their contributing or something that accompanies it (e.g., psychic benefits or the sense that one has done the right thing).[66]

---

[66] Buchanan, "The Right to a Decent Minimum of Health Care," 70–2, provides an argument that noncontribution will be a dominant strategy even if one values one's

One can get out of this problem by assuming that potential contributors value that charity be provided more than they value that they
are the ones providing it. Let us assume, for the sake of the argument,
that a significant number of people think this way. For them provision
of charity seems to be a public good: noncontributors cannot easily be
excluded from enjoying the benefits generated when others provide
charity, and one's enjoying those benefits does not seem to diminish
others' enjoyment. Some economists go on to argue that for people
like this, noncontribution will be a dominant strategy. If the potential
contributor thinks that an adequate amount of charity will be provided, then he will free ride because he does not value contributing
when others have provided an adequate amount. If he thinks that
others will not provide an adequate amount of charity, then he lacks
assurance that his contribution will be able to produce an adequate

own contribution to charity. His argument goes as follows. We imagine potential contributors to charity realizing that some of the most important forms of aid, such as the
provision of sophisticated medical technology, require coordinated collective giving
and may very well be more effective than any uncoordinated giving that I or some
others might perform. When deciding whether to give aid to such a coordinated
collective effort, the potential donors reason as follows. Suppose enough others will
contribute to make the project that requires coordinated aid a success. In that case,
his contribution will provide little benefit, for it is not *his* aid but others' that was
decisive to the success of the project; he incurs a cost by giving to this project because
by giving he loses opportunities to channel the same resources into alternative individual charitable acts whose success does not depend upon actions of others. Thus it
will more rational for him to "free ride" (in scare quotes because it's not free riding
in the literal sense) and provide aid to a project whose success does not depend
upon others. Suppose the potential contributor thinks that not enough others will
give. Then lacking assurance that his contribution will not be wasted, he performs
an individual act of charity whose success does not depend upon others. If enough
potential contributors think this way, then an insufficient amount of aid will be given
to those important large-scale projects that require coordinated giving.

Buchanan's argument fails because it depends on the assumption that after a
certain threshold has been reached, and the project's success assured, one's contribution doesn't add any significant benefit. This assumption is clearly crucial to
the argument, for without it, even if the potential contributor's contribution is not
decisive, it can still produce nontrivial *benefits*, and as such the temptation not to contribute will diminish sharply. And although it's possible that there are goods like
the sort Buchanan presupposes, he provides no evidence that the most important
elements of assistance for the needy are like this. His own example of medical technology belies his argument: even after sufficient funds have been reached to provide,
say, some complicated medical equipment, more funding hardly produces nontrivial
benefits (e.g., the equipment can be made more widely available, more people can
be trained how to use it).

amount without others' contributions. Here again, he will refrain from donating. Thus, no matter what a donor thinks others will do, he will withhold his contribution.[67]

This argument has two problems, however. First, the claim that there is an assurance problem is flawed. There is an assurance problem only if a potential donor does not value his contribution (or values it less than its cost) if it fails to produce, in conjunction with others, a *sufficient* reduction in the problem of involuntary disadvantage.[68] It is this assumption that supports the claim that the potential donor will prefer withholding his contribution if he thinks enough others will not contribute. If he thought that there was some net value in helping reduce the problem even if a sufficient reduction was not achieved, he would contribute even if others did not. It is hard to see, however, why a potential donor of this type would place no or almost no value on the partial reduction of poverty or disadvantage. Even if someone thinks that one should address the whole problem, this implies not that addressing the parts has virtually *no* value, but only that doing so has less value than addressing the problem in its entirety.[69]

---

[67] An argument of this sort seems to have originated with Milton Friedman, *Capitalism and Freedom* (Chicago: University of Chicago Press, 1962), 190–1. Since then the argument has been employed by a variety of economists. See Robert Sugden, *Who Cares? An Economic and Ethical Analysis of Private Charity and the Welfare State* (London: Institute of Economic Affairs, 1983), 11–22, and the references cited therein. Friedman's argument only refers to the lack of assurance that others will contribute sufficiently. That won't show that noncontribution is a dominant strategy; one also needs to mention that free riding will occur when others do contribute sufficiently. Hence I mention the motives of lack of assurance and free riding.

[68] This seems implicit in Friedman's presentation of the argument: "we might all of us be willing to contribute to the relief of poverty, *provided* everyone else did" (*Capitalism and Freedom*, 191, his emphasis). One explanation of why I need assurance that everyone else contributes is that I only value relieving the problem if a certain threshold of relief is produced.

[69] As pointed out by Robert Nozick, *Anarchy, State, and Utopia* (New York: Basic Books, 1974), 267. It is possible, admittedly, that some people might hold the view that what really matters is simply the expressive value being realized by a collective commitment to poverty relief, which doesn't require that poverty actually be relieved, and that cannot, by definition, be done unless nearly everyone participates, which requires coercion. The only thing that really matters, in other words, is a collective commitment; everything else is secondary and unimportant. It is very doubtful, however, that enough people hold this view to generate a public-good problem regarding voluntary contributions to charity. I discuss whether arguments about expressive commitments can be used to support a communitarian case for state welfare in section 9.2.2.

Thus it seems that there are good grounds for contributing to charity even if one thinks others will not adequately contribute. If this is so, then there is no dominant strategy here: I will not contribute (free ride) if others give a sufficient amount, but I will give if others do not. In game theory parlance, we have a game of "chicken" here. There is no settled view about what is a rational strategy in a game of chicken, but noncontribution is clearly not a dominant strategy.

A second problem with the public-goods argument is it is plausible that there really is no free-rider problem either. That's because it is not obvious what amount of charity is "sufficient," and therefore one should probably reason as if providing sufficient charity is not a real option. In these circumstances, contribution becomes a dominant strategy: one gives because one is never sure that others have given a sufficient amount, and one values the bringing about of a partial reduction of poverty or disadvantage.

Because neither the historical evidence nor the public-goods argument supports the claim that private charity would be insufficient were state welfare abolished and because the sensitivity of private aid to the amount of state welfare provided suggests that private aid might well rise if state welfare were ended, it is hard to see what basis there is for claiming that private aid will be insufficient in the absence of state welfare. I have not, it's worth emphasizing, *proved* that private aid will be sufficient. That is probably impossible to prove. We need to keep in mind, however, where the burden of proof lies here. So far, I have argued that egalitarians should view private charity as no worse (and possibly better) than state welfare. To raise the question "but will private charity be enough?" as a way of showing that state welfare is better, one needs a positive argument that private aid will be insufficient. If such an argument is lacking – and the common ways of providing such an argument seem to fail – then the case I have made in this chapter still stands. Egalitarianism and prioritarianism should consider private charity to be at least as just as state welfare.

Appendix C

Mutual Aid or Friendly Societies

Fraternal societies[70] were voluntary associations formed along ethnic, occupational, and sometimes ideological or religious lines that provided low-cost medical care, life and accident insurance, death and burial benefits, and assistance during periods of unemployment. They were guided by the principle of reciprocity, not charity, and were funded by their members' dues. Those who were aided were then expected, when they were able, to provide help to fellow members in need, pay dues, and attend meetings. These meetings often took place at lodges, which were the centers of social life as well as places where one could get medical care from the lodge doctor, find out about job opportunities, and so forth. Fraternal societies did provide help for those who could not pay them back (e.g., like charities, many mutual-aid societies ran orphanages), but even though the mutual-aid societies did offer a safety net, their main concern was not charity.

Fraternal or friendly societies were at least as important, if not more important, than charities in the voluntary provision of welfare services. In the United States, they were particularly vital in the lives of certain groups, such as blacks and immigrants from eastern and southern Europe.[71] Up until 1920, they dominated the market for life and health insurance, to the dismay of commercial life insurance and organized

---

[70] See David T. Beito, *From Mutual Aid to the Welfare State: Fraternal Societies and Social Services, 1890–1967* (Chapel Hill: The University of North Carolina Press, 2000) and David G. Green, *Reinventing Civil Society: The Rediscovery of Welfare without Politics* (London: Institute for Economic Affairs, 1993).

[71] Beito, *From Mutual Aid to Welfare State*, 2.

medicine. Historian David Green estimates that by 1910 in England three-fourths of the working male population belonged to one friendly society or another (women often had their own society, but as time went on spouses and children received benefits from the husband's society).[72] Furthermore, fraternal societies overcame a problem endemic to charities – the distance between donors and recipients when they come from different backgrounds, classes, or milieus. Because mutual-aid societies were founded on dues and because the sense of identification between members in ethnically or occupationally based societies was quite strong, there was little of the sometimes alienating sense of noblesse oblige and paternalistic meddling that can haunt even the best charities. Yet despite their importance and their moral attractiveness, it is not clear that mutual-aid societies can be considered a viable alternative to today's welfare state. This is because they were primarily combinations of an insurance society, a social club, and a community. Thus, the benefits provided by the welfare state that correspond to (some of) what mutual-aid societies offered is (for the most part) social insurance, not state welfare. And, in any event, with the rise of widespread commercial insurance, it is hard to see how these societies could play an important role today were the welfare state to disappear.[73]

It is worth pointing out that, despite their differences, fraternal societies and charities had a great deal in common. Both distinguished between the deserving and undeserving. For example, mutual-aid societies were less likely to offer medical treatment to those whose medical problems were caused by venereal disease or excess drinking.[74] Like charities, they rejected automatic aid – fear of malingerers was widespread, and aid to able-bodied adults was considered a right only for those who paid dues. Both offered personal, not impersonal, aid. And both stressed reciprocity, that is, aid was based on some ability to pay back or contribute in some way – although this was easier for fraternal societies because they were founded on dues, whereas charities had to rely on less formal modes of reciprocity.

[72] Green, *Reinventing Civil Society*, 66.
[73] Perhaps, though, the provision of insurance benefits tied to a social network might emerge amidst immigrant groups who are not comfortable with commercial insurance. In any event, because I wish to stick with real institutional alternatives that exist today, I will focus on charities and not fraternal societies as the alternative to state welfare because the former are today far more important than the latter.
[74] Beito, *From Mutual Aid to Welfare State*, 10–11, 44–5, 49–62.

7

Welfare or Means-Tested Benefits, Part II

In Chapter 6 I argued that egalitarianism and its prioritarian cousin should consider private charity to be at least as just as state conditional welfare. In this chapter I come to the same conclusion with regard to the positive-rights theory, communitarianism, and the requirement of epistemic accessibility.

7.1 The Right to Welfare

If one thinks that there is a basic right to welfare, it may seem obvious that state welfare is preferable to voluntary aid. After all, no one who receives aid from charitable institutions or donors has a *right* to that aid. So how could state welfare fail to be clearly superior to a voluntary alternative? However, things are not quite what they seem. If one believes that there is a right to welfare, it does not follow that state welfare has a clear and easy victory over voluntary assistance.

7.1.1 *The Content of the Right*
A legal right to welfare is either a right of the needy or those below a certain income to cash transfers or certain services, or a right to have or obtain a certain level of well-being that these transfers and aid are supposed to provide. If a right to welfare is the former, then virtually by definition state welfare beats voluntary aid. Whether unconditional or conditional state aid is better is unclear because this depends on who should be the bearers of the right. If it is anyone who falls below

a certain income, then unconditional state welfare is superior. If it is anyone who falls below a certain income and is willing to work or take responsibility for his or her life (if possible), then conditional state aid is superior for reasons discussed in section 6.4.

If a legal right to welfare is a right to have or obtain a certain level of well-being, then matters become more complicated. Conditional aid beats unconditional aid because the former is more focused on the need of many recipients to alter their character traits, skills, and abilities, and thus its form of aid is better at connecting with what nondisabled adult recipients need. It may seem that conditional state aid is clearly superior to voluntary aid because, again, only the former gives its recipients a right to have or obtain well-being. But is this correct? It is generally acknowledged that the two core elements of a moral right are that it typically trumps or defeats nonrights moral claims and that it is something one is entitled to, that is, one can legitimately demand that it be upheld or honored. However, welfare rights create significant conflicts with each other because even in an affluent society not everyone's needs can be met. The state must then pick and choose which needs are to be met (or whose needs are to be met or in what form they are to be met) and in doing so, the sense in which there really are welfare rights becomes diluted if not transformed. Rather than one having a right to well-being that others (especially the government) *must* respect or honor, welfare beneficiaries become closer to supplicants who are at liberty to press their claims but are not entitled to them in a full-blown sense.[1] Thus, contrary to appearances, a legal right to have or obtain well-being does not really provide its recipients with a moral right.

One might object that a right to have or obtain well-being need not be understood in such an open-ended and vague way, and when it is understood in a more precise manner, the problem of endless conflicts is sharply diminished. Many defenders of welfare rights insist that the right is to have only one's *basic* needs met (when this is economically feasible) and that the notion of a basic need has definite

---

[1] See David Kelly, *A Life of One's Own: Individual Rights and the Welfare State* (Washington, DC: The Cato Institute, 1998), 133. Kelly is mistaken, however, when he says that welfare rights turn *all* rights into privileges. I don't see why, e.g., the right not to be assaulted or murdered becomes a mere privilege because the government is attempting to enforce welfare rights.

parameters. So, for example, David Copp argues that basic needs are things *anyone* would require in *some* quantity and in *some* form in order to avoid a blighted and harmed life: examples would be the need for nutritious food and clean water, to preserve the body intact, for periodic sleep and relaxation, for companionship, for education, and for self-respect and self-esteem. In some cases, state welfare in an affluent society can enable everyone to have their basic needs met (e.g., cash to purchase a nutritious diet); in other cases, it can provide institutions that enhance one's ability to meet these needs (e.g., institutions that foster self-esteem and self-respect).[2] Because welfare rights are upheld if all the beneficiaries get or are able to obtain their basic needs, and because everyone having or obtaining basic needs only requires that everyone have or obtain *some* degree of the items that are needed to avoid a blighted and harmed life, then the argument I gave earlier has been refuted. State welfare can provide all its beneficiaries with the content of welfare rights. Serious conflicts will arise with attempts to satisfy nonbasic needs, but that is not something, on the most plausible understanding of welfare rights, to which one is entitled.

In order for this reply to succeed, I suspect that the notion of a harmed or blighted life will have to be interpreted in a very minimal manner, for otherwise some or perhaps many people will need a considerable quantity of needed items in order to avoid being harmed or blighted. Let us suppose, then, that a very minimal sense of welfare rights overcomes the problem of welfare rights creating serious conflicts with one another. That reply would produce a different problem, namely that the level of well-being welfare rights provide would be significantly below that which charity could be expected to provide. If welfare rights provide for the basic needs of its beneficiaries in only a very minimal sense, and that is all they can legitimately demand be provided, then given the diversity of individuals' needs, it is likely that charity, with its greater flexibility and hence greater attentiveness to differences in what individuals need, would be significantly better in providing many of its beneficiaries a better level of well-being. And once the gap between the level of well-being provided by welfare rights and charity becomes significant, it becomes unclear that

[2] David Copp, "The Right to an Adequate Standard of Living," *Social Philosophy and Policy* 9, no. 1 (Winter 1992): 252–3.

the superiority of welfare rights in providing an entitlement to welfare makes it better, from a rights perspective, compared to charity. To see why, consider a thought experiment about basic negative rights. On Planet Bruised, a right not to be assaulted is considered justified and is enforced, but all that this means is that the most brutal assaults are considered rights violations; more moderate or mild assaults are not considered as rights violations (or serious ones) and are erratically protected by the government or whatever agencies enforce rights. On Planet Virtuous, by contrast, there is no sense that people have a *right* not to be assaulted, but the level of assaults is quite low because people generally believe it is demeaning or vicious to assault someone. So although there are few assaults on Planet Virtuous, if they do occur there is no sense that the victim has been wronged, only a sense that the perpetrator acted in an unworthy manner. Now which society gets closer to fulfilling the content of the right not to be assaulted? It is far from clear: is it worse, from a rights perspective, not to be able to press claims in the rare cases in which assaults occur or better to be able to press claims but be frequently subject to assaults? By analogy,[3] if all welfare rights are required to do is to help its beneficiaries obtain one's basic needs in a very minimal sense, then it is unclear that this is closer to fulfilling the content of right to welfare than a system of charity, which better provides for one's basic needs.

A defender of a right to well-being might reply that I have overlooked that welfare rights do not completely supplant private charity. Thus, the fact that state welfare will be inferior in delivering a level of well-being that charity delivers is irrelevant because state welfare and charity will coexist, and their combination is exactly what a defender of a right to well-being (in the minimal sense described in the preceding text) should want. The right to well-being provides minimal well-being as a right, and, combined with charity, we get an adequate

---

[3] Admittedly, this analogy has the problem that when judging the thought experiment with Planets Bruised and Virtuous, we have an independent notion of the right not to be assaulted, and thus judge Planet Bruised to have a great deal of assaults and rights violations. However, in comparing a system of minimal welfare rights with charity, we are *not* assuming that the former protects those rights at the cost of allowing a great deal of welfare-rights violations. Nevertheless, because the content of a right to well-being is rather fuzzy, it seems legitimate to say that a system that protects a right to minimal well-being is not obviously superior to a nonrights system that provides more well-being.

level of well-being. Compared with charity alone, this combination is better because both alternatives can be expected to provide an adequate level of well-being, but only welfare rights provide the more minimal aspects of that well-being as a right.

This is a legitimate point – *provided* welfare rights won't have a serious crowding out effect on private charity. However, as I argued in section 6.6, although state welfare does crowd out some degree of private contributions, it is unclear how much crowding out does occur. This means, then, that it is uncertain whether or not state welfare plus charity will deliver a roughly equivalent level of well-being that charity alone will deliver. If it is roughly equivalent, then, given that only state welfare provides its beneficiaries with a right to aid, state welfare is superior in providing the content of welfare rights. If state welfare is worse than charity in terms of delivering a certain level of well-being to its recipients – particularly if it is significantly worse – then state welfare's advantage over charity in its providing its recipients with a legal right is negated by its relative deficiency in supplying or helping recipients obtain well-being.

To summarize this section: if a legal right to welfare is a right to cash or certain services, then state welfare is clearly better at fulfilling the content of the right than voluntary aid, though whether state aid should be conditional or unconditional remains open. If a legal right to welfare is a right to have or obtain a certain level of well-being, then conditional aid is better than unconditional aid at fulfilling the content of the right. But it is unclear whether conditional state or private aid is better. Whatever advantages the former has, because it provides a right to that aid, may be canceled out by its only providing that right if the aid is minimal, and if the aid it delivers is (in combination with what private charity has not crowded out) not significantly less than what private charity delivers. Thus, overall, the apparent advantage that state welfare has over private aid in fulfilling the content of welfare rights may be illusory.

7.1.2 The Grounds of the Right

Let us now turn our attention to the content of a legal right to welfare to the grounds of this right. Or to put matters another way, let us shift our attention to the moral right to welfare, that is, to arguments that the legal right to welfare should exist or be protected. In previous chapters I discussed a common two-step argument for basic positive rights. Step one is that persons need a certain level of well-being in order that basic negative rights have value or to enable them to exercise and/or develop their capacities for moral agency. Step two is that certain welfare-state institutions are the best way to meet these needs. Many defenders of positive rights believe that the best institutional form for meeting these needs is social insurance. The reason is that social insurance is universal, and it is founded on contribution, rather than deprivation. Thus it avoids the problem that welfare rights in a market society have, which is that they run the serious risk of undermining self-respect because they imply or suggest that the recipients are purely dependent on others to provide for one's (material) needs. Positive rights through social insurance are based on reciprocity, not asymmetrical relations of dependence, and thus balance positive rights with the notion of responsibility inherent in the idea of a moral agent. Now in Chapters 4 and 5 I've argued that this argument supports private compulsory insurance as better than social insurance. But now we face a different issue. Even if insurance – whether social or private – is the preferred institutional form for fulfilling positive rights, income-based programs may still be necessary as a supplement for those unable to work or contribute and for those who don't work or contribute now but could in the future. How, if at all, does this argument apply to such programs?

This two-step argument supports conditional aid as superior to unconditional aid for three reasons. First, conditional aid obviously embodies a reciprocity condition (for nondisabled adults), while unconditional aid does not. Second, conditional aid, by taking measures to prevent able-bodied adults from receiving welfare over the long term, avoids or lessens the division of the (nondisabled) adult population into a class of dependents and those who support them. Third, the whole *raison d'être* of conditional aid is to help recipients take responsibility for themselves and become productive members of society, while this is not true of unconditional aid.

However, one might object that if the preceding argument is supposed to ground welfare rights as parallel to basic negative rights, then the rights that are grounded should not be conditional on the person taking responsibility for his plight. Consider, for example, the right not to be assaulted. Suppose I know that there have been a great deal of muggings in a certain area at night, particularly for people who dress in expensive clothes, but I nevertheless repeatedly walk through that area at night wearing expensive clothes and get mugged numerous times. Though I am to a significant extent responsible for being assaulted, my rights have still been violated. I acted irresponsibly, but my right not to be assaulted was not conditional on my acting responsibly.[4] A related point is that only a right to unconditional aid gives the right holder the kind of control that implies he is an independent agent, to do what he wants (within the limits set by the rights of others) with the aid to which he is entitled, even if he does the wrong thing. Conditional aid is, in a sense, paternalistic: the aim is to get the recipient to behave in a certain way, join the work force, acquire certain skills and abilities, and change his habits, and so forth, so that he will live a better, more responsible life. In other words, a right to conditional aid lacks the idea that the right holder has the right to do the wrong thing, which is a central feature of negative liberty rights. However, if the grounds for welfare rights are supposed to show that welfare rights are parallel with basic negative rights, then a right bound by paternalistic conditions or that lacks the idea of a right to do the wrong thing must be rejected because no such conditions are part of the latter rights.

In one sense, this objection is sound: it shows that if one thinks that basic negative and positive rights are symmetrical, then one cannot support a welfare right to conditional aid. But because the premises or steps that are supposed to justify welfare rights do seem to support conditional aid, then the more reasonable alternative here is to give

---

4 The example comes from Norman Barry, "The Philosophy of the Welfare State," *Critical Review* 4 (Fall 1990): 556. I've altered his example so that the person is repeatedly mugged because I wanted an example of someone who can be held (partially) responsible for his plight (backward-looking judgment) and who has (in part) failed to take responsibility for his actions (forward-looking assessment). I.e., the person who gets mugged in my version of the example is partially to blame for being mugged, and, by not altering his actions after being mugged, does not really take a proactive kind of attitude toward his life. I made this alteration in Barry's example because I did not want the example to depend on a view about which kind of responsibility is more important because the defenders of basic positive rights are not explicitly committed to any such view.

up the claim of symmetry. To argue that welfare rights must be rights to unconditional aid would be to ignore the logic of the argument for the sake of a claim about symmetry between basic negative and positive rights. It makes more sense to drop the symmetry claim, however, if one wishes to stick with the two-step justification.

What about the choice between conditional state aid and private conditional aid? Because only the former provides a right to such aid, it seems obvious that only the former is compatible with the two-step argument for welfare rights. However, there is a worrisome feature about this seemingly obvious point. Once we grant that an essential part of the justification of giving welfare recipients a right to conditional aid is to enable able-bodied adult recipients to be productive and responsible moral agents, then it becomes unclear why one shouldn't favor the system that more effectively promotes that aim, even if that system lacks the legal recognition of a welfare right. Or to put it another way, once welfare policy is supposed to be paternalistic, it's not obvious why state paternalism is better than private paternalism. The response to my worry is that because moral rights generally trump other moral considerations, then even if private conditional aid is more effective in getting recipients into the work force (e.g., enabling them to learn new skills, habits), it doesn't matter, if we are working within the perspective that positive rights are needed to give negative liberty rights value or to provide conditions for the exercise and/or development of moral agency. That would seem to be a good response – *if* the rights instantiated by a system of state conditional welfare were typical moral rights. But, as we have already discussed, they are not. They lack, crucially, the right-to-do-wrong feature that exists with negative liberty rights, that is, the idea that the right holder has the freedom or discretion to exercise his right as he wants, even if he acts wrongly in doing so. Welfare recipients in a system of conditional aid may not do what they want with their aid, as we have seen; in this sense, they must act rightly (i.e., take steps to be productive, enter the work force). It's unclear if a right in this restricted sense really does take priority over or trump other considerations.[5] If it does, then state conditional aid

---

[5] There are good arguments on both sides of this question. On the one hand, one could argue that there is no necessary connection between the trumping feature of moral rights and the right-to-do-wrong feature. All rights have the former, but only

is obviously superior to private conditional aid from the standpoint of the two-step argument for positive rights; if it doesn't, then it is not obviously superior.

There is a somewhat different way to put the problem with the argument that it is obvious that because only state conditional aid provides a right to aid, state conditional aid must be superior to private conditional aid. It seems that if we are only using internal arguments and thus are precluded from criticizing the premises or principles used in these arguments, then we *have* to end up with a conclusion that some institutional instantiation of some type of positive rights is needed – the only questions are what institutional form or what type of positive rights are needed. However, it is not clear that the premises of the positive-rights arguments that we have been examining do involve the claim that there are basic positive rights. They may only involve the claim that one needs certain material *goods* in order that these rights have value or in order to exercise and/or develop one's capacity for moral agency, and then an *inference* is made that these goods require some kind of positive rights.[6] I didn't draw attention to this when I discussed the choice between social and compulsory private insurance because it didn't matter, as both institutions involve compulsory insurance and provide some kind of legal right. However, with the choice between state welfare and private charity, this point becomes more important and leaves open the possibility that the two-step argument does not justify state welfare as superior to private charity.

---

negative liberty rights have the latter. Because welfare rights aren't liberty rights, it is not surprising they lack that feature, which doesn't imply that they lack the trumping feature. On the other hand, one could argue that without the right-to-do-wrong feature, rights are the right to do what is right or morally neutral, and that the values or interests protected by such a right aren't so important or weighty that they must trump other considerations. So if those values (e.g., getting the welfare recipient into the work force, becoming productive) are better promoted without a legal right, then we should favor that alternative.

[6] It also depends on at what point in the argument the inference from needing material goods to requiring rights occurs. The longer the argument and the more steps or inferences within the argument, then the more legitimate it is, when one is limiting oneself to internal arguments that don't challenge the principles or premises of the argument or perspective, to criticize the inference. My reading of Plant, Moon, Waldron, Gewirth, and Jacobs – the authors I cited as representative of the view that positive rights are needed to give negative rights value or enable one to exercise and/or develop one's moral agency – is that they vary concerning when this inference is made in their arguments.

Thus, although it is clear that conditional aid is superior to unconditional aid from the standpoint of the two-step positive-rights arguments, it remains unclear that state conditional aid really defeats private conditional aid.

Before concluding this section, we should also look at another argument for basic positive rights, based not on moral agency or making negative rights valuable, but on mutual respect. Recall that some philosophers argue that to treat people as moral equals and live in a society in which people interact based on mutual respect requires that no one is humiliated because of her personal characteristics and that rigid hierarchies and class divisions are absent. This, in turn, they argue, requires guaranteed access to basic goods. What would this rationale for basic positive rights imply as far as welfare policy is concerned?

At first glance, this rationale may seem to support a right to unconditional aid. After all, it might be thought, conditional aid is humiliating in an important respect. In order to qualify for aid, one has to admit – to oneself and to the officials administering the aid – that one is or has been incompetent in finding employment or sufficient employment to support oneself (and one's dependents). Although this may not be a problem when the job market is poor (e.g., during a recession), when jobs are plentiful it seems like "shameful revelation," as Jonathan Wolff calls it,[7] to reveal this information. Whereas if one has an unconditional right to aid, one is not compelled to admit to oneself or others that one is incompetent.

However, there are some problems with this argument. As I discussed in sections 6.4.3 and 6.4.4, what officials administering conditional welfare care about most of all is *that* one is working or taking steps to enter the work force, not *why* one hasn't until now done so.[8]

---

[7] Jonathan Wolff, "Fairness, Respect and the Egalitarian Ethos," *Philosophy and Public Affairs* 27, no. 2 (1998): 113–15. Wolf's argument is directed against egalitarianism, not the basic rights argument I am investigating, but his argument can be applied to the latter.

[8] Admittedly, if one hasn't take serious steps to enter into the work force after one has applied for or received benefits, officials may want to know why in order to ascertain whether a cutoff of aid is in order. But the primary motivation is to get recipients into the work force, so causal explanations about subsequent failures to do so are a secondary matter.

Hence one doesn't have to admit to the officials anything about one's (alleged) incompetence in finding work or making sufficient income. Admittedly, one may have to admit this to oneself – but might not it also be the case that in a system of unconditional aid one would have to admit to oneself something that is humiliating? This leads to the main problem with the argument, which is the lack of comparative institutional evaluation. Suppose it is true that in a good job market potential welfare recipients will have to, at some point, admit to themselves that they have not been terribly competent in finding a job or in taking steps to enter the work force, and suppose it is true that this is humiliating and damaging to one's self-respect and to the respect others shows you. The relevant question is whether this is less humiliating and damaging to one's self-respect than unconditional aid that suggests, as Moon pointed out, that some able-bodied or nondisabled adults are unable or unwilling to support themselves through productive activity. Both policies may produce some damage to one's self-respect and to the respect others show you, but there are three reasons to believe conditional aid is less damaging than unconditional aid.

First, both the data from welfare reform and commonsense observations about moral hazard indicate that recipients are likely to receive benefits for fewer periods of time when aid is conditional than when it is unconditional. Because presumably damage to respect and self-respect is worse the longer it persists, the reduced time spent on welfare is a plus for conditional aid. This point is perhaps reinforced when we consider the matter intergenerationally: a child whose (able-bodied) parents have always been receiving welfare is likely to start out adulthood with more obstacles to obtaining self-respect and the respect of others than one whose parents have been receiving welfare for a shorter period of time.

Second, the attitude of the public toward welfare recipients is likely to be more respectful when aid is conditional. This is not just the point that the public, at least in some welfare states, dislikes unconditional aid. It is rather that, in light of the inevitable public ignorance about the details of welfare policy, what one is likely to find is a generalized negative disrespectful attitude toward welfare recipients when there is no strong link between welfare and work. Even if a welfare recipient in a system of unconditional aid is making a serious attempt to get into the work force, the presence of public ignorance means that this generalized attitude of disrespect is likely to stick to her, whereas in conditional aid this is less likely to be a problem.

Third, there is the retrospective attitude of the recipients toward the program once they are in the work force. Even if Wolff is right that the recipients are likely to experience shameful self-revelation when in a good job market they have to reveal some damaging facts about themselves, one would think that this to some extent could be mitigated or cancelled out by a retrospective approval of the welfare program once one is in the job market. Whereas with unconditional aid, there could be resentment once one is in the job market that the attitude of the program was so indifferent regarding providing help in finding employment. This is, admittedly, the most speculative of the points I have raised here, although perhaps the (admittedly fragmentary) data I cited in Chapter 6 (n. 40), regarding recipients' attitudes toward welfare reform backs it up.

Thus conditional aid seems more compatible with a society based on mutual self-respect than unconditional aid does. What about the choice between private and state conditional aid? This is a close call. On the one hand, getting aid on the basis of charity may be more humiliating than receiving aid as a right. I pointed out in the appendix to Chapter 6 that there is always a risk, even in the best functioning private charities, of a gulf between recipients and those who supply the aid. If this gulf between those who receive aid and those who supply it is larger than what exists in state welfare, then the mutual respect argument favors state conditional aid. On the other hand, I pointed out in sections 6.3 and 6.4 that those supplying charity (when charities are independent of the state) are probably more genuinely concerned with and are more focused on the recipient's well-being than government welfare officials, which may reduce the separation between those who supply the aid and those who receive it. This increased concern for and focus on the recipients' well-being, plus the increased efficiency in getting recipients into the work force – which, of course, reduces the separation between recipients and those supplying the aid – may make private charity at least as justified from the perspective of the mutual respect argument.

Thus, whether the grounds of the right to welfare are based on moral agency or mutual respect, we get fairly weighty reasons in favor of conditional aid, but, contrary to appearances, we do not get a decisive argument for state conditional welfare.[9]

7.1.3 Sterba's Argument

An important challenge to the conclusion of the last section is the view of James Sterba, who argues that libertarianism entails support for welfare rights. Because libertarianism maintains that all basic rights are negative liberty rights and there are no welfare rights and, in addition, is opposed to all welfare-state institutions, Sterba's argument, if sound, would turn my argument of the last section on its head. Whereas I have argued that premises that are supposed to support welfare rights fail to do so, Sterba argues that premises that are supposed to oppose welfare rights would actually succeed in supporting them. Sterba's overall project also stands mine on its head: whereas I aim to show that the political values or principles that predominate in contemporary political philosophy should converge on opposing the welfare state and supporting market alternatives, Sterba's aim is to show that these values or principles should converge on supporting the welfare state. Although Sterba and I do not focus on the same political principles or values (e.g., Sterba discusses the implications of feminism, which I don't, and I discuss the implications of egalitarianism, which he doesn't) nevertheless, we can't both be right.

---

9 The reader may wonder why I have only applied very general arguments for basic positive rights to the choice of state welfare versus private charity and have not discussed any arguments for a right to welfare that are independent of these general arguments. The reason is twofold. First, in contemporary political philosophy most arguments for welfare rights are applications of this general argument. This is unlike the case for the right to health care, which is sometimes made independently of arguments that basic positive rights are needed to give negative rights value, exercise and/or develop one's moral agency, or have a society founded on mutual respect. Second, the only argument for a right to welfare that would not be based on these general arguments would probably be an argument based on the duty to be charitable. But such arguments are unlikely to support state welfare because charity requires that one exercise discretion in choosing which beneficiaries to aid and how to aid them. For more detail on why arguments about charity are quite different than arguments for welfare rights, see Douglas Den Uyl, "The Right to Welfare and the Virtue of Charity," *Social Philosophy and Policy* 10 (1993): 192–224. However, see n. 14 for a qualification of this point.

Sterba[10] divides libertarianism into two types: Spencerian and Lockean libertarianism. The former defines liberty as being unconstrained from doing what one wants or is able to do. It takes a right to equal liberty as the basic right, and all other rights, such as a right to life and private-property rights, are derived from it. Lockean libertarians take a set of rights as basic (e.g., the right to life, property rights) and define liberty as the absence of constraints in the exercise of these rights. In other words, Spencerian libertarians define liberty in a morally neutral way so that any interference with what a person wants or is able to do is a restriction on her liberty – thus all laws that attach penalties to actions are restrictions of liberty – while for a Lockean only rights violations are restrictions on liberty. Because Lockean libertarianism is the predominant form of libertarianism, and because Sterba's arguments against it are a bit simpler, I will focus on that version of libertarianism.

Sterba argues as follows. A "typical conflict situation between the rich and poor"[11] is one in which the former have more than enough goods and resources to satisfy their basic needs, while the poor lack goods and resources to satisfy their basic needs, even though they have tried all the means available to them that libertarians regard as legitimate (e.g., charity) for obtaining their basic needs. Suppose the poor then try to take from the rich what they require to meet their basic needs, and the rich prevent the poor from doing so. Regarding a Lockean view, does this violate the poor's rights? Sterba says yes, giving a two-part argument. The first part is that if the rich do prevent the poor from taking what they require to meet their basic needs they will, as a result, sometimes starve to death, or if that does not occur, they will be "physically and mentally debilitated."[12] If the rich's actions lead to the death of the poor, then the rich will be killing the poor, regardless of whether this is done intentionally or unintentionally.

---

[10] Sterba has written a variety of articles and books on this topic. I focus on the latest versions of the argument found in *Justice for Here and Now*, ch. 3, and "Welfare Libertarianism," in *Political Philosophy: Classic and Contemporary Readings*, Louis P. Pojman, ed. (New York: McGraw-Hill, 2002), 216–28.

[11] Ibid., 218. This description of the conflict situation comes from Sterba's discussion of Spencerian libertarianism; however, the conflict situation does not change from one form of libertarianism to another but only changes the way the two forms respond to the conflict.

[12] Ibid., 221.

The second part of the argument is that such killing is unjust and hence a violation of the Lockean right to life, which is a right not to be killed unjustly. Sterba believes that libertarians will respond that such killing is not unjust because it is a legitimate exercise of one's property rights. Sterba rejects this claim. He distinguishes two views of property rights: that they are not conditional on the resources and opportunities available to others and that they are conditional. More specifically, the former view holds that the rich have a right to their property even if the poor, through no fault of their own, lack goods and resources to meet their basic needs, while the latter view holds that the rich lack property rights in their surplus goods and resources if the poor, through no fault of their own, need these resources to satisfy their basic needs. Sterba argues that the conditional view is the one Lockean libertarians must endorse. He makes this argument by appealing to two principles for resolving moral conflicts that he thinks virtually all philosophers, including libertarians, must accept. The first principle is his version of the *ought* implies *can* principle, which reads as follows:

People are not morally required to do what they lack the power to do or what would involve so great a sacrifice that it would be unreasonable to ask them to perform such an action and/or, in the case of severe conflicts of interest, unreasonable to require them to perform such an action.

The second principle, which is the contrapositive of the first principle, is the conflict resolution principle, which reads as follows:

What people are morally required to do is what is either reasonable to ask them to do, or, in the case of severe conflicts of interest, reasonable to require them to do.[13]

The upshot of these two principles is that it is not morally required to ask someone to do something that is unreasonable, and in severe conflicts of interest it is required that people do what is reasonable. Because the conflict situation described by Sterba – which he thinks is typical of a conflict between rich and poor – is a severe conflict of interest, then it is required that the poor be allowed to take the surplus of the rich and the rich let them do so. Otherwise, the poor would either be

---

[13] Ibid., 218–19.

required to not interfere with the rich's property rights, which means they would be required to let themselves be killed, which is unreasonable, or it would be permissible for the poor to try to take the surplus, but also permissible for the rich to try to hold on to their surplus, which would produce a power struggle in which the poor would lose. Thus, concludes Sterba, only the conditional view of property rights is justified. That view gives the poor a welfare right to take the surplus possessions of the rich.

Sterba notes that such a right is, at first glance, not equivalent to a positive welfare right, because the rich's obligations here are simply to refrain from interfering with the poor's taking of their surplus, and thus the right is a negative right. However, Sterba points out that this is of little practical significance because

in recognizing the legitimacy of negative welfare rights, libertarians will come to see that virtually any use of their surplus possessions is likely to violate the negative welfare rights of the poor by preventing the poor from rightfully appropriating (some part of) their surplus goods and resources. So, in order to ensure that they will not be engaging in such wrongful actions, it will be incumbent upon them to set up institutions guaranteeing positive welfare rights for the poor. . . . Furthermore, in absence of adequate positive welfare rights, the poor, either acting by themselves or through their allies or agents, would have some discretion in determining when and how to exercise their negative welfare rights. In order not to be subject to that discretion, libertarians will tend to favor the only morally legitimate way of preventing the exercise of these rights: They will set up institutions guaranteeing adequate positive welfare rights.[14]

Finally, Sterba notes that the welfare right established by this argument requires that the poor take advantage of whatever opportunities there are for mutually beneficial work, and, if they fail to do so, the obligation of the rich to let the poor have their surplus possessions or to establish a positive welfare is either canceled or lessened. Furthermore, the poor are required to return the equivalent of any surplus

---

[14] Ibid., 222. Jeremy Waldron provides a similar defense of positive welfare rights, which is based upon the negative right not to have force used against one while one is satisfying one's basic needs, when there seems to be no other way to meet those needs. See "Welfare and the Images of Charity," in *Liberal Rights*, ch. 10. Waldron describes his argument as providing a rationale for the enforcement of charity. For reasons I pointed out in n. 9, I think this is a misdescription of his argument.

possession once they have obtained their basic need. In other words, the right Sterba thinks he has established using libertarian premises is a right to conditional aid. (Notice, however, that a right to *conditional* aid is different from Sterba's argument that property rights are *conditional* upon the poor having their basic needs met. The former refers to the *content* of a right – in this case, a right to welfare – the latter to the *grounds* of a right – in that case, property rights.)

7.1.4 Why Sterba's Argument Fails

Suppose, for the sake of the argument, that libertarians should accept Sterba's argument in its entirety. It still wouldn't follow that the argument yields a welfare right, if by a welfare right we mean the kind of income-tested benefits provided by the welfare state. All it yields is a right to *subsistence*, to the amount necessary to avoid being killed by a refusal of the rich to provide aid or let the poor appropriate the rich's resources. The linchpin of Sterba's argument is that if the rich prevent the poor from appropriating their "surplus," then they will be *killing* them. If this preventing simply harms the poor, leaves them no worse off than they were prior to the prevention, or is not a significant causal factor in a subsequent death, then there is no killing. If there is no killing, then there is no unjust killing, and if there is no unjust killing, then there is no violation of the negative right to life as Lockean libertarians understand it. And if there is no violation of the right to life in not allowing the poor to appropriate the rich's "surplus," then it is a legitimate exercise of their property rights for them to prevent the appropriation. Sterba, however, clearly wants more than a right to subsistence: he wants a right for the poor to have their basic needs met (provided they cannot meet their basic needs through the market or charity), and he defines basic needs as those which if not satisfied lead to deficiencies with respect to a standard of physical and mental well-being. "Thus a person's need for food, shelter, medical care, protection, companionship, and self-development are, at least in part, needs of this sort."[15] Clearly, if the rich's preventing the poor from appropriating the rich's surplus leads to the poor's basic needs not being satisfied, then they need not be killed: being made deficient in mental or physical well-being is quite different from being killed. And

[15] Sterba, *Justice for Here and Now*, 194, n. 5.

even if they are killed, with regard to some of these needs, such as medical care, no libertarian would acknowledge that this is an unjust killing (and neither would many nonlibertarians, considering that fulfilling some people's basic medical needs could easily entail bankruptcy).[16]

Sterba could give two kinds of responses to my point that there is a big gap between the type of welfare right he thinks libertarian premises establish, and the right to subsistence that he has established, assuming for the time being that libertarianism should accept the argument in its entirety. First, he might argue that once he has established a right to subsistence, this will, in turn, provide support for a full-fledged welfare right. A right to bare subsistence might leave recipients vulnerable to starvation or severe malnutrition, if the aid provided turns out to be insufficient. Only if recipients have a guarantee of an amount greater than subsistence will subsistence be guaranteed. This reply, however, seems very close to the fallacious argument that because we can't draw a precise line between A and B, there really isn't a difference between A and B. Admittedly, there is no precise way to delineate what would be needed for subsistence. But this doesn't mean that in order to provide a right to subsistence one needs to provide a right sufficient for the poor to satisfy their basic needs.[17] More important, the response forgets that to establish a welfare right that will provide for the poor's basic needs, Sterba must show that without doing so, the poor will, according to libertarian standards, be unjustly killed. Given how Sterba defines basic needs, he does not show this.

---

[16] Notice that Sterba's definition of basic needs is much more expansive than Copp's minimalist definition I discussed in section 7.1.1. A right to have one's basic needs met, in Copp's sense of the term, is much closer to a right to subsistence.

[17] Perhaps a more promising strategy for Sterba might be to predict that a right to subsistence will lead to political pressures to expand or alter the right so that it becomes a right to have one's basic needs met. In other words, he might argue that even though a line *can* be drawn between a right to subsistence and a right to have one's basic needs met, that line *won't* be drawn and the former will be transformed into the latter. Although it is not uncommon for legislatures or judges to transform or alter rights in this manner, given the considerable gulf between a right to subsistence and a right to have one's basic needs met, Sterba would need to provide some strong reasons to believe such a transformation will be likely to occur in this case. In any event, even if Sterba were to support that empirical claim, he would still face the other problem I note in the text, which is that the linchpin of his case that libertarianism must support a welfare right to have one's basic needs met is that if they don't support such a right, they will be supporting the unjust killing of the poor – and that claim of Sterba's is false.

Another response Sterba might give is that even if he has only established that libertarian premises support a right to subsistence, he has still shown that libertarians must support a basic positive right. This is still important, because it shows that even viewpoints supposedly opposed to basic positive rights or any kind of welfare state must support some kind of basic right and some kind of welfare state. This response is correct – *provided* that the premises Sterba uses in his arguments are ones libertarians must accept. However, they aren't. Sterba, the reader will recall, says that he has described a *typical* conflict between the rich and the poor. Because the severe conflict he has described is equivalent to voluntary solutions to the poor's plight (e.g., charity) being so inadequate that they must have access to the rich's surplus in order to avoid being killed, Sterba is endorsing a very strong version of the objection discussed in section 6.6, that charity will fail to be enough. The usual ways of arguing for that view fail. Thus, Sterba hasn't shown that libertarian premises yield a positive right to subsistence.

Sterba would likely reply as follows: to concede that if his premises were true, then libertarians would have to support a basic positive right is extremely significant, for it means that there is really no fundamental disagreement between advocates of basic positive rights and libertarians.[18] Because Sterba's argument for basic positive rights depends on the poor having taken advantage of whatever employment opportunities and voluntary welfare assistance is available, then both he and libertarians agree that if those opportunities and assistance aren't available (or aren't available in sufficient amounts to avoid the poor being killed by its absence), a basic positive right is justified. Sterba and libertarians thus only disagree about whether those opportunities and assistance are available. Or to put matters another way, Sterba would likely reply that he has succeeded in showing that even libertarians must agree that a conditional positive right to subsistence is justified: if certain conditions are absent – the existence of sufficient employment opportunities and welfare assistance – then the poor have a right to the resources of the rich that are necessary to prevent the poor from being killed. (Recall that a *conditional right to aid* should not be confused with a *right to conditional aid*. The former refers to

---

[18] Sterba makes this kind of reply in "Welfare Libertarianism," 225 and 227.

conditions in the grounds of the right; the latter refers to conditions in the content of right, such that aid is only given to those who work or who take serious steps to enter the work force.)

This reply, however, misconstrues the nature of arguments for basic rights, as well as argumentation in political philosophy, at least when the issues are institutional. Sterba thinks a welfare state and basic positive rights are justified; libertarians do not. This is a fundamental disagreement about what kinds of institutions should exist. Sterba labels these disagreements as merely "practical,"[19] but these "practical" disagreements are precisely what this disagreement is all about, as well as many disagreements in political philosophy. Consider, for example, a debate about whether or not pornography should be censored by the government. A common argument for censorship is that viewing pornography (or certain kinds of pornography) directly causes a sharp increase in rape and other crimes against women. Those who oppose censorship often argue that there is no empirical evidence for this alleged direct causal connection but concede that if there were such a direct connection, censorship would be justified. So we have a disagreement here: one side favors censorship, the other side opposes it. Following Sterba's logic, we would have to say that the two sides do not really fundamentally disagree, and there is only a practical disagreement because both agree that if pornography did directly cause a sharp increase in rape, censorship would be justified. That would be an odd description of a debate in which the two sides favor completely opposite policies: one side favors a free market in sexually explicit material, and the other side wants the government to prohibit that market. Of course, the disagreement between the two sides isn't as deep as it would be if the anticensorship side maintained that *no* amount of empirical evidence of a direct causal connection between pornography and rape could provide support for censorship. But to maintain that only *that* kind of disagreement is a fundamental disagreement is to relegate many kinds of disagreements in political philosophy about what institutions we should have as insignificant.[20]

---

[19] Ibid.

[20] Suppose we were to apply Sterba's point to argumentation in general. Then we'd have to say that if two sides agree that certain premises logically entail a conclusion

We can put the point another way by focusing on the problems with Sterba's claim that both libertarianism and his defense of the welfare state favor a conditional right to welfare. Both agree that if certain conditions were met – markets and charities working so badly that the poor will be killed unless they take some of the rich's surplus – a basic positive right would be justified. However, *all* rights are conditional in *that* sense: their justification depends on the existence or absence of certain (empirical) conditions. Consider an uncontroversial right, the right not to be assaulted or battered. This right depends upon the fact that humans suffer pain and physical harm when they are physically attacked; if humans liked such assaults or did not feel pain, then it would be hard, perhaps impossible, to justify the right. Of course, this fact is recognized by all and is not controversial, although it is controversial whether markets and charities would fail as badly as Sterba thinks they do. But whether the empirical conditions that ground a right are controversial or not is a separate issue from the fact these conditions are necessary to ground a right. To say that libertarianism and Sterba's defense of the welfare state agree on a conditional right is to make the agreement sound deeper that it is because, at some level, everyone agrees that rights are conditional: the interesting question is the nature of these conditions and whether they exist.

So far I've argued that even if one accepts Sterba's argument in its entirety, the conclusion he will have established is that there is a positive right to subsistence, not a welfare right. I've also argued that Sterba's empirical claims about the insufficiency of aid in a libertarian society – such that the lack of aid will kill the poor – are weak or false, and that contrary to what Sterba says, the view that they are weak or false illustrates a major disagreement between libertarianism and Sterba's

---

(i.e., agree that the argument is valid) that there is no fundamental disagreement, even if one side thinks the premises are false (i.e., one side thinks the argument, though valid, is unsound). But clearly disagreements about whether an argument is sound are as fundamental as disagreements about whether an argument is valid: they are just different kinds of disagreement. If Sterba's premises yield a positive right to subsistence, then the argument is valid, but if the premises are false, or at any rate libertarians should not accept them, then Sterba's argument is unsound or at least has not been shown to be sound. The disagreement between Sterba and libertarianism is the latter kind of disagreement. Because disagreements about validity and soundness are equally fundamental, there seems to be no basis for considering only the former kind as fundamental.

ense of basic positive rights. But there's an additional problem: even if Sterba's claims were empirically true, conceptually, his claims about reasonableness are in serious trouble.

Sterba maintains that (a) in a libertarian society aid for the poor will be so stingy that the lack of aid will kill them, and (b) faced with (a), the only reasonable solution for people in a libertarian society is to establish or endorse a right to state aid. But are (a) and (b) consistent with one another?

First, notice that bringing about the situation in (a) is quite unreasonable. This is true whether we make an assessment of the reasonableness of (a) from the standpoint of an individual decision maker, or from a social or collective standpoint, where we evaluate the reasonableness of a libertarian society being so stingy. Regarding virtually any moral theory, as well as Sterba's view (which is that morality is a reasonable compromise between self-interested and altruistic reasons),[21] it is, in general, not reasonable for an individual to be so stingy and uninterested in other people's well-being. From a collective point of view, we get an even stronger "no," for if a libertarian society were to be so stingy, its stinginess would lead to a severe conflict of interest in which the rich's well-being is at the expense of the poor, and presumably it is unreasonable to do something that creates a severe conflict of interest when one can avoid doing so at a lower cost (e.g., giving sufficient aid). But if people are being unreasonable in doing (a), how could they then turn around and do what Sterba says is reasonable and vote for state aid? Admittedly, Sterba doesn't say they *will* do what is reasonable, but if unreasonable people *can't* do what is reasonable, then given the *ought* implies *can* principle, people will be barred from saying that they *should* do what is reasonable. In short, if people living in a libertarian society are unreasonable enough to do (a), then they can't then do (b), which means one is barred from saying that they should. Endorsing (a) precludes one from endorsing (b).

Sterba might have a reply to this argument. He might say that having done what is unreasonable, a typical individual person living in a libertarian society will recognize his unreasonableness and become reasonable and vote for aid. Although this may avoid the incoherence described in the preceding text, it creates another problem: if having

---

[21] Sterba, *Justice for Here and Now*, 21–32.

recognized that they are acting unreasonably, why won't people living in a libertarian society reverse course and give aid rather than voting for aid? The former seems far more reasonable, for a variety of reasons:

1. Aid will work faster. It takes time for elections to occur, to set up a welfare bureaucracy (there will be none in place in a libertarian society), and to distribute aid. Because there will be at least some charities in place, a faster way to fix one's unreasonableness is to give more aid.

2. Fixing one's unreasonableness by giving aid decisively eliminates one's unreasonableness; voting for state aid does no such thing because only if a majority of voters vote for state aid (or acquiesce in a democratic process that produces a right to aid) will state aid come about. *Ceteris paribus*, it's more reasonable to decisively fix one's unreasonableness than to choose an alternative that does not do so. However, I did point out in section 6.6 that the costs of expressing one's preferences are cheaper than acting on those preferences, which means that the costs of voting for aid are cheaper than giving aid. Would these cheaper costs show that it is at least as reasonable to vote for aid even though it doesn't decisively fix one's unreasonableness? I don't think so, because of point three.

3. In a libertarian society, to vote for state aid is to express one's preference for a major institutional change when there is a viable alternative that avoids such change, namely nonstingy private charity. One can assume that in order for a libertarian society to exist, a significant number of people must oppose political solutions to solve social problems and favor voluntary ones. Thus, to vote for state aid in a libertarian society involves a major ideological shift in the preferences of many of its members. This makes expressing a preference for state aid more costly, for many members of a libertarian society, than a normal preference shift. In this case, it may not be cheaper to vote for aid than to give aid, and thus the argument in (2) stands: it is more reasonable to decisively fix one's unreasonableness by giving aid rather than to vote for aid.

To summarize the results of this section: even if libertarians should accept Sterba's argument in its entirety, this would not yield a right to welfare but a right to subsistence, which is much less extensive than the kind of positive rights provided by welfare states. There is no reason for libertarians to accept these premises, for they rest on the unsupported empirical view that private charity and markets will work so badly that the poor will be killed unless they appropriate the rich's surplus. Contrary to Sterba's claim, this kind of disagreement between libertarians and Sterba is a fundamental one because they disagree whether or not, given conditions in the real world, a positive right to subsistence is justified. Finally, even if charity in a libertarian society would be as stingy as he says it would be, the more reasonable solution in the face of such stinginess would be to give more aid, not to endorse a right to state aid.

7.2 Communitarianism and Welfare

At first glance, it seems obvious that communitarianism must decisively favor conditional aid. After all, unconditional aid seems like a one-sided, unreciprocal arrangement: able-bodied recipients get benefits without any obligation to work, and the donors are required to provide income to nondisabled recipients without necessarily getting anything in return from the recipients. I argue that this first impression *is* correct: communitarian arguments for conditional aid are far stronger than any countervailing considerations. However, whether communitarianism should favor state or private conditional aid turns out to be a far more difficult matter.

7.2.1 *Communitarian Arguments for Conditional Aid*

Recall that there are five communitarian criteria that are used to make institutional comparisons: universality, shared responsibility, reciprocity, fidelity, and participation and responsiveness. Although welfare only goes to the poor or needy and is not a universal program, communitarians should favor a welfare policy that helps insure that everyone is treated as a full-fledged member of the relevant community or, to put it another way, helps sustain a sense of solidarity between the recipients and the rest of the community. Conditional aid has a significant advantage in this regard, because it requires that able-bodied adults work or take serious steps to enter the work force in order to receive aid, while unconditional aid provides aid without requiring work or taking serious steps to enter the work force. The latter separates the recipients from the rest of the community by enabling (or perhaps encouraging) them to violate the norm linking work with income that other able-bodied adults follow.[22] Furthermore, conditional aid is far superior to unconditional aid because it involves an equitable sharing of responsibility: the nonneedy support the needy in exchange for the latter working and taking steps to become productive members of the community. Unconditional aid, by contrast, is not a reciprocal arrangement: donors must support recipients and recipients are not required to do anything in order to receive the aid. As for fidelity, both systems are roughly equal: their promises are relatively easy to understand, and both tend to fulfill those promises. Unconditional aid, if the aid level is high enough, does enable recipients to avoid severe deprivation and boost their income, and conditional aid's work requirement and its programs, which enable the poor to improve their skills or alter their behavior, does enable recipients to enter the work force and become more productive citizens. Of course, unconditional aid can be set so low that its recipients are severely deprived, and, as I discussed earlier, conditional aid may have rather loose work requirements and its programs may be run inefficiently, but neither system seems inherently more or less likely to fail to live up to its promised goals.

One objection to the preceding is to argue that because welfare is a selective, nonuniversal program, it inevitably treats its recipients as different from ordinary citizens, regardless of what form it takes, and thus is worse in promoting solidarity than universal programs such as social insurance. Communitarians should favor treating welfare like social insurance as much as possible. How could this be done? One possibility is to view welfare recipients as unemployed and consider them entitled to unemployment assistance even if they haven't worked or worked very erratically.[23] One could replace welfare with what looks like a social-insurance program by giving all nonworking adults assistance of this sort. A somewhat different twist on this idea is to replace welfare with a family security program that would be analogous

---

[22] A defender of unconditional aid might reply that a superior way of integrating the poor and needy into the community is to make welfare more like social insurance: a universal benefit to which all citizens are entitled. I discuss that objection in the following text.

[23] Lawrence Mead, "Citizenship and Social Policy: T. H. Marshall and Poverty," *Social Philosophy and Policy* 14, no. 2 (Summer 1997): 210, mentions, but does not endorse, this argument.

to SS for the elderly. A family security program would have two central components: all parents, regardless of income or family structure, would be entitled to a refundable tax credit, and there would be a federal program of job training and subsidies for the unemployed, displaced workers, and new entrants into the work force.[24] Like SS, which gives lower income workers a higher percentage of their earnings than upper income workers, so too family security benefits, although open to all regardless of income or family status, could be designed so as to give a disproportionate amount to lower income recipients.

A different way to make welfare more like social insurance is to give all citizens some form of unconditional aid: everyone would be entitled to a minimal basic income, and so the only difference between the poor and everyone else would be that the poor have no or few alternative sources of income than this guaranteed basic income.[25]

However, it is hard to reconcile any of these proposals with communitarianism. As for the first proposal, it involves trying to increase solidarity by semantics. Even if we call the aid that is received without any work requirement *unemployment assistance* or *family security*, it still remains a fact that some people who receive this aid will do so because they had worked and others will just receive it, period.[26] It's hard to

---

[24] Theda Skocpol, "Targeting within Universalism: Politically Viable Policies to Combat Poverty in the United States," in *The Urban Underclass*, Christopher Jencks and Paul E. Petereson, eds. (Washington, DC: The Brookings Institution, 1991), 429–31. Family security also includes NHI and mandatory parental leave, neither of which is relevant for my discussion in this chapter.

[25] Bill Jordan, "Basic Income and the Common Good," in *Arguing for Basic Income: Ethical Foundations for a Radical Reform*, Philippe Van Parijs, ed. (London: Verso Publishing, 1992), 155–77, and Michael Freeden, "Liberal Communitarianism and Basic Income," in ibid., 185–91.

[26] Goodin, "Social Welfare as a Collective Responsibility," in Schmidtz and Goodin, *Social Welfare and Individual Responsibility*, 184–8, argues that because there are not enough jobs to employ all those who want to work, those who are unemployed are doing the employed a favor by letting the latter obtain jobs. Welfare is, in effect, compensation for structural unemployment. Goodin doesn't claim that this argument is a communitarian one, but it's worth noting that were a communitarian to try to adopt it, it would fail, because it's utterly implausible that the employed would adopt Goodin's view. (Also, Goodin's view requires establishing that the low unemployment in the United States through much of the 1990s will not be repeated, and that high unemployment isn't a sign of government-created rigidity in the labor market – two daunting tasks. In November 2006, the unemployment rate in the United States was 4.5 percent, which is pretty low. For monthly data on unemployment in the United States see http://www.bls.gov/cps/ (accessed December 2006).

believe that the hostility or suspicion of aid to able-bodied adults who don't work will disappear because we change a label.[27] As for the basic income proposal, at one level it makes perfect sense: if the reason for the separation between welfare recipients and the rest of the adult public is that the latter maintain a norm between work and income, and the former does not, or does so much less, then the separation between them will end if no one follows this norm. But this proposal involves radically changing one of the most basic social norms of Western communities, indeed virtually all communities, and it's hard to see why communitarians should favor that, for two reasons. First, some communitarians, such as Michael Walzer, do political philosophy by judging institutions in terms of how well they fit with a community's norms.[28] That would preclude us from asking whether the community's norms should be radically changed. Second, even for communitarians who reject this kind of relativist or contextualist methodology, it is very hard to see what basis there would be for claiming that a society with a universal basic income would promote a stronger or better sense of community or solidarity between its members than one in which the norm linking work and income is maintained for many of its poorest and most disadvantaged members by a system of conditional aid. After all, communitarians often argue that a serious problem today in many Western societies is that there is too much of an emphasis on rights and not enough on responsibilities: they generally argue that sustaining or strengthening solidarity involves *strengthening* the bonds of obligation citizens feel toward each other. It's hard to see how *eliminating or weakening* the responsibility to work would be an improvement from a communitarian perspective. Communitarians should not bother with the alternative of unconditional aid for all.[29]

---

[27] A similar point is made by Mead, "Citizenship and Social Policy," 209.

[28] Walzer, *Spheres of Justice*, ch. 1, 13.

[29] I do not see anywhere in Bill Jordan and Michael Freeden's communitarian arguments for basic income where they take the points I raise into consideration. Jordan argues that many of the poor are excluded from the job market and that a basic income "would give the excluded minority access to the market system of fairness" and that by giving everyone an entitlement to income it would be a mechanism for "including all in the common good." Jordan, "Basic Income and the Common Good," in Van Parijs, *Arguing for Basic Income: Ethical Foundations for a Radical Reform*, 172. Jordan's first point is odd because a basic income gives income without work or production, while markets provide income for work or production. His second point doesn't explain why a common good of a basic income is better than a common good

Another possible communitarian defense of unconditional welfare is that welfare recipients' disadvantages, which are, for the most part, due to no fault of their own, are the main reason for their exclusion from the community, and that only an unconditional entitlement will bring them back in as full-fledged members.[30] Perhaps one could add to this point that even if conditional aid is not explicitly premised on the assumption that the recipients are to blame for their plight, the programs that are designed to make recipients more productive citizens will be taken that way, and they will further exacerbate the division between welfare recipients and the public unless the programs do not require work in exchange for benefits. There are two problems with this possible communitarian defense. First, the argument is a non sequitur. Why is an unconditional welfare entitlement a better way of promoting ties between welfare recipients and the communities of which they are a part than conditional welfare? Even if welfare recipients' plight is for the most part not of their own making, the issue for a communitarian is how to help bridge the gap between recipients and donors. This argument for unconditional welfare might make sense in some version of an egalitarian theory that would see unconditional entitlement as fair compensation for unchosen disadvantages (I don't think such an argument succeeds; see section 6.4.3). But one could only link such egalitarianism with communitarianism if the former was a necessary means to sustaining solidarity or to making welfare recipients full-fledged citizens, and we've already seen that giving income without any work in exchange does not do that. Second, as I discussed in section 6.4.3, most welfare recipients are eager to accept offers of work. Although some may be so demoralized by their plight so as not to voluntarily accept such offers, and thus the work requirement of conditional welfare dragoons them into working, this is overshadowed by recipients who are pleased to get into the work force. Furthermore,

---

linked with a responsibility or obligation of all able-bodied adults to work. Freeden ties basic income "indirectly" to "direct contribution to communal purposes, based on some measure of reciprocity" and "directly" to "sharing and consumption of available social goods as facets of human needs." Freeden, "Liberal Communitarianism and Basic Income," in ibid., 186. The first point has the same problem as Jordan's first point (how is unconditional income justified in terms of reciprocity?) and the second point has the same lacuna that occurs with Jordan's second point.

[30] Alan Wolfe, "The Right to Welfare and the Obligation to Society," *The Responsive Community* 1, no. 2 (Spring 1991): 19, implies something like this.

the work requirement lessens the alienation and hostility of donors, which is an important benefit.

Yet another defense of unconditional welfare has recently been given by Amitai Etzioni. Rather than justifying unconditional aid as a way to bring into the community those who are poor or unemployed through no fault of their own, he argues that a decent or good community would not completely cut off aid even if the recipients act irresponsibly. Etzioni favors lowering benefits somewhat for those who don't but can work, but says that cutting them off or sharply reducing their benefits is too exclusionary. Thus Etzioni appears to favor something closer to a European style of welfare reform in which full benefits are conditional upon entering a job training program or the like, but no one's benefits are ever completely cut off or sharply reduced. Etzioni considers this a requirement of decency or humanity – part of the communitarian value of assuming responsibility for all members of the community.[31]

This is perhaps the most promising defense of unconditional aid because it does argue for different obligations for able-bodied adults who work and those who don't, which seems essential for a communitarian argument. But the argument still seems defective because it doesn't address the problem of lack of reciprocity or an unequal sharing of responsibility. The able-bodied who won't work are still guaranteed lifetime income simply for existing, while the able-bodied who do work get income because they worked. Perhaps Etzioni's thought is that cutting off or sharply reducing benefits is disproportionate, while reducing benefits somewhat is not. There is a qualitative difference between the able-bodied who work and those who don't, and so a mere reduction in benefits seems more disproportionate. (Also, because Etzioni talks about everyone being entitled to a "rich minimum,"[32] it seems that he is talking about a fairly minor reduction in benefits.) Or perhaps Etzioni is worried about the problem I have discussed earlier – that the moral error in cutting off benefits for those who are too demoralized to work is greater (in this case, involves greater inhumanity or lack of decency) than the moral error of keeping benefits for those who can work. However, the reply to that kind of

---

[31] Amitai Etzioni, the forward to Gilbert, *Transformation of the Welfare State*, xiv–xvi.
[32] Ibid., xvi.

argument is also similar to what I said earlier: the numbers of people involved in the former error are much smaller than in the latter error. Furthermore, it is not clear how on communitarian grounds one can say that it is more inhumane or indecent to cut off or sharply reduce benefits for able-bodied adults than to keep subsidizing people who, by failing to work, are not developing the basic capacities for making something of their lives that all other citizens are developing.

7.2.2 *The Uneasy Communitarian Case for State Conditional Welfare*

From a communitarian perspective, both state conditional aid and private aid have some comparative advantages. The former compels all the nonneedy to help welfare recipients. Because communitarians favor shared responsibility, a system of purely private aid, which allows the nonneedy to escape their responsibilities to the poor and deprived, is, *ceteris paribus*, an inferior system.[33] However, although state welfare has a *broader* sharing of responsibility, private aid involves a *deeper* sense of responsibility because donors are far more actively involved in helping recipients than in state welfare in which the main involvement is simply noticing that part of one's paycheck goes to help welfare recipients. Communitarians should consider that deeper involvement a plus because they value citizen participation. In addition, a voluntary system provides a kind of flexible and individualized involvement that is lacking in political systems.[34] It is flexible because one can donate time, money, advice – or any combination thereof – to a charity in accordance with one's preferences, while, unless one works for a welfare department, one's participation is simply as a taxpayer. It is individualized because the decentralization of the system enables one to shape the nature of one's endorsement. If I wish to aid a specific group with a specific kind of program, I can do so in a private system, while even a decentralized political system still has the one-size-fits-all problem. If I don't like the way the charity aids its recipients I can leave it, stop sending it money, and join or endorse one that shares my values or preferences. This makes private charities more responsive to

---

[33] In addition, communitarians might worry that voluntary aid, by allowing some to shirk their responsibilities, could create a kind of downward spiral in light of resentment over the presence of some free riders.

[34] Here I adapt some arguments of N. Scott Arnold, "Postmodern Liberalism and the Expressive Function of Law," *Social Philosophy and Policy* 17, no. 1 (2000): 98–101.

the particularized ways in which I can express my responsibility and desire to aid the poor and unfortunate, also a communitarian plus, because communitarians stress that institutions that help communities construct or discover a common good should be responsive to different views about the best way to realize this common good.

So which is better from a communitarian point of view?: state conditional aid that requires all to be responsible for the needy and poor or a private system that involves a less broad but deeper sense of responsibility of the donors to the recipients, and also allows that responsibility to be expressed in a more flexible and individualized manner? I'm not aware of any communitarian principles or arguments that show what to choose when there is a conflict between two ways of sharing responsibility, one that is broader and the other that is less broad but deeper, and expressed in a way that is responsive to different ways of understanding that responsibility.

One way to try to break this deadlock is to argue that state welfare has another advantage that is lacking with private aid, namely that legislation expresses a social commitment to aiding welfare recipients that is lacking in a decentralized, voluntary system. However, arguments about the expressive value of legislation work best when the message of the legislation is quite clear to those who vote for them and when the message remains clear during the existence of these laws and is affirmed and understood by the citizens. Both of these conditions are absent with state welfare. When the United States changed from a system of unconditional welfare (AFDC) to conditional welfare (TANF) in 1996, it was politically contentious: did adding a work requirement and placing a time limit on benefits mean that we were forcing recipients to take responsibility for themselves, or was it rather a vindictive attempt to blame the victim? Were we reaching out to help the welfare recipients become more productive citizens or were we abandoning them?[35] That defenders and opponents of welfare reform in the United States could find different messages being sent by its adoption suggests that interpreting "the" message of state welfare

---

[35] To get a flavor of the disagreements between proponents and opponents of the 1996 welfare reform bill, compare Jeff Jacoby, "Welfare Catastrophe? No, It's a Modest Reform," *The Boston Globe*, August 6, 1996, A15 and Robert Herbert, "Welfare Hysteria," *The New York Times*, August 5, 1996, A17.

is a murky business. Furthermore, the fact that there was a long time lag between the unpopularity of unconditional welfare with the voters and a change in the laws means that it is also a hazardous business to argue that the message of state conditional welfare will remain clear to the voters during its existence and be affirmed by them.[36]

So it doesn't appear focusing on the message sent by a political endorsement of state (conditional) welfare will tip the balance in its favor. We still face the conflict of greater breadth of responsibility versus greater depth of responsibility and a more individualized way of expressing that sense of responsibility. Perhaps the most promising communitarian argument is to argue that because state welfare is compatible with private aid, while a purely private system of aid rules out state aid, that state welfare is better because it gives us the best of both worlds: a broader sense of responsibility combined with the depth of responsibility and individualized way of expressing it that occurs with private aid. This argument perhaps tips the balance in favor of state aid, but it is an uneasy communitarian case. It's uneasy for two reasons: state aid crowds out some degree of private aid (see section 6.6), and the type of responsibility assumed by voluntary donors when the state provides welfare tends to be less deep than the kind of responsibility assumed when the state is not involved. Still, because state aid is compatible with some kind of private aid, and some of this will involve the more active kind of assumption of responsibility that communitarians favor, it is probably safe to say that communitarians should favor state welfare.

7.3 Public Justification, Epistemic Accessibility, and Welfare

In Chapters 4 and 5 I've argued that private compulsory insurance is far easier to publicly justify than the two largest social-insurance

---

[36] On the evolution from AFDC to TANF, and the unpopularity of the former, see Hugh Heclo, "The Politics of Welfare Reform," in Blank and Haskins, *The New World of Welfare*, 170–94, and Mead, "The Politics of Conservative Welfare Reform," in ibid., 201–17. It's worth noting that starting in 1967, laws were passed that provided incentives for welfare recipients to work. Not until 1988, however was there any enforceable obligation included in these laws. The year 1996, rather than 1988, is still the crucial turning point because that is when the federal entitlement to AFDC ended.

programs, NHI and SS. However, matters are more complicated when we turn to income-based programs.

Consider, first, unconditional versus conditional state aid. The purer the unconditional aid – the more it provides benefits to those below a certain income without requiring anything in return – the easier it is for recipients, administrators, and voters to understand. Conditional state aid, by contrast, is more complicated because the aim is to change the recipient's behavior. It's likely that a significant number of TANF applicants and recipients of TANF do not understand all the rules,[37] and, as I pointed out earlier (see Chapter 6, n. 48), welfare administrators are sometimes negligent in explaining them clearly. Thus unconditional aid is clearly better than state conditional aid in being easier for those who live under it to understand.

The comparison of private conditional aid with unconditional aid is more complicated. Those who contribute to charity will have a tendency to monitor their contributions and get more personally involved with recipients of aid than taxpayers who provide the funds for state welfare. Furthermore, to the extent that meeting the goals of the charity requires making them clear to the recipients, administrators of the programs will have a greater tendency to do that than state administrators of aid. Nevertheless, because the aim in private aid as well as in state conditional aid is to change behavior, there is no doubt that the content of the rules will be more complicated than in a pure system of unconditional aid. So evaluating the epistemic accessibility of unconditional aid versus private conditional aid means evaluating the extent to which the simplicity of the rules (which favors unconditional aid) is or is not more important than the incentives to clearly communicate them (which favors private aid). I can think of no way to answer that question, so it appears that unconditional aid and private conditional aid are on a par, with state conditional aid being worse.

However, there are two further complications to consider. First, only the pure form of unconditional aid – cash for low-income persons, without any obligation on the recipients' part – is simple and easy to understand and explain. As I mentioned in section 6.2, that kind of welfare is now gone. Every welfare state now has a variety of programs

---

[37] Pavetti and Bloom, "State Sanctions and Time Limits," in Blank and Haskins, *The New World of Welfare*, 251–2.

to get recipients into the work force, and fairly complicated rules about entry into and eligibility for those programs, and rules about behavior that the program is trying to encourage (but does not enforce or enforces half-heartedly). This seems to tip the balance in favor of private aid because the less pure systems of unconditional aid and systems of private aid have complicated rules, but the latter does a better job at explaining them to the donors and recipients of aid.

Now it may be objected that the disappearance of pure systems of unconditional aid is a temporary, contingent matter, and thus we cannot dismiss such systems as no longer being viable. However, even if this objection is sound, another consideration may tip the balance in favor of private aid. The pure form of unconditional welfare is, at least in some welfare states (e.g., the United States),[38] fairly unpopular with the public. Because the public has a decent understanding of how this system works and their rejection of unconditional welfare is reasonable – they believe it is unfair that they are required to provide able-bodied adults income without the latter ever being required to work, and they believe that long-term dependence on government welfare is bad for the recipients – then this form of welfare must be rejected. Although I have used the idea of public justification to generate a requirement of epistemic accessibility, public justification also means that if a reasonably well-informed public rejects a certain institution (or at least if it rejects it on reasonable grounds), it cannot be publicly justified. With the pure form of state unconditional aid out of the running because it is rejected on reasonable grounds by the public, my argument that private conditional aid is somewhat more epistemically accessible than the less pure forms of state unconditional aid remains intact. Because that argument applies to state conditional aid as well – as it is at least as complicated as the less pure forms of state unconditional aid – then the requirement of public justification and epistemic accessibility provides some reason to favor private charity.

7.4 Conclusion: The Uncertain Choice between State and Private Conditional Aid

Two main results stand out in the two chapters on welfare: conditional aid is superior to unconditional aid from virtually all perspectives,

[38] See n. 35.

but there is no clear winner between state and private conditional aid. Rather than giving a detailed summary of all the arguments in these chapters, I will instead sketch the main considerations that favor conditional aid and indicate why the choice between state and private conditional aid remains uncertain.

Conditional aid has three main advantages over unconditional aid. First, it is a far more reciprocal arrangement than unconditional aid. Recipients get donors' funds, but able-bodied or nondisabled adult recipients must, in a fairly short period of time, work or take serious steps to enter the work force. Whereas, unconditional aid, even in its less permissive forms, allows recipients to enjoy welfare without any enforceable obligation. This is the main reason why communitarians, with their stress on reciprocity and maintaining solidarity between recipients and donors, must favor conditional aid. Second, conditional aid is far better in both discovering whether recipients are willing to take responsibility for their future and inducing them to do so. You can't really discover whether or not recipients are willing to take responsibility for their future in the way ordinary working adults do, unless you see how they respond to offers to get them out of their present situation and apply a penalty for failure to take up the offer. Only conditional aid does that, which is a main reason that egalitarians, who should want those who have been bruised by bad brute luck to take responsibility for their lives, must favor it. Third, conditional aid is better at delivering what many recipients really need. What they need is not just material aid, which both systems supply, but a system that enables them to learn skills and change their habits and character traits to the extent that these are preventing them from taking responsibility and internalizing the norm linking income with work, a norm that is essential if receiving welfare is not to undermine self-respect. Conditional aid is better attuned to these needs because it is more likely to provide these programs and induce recipients to use them. This point gives both egalitarians, communitarians, and some positive-rights theorists a reason to prefer conditional aid because whether it is in the name of justice, solidarity, or self-respect, all of these theorists want the kind of aid that is tailored to what recipients really need, rather than an unconditional entitlement.

By contrast, unconditional aid has only two positive virtues. First, in its pure form, it is an extremely simple and comprehensible program. Those below a certain income get aid. Period. Worries about the public not understanding this system or the way it operates are virtually nil. Second, if one thinks that the content of a welfare right, a right to aid, is simply a right to cash or services for the needy, without any obligation on the part of recipients, then unconditional aid obviously fits the description perfectly.

However, neither of these advantages really counts for much. Pure unconditional aid is no longer a viable welfare-state option. Even if it was, it is unclear that its simplicity and comprehensibility would help justify it because pure unconditional aid tends to be quite unpopular, at least in certain countries, and the reasons for its unpopularity seem reasonable and reflect some of the reasons that communitarians, egalitarians, and some positive-rights theorists reject it. As for unconditional aid being the obvious match for the content of a positive right of needy people for cash assistance or certain services, this is less impressive if the grounds of a positive right tend to support conditional aid. When there is a conflict between the grounds of a right and some view about the content of that right, the former seems to be the more weighty consideration. As I argued in section 7.1.2, the typical ways that positive rights are supported tend to support a right to conditional aid.

The choice between state and private conditional aid, by contrast, is not so simple. Private charities have three comparative advantages. First, they are more effective in getting people to take responsibility for their future than state conditional welfare because they are more decentralized, more effective at monitoring the results of their efforts, and better at reducing moral hazard. This means that charities are more effective at promoting the egalitarian goal of getting recipients to take responsibility for their future, and giving them what they really need. Second, private aid instills a deeper and more active sense of responsibility among the donors, who will tend to be more actively involved in helping recipients than are taxpayers. This is a reason why communitarians should appreciate the way charities give depth to the idea of shared responsibility. Third, charities will tend to do a better job at communicating to donors and recipients the rules under which they operate. And this is a reason why private aid will tend to be run in a more comprehensible manner than state conditional aid. However, these advantages are pretty much canceled out by the disadvantage that charity is voluntary and, as such, doesn't require everyone to take responsibility for aiding the needy. That is an important drawback for communitarians who want all the nonneedy to assume that responsibility, as well as for positive-rights theorists who want aid to the needy to be a matter of enforceable obligation. And although egalitarians can appreciate the greater efficiency of private conditional aid in promoting the goal of getting recipients to take responsibility for their future, that efficiency, by itself, is not a strong enough reason for egalitarians to prefer charities to state conditional welfare.

8

Conclusion

8.1 Introduction

So far I have argued that all the nonlibertarian political philosophies or perspectives that form the framework of this book should consider private compulsory insurance to be superior to the two main forms of social insurance, NHI and SS, and conditional (state or private) welfare to be superior to unconditional state welfare. Thus, in answer to the question of this book – is the welfare state justified? – the answer is no, according to the main nonlibertarian perspectives in political philosophy, if by the welfare state we mean a state in which social-insurance institutions are dominant.

Another way to look at the significance of my arguments is that they show that the dominant nonlibertarian perspectives in political philosophy have institutional implications that are closer to libertarianism than they believe. Although libertarianism would consider voluntary private insurance to be the most just form of insurance, it would, I believe, consider compulsory private insurance to be more just than social insurance, and so in that sense my book shows that there is more institutional convergence in political philosophy than is commonly believed. That is, both the dominant nonlibertarian perspectives in political philosophy (egalitarianism and its prioritarian cousin, positive-rights theory, communitarianism, and the requirement of epistemic accessibility common to many forms of liberalism) and libertarianism should agree that private compulsory insurance is more just than social insurance (at least the two main forms of social insurance, NHI and SS). And although libertarianism would maintain that state conditional welfare is inferior to private conditional welfare, whereas the mainstream perspectives that form the framework of this book would find neither form of conditional welfare better than the other, there would be some convergence between the consensus perspectives in contemporary political philosophy and libertarianism in that both would agree that unconditional state welfare is unjust.

Many authors in political philosophy argue that they are right and that their opponents are wrong. One suspects few of them change their opponents' minds, mainly because most of their books argue their opponents' principles are wrong, and, as I noted in Chapter 1, it is hard to change peoples' minds about basic principles. I have dedicated this book, in all seriousness, to academic supporters of the welfare state because I hope that, as I have not objected to their principles but instead have argued that they have misunderstood the institutional implications of their principles and/or have misunderstood how welfare institutions work compared with feasible market alternatives, this book may actually change some people's minds.

Having said that, it is only fair to note in this concluding chapter that, in a sense I alluded to Chapter 1, my arguments are incomplete. Even if compulsory private insurance is clearly better or more just than social insurance, according to virtually all perspectives in political philosophy, and conditional private or state welfare is more just than unconditional state welfare, it could be that the transition from unjust welfare-state institutions to just feasible alternatives creates such evils or injustice that it would be better or more just to remain with the status quo. Thus, in order to remedy this incompleteness in my arguments, I must show that the transition from these unjust institutions does not create such injustice that it would be better to stay with the status quo.[1]

It would, however, take another book to thoroughly discuss whether all of the perspectives should support a shift from NHI and SS to MHI

---

[1] Of course, the transition from X to Y could simply mean eliminating X and starting Y immediately. However, as I shall use the term, this is still a transition, because it raises the question of the justice of cutting off people who have come to depend upon X, and also because, at least in the case of social insurance, so many people feel entitled to these benefits that an immediate cutoff is not feasible.

and CPP (and from unconditional government welfare to conditional
welfare, in the case of those welfare states that have not shifted away
from unconditional government welfare). To see whether the problem
of transition is manageable, I will discuss whether the U.S. system of
SS can be transformed to CPP without creating such injustice that it
would be better to stick with SS, or to put the point positively, whether
SS can be transformed to CPP in a just manner. I argue that there is a
way, in the United States, of instituting CPP and phasing out SS that
all the perspectives should support. I will then wrap up the chapter by
seeing where things stand for supporters of the welfare state in light
of the arguments in this chapter.

8.2 The Problems with SS and the Transition Problem

As I argued in Chapter 5, if we were starting from scratch, none of
the perspectives that form the framework of this book would choose
SS; all would choose CPP. To remind the reader, SS, but not CPP, is
a PAYGO system and has intergenerational inequalities that are completely unchosen. Except in the early stages of a PAYGO system, investment in the capital private market provides much higher rates of return
than a tax and transfer system. CPP's safety net has more progressive
intragenerational redistribution than SS, which is barely, if at all, progressive. In CPP, everyone has a right to one's pension, which gives
everyone (not just the affluent) real inheritable wealth, thus helping
to greatly minimize the present wealth gap between those who own
capital and those who don't. An additional benefit of this right is that
it enables all citizens to take responsibility for planning their retirement, and therefore being treated with the same dignity the more
affluent are treated with when they manage their own voluntary private accounts. These are all good reasons why egalitarians and their
prioritarian cousins should favor CPP.

Positive-rights theorists should favor CPP because, as mentioned in
the preceding text, it gives all citizens a right to their pension, thus
giving all generations real security, unlike a PAYGO system in which
earlier generations are made more secure at the price of reducing
security for later generations.

As for communitarians, whatever advantages SS has over CPP in
virtue of its system of shared collective responsibility (which is largely

symbolic – the living can't really share responsibility with the dead) are dwarfed by its intergenerational inequities and failure to keep its promises. These inequities and the failure to keep promises present a real threat of creating social division and undermining solidarity between the old and the young.

Finally, the case for CPP was perhaps the strongest based on the requirement of epistemic accessibility. Epistemic accessibility means major social and political institutions are not justified to the extent that support for them is due to the public being misled and/or being misinformed. SS relies on misleading rhetoric and deception, and accurate information about its functioning is very hard to obtain. By contrast, it is not that difficult for an ordinary person to obtain reasonably accurate or reliable information about CPP, which has both the contractual obligation and the incentives provided by a competitive market to provide accurate and timely information.

But because we aren't starting from scratch and presently have an unjust system, what should be done? Before we discuss the transition problem in moving from an unjust system (SS) to a just one (CPP) and whether in doing so we create or manifest such injustice that it would be better to stick with SS, we ought to note SS's impending financial problems (or crises, if one prefers). As I noted in Chapter 5, the U.S. SS system is almost a pure PAYGO system, which means payroll taxes are not invested and if there is a surplus of payroll taxes over revenues in any year that surplus is spent by the government. The impending financial problem or crisis is that when the bulk of baby boomers start to retire close to 2018 the system will run annual deficits. An SS trust fund that now shows huge surpluses of close to $1.5 trillion[2] is supposed to provide funds to handle those deficits. However, as I noted in Chapter 5 (n. 8), the trust fund contains no real assets, only special issue bonds – IOUs issued from one part of the government to another. Thus, when the annual deficits start, the government will not have money to pay all the promised benefits. Calling in the IOUs in the trust fund means – assuming that the system remains as it is, and there is no investment of workers' contributions – the government

[2] Peter A. Diamond and Peter R. Orszag, *Saving Social Security: A Balanced Approach* (Washington, DC: The Brookings Institution, 2005), 25. This was the figure in 2004.

is going to have to raise taxes and/or cut benefits and/or get the funds from general revenues.[3] (Notice this is just exactly what it would have to do if there was no trust fund, which is why the term is quite misleading.) And even if we accepted the fiction that the trust fund contained assets to pay promised benefits, those get exhausted by 2042, and the system could only pay close to three-quarters of every dollar of promised benefits.[4]

The upcoming financial problems or crises of the U.S. SS system are a function of the injustice of the system. It is unjust that instead of having real assets to pay its promises, SS has huge unfunded liabilities, which is what happens in the late stages of a PAYGO. It is unjust if taxes get increased and/or benefits cut, thus further reducing the rate of return for generations that had the bad luck to be born at the wrong time. It is unjust that the beneficiaries have no legal right to their pension, thus allowing the government to be continually changing the rules of the game (i.e., changing the tax rate and benefit structure). It is unjust that the promised benefits to retirees are at risk because the system is a PAYGO system that did not make investments that would provide assets to keep its promises. And it is unjust that SS's rhetoric about trust funds misleads a great deal of the public into thinking that the annual surplus of taxes over revenue that has occurred for almost the last twenty years is being saved for the time when shortfalls occur, whereas the truth is that the surpluses are spent by the U.S. Treasury and so the trust fund is just a record of transfers from SS to the rest of the government.

Put this way, it looks like the case for getting rid of SS and replacing it with CPP seems overwhelming. SS is an unjust system, and its upcoming financial problems are reflections of its injustice. But the problems with SS aren't going to magically disappear if we institute CPP. For one thing, people have come to rely on SS, and it would be unfair, on any theory of justice, to simply cut them off. Furthermore, if we allow people to opt out of SS and have a system of private accounts, the people opting out won't be paying SS taxes, and there will be less money to pay for retirees. So some way must be found to pay for the

---

[3] I assume here no massive inflation (printing of a huge amount of money) to solve the problem. Strictly speaking, that could be considered another way to get the funds, but I assume the political and economic climate in the United States rules this out.

[4] Diamond and Orszag, *Saving Social Security,* 29

transition to CPP, and it is possible that the ways of paying for the transition involve injustice.

Thus, we are now in a position to clarify the choice before us. In the long run, it is better to get rid of an unjust system (SS) and replace it with one that is more just (CPP). But in the short and medium run, it seems like the transition to a CPP could create injustices of its own, and it is an open question whether the problems in instituting a system of private accounts are so great that it would be better to stick with the status quo, even though, given my arguments in Chapter 5 and the upcoming financial problems of SS, that means sticking with an unjust system.

I shall compare two plans for handling SS's upcoming problems to show that it is more just to move to a plan that institutes private accounts (and eventually abolishes SS altogether). One is a plan by the libertarian think tank, the Cato Institute, which provides a way of instituting private accounts, solving SS's financial problems, and eventually abolishing SS altogether.[5] The other is a plan set out by two economists of the Brookings Institution self-described as "saving" SS, solving its financial problems, and yet not instituting compulsory private accounts.[6] My argument in favor of Cato's plan is simple: even if we give as much benefit of the doubt as possible to the Brookings plan, in the short and medium run Cato's plan is more just than the Brookings plan, and because in the long run the Cato plan abolishes an unjust system, the Cato plan is more just, all things considered.[7]

So the next task is to describe the two plans and then evaluate them using the perspectives that frame this book: egalitarianism and its prioritarian cousin, positive-rights theory, communitarianism, and epistemic accessibility.

One final point before I begin that comparison: there is always great uncertainty in long-range financial predictions. To avoid comparing

---

[5] See Tanner, "The 6.2 Percent Solution," in Tanner, *Social Security and Its Discontents*, 281–308, and Michael Tanner, "A Better Deal at Half the Cost: SSA Scoring of the Cato Social Security Reform Plan," *Cato Institute Briefing Papers*, no. 92 (April 26, 2005).

[6] Diamond and Orszag, *Saving Social Security*, in particular, ch. 3.

[7] There are other plans for reforming SS, but I picked these because of their stark contrasts and because they seem to me the most thorough. I ignore permutations of these plans. E.g., I ignore plans that, like the Brookings Plan, call for saving SS without private accounts but favor government investment of some of the SS surplus, and I ignore plans for introducing private accounts like Cato's but don't call for eventually abolishing SS (e.g., President Bush's plan).

apples and oranges, I rely on the "scoring" of the two plans by the
Office of the Actuary of the Social Security Administration (SSA).[8] In
this scoring, payroll tax increases (as we shall see, this is part of the
Brookings plan) have no negative financial impact on the economy,
and a large rise in the number of investors (a feature of the Cato plan)
has no positive impact on the economy. I think both assumptions are
wrong but will use them here to avoid unnecessary complications. I will
also use the SSA's figure that SS has unfunded liabilities in the range of
$11 trillion to almost $13 trillion,[9] though economists disagree about
how to estimate SS's unfunded liabilities.[10]

8.3 The Cato Plan

The heart of the proposal is that all workers under the age of 55 would
have the choice of diverting their half of the SS tax (6.2 percent)
into a private account that they would own. The employer's portion
(also 6.2 percent) would pay for disability insurance and survivors'
benefits and to partially fund benefits for those already retired or near
retirement, whose benefits would stay the same. (In the following text
I discuss other sources of revenue to pay for the transition to CPP.)
Workers choosing private accounts would forego any future accrual of
SS benefits.

However, although workers choosing private accounts would forego
any future accrual of SS benefits, they do get some credit for the years

---

[8] Strictly speaking, the SSA "scored" a plan similar to Cato's introduced by Representatives Johnson and Flake. See http://www.ssa.gov/OACT/solvency/SJohnson_20050215.pdf. For a discussion of the SSA's scoring of the Johnson-Flake plan, see Tanner, "A Better Deal at Half the Cost." For the SSA's scoring of the Brookings plan, see http://www.ssa.gov/OACT/solvency/DiamondOrszag_20031008.html (both accessed June 2006).

[9] Tanner, "A Better Deal at Half the Cost," n. 12, gives the figure of $12.8 trillion. I say between $11 trillion and $13 trillion because it depends on whether or not the SS trust fund is considered an asset. Tanner gets his figure by adding the SSA estimate of $11.1 trillion in liabilities and adding the $1.7 trillion in the SS trust fund as a liability to the government, rather than an asset (e-mail from Michael Tanner, July 5, 2006). The 2005 Report of the Board of Trustees of the Federal Old age and Survivors Insurance and Disability Trust Funds, March 2005, is found at http://www.ssa.gov/OACT/TR/TR05/trTOC.html (accessed June 2006). The figure of $1.7 trillion in the SS trust fund can be found on p. 2 and the $11.1 trillion figure can be found on p. 58.

[10] For a discussion of these disagreements, see http://www.concordcoalition.org/issues/socsec/issue-briefs/SSBrief4-Measurement.htm (accessed June 2006).

they paid into the system in the form of recognition bonds. These bonds would not pay interest and would be tradable in bond markets, but proceeds from the sale of the bonds would have to be redeposited in a worker's individual account until the worker became eligible to make withdrawals. Notice, then, that the recognition bonds make exiting out of SS more attractive by giving workers the greater rate of return in private accounts *and* by giving them some credit for the years they were forced to pay into SS.[11]

Those just entering the work force would have to choose the private accounts, so eventually no one is in the SS system. Workers also have the option of contributing an additional 10 percent of their wages to their private account if they so desire.

Because the Cato plan does not cut benefits for those retiring or near retirement, it is fair to retirees. However, because the employers' share of the SS tax only partially funds retirement benefits, less taxes will be collected to pay retirees as younger workers opt out of SS, and some way must be found to pay for the recognition bonds. So how does the Cato plan pay for the transition to CPP in the short and medium run? How does it reduce and eventually retire the large SS debt?

For the short and medium run (say, over the next forty years), the Cato plan relies on first, changing the benefit formula (or if one prefers, cutting future benefits), second, borrowing money (bonds sold to the general public, not the IOUs issued from one part of the government to another in the SS trust fund), third, spending cuts, and fourth, redirection of some general revenues.

Regarding the first point, right now the benefit formula in SS is determined by a number of factors. One factor is that benefits are tied to average wage growth. The Cato plan proposes changing this, starting in close to ten years and phasing it in gradually over a thirty-five-year period, so that SS benefits are tied to price inflation, rather than average wage growth, because prices grow more slowly than wages, as a general rule.

---

[11] Another way to look at the recognition bonds is that they are prepayment for some future SS benefits. Looked at that way, they are not strictly speaking a "cost of transition" but simply a way of paying now some of the future costs of SS. Milton Friedman argues this way in "Speaking the Truth about Social Security Reform," in Tanner, *Social Security and Its Discontents,* 310–11.

Regarding the second point, borrowing money means, of course, raising taxes. These won't be payroll taxes, which Cato does not raise, but income taxes. As I shall discuss in section 8.5, one way to look at this borrowing is that it makes explicit the unfunded liabilities that already exist in SS, and thus does not create new debt.

Regarding the third point, the Cato plan calls for cutting corporate welfare, by which they mean direct grants to corporations. This money would instead go to pay for the short- and medium-run transition costs.

Regarding the fourth point, the Cato plan calls for redirecting some corporate taxes to pay for the transition and redirecting some SS taxes that are presently used to fund Medicare to fund the transition.

According to the figures Cato uses (which were endorsed by the SSA), the SS part of the system starts to run surpluses close to 2046. This is because the big bump in costs from the recognition bonds is largely gone, there are fewer retirees to pay (on the assumption that most people who had the choice between SS and CPP have chosen the latter because of their greater rate of return, desire to be an investor, etc.), and all new workers are no longer in the SS system.[12] According to the SSA, the SS part of the system will have surpluses of more than $1.8 trillion by 2080. Because the Cato plan intends to get rid of SS, it does not use these surpluses as they are used today in the SS trust fund (i.e., transferred to the U.S. Treasury general revenues), but instead uses the surpluses to pay down the debt that was incurred in the short- and medium-run period. In other words, the taxes that were used during the short and medium run for the transition are now used for debt repayment.[13] Thus all the SS liabilities get repaid, and as eventually there is no one in the SS system, SS is abolished.

Other features of Cato's plan are familiar from my description of a CPP system in Chapter 5. A minimum pension is guaranteed and funded by general revenues that would be significantly larger than the current minimum guarantee. One can choose, within limits, with whom to invest your money and how to invest it. At retirement, workers could choose an annuity, a programmed withdrawal option, or the combination of an annuity and a lump-sum payment. Regulations prevent excessively risky retirement option (e.g., taking all of one's

[12] E-mail from Michael Tanner, clarifying the SSA's scoring, June 19, 2006.
[13] Ibid.

retirement in a lump sum). However, two distinctive features of the Cato plan are worth noting: one involving more regulation and control, one involving less.

On the side of more regulation and control, the Cato plan allows for substantial investment options only once one has reached a certain "trigger point" of funds. Before that point, investors have only three options, all involving various mixes of stocks and bonds (with a default option for those who decide not to choose). On the side of less regulation and control, once an individual has enough in his or her pension savings account to purchase an annuity of 120 percent of the poverty level, he or she can opt out of CPP.

To summarize then, the Cato plan allows and encourages workers under fifty-five to opt out of SS and compels new workers to participate in CPP (at least until they have accumulated enough in their account to pay for a sizeable postretirement annuity). The Cato plan pays for retirees' benefits and the short- and medium-run transition costs by a combination of present SS taxes (the employer's portion), gradual cuts in the benefit formula, raising of income taxes (borrowing money), cuts in government spending, and redirection of some money from general revenue.[14] Eventually, the SS part of the system goes into balance and the money used for transition costs is used to pay down the debt incurred during the short- and medium-run period, and SS is eventually abolished when no one is left in the system, and everyone is either in CPP or has enough in their retirement accounts to opt out of CPP.

8.4 The Brookings Plan

Peter Diamond and Peter Orszag of the Brookings Institution have set out a detailed plan designed to "save" SS without instituting private accounts. Here are the main elements of their plan:[15]

1. Payroll tax increases. This is done right now by increasing the maximum taxable earnings that are subject to payroll taxes (in 2006, wages above $94,200 are not subject to the payroll tax) by 0.5 percent

---

[14] About half the transition costs are paid for by borrowing. E-mail from Michael Tanner, May 18, 2006.
[15] Diamond and Orszag, *Saving Social Security*, ch. 5.

and, starting in 2023, increasing the payroll tax for all. In addition, the wealthy (i.e., those above the maximum taxable earnings) are subject to an additional payroll tax increase.

2. Increasing the number of taxpayers. State and local workers who are now exempt from the SS are brought into it and start paying payroll taxes.

3. Benefit cuts. The benefit formula is annually and automatically adjusted downward for projected increased life expectancy. One of the (many) factors contributing to the upcoming financial problems or crises of SS is that retirees are living a great deal longer than they used to, which is one reason the amount of money promised retirees will soon far outstrip what is sustainable given the current tax rates, which were estimated based on the assumption of a somewhat lower life expectancy. These annual reassessments will affect only those fifty-nine years of age and younger, so present and near retirees' benefits are not changed. In addition, the top 15 percent of earners get a reduction in benefits phased in through 2031.

4. Additional funds. The Brookings plan leaves open the possibility that additional funds could come from general revenue. Perhaps from a reformed estate tax, meaning that the present plan to reduce estate taxes would be canceled and part of the money from estate taxes would go into the SS system. Diamond and Orszag are not explicitly committed to this, so it is not a necessary element of their plan.

5. More features. There are other features to the Brookings plan designed to protect vulnerable beneficiaries that are worth a mention, such as those with low lifetime earnings. The most important of these is that minimum wage workers with at least thirty-five years of work would receive a benefit equal to the poverty level, phased in through 2012. After 2012, the benefit level for these workers would increase above poverty level.

So, in sum, in the short and medium run, the Brookings plan relies on a combination of payroll tax increases and benefit cuts. The plan also tries to make the system more progressive by adding increased taxes to the top earners and decreased benefits for them. As I noted in Chapter 5, SS as it stands has barely if any progressive redistribution, and it may be that the Brookings plan would clearly make it progressive. It is also worth noting that the Brookings plan does not call for any tax increases other than payroll increases, except perhaps that a planned estate tax reduction on those with substantial estates would be canceled, and in that sense income taxes are raised. Nor does it plan to raise revenue by having the government borrow money from the public.

What about the long run? According to the SSA, the Brookings plan will be in actuarial balance on average over a seventy-five-year period. However, we need to understand what the SSA means by this. The SSA is using the SS trust fund as part of its accounting.[16] Because there are no real assets in the trust fund, and any surplus is turned over to the U.S. Treasury to be spent by the government, then any year when expenditures exceed revenues, the government can only pay what has been promised by doing what it would have to do if there were no trust fund (e.g., raise taxes, cut benefits, or get the money from general revenue).[17] Because Diamond and Orszag are not really committed to getting money from general revenues, this means that in the long run, when there are years when expenditures exceed revenues, the Brookings plan will require further payroll tax increases and/or further benefit cuts.[18] Therefore, Brookings saves SS by payroll tax increases and benefit cuts in the short, medium, *and* long run.[19]

---

[16] At one point in their scoring of the Diamond-Orszag plan, the SSA says, "Moreover, the solvency for the 75-year long range period would be deemed sustainable for the foreseeable future as indicated by the stable ratio of Trust Fund *Assets* (my emphasis) to annual program cost (TFR) at the end of the period." Also see n. 9.

[17] Peter Diamond in an e-mail to me on May 11, 2006, said that in their plan "there are individual years when expenditures exceed revenues, but that is what the trust fund has been built up for." See also Diamond and Orszag *Saving Social Security*, 51, where they say the bonds held by the trust fund are an asset to the fund. But the trust fund is also a liability to the federal government, because to redeem these special issue bonds the government has to raise taxes, cut benefits, find the money from general revenue, etc.

[18] Because Diamond and Orszag only mention payroll tax increases and do not mention income tax increases as a way to finance SS, I have not listed the latter as a possible future income source, but strictly speaking it can't be ruled out.

[19] It's only fair to note that Peter Orszag does favor some reforms that would make it easier for workers to have voluntary pensions, namely making enrollment in them the default option for companies that offer them. However, these reforms do not seem to be part of the Brookings plan to save SS. See his testimony to the Senate at http://apps49.brookings.edu/views/testimony/orszag/20050426.pdf (accessed June 2006).

8.5 Comparing the Two Plans

In the long run, the Cato plan is obviously more just than the Brookings plan, because it gets rid of an unjust system, while the Brookings plan keeps it. What about the short and medium run?

For two of the four perspectives, positive-rights theory and the requirement of epistemic accessibility common to many forms of liberalism, Cato's plan is clearly superior. Pension savings accounts provide one with a legal right to one's pension, but SS does not. True, not everyone in the short and medium run will have a private-pension savings account in the Cato plan because, particularly in the short run, retirees and near retirees are likely to stay in the SS system. But many people will have private accounts, in particular, all new entrants to the work force and many of those under fifty-five.

As for epistemic accessibility, the Brookings plan keeps SS with all of its complexities and complications that make it very hard for an ordinary person to understand and persists in using at least some of the rhetoric that misleads people into thinking that SS is like private pensions, specifically the SS trust fund. The Cato plan is clearly better, because a great deal of people will be in a private system, which is, as I argued in Chapter 5, pellucid compared to SS. Of course, many of the people in CPP will also be getting some money from the years they were forced to pay into the SS system (the recognition bonds), and this could make the complexity of the CPP system during the short and medium term less epistemically accessible than it is in the long run when people will only have private pensions (or have accumulated enough assets to opt out of the system), but it is still the case that people in the CPP system will be out of the PAYGO SS system, with all its mind-numbing complexity and misleading terminology and rhetoric.

Because the Cato plan is more just than the Brookings plan in the long run, and it is clearly superior in the short and medium run from the perspectives of positive-rights theory and the requirement of epistemic accessibility, the questions remaining are how egalitarians (and their prioritarian cousins) and communitarians would rank the systems in the short and medium run. I begin first with egalitarians and their prioritarian cousins.

One possible advantage of the Brookings plan for egalitarians is that the reforms they propose would make the system more progressive than in the Cato plan.[20] I have not seen any comparative evaluation of the two plans to know whether this is so. Cato provides the redistribution through a minimum pension guarantee (one that is larger than the current minimum benefit provided by SS) financed by general revenues (i.e., progressive income taxes), although Brookings makes the system more progressive through increasing payroll taxes on those earning more than the taxable maximum, reducing their benefits disproportionately, and by raising the minimum benefit for low-wage earners. But for the sake of the argument, let us say that the Brookings plan does make redistribution within the SS system more progressive than in the Cato plan. (This wouldn't necessarily count as an advantage for a prioritarian, who cares not about relative inequalities but about the absolute level of the involuntarily worst off.)

Another possible advantage for egalitarians as well as their prioritarian cousins is that the Brookings plan does not call for any increased government debt. The upcoming financial problems or crises of SS are handled solely internally within the system by payroll tax increases and benefit cuts,[21] whereas Cato handles it in part by borrowing. Egalitarians and prioritarians might plausibly argue that it is unfair to increase the burden on taxpayers for an actuarial imbalance that is not their fault, and, to the extent that the bondholders will be wealthy individuals, the burden on future taxpayers may be disproportionately falling on the involuntarily disadvantaged.

Although this is not a bad objection, it is subject to two strong rebuttals. First, although the Cato plan does in the short and medium run increase the burden on taxpayers by borrowing, all that is really being done here is explicitly recognizing the debt that already exists. PAYGO systems in their late stages have enormous unfunded liabilities. The SSA estimates the liability in the range of $11 trillion to almost $13 trillion. If it was on the books rather than not being part of the

---

[20] Recall that in Chapter 6 I argued that there is really no firm egalitarian argument for income redistribution when looked at from the side of the "donors." This means it is unclear as to whether egalitarians would want SS to engage in income redistribution at all. But for the sake of the argument, and to give as much possible benefit of the doubt to arguments for the Brookings plan, I ignore my arguments in Chapter 6 in this chapter.

[21] Recall that Diamond and Orszag mention also some general revenue transfers or reforming the estate tax, but as they are not committed to this, I omit it here.

official budget, the Cato plan's borrowing would look more benign. Because the borrowing is part of a long-run plan to eliminate the unfunded liabilities, one could turn the argument around and say that Cato is being fair by reducing the SS debt, a legacy of its injustice, in a reasonable period of time.

The other rebuttal to the argument that the Cato plan is unfair in burdening taxpayers by borrowing is that the Brookings plan burdens all in the SS system by increasing payroll taxes and reducing benefits, thus reducing the rate of return for a generation that has already, because it has the misfortune to be born in the late stages of a PAYGO system, a lousy (and way below market) rate of return. The Cato plan does increase income taxes, but it does so largely as a way of getting people into a CPP system that significantly increases the rate of return.[22] This is because most of the need for the borrowing arises to pay the cost of the recognition bonds, rather than from allowing workers to redirect their taxes to individual accounts, and the recognition bonds provide those under fifty-five a further incentive to exit an unjust SS system.[23]

This point about the rate of return leads to what is a decisive egalitarian and prioritarian argument for the Cato plan in the short and medium run. The Cato plan, but not the Brookings plan, gives everyone a pension savings account, individual ownership, and real wealth they can pass on to their designated beneficiaries. As I argued in Chapter 5, this should be viewed as a huge advantage for egalitarians and prioritarians. Many of the more affluent members in today's welfare states now have this kind of individual ownership and control because many of them have a private-pension or retirement account to complement their payments from SS. In the short and medium run, the Cato plan enables the poor and the less affluent to enter and participate

[22] The SSA estimates that a portfolio consisting solely of stocks would have a return of 6.5 percent, and if we lower this to account for asset allocation (i.e., that the portfolios will consist of a mixture of stocks and bonds) it is still probably more than double that of SS's rate of return, which is close to 2 percent. See Tanner, "A Better Deal at Half the Cost," 3, and Michael Tanner, "The Better Deals: Estimating Rates of Return under a System of Individual Accounts," *Cato Institute Project on Social Security Choice* no. 31 (October 22, 2003), 12.
[23] Ibid., 6–7.

in this system of individual ownership and control, by making them all investors in their retirement, all owners of capital. This is a very strong reason for egalitarians and prioritarians to favor the Cato plan because, after forty years, we are talking about a significant nest egg at retirement and a substantial period during which one had one's own account with a higher rate of return than would exist in the Brookings plan.

Even if we concede that the Brookings plan is better for egalitarians because it has more progressive redistribution within the system, this is more than counterbalanced by the greater rate of return and system of individual ownership and control that the Cato plan provides for less affluent members. As for the injustice of putting greater burdens on taxpayers in the short and medium run by borrowing to pay for some of the transition costs, this is arguably a legacy of the injustice of SS and its unfunded liabilities and is also due largely to a way to provide incentives for workers age fifty-five and under to exit an unjust system. Thus, overall, egalitarians and prioritarians should favor the Cato plan for the short and medium run.[24]

Let us now turn to communitarian evaluation of the two plans in the short and medium run. Recall that communitarians use four criteria to evaluate choices of pension systems: universality, shared responsibility, reciprocity, and fidelity. Both systems are universal. I argued in Chapter 5 that although SS may have a more communitarian sense of shared responsibility (because CPP is largely an individualist system with a residual safety net), communitarians should prefer CPP because the intergenerational inequities of SS and the inherent inability of PAYGO systems to keep their promises in their later stages were too high a price for communitarians to pay to endorse SS. What about during the transition period? The Brookings plan keeps the more communitarian sense of shared responsibility, while the Cato plan during this period is a mixture of those who are in CPP and those who stay in SS; on this criterion, Brookings is superior. However, the Brookings plan maintains

---

[24] In addition, Cato's benefit cuts are fairer than Brookings's cuts. Neither plan reduces benefits for retirees or near retirees, and so are equally fair to those who have become dependent on the system through no fault of their own. But by the time Cato's benefits cuts start, those subject to them have had a chance to opt out of the system if they want to, whereas in the Brookings plan, there is no exit.

and deepens the intergenerational inequities. By raising payroll taxes and cutting benefits, it worsens the rate of return younger workers can look forward to as opposed to the rate of return retirees received during the earlier stages of PAYGO, whereas the Cato plan at least significantly boosts the rate of return for people who are in the CPP system. Furthermore, both the Cato plan and the Brookings plan show that SS cannot keep its promises: benefits will be cut at some point. The Cato plan is superior here, because it at least allows workers to opt out of the SS system and enter into a defined-contribution system in which, absent fraud, the system keeps its promises of delivering a market rate of return. Though Diamond and Orszag try valiantly to bring stability to a PAYGO system by its annual readjustment to benefits based on increasing life expectancy, their plan still, by Diamond and Orszag's own admission, relies on the trust fund to keep its actuarial balance, which means further changes in the relationship between taxes and benefits. Overall, the communitarian evaluation of the short and medium run favors the Cato plan: it is more equitable and keeps its promises, even if it is a more individualist system of responsibility for one's retirement than the Brookings plan.

So, all four perspectives should favor the Cato plan in the short and medium run. Because only the Cato plan gets rid of SS in the long run, using the Cato plan for a transition from SS to CPP and its eventual abolition should be endorsed by all the perspectives that form the framework that has guided this book.

8.6 Where Things Stand

This chapter shows that the transition problem is manageable with regard to the SS system in the United States. CPP is more just than SS (within the perspectives that form the framework of this book), and the transition from SS to CPP can be accomplished in a just manner.

Perhaps there is something idiosyncratic about the U.S. SS system such that the preceding conclusion cannot be generalized to SS systems in other welfare states, but I doubt it. All late stage PAYGO systems are facing similar problems: either right now or very soon less money will be coming in (taxes) than what is supposed to go out (promised benefits), and one has essentially the same kind of solutions: "saving" an unjust system as Brookings does, or moving toward a system of private investment the way Cato does and eventually abolishing SS.[25] If the Cato plan can do the latter in a just manner in the United States, it should be possible to devise a similar plan for other SS systems.

Of course, the preceding remarks do not prove that a just transition from SS to CPP is generalizable across countries. Nor have I shown that a just transition from unjust NHI to just MHI is possible, nor have I discussed the transition issue vis-à-vis moving from unconditional welfare to conditional state or private welfare. I conclude this book by examining the best and worst case scenarios for supporters of the welfare state regarding the transition issue, taking the arguments in Chapters 3 through 7 to be sound.

The best-case scenario is that, although present-day welfare institutions are unjust, and there are feasible just alternatives, we have no assurance, except perhaps in specific countries (e.g., the U.S. SS system), that the transition to these just institutions will be just. So we should be cautious in making any changes to what are admittedly unjust institutions. This would be quite a change for supporters of the welfare state. Instead of seeing welfare-state institutions as embodying just principles, they would say that although we wouldn't choose these institutions if we were starting from scratch, until we know that there is a just way to end them we should leave them be. This would be, in the literal sense of the term, a conservative defense of the welfare state.

The worst-case scenario for supporters of the welfare state is that these institutions are unjust, and because there are just feasible alternatives and a just way to make the transition to them, we should be taking steps right now to make the transition to just alternatives and eventually abolish the unjust institutions.

Academic supporters of the welfare state may find both scenarios depressing, and although I said in section 8.1 that I had some hope this book would change some people's minds, I get no joy from depressing people, particularly because some of the academic supporters of the welfare state are my friends and colleagues. I wish to conclude on a hopeful note by stressing the matter of convergence.

I wrote this book with the thought that the divisions between different perspectives in political philosophy are less than we think.

---

[25] I ignore permutations of these solutions: adding government investment as a way to "save" the system or adding private accounts without abolishing SS.

Although we disagree on basic principles, maybe if we understood the facts and how alternative institutions operate, we would find common ground on institutional questions. This is, I think, a message of hope. Despite seeming intractable disagreements in political philosophy, in another sense (i.e., having to do with the institutions that should be in place), we agree on a great deal more than we realize.

Select Bibliography

Aaron, Henry J., and William B. Schwartz. *The Painful Prescription: Rationing Hospital Care.* Washington, DC: The Brookings Institution, 1984.

Almy, Frederic. "The Relation between Private and Public Outdoor Relief–I" and "The Relation between Private and Public Outdoor Relief–II." *Charities Review* 9, no. 1 (1899): 22–33 and 65–71, respectively.

Anderson, Elizabeth. "What Is the Point of Equality?" *Ethics* 109, no. 2 (1999): 287–337.

Andre, Clare, Manual Velasquez, and Tim Mazur. "Voluntary Health Risks: Who Should Pay?" *The Responsive Community* 4, no. 3 (Spring 1994): 73–7.

Arneson, Richard J. "Equality," in *The Blackwell Guide to Social and Political Philosophy*, Robert L. Simon, ed. Malden, MA: Blackwell Publishing, 2002a, 85–105.

_____. "Why Justice Requires Transfers to Offset Income and Wealth Inequalities," *Social Philosophy and Policy* 19, no. 1 (Winter 2002b): 172–200.

_____. "Egalitarianism and the Undeserving Poor," *The Journal of Political Philosophy* 5, no. 4 (December 1997): 327–50.

Arnold, N. Scott. "Postmodern Liberalism and the Expressive Function of Law," *Social Philosophy and Policy* 17, no. 1 (2000): 87–109.

Attarian, John. *Social Security: False Consciousness and Crisis.* New Brunswick, NJ: Transaction Publishers, 2001.

Barr, Nicholas. *The Economics of the Welfare State.* Stanford: Stanford University Press, 1993.

_____. "Economic Theory and the Welfare State: A Survey and Interpretation," *Journal of Economic Literature* 30 (June 1992): 741–803.

Barry, Norman. *Welfare*, 2nd ed. Buckingham: Open University Press, 1999.

_____. "The Philosophy of the Welfare State," *Critical Review* 4 (Fall 1990): 545–68.

Beach, William W., and Gareth E. Davis. *Social Security's Rate of Return.* Washington, DC: The Heritage Foundation, January 15, 1998.

Beiner, Ronald. "What Liberalism Means," *Social Philosophy and Policy* 13 (Winter 1996): 190–206.

Beito, David T. *From Mutual Aid to the Welfare State: Fraternal Societies and Social Services, 1890–1967.* Chapel Hill: The University of North Carolina Press, 2000.

Bersharov, Douglas. "The Past and Future of Welfare Reform," *The Public Interest* (Winter 2003): 4–21.

Biggs, Andrew. "Personal Accounts in a Down Market: How Recent Stock Market Declines Affect the Social Security Reform Debate," in *Social Security and Its Discontents: Perspectives on Choice,* Michael D. Tanner, ed. Washington, DC: The Cato Institute, 2005, 333–56.

Blank, Rebecca M., and Ron Haskins, eds. *The New World of Welfare.* Washington, DC: Brookings Institution Press, 2001.

Blaxter, Mildred. "A Comparison of Measures of Inequality in Morbidity," in *Health Inequalities in European Countries,* John Fox, ed. Aldershot: Gower Publishing, 1989, 199–230.

Blitz, Rudolph C., and John J. Siegfried. "How Did the Wealthiest Americans Get So Rich?" *Quarterly Review of Business and Economics* 32 (Spring 1992): 5–26.

Brennan, Geoffrey, and Loren E. Lomasky. *Democracy and Decision: The Pure Theory of Electoral Preference.* New York: Cambridge University Press, 1993.

Breslow, Lester, and James E. Enstrom. "Persistence of Health Habits and Their Relationship to Mortality," *Preventive Medicine* 9, no. 4 (1980): 469–83.

Brock, Dan W. "Priority to the Worse Off in Health-Care Resource Prioritization," in *Medicine and Social Justice: Essays on the Distribution of Health Care,* Rosamond Rhodes, Margaret P. Battin, and Anita Silvers, eds. Oxford: Oxford University Press, 2002, 362–72.

Brody, Baruch. "Liberalism, Communitarianism, and Medical Ethics," *Law and Social Inquiry* 18 (Spring 1993): 393–406.

Buchanan, Allen. "Health-Care Delivery and Resource Allocation," In *Medical Ethics,* Robert Veatch, ed. Sudbury, MA: Jones and Bartlett, 1997, 321–59.

———. "The Right to a Decent Minimum of Health Care," *Philosophy and Public Affairs* 13 (Winter 1984): 55–78.

Bunker, John P., Deanna S. Gomby, and Barbara Kehrer, eds. *Pathways to Health: The Role of Social Factors.* Menlo Park, NJ: Henry J. Kaiser Family Foundation, 1989.

Cassell, Christine, et al. *Core Values in Heath-Care Reform: A Communitarian Approach.* Washington, DC: The Communitarian Network, 1993.

Chapman, Audrey R., ed. *Health Care Reform: A Human Rights Approach.* Washington, DC: Georgetown University Press, 1994.

Choi, Young Back. "On the Rich Getting Richer and the Poor Getting Poorer," *Kyklos* 52 (June 1999): 239–58.

Cohen, G. A. "On the Currency of Egalitarian Justice," *Ethics* 99, no. 4 (1989): 906–44.

_____. "The Structure of Proletarian Unfreedom," *Philosophy and Public Affairs* 12 (Winter 1983): 3–33.

Cook, Fay Lomax, and Lawrence R. Jacobs. "Assessing Assumptions about Attitudes towards Social Security: Popular Claims Meet Hard Data," in *The Future of Social Insurance: Incremental Action or Fundamental Reform*, Peter Edelman, Dalls L. Salisbury, and Pamela J. Larson, eds. Washington, DC: Brookings Institution, 2002, 82–110.

Copp, David. "The Right to an Adequate Standard of Living," *Social Philosophy and Policy* 9 (Winter 1992): 231–61.

Coulter, Angela, and Chris Ham, eds. *The Global Challenge of Health Care Rationing*. Buckingham: Open University Press, 2000.

Cox, W. Michael, and Richard Alm. *Myths of Rich and Poor: Why We're Better Off Than We Think*. New York: Basic Books, 1999.

D'Agostino, Fred. "Public Justification," in *The Stanford Encyclopedia of Philosophy*, Edward N. Zalta, ed. Fall 1996 ed., http://plato.stanford.edu/archives/fall1997/entries/justification-public/.

Daniels, Norman. "Four Unsolved Rationing Problems: A Challenge," *Hastings Center Report* 24 (July–August 1994): 27–9.

Daniels, Norman, and James E. Sabin. *Setting Limits Fairly: Can We Learn to Share Medical Resources?* New York: Oxford University Press, 2002.

Daniels, Norman, Bruce Kennedy, and Ichiro Kawachi. *Is Inequality Bad for Our Health?* Boston: Beacon Press, 2000.

Daniels, Norman, Donald W. Light, and Ronald L. Caplan. *Benchmarks of Fairness for Health Care Reform*. New York: Oxford University Press, 1997.

Demsetz, Harold. "Information and Efficiency: Another Viewpoint," *Journal of Law and Economics* 12 (1969): 1–22.

Derthick, Martha. *Policymaking for Social Security*. Washington, DC: Brookings Institution, 1979.

Diamond, Peter A., and Peter R. Orszag. *Saving Social Security: A Balanced Approach*. Washington, DC: The Brookings Institution, 2005.

Dimson, Elroy, Paul Marsh, and Mike Staunton. *Triumph of the Optimists*. Princeton: Princeton University Press, 2002.

Dixon, Anna, and Elias Mossialos, eds. *Health Care System in Eight Countries: Trends and Challenges*. London: European Observatory on Health Care Systems, London School of Economics and Political Science Hub, 2002.

Dworkin, Ronald. *Sovereign Virtue: The Theory and Practice of Equality*. Cambridge, MA: Harvard University Press, 2000.

_____. "Justice in the Distribution of Health Care," *McGill Law Review* 38, no. 4 (1993): 883–98.

_____. "Why Liberals Should Care about Equality," in *A Matter of Principle*. Cambridge, MA: Harvard University Press, 1983, 205–13.

Eliasson, Nils. *Protection of Accrued Pension Rights: An Inquiry into Reforms of Statutory and Occupational Pension Schemes in a German, Norwegian and Swedish Context*. Lund, Sweden: Akademibokhandeln, 2001.

Emanuel, Ezekiel J. *The Ends of Human Life: Medical Ethics in a Liberal Polity.* Cambridge, MA: Harvard University Press, 1991.

Emanuel, Ezekiel J., and Linda L. Emanuel. "Preserving Community in Health Care," *Journal of Health Politics, Policy, and Law* 22, no. 1 (1997): 147–84.

Epstein, Richard A. *Mortal Peril: Our Inalienable Right to Health Care?* Reading, MA: Addison-Wesley Publishing Company, 1997.

————. *Antidiscrimination in Health Care: Community Rating and Preexisting Conditions.* Oakland, CA: The Independent Institute, 1996.

Esmail, Nadeem, and Michael Walker. *Waiting Your Turn: Hospital Waiting Lists in Canada.* Vancouver: The Fraser Institute, 2002.

Etzioni, Amitai. *The Essential Communitarian Reader.* Lanham, MD: Rowman and Littlefield, 1998.

Etzioni, Amitai and Laura Brodbeck. *The Intergenerational Covenant: Rights and Responsibilities.* Washington, DC: The Communitarian Network, 1995.

Evans, R. G., Morris L. Barerm, and Theodore R. Marmor, eds. *Why Are Some People Healthy and Others Not? The Determinants of Health of Populations.* New York: Aldine DeGruyter, 1994.

Feigenbaum, Susan. "Body Shop Economics: What's Good for Our Cars May Be Good for Our Health," *Regulation* 15 (Fall 1992): 25–31.

Feldstein, Martin. "The Future of Social Security Pensions in Europe," *National Bureau of Economics Research Working Paper 8487*, available at http://www.nber.org/papers/w8487.

Feldstein, Martin, ed. *Privatizing Social Security.* Chicago: University of Chicago Press, 1998.

Feldstein, Martin and Horst Siebert, eds. *Social Security Pension Reform in Europe.* Chicago: University of Chicago Press, 2002.

Ferrara, Peter J. *Social Security: The Inherent Contradiction.* Washington, DC: The Cato Institute, 1980.

Ferrara, Peter J., and Michael Tanner. *A New Deal for Social Security.* Washington, DC: Cato Institute, 1998.

France, George, and Francesco Taroni. "Evolution of Health Care Reform in Italy." Presented at European Health Care Discussion Group at London School of Economics, available at http://healthpolicy.stanford.edu/GHP/GeorgeFrancepaper.pdf.

Freeman, Richard. *When Earnings Diverge: Causes, Consequences and Cures for the New Inequality in the U.S.* Washington, DC: National Policy Association, 1997.

Friedman, Milton. "Speaking the Truth about Social Security Reform," in *Social Security and Its Discontents*, Michael Tanner, ed. Washington, DC: The Cato Institute, 2004, 309–12.

————. *Capitalism and Freedom.* Chicago: University of Chicago Press, 1962.

Gauld, Robin, and Sarah Derrett. "Solving the Surgical Waiting List Problem? New Zealand's 'Booking System,'" *International Journal of Health Planning and Management* 15 (2000): 259–72.

Gaus, Gerald. "Why All Welfare States (Including Laissez-Faire Ones) Are Unreasonable," *Social Philosophy and Policy* 15 (Summer 1998): 1–33.

Geyer, Siegried, and Richard Peter. "Income, Occupational Position, Qualification and Health Inequalities – Competing Risks? (Comparing Indicators of Social Status)," *Journal of Epidemiology and Community Health* 54, no. 4 (2000): 299–305.

Gilbert, Neil. *Transformation of the Welfare State: The Silent Surrender of Public Responsibility*. New York: Oxford University Press, 2002.

Glaser, William. *Health Insurance in Practice: International Variations in Financing, Benefits, and Problems*. San Francisco: Jossey-Bass Publishers, 1991.

Goodin, Robert E. "Treating Likes Alike, Intergenerationally and Internationally," *Policy Sciences* 32, no. 2 (1999): 189–206.

Goodin, Robert E., Julian Le Grand, and D. M. Gibson, eds. *Not Only the Poor: The Middle Classes and the Welfare State*. London: Allen and Unwin, 1987.

Goodman, John C., and Gerald L. Musgrave. *Patient Power: Solving America's Health Care Crisis*. Washington, DC: The Cato Institute, 1992.

Gottschalk, Peter, and Sheldon Danziger. "Income Mobility and Exits from Poverty of American Children, 1970–1992," in *The Dynamics of Child Poverty in Industrialized Countries*, Bruce Bradbury, Stephen P. Jenkins, and John Micklewright, eds. Cambridge: Cambridge University Press, 2001, 135–53.

Gratzer, David. "The ABCs of MSAs," in *Better Medicine: Reforming Canadian Health Care*, David Gratzer, ed. Toronto: ECW Press, 2002, 287–307.

Green, David G. *Reinventing Civil Society: The Rediscovery of Welfare without Politics*. London: Institute for Economic Affairs, 1993.

Ham, Chris. "Synthesis: What We Can Learn from International Experience," *British Medical Bulletin* 51 (October 1995): 819–30.

Harrison, S. "A Policy Agenda for Health Care Rationing," *British Medical Bulletin* 51 (October 1995): 885–99.

Hayek, F. A. "Competition as a Discovery Procedure," in *New Studies in Philosophy, Politics, Economics, and the History of Ideas*. Chicago: University of Chicago Press, 1978, 179–90.

Herzlinger, Regina. *Market Driven Health Care*. Reading, MA: Addison-Wesley Publishing Company, 1997.

Himmelfarb, Gertrude. *The De-Moralization of Society*. New York: Alfred Knopf, 1994.

Holzmann, Robert, and Joseph E. Stiglitz, eds. *New Ideas about Old Age Security*. Washington, DC: World Bank Publications, 2000.

Holzmann, Robert, Richard P. Hinz, et al. *Old-Age Income Support in the 21st Century: An International Perspective on Pension Systems and Reform*. Washington, DC: The World Bank, 2005.

Hurst, Erik, Ming Ching Luoh, and Frank P. Stafford. "The Wealth Dynamics of American Families, 1984–1994," in *Brookings Papers on Economic Activity*, William C. Brainard and George L. Perry, eds. Washington, DC: Brookings Institution, 1998, 276–337.

Illsley, Raymond. "Comparative Review of Sources, Methodology and Knowledge [of Health Inequalities]," *Social Science and Medicine* 31, no. 3 (1990): 229–36.

Irvine, Carl, Johann Hjertqvist, and David Gratzer. "Health Care Reform Abroad," in *Better Medicine: Reforming Canadian Health Care*, David Gratzer, ed. Toronto: ECW Press, 2002, 248–68.

Jacobs, Lesley. *Rights and Deprivation*. Oxford: Oxford University Press, 1993.

James, Estelle. *Social Security Reform around the World: Lessons from Other Countries*. Dallas: National Center for Policy Analysis Report no. 253, August 2002.

Jensen, Gail A. "Making Room for Medical Savings Accounts in the U.S. Healthcare System," in *American Health Care: Government, Market Processes, and the Public Interest*, Roger D. Feldman, ed. New Brunswick, NJ: Transaction Publishers, 2000, 119–43.

Jensen, Gail A., and Michael A. Morrisey. "Employer-Sponsored Health Insurance and Mandated Benefit Laws," *The Milbank Quarterly* 77, no. 4 (1999): 1–21.

Jianokopolos, Nancy A., and Paul L. Menchik. "Wealth Mobility," *Review of Economics and Statistics* 79 (February 1997): 18–32.

Jost, Timothy Stolftzfus. "The Role of the Courts in Health Care Rationing: The German Model," *Journal of Contemporary Health Law and Policy* 18 (2002): 613–18.

———. "Health Care Rationing in the Courts: A Comparative Study," *Hastings International and Comparative Law Review* 21 (Spring 1998): 653–81.

Katz, Michael B. *In the Shadow of the Poorhouse: A Social History of Welfare in America*, 10th anniv. ed. New York: Basic Books, 1996.

Kelly, David. *A Life of One's Own: Individual Rights and the Welfare State*. Washington, DC: The Cato Institute, 1998.

Kirzner, Israel. *Competition and Entrepreneurship*. Chicago: University of Chicago Press, 1973.

Klein, R., P. Day, and S. Redmayne. "Rationing in the NHS: The Dance of the Seven Veils – In Reverse," *British Medical Bulletin* 51 (October 1995): 769–80.

Kukathas, Chandran. "Liberalism, Communitarianism, and Political Community," *Social Philosophy and Policy* 13 (Winter 1996): 80–104.

Kymlicka, Will. *Contemporary Political Philosophy: An Introduction*, 2nd ed. New York: Oxford University Press, 2002.

Lachman, Margie E., and Suzanne L. Weaver. "The Sense of Control as a Moderator of Social Class Differences in Health and Well-Being," *Journal of Personality and Social Psychology* 74, no. 3 (2001): 763–73.

Lenaghan, Jo, ed. *Hard Choices in Health Care*. London: BMJ Publishing Group, 1997.

Liebman, Jeffrey. "Redistribution in the Current U.S. Social Security System," in *The Distributional Aspects of Social Security and Social Security Reform*, Martin Feldstein and Jeffrey B. Liebman, eds. Chicago: University of Chicago Press, 2002, ch. 1.

Lofgren, Ragnar. *Health Care Waiting List Initiatives in Sweden*. Vancouver: The Fraser Institute, 2002.

Marmot, Michael. "Social Inequalities in Mortality: the Social Environment," in *Class and Health*, Richard G. Wilkinson, ed. London: Tavistock Publishing, 1986, 21–33.

Marmot, Michael G., et al. "Health Inequalities among British Civil Servants: The Whitehall II Study," *Lancet* 337 (June 8, 1991): 1387–93.

Matisonn, Shaun. "Medical Savings Accounts in South Africa," *National Center for Policy Analysis* (June 2000).

Maxwell, R. J. "Why Rationing Is on the Agenda," *British Medical Bulletin* 51 (October 1995): 761–68.

Mayer, Susan. *What Money Can't Buy*. Cambridge, MA: Harvard University Press, 1997.

McGinnis, J. Michael, and William. H. Foege. "Actual Causes of Death in the United States," *JAMA* 270 (November 1993): 2207–12.

McGinnis, J. Michael, Pamela Williams-Russo, and James R. Knickman. "The Case for More Active Policy Attention to Health Promotion," *Health Affairs* 21, no. 2 (2002): 78–93.

McKerlie, Dennis. "Justice between the Young and the Old," *Philosophy and Public Affairs* 30, no. 2 (2002): 152–77.

Mead, Lawrence. "Citizenship and Social Policy: T. H. Marshall and Poverty," *Social Philosophy and Policy* 14 (Summer 1997): 197–230.

Mellor, Jennifer M., and Jeffrey Milyo. "Income Inequality and Health Status in the United States: Evidence from the Current Population Survey," *The Journal of Human Resources* 37, no. 3 (2002): 510–39.

Menzel, Paul. *Strong Medicine: The Ethical Rationing of Health Care*. New York: Oxford University Press, 1990.

Miller, David. "Equality and Justice," in *Ideals of Equality*, Andrew Mason, ed. Oxford: Blackwell Publishing, 1998, 21–36.

Miller, Tom. "Improving Access to Health Care without Comprehensive Health Insurance Coverage: Incentives, Competition, Choice, and Priorities," in *Covering America: Real Remedies for the Uninsured. Volume 2: Proposal Summaries*, Eliot Wicks, ed. Washington, DC: Economic and Social Research Institute, November 2002.

Mittelstaedt, H. Fred, and John C. Olsen. "An Empirical Analysis of the Investment Performance of the Chilean Pension System," *Journal of Pension Economics and Finance* 2, no. 1 (2003): 7–24.

Moon, J. Donald. "Introduction: Responsibility, Rights and Welfare," in *Responsibility, Rights and Welfare*, J. Donald Moon, ed. Boulder, CO: Westview Press, 1988a, 4–8.

———. "The Moral Basis of the Democratic Welfare State," in *Democracy and the Welfare State*, Amy Gutmann, ed. Princeton: Princeton University Press, 1988b, 27–52.

Mooney, Gavin. "'Communitarian Claims' as an Ethical Basis for Allocating Health Care Resources," *Social Science and Medicine* 47 (November 1998): 1171–80.

Morrisey, Michael A. "State Health Care Reform: Protecting the Provider," in *American Health Care: Government, Market Processes, and the Public Interest*, Roger D. Feldman, ed. Oakland, CA: The Independent Institute, 2000, 229–68.

Murphy, Liam, and Thomas Nagel. *The Myth of Ownership: Taxes and Justice*. New York: Oxford University Press, 2002.

Nagel, Thomas. *Equality and Partiality.* New York: Oxford University Press, 1991.

Newdick, Christopher. "Judicial Supervision of Health Resource Allocation – The U.K. Experience," in *Readings in Comparative Health Law and Bioethics,* Timothy Stoltzfus Jost, ed. Durham, NC: Carolina Academic Press, 2001, 66–9.

Nightingale, Demetra Smith. "Work Opportunities for People Leaving Welfare," in *Welfare Reform: The Next Act,* Alan Weil and Kenneth Feingold, eds. Washington, DC: The Urban Institute Press, 2002, 103–20.

Normann, Gorman, and Daniel J. Mitchell. "Pension Reform in Sweden: Lessons for American Policymakers," *Heritage Foundation Backgrounder* (June 29, 2000), 1381.

Nozick, Robert. *Anarchy, State, and Utopia.* New York: Basic Books, 1974.

Olasky, Marvin. *The Tragedy of American Compassion.* Washington, DC: Regnery Gateway, 1992.

O'Neill, June. "The Trust Fund, the Surplus, and the Real Social Security Problem," *Cato Project on Social Security Privatization* (April 9, 2002): 1–9.

Ozar, David T. "What Should Count as Basic Health Care?" in *Philosophical Issues in Human Rights,* Patricia Werhane, A. R. Gini, and David T. Ozar, eds. New York: Random House, 1986, 298–310.

Parfit, Derek "Equality or Priority," in *Ideals of Equality,* Andrew Mason, ed. Oxford: Blackwell Publishers, 1998, 1–20.

Pauly, Mark, and Brad Herring. *Pooling Health Insurance Risks.* Washington, DC: AEI Press, 1999.

Plant, Raymond. *Modern Political Thought.* Cambridge: Basil Blackwell, 1991.

Rakowski, Eric. *Equal Justice.* Oxford: Oxford University Press, 1991.

Ramsay, Cynthia. "Medical Savings Accounts: Universal, Accessible, Portable, Comprehensive Health Care for Canadians," *The Fraser Institute Critical Issues Bulletin* (May 1998).

Rawls, John. *Justice as Fairness: A Restatement.* Cambridge, MA: Harvard University Press, 2001.

———. *A Theory of Justice.* 2nd ed. Cambridge, MA: Harvard University Press, 1999.

Redwood, Heinz. *Why Ration Health Care? An International Study of the United Kingdom, France, Germany, and the Public Sector Health Care in the USA.* London: Institute for the Study of Civil Society, 2000.

Rodriguez, L. Jacobo. *Chile's Private Pension at 18: Its Current State and Future Challenges.* Washington, DC: Cato Project of Social Security Privatization, July 30, 1999.

Rose, Stephen. "Is Mobility in the United States Still Alive? Tracking Career Opportunities and Income Growth," *International Review of Applied Economics* 13 (September 1999): 417–37.

Sagan, Leonard A. *The Health of Nations: True Causes of Sickness and Well-Being.* New York: Basic Books, 1987.

Salamon, Lester M., et al. *Global Civil Society: Dimensions of the Nonprofit Sector.* Baltimore: The John Hopkins Center for Civil Society Studies, 1999.

Sawhill, Isabel V. "Still the Land of Opportunity?" *Public Interest* 135 (Spring 1999): 3–18.

Scandlen, Greg. "MSAs Can Be a Windfall for All," *NCPA Policy Backgrounder* (November 2, 2001): 1–21.

Scheffler, Samuel. "What Is Egalitarianism?" *Philosophy and Public Affairs* 31, no. 3 (2003): 5–39.

Schmidtz, David. "Equal Respect and Equal Shares," *Social Philosophy and Policy* 19 (Winter 2002): 244–74.

Schmidtz, David and Robert E. Goodin. *Social Welfare and Individual Responsibility*. Cambridge, MA: Cambridge University Press, 1998.

Scott, Ellen K., Kathryn Edin, Andrew S. London, and Joan May Mazelis. "My Children Come First: Welfare-Reliant Women's Post-TANF Views of Work-Family Tradeoffs and Marriage," in *For Better and for Worse: Welfare Reform and the Well-Being of Children and Families*, Greg J. Duncan and P. Lindsay Chase-Lansdale, eds. New York: Russell Sage Foundation, 2001, 132–53.

Sen, Amartya. "Health Equity: Perspectives, Measurability and Criteria," in *Challenging Inequities in Health: From Ethics to Action*, Timothy Evans, Margaret Whitehead, Finn Diderischen, Abbas Bhuiya, and Meg Wirth, eds. New York: Oxford University, 2001, 68–75.

Shapiro, Daniel. "Liberalism, Basic Rights, and Free Exchange," *Journal of Social Philosophy* 26 (Fall 1995a): 103–26.

———. "Liberalism and Communitarianism," *Philosophical Books* 36 (July 1995b): 145–55.

Shipman, William G. *Retirement Finance Reform Issues Facing the European Union*. Washington DC: The Cato Social Security Policy Studies, January 2, 2003.

Shriver, Melinda L., and Grace-Marie Arnett. "Uninsured Rates Rise Dramatically in States with Strictest Health Insurance Regulation," *Heritage Foundation Backgrounder* (August 14, 1998).

Skocpol, Theda. "Targeting within Universalism: Politically Viable Policies to Combat Poverty in the United States," in *The Urban Underclass*, Christopher Jencks and Paul E. Peterson, eds. Washington, DC: The Brookings Institution, 1991, 411–36.

Smith, James. "Inheritances and Bequests," in *Wealth, Work, and Health: Innovations in Measurement in the Social Sciences*, James P. Smith and Robert J. Willis, eds. Ann Arbor: University of Michigan Press, 1999, 121–49.

Solow, Robert. "Who Likes Workfare?" in *Work and Welfare*, Amy Gutmann, ed. Princeton: Princeton University Press, 1998, 3–54.

Sorrentino, Constance, and Joyanna May. "U.S. Labor Market in International Perspective," *Monthly Labor Review* 125 (June 2002): 15–35.

Steptoe, Andrew, and Jane Wardle. "Locus of Control and Health Behavior Revisited: A Multivariate Analysis of Young Adults from 18 Countries," *British Journal of Psychology* 92, no. 4 (2001): 643–57.

Sterba, James. "Welfare Libertarianism," in *Political Philosophy: Classic and Contemporary Readings*, Louis P. Pojman, ed. New York: McGraw-Hill, 2002, 216–28.

Strossberg, Martin, Joshua M. Weiner, and Robert Baker, with Alan I. Fein, eds. *Rationing America's Medical Care: The Oregon Plan and Beyond.* Washington, DC: The Brookings Institution, 1992.

Sweatman, Louise R., and Diane Wollard. "Resource Allocation Decisions in Canada's Health Care System: Can These Decisions Be Challenged in a Court of Law?" *Health Policy* 62, no. 3 (2002): 275–90.

Takala, Tuija. "Justice for All? The Scandinavian Approach," in *Medicine and Social Justice,* Rosamond Rhodes, Margaret P. Battin, and Anita Silvers, eds. Oxford: Oxford University Press, 2002, 183–90.

Tanner, Michael. "A Better Deal at Half the Cost: SSA Scoring of the Cato Social Security Reform Plan," *Cato Institute Briefing Papers* (April 26, 2005): 1–13.

———. "The 6.2 Percent Solution," in *Social Security and Its Discontents,* Michael Tanner, ed. Washington: DC: The Cato Institute, 2004, 281–308.

———. *The Poverty of Welfare: Helping Others in Civil Society.* Washington, DC: The Cato Institute, 2003.

Temkin, Larry. "Justice and Equality: Some Questions about Scope," *Social Philosophy and Policy* 12 (Summer 1995): 72–104.

Tullock, Gordon. *The Economics of Income Redistribution.* Boston: Kluwer-Nijhoff Publishing, 1983.

U.S. Congress, Office of Technology Assessment. *International Health Statistics: What the Numbers Mean for the United States.* Washington, DC: U.S. Government Printing Office, November 1993.

Uyl, Douglas Den. "The Right to Welfare and the Virtue of Charity," *Social Philosophy and Policy* 10 (1993): 192–224.

Valkonen, Tapni. "Adult Mortality and Levels of Education," in *Health Inequalities in European Countries,* John Fox, ed. Brookfield, VT: Gower, 1989, 142–72.

Vallentyne, Peter. "Brute Luck, Option Luck, and Equality of Initial Opportunities," *Ethics* 112, no. 3 (2002): 531–8.

———. "Self-Ownership and Equality: Brute Luck, Gifts, Universal Dominance and Leximin," *Ethics* 107, no. 2 (1997): 321–43.

Van de Ven, P. M. M. "Choices in Health Care: A Contribution from the Netherlands," *British Medical Bulletin* 51 (October 1995): 781–90.

Van Doorslaer, Eddy, Xander Koolman, and Frank Puffer. "Equity in the Use of Physician Visits in OECD Countries: Has Equal Treatment for Equal Need Been Achieved?" in *Measuring Up: Improving Health System Performance in OECD Countries.* OECD: Paris, 2002, ch. 11.

Wagner, Richard. *To Promote the General Welfare: Market Processes Versus Political Transfers.* San Francisco: Pacific Research Institute for Public Policy, 1989.

Waldron, Jeremy. *Liberal Rights: Collected Papers.* New York: Cambridge University Press, 1993.

Walzer, Michael. *Spheres of Justice: A Defense of Pluralism and Equality.* New York: Basic Books, 1983.

Wasley, Terree P. *What Has Government Done to Our Health Care?* Washington, DC: Cato Institute, 1992.

Weaver, Carolyn L. *The Crisis in Social Security.* Durham, N.C.: Duke University Press, 1982.

Weidner, Gerid. "Why Do Men Get More Heart Disease than Women? An International Perspective," *American Journal of College Health* 48 no. 6 (2000): 291–4.

Weinstein, Michael. "America's Rags to Riches Myth," *New York Times* (February 18, 2000).

White, Joseph. *Competing Solutions: American Health Care Proposals and International Experience.* Washington, DC: The Brookings Institution, 1995.

Woodroofe, Kathleen. *From Charity to Social Work in England and the United States.* London: Routledge, Kegan, and Paul, 1962.

Wolfe, Alan. "The Right to Welfare and the Obligation to Society." *The Responsive Community* 1, no. 2 (Spring 1991): 12–22.

Wolff, Jonathan. "Fairness, Respect and the Egalitarian Ethos," *Philosophy and Public Affairs* 27, no. 2 (1998): 97–122.

World Bank Policy Research Report. *Averting the Old Age Crisis: Policies to Protect the Old and Promote Growth.* New York: Oxford University Press, 1994.

Ziliak, Stephen T. "The End of Welfare and the Contradiction of Compassion," *Independent Review* 1, no. 1 (1996): 55–74.

Zogby, John, et al. "Public Opinion and Private Accounts: Measuring Risk and Confidence in Rethinking Social Security." *Cato Project on Social Security Choice* no. 29 (Washington, DC: The Cato Institute, January 6, 2003).

Index